The Forfeiture of Leases

AUSTRALIA
The Law Book Company
Brisbane - Sydney - Melbourne - Perth

CANADA
Carswell
Ottawa - Toronto - Calgary - Montreal - Vancouver

Agents
Steimatzky's Agency Ltd., Tel Aviv
N.M. Tripathi (Private) Ltd., Bombay
Eastern Law House (Private) Ltd., Calcutta
M.P.P. House, Bangalore
Universal Book Traders, Delhi
Aditya Books, Delhi
MacMillan Shuppan KK, Tokyo
Pakistan Law House, Karachi, Lahore

The Forfeiture of Leases

by

Mark Pawlowski

LL.B (Hons), BCL (Oxon), ACIArb., of the Middle Temple, Barrister,
Senior Lecturer in Law, School of Law, University of Greenwich,
Visiting Lecturer in Land Registration, University College London

London
Sweet & Maxwell
1993

Published in 1993 by
Sweet & Maxwell Limited of
South Quay Plaza
183 Marsh Wall
London E14 9FT
Phototypeset by MFK Typesetting Ltd. of
Hitchin, Hertfordshire
Printed and bound in Great Britain
by Hartnolls Ltd., Bodmin

No natural forests were destroyed to make this product;
only farmed timber was used and replanted

A CIP catalogue record for this book is
available from the British Library

ISBN 0-421-48640-6

Foreword

There is hardly a subject which gives rise to as much litigation as the law of forfeiture. Some of the litigation is uncontested; much highly controversial. In either case, the pitfalls for practitioners, and for the judiciary are legion in a "field—one might say a minefield—in which it is necessary to tread with difidence and warily" (see p. 139). Moreover, not infrequently an unforeseen point of difficulty not dealt with by a standard textbook arises during the trial. This book fills a gap, and will be of great help to practitioners. Any judge trying a possession list will be comforted by having it at his—or her—elbow.

It is very much a practitioner's book yet it is based on a comprehensive, indeed profound knowledge of the subject. One of its advantages is the analysis of comparatively recent case law; another is brevity of clear and definite views. There is no fudge, and answers can be found at a glance.

As one would expect, the book deals with the right to and effect of forfeiture, waiver and relief. One example of its usefulness is its summary of the factors which the Court should take into account in exercising its discretion to grant relief. Other topics are also covered, such as forfeiture of options to renew leases. That besides, the book deals with forfeiture in the context of a contract of sale or hire purchase, a building contract, and in relation to deposits, mortgages and the transfer of proprietary or possessory interest in property other than land. Last, it even refers to forfeiture in criminal law.

In addition to the text, there are separate sections setting out the relevant legislation and a selection of forms.

My main regret is that the book was not written half a century ago; happily, its readers will not look to the past but to the future.

June 9, 1993   *His Hon. Judge Dobry, C.B.E., Q.C.*

For my wife, Lidia

Ubi to Caia, ibi ego Caius

Preface

This book is intended to provide a comprehensive guide to the law of forfeiture of leases aimed predominantly at the legal practitioner. It is hoped, however, that it will also provide a useful source of reference for teachers and students of the law of landlord and tenant.

The contents deal with all aspects of forfeiture in the leasehold context. The various principles underlying each subject area are illustrated by numerous extracts from the judgments of leading cases, whilst other cases not specifically mentioned in the main text are referred to in the footnotes as an aid to further research. In addition, the main statutory provisions relating to the forfeiture of leases and a selection of forms are set out for the convenience of the reader.

The subject of forfeiture lies at the forefront of much litigation in the context of both commercial and residential leases. The forfeiture of the lease is, of course, the primary remedy of a landlord faced with a tenant who has defaulted in the payment of his rent or other obligations in the lease. At the same time, the lease will invariably be a valuable asset which the tenant will seek to preserve in most cases by seeking relief from forfeiture.

The law, however, is obscure and, in many respects suffers historically from a combination of piecemeal development of common law rules and equitable principles and *ad hoc* statutory intervention. At the same time, it is an expanding area of law and this is reflected in a spate of recent decisions (see, for example, *Billson* v. *Residential Apartments Ltd.* [1992] 2 W.L.R. 15, (H.L.), (physical re-entry); *W.G. Clark (Properties) Ltd.* v. *Dupre Properties Ltd.* [1991] 3 W.L.R. 579, (denial of landlord's title); *Van Haarlam* v. *Kasner* [1992] 36 E.G. 135; *Iperion Investments Corporation* v. *Broadwalk House Residents Ltd.* [1992] 2 E.G.L.R. 235; *Darlington Borough Council* v. *Denmark Chemists Ltd.* [1993] 02 E.G. 117, (C.A.) and *United Dominions Trust Ltd.* v. *Shellpoint Trustees Ltd.* [1993] E.G.C.S. 57, (C.A.) (mortgagee's claim to relief from forfeiture).

In 1985, the Law Commission, as part of its programme for the codification of the law of landlord and tenant, published a Report entitled *Forfeiture of Tenancies* ((1985) Law Com. No. 142) which examined various defects in the current law and recommended the replacement of the present structure with an extirely new system. Over seven years have now passed since the publication of this Report but there is still little expectation that the Law Commission's recommendations will become law in the foreseeable future. In this connection, Chapter 12 sets out the major defects highlighted by the Commission and outlines the main proposals of the new scheme.

I would like to thank Professor David Wills, School of Land and Construction Management, University of Greenwich, for his kind indulgence in excusing me from various administrative duties within the School during the past year to enable me to complete this work. I also wish to express my sincere gratitude to Mr. Jolyon Hall and Mrs. Elizabeth Anker of the University of Warwick Library for their co-operation in allowing me to use the facilities of the Library over many painstaking months. In particular, I would like to thank them for their kind permission to let me use my word-processor in the Law and British Official Publications Room. I also wish to thank Butterworth & Co. (Publishers) Ltd. for their kind permission to reproduce various extracts from Halsbury's Statutes.

I am also very much indebted to my wife, Lidia, for putting up with my absences from home to visit the library and who has been a constant source of encouragement in my efforts.

The forfeiture of leases is, without doubt, a complicated and technical area of the law and it hoped that this book will shine a beam of light in a dark tunnel!

The law is stated to be as at May 1, 1993.

May 1993
Mark Pawlowski
School of Law
University of Greenwich

Contents

CONTENTS

Part III: Relief against Forfeiture

Part IV: Proposals for Reform

Part V: Main Statutory Provisions

Part VI: Selection of Forms

Table of Cases

Table of Statutes

Commonwealth

Australia

New Zealand

Table of Statutory Instruments

Part I: Introduction

Chapter One

Introduction

Overview of subject

(1) *The right of forfeiture*

The right of a landlord to forfeit[1] a lease may arise in a variety of different ways. Most commonly, the landlord may forfeit under a proviso for re-entry contained in the lease for breach of covenant on the part of the tenant. Alternatively, a lease may be granted upon condition so that, on the happening of the event specified in the condition, the landlord will be entitled to forfeit without recourse to a proviso for re-entry. The event in question may be an entirely neutral one (for example, the grant of planning permission for a particular use) or it may be an act or omission on the part of the tenant (for example, not to assign, underlet or part with possession of the demised premises). In the latter case, it is more usual to phrase the relevant obligation in the form of a covenant coupled with a forfeiture clause because a breach of covenant, unlike a breach of condition, will entitle the landlord to claim damages in addition to his remedy of forfeiture. A forfeiture may also be incurred by breach on the part of the tenant of an implied condition of the lease in circumstances where the tenant denies or disclaims the landlord's title to the property comprised in the lease. The denial (or disclaimer) may take three distinct forms (a) denial by matter of record (b) denial by act *in pais* or (c) disclaimer by a yearly or other periodic tenant.

---

[1] Forfeiture denotes the loss, destruction or termination of a proprietary or possessory right in property: see, *e.g. Scandinavian Trading Tanker Co. AB* v. *Flota Petrolera Ecuatoriana, The Scaptrade* [1983] 2 All E.R. 763, 767, *per* Lord Diplock; *Sport International Bussum BV* v. *Inter-Footwear Limited* [1984] 1 W.L.R. 776, (H.L.); *B.I.C.C. plc* v. *Burndy Corporation* [1985] Ch. 232, 252, (C.A.), *per* Dillon L.J.; *Comco Constructions Proprietary Limited* v. *Westminister Properties Proprietary Limited* (1990) 2 W.A.R. 335; (1991) 7 Const. L.J. 49, (Supreme Court of Western Australia), *per* Brinsden J.; *Underground (Civil Engineering) Limited* v. *Croydon London Borough Council* [1990] E.G.C.S. 48, *per* Mr T. A. Morison, Q.C., (sitting as a deputy judge of the High Court). See also, in a different context, *Re Sumner's Settled Estates* [1911] 1 Ch. 315, 319, *per* Eve J.

3

A denial by matter of record will arise when the tenant, in the course of his pleadings, expressly denies his landlord's title and is thereby estopped by the record from re-asserting his lease or tenancy. This form of denial was discussed in *Warner* v. *Sampson*[2] in which the Court of Appeal held that a general traverse in the tenant's pleadings did not involve the affirmative setting up by the tenant of a title adverse to that of the landlord as it merely put the landlord to proof of the allegations traversed.

A denial by act *in pais* will arise when the tenant deliberately attempts to set up an adverse or hostile title either in himself or in a stranger in the face of the landlord's title.

The disclaimer of the lease (whether by words or acts) by a yearly or other periodic tenant will operate as a waiver by the tenant of the usual notice to quit. The effect of such a disclaimer, therefore, is that the landlord may terminate the tenancy forthwith without serving the appropriate notice to quit on the tenant. The principle appears to be founded on the doctrine of estoppel since the landlord is not obliged to determine the tenancy by notice to quit because the tenant has already asserted by words or conduct that it has no existence.

Finally, mention should be made of section 35(2) of the Sexual Offences Act 1956 under which a landlord is given a statutory right to determine the lease where the tenant is convicted of knowingly permitting the whole or part of the demised premises to be used as a brothel and the tenant fails to assign the lease within three months of being required to do so by the landlord.

(2) *Exercise of the right of forfeiture*

An act of forfeiture on the part of the tenant only renders the lease voidable at the instance of the landlord. This is so even where the proviso for re-entry expressly provides that the lease shall be "void" or "cease to have effect" upon the tenant's default. Since the lease is only made voidable, the landlord is obliged to make an election either to forfeit the lease or to treat the lease as continuing. (In the latter case, he is said to waive the forfeiture). Moreover, once the landlord has made his election one way or the other, it will be irretractable.

In order for the landlord to bring about an effective forfeiture of the lease, he must take some positive and unequivocal step to signify to the tenant his intention of treating the lease as at an end as a consequence of the tenant's breach of covenant or condition in the lease. Under a proviso for re-entry, he may do this either by actually (physically) re-entering onto the demised premises or by suing for possession or seeking a

---

[2] [1959] 1 Q.B. 297, (C.A.). See further, Chap. 2.

declaration of title to possession of the premises. If the landlord adopts the former method, he must be careful not to infringe the provisions of section 6 of the Criminal Law Act 1977 which prohibit the landlord from using or threatening violence for the purpose of securing entry onto the premises. Moreover, actual re-entry is not available to a landlord where the premises are let as a dwelling and whilst any person is lawfully residing therein.[3] In view of these difficulties, the more usual course in practice is for the landlord to initiate proceedings for possession where the service of the writ (or summons) will operate in law as a notional re-entry. The writ (or summons) must, however, contain an unequivocal demand for possession and this will not be so if it claims relief consistent with the continuation of the lease (for example, an injunction to restrain future breaches of covenant).

Where, on the other hand, the right to forfeit arises out of a proviso which renders the lease void upon the tenant's breach without reference to any pre-requisite of "re-entry" in order to bring about a forfeiture of the lease, the landlord may signify his intention to forfeit by simply giving notice of his intention to the tenant.

(3) *The effect of forfeiture*

Once the landlord has effectively elected to forfeit the lease (whether by actual re-entry or the service of proceedings for possession), he cannot rely upon any subsequent breaches of covenant on the part of the tenant because, having elected to forfeit the lease, he is estopped from treating the lease (and the covenants in the lease) as still on foot. Moreover, the landlord cannot seek interlocutory relief to restrain breaches of covenant once he has unequivocally elected to forfeit the lease. This will not, however, preclude him from seeking interlocutory relief against the tenant based on a proprietary right operating outside the lease, regardless of his election to treat the lease as forfeited. For example, the landlord may be able to seek an injunction or claim damages founded on a cause of action in tort. Moreover, he will not be precluded from recovering rent which accrued due prior to re-entry.

Since the tenant is no longer bound by the covenants in the lease, it follows that he will no longer be bound to pay rent but, assuming he continues in possession of the premises, he will be liable for mesne profits which are technically damages for trespass.

Invariably, the tenant will seek relief from forfeiture and during the "twilight period"[4] between forfeiture and the determination of the tenant's application for relief, the tenant may continue to enforce the

---

[3] s. 2 of the Protection from Eviction Act 1977.
[4] *Meadows* v. *Clerical, Medical and General Life Assurance Society* [1981] Ch. 70, 78, *per* Sir Robert Megarry V.-C.

landlord's covenants in the lease.[5] The service of proceedings by the landlord will not, therefore, by itself operate so as to bring about a termination of the lease. The matter must go a stage further and a judgment obtained by the landlord for possession of the premises before the lease is finally treated as determined. However, once judgment is obtained, the determination of the lease will relate back to the date of forfeiture. Moreover, the effect of the forfeiture will be to determine not only the lease but all other derivative interests created under it.

(4) Forfeiture for non-payment of rent

A landlord cannot forfeit a lease for non-payment of rent in the absence of a proviso for re-entry or condition contained in the lease. Moreover, at common law, in the absence of express words in the lease dispensing with a formal demand, the landlord can only forfeit for non-payment of rent if he has made a formal demand for the rent. Since the conditions for making such a demand are very stringent, a modern lease will invariably exempt the landlord from this requirement by providing that a forfeiture may take place if the rent is unpaid for a specified period "whether formally demanded or not."

A formal demand will also be unnecessary if at least six months' rent is in arrear before the date of service of the writ and no sufficient distress is to be found on the demised premises countervailing the arrears then due.[6]

(5) Forfeiture for other breaches of covenant

In cases other than non-payment of rent, the landlord cannot forfeit unless he has first served notice on the tenant (a) specifying the particular breach complained of (b) if the breach is capable of remedy, requiring the tenant to remedy the breach and (c) in any case, requiring the tenant to make compensation in money for the breach. Further, the landlord cannot enforce his right of forfeiture until the tenant has failed within a reasonable time after service of the notice to remedy the breach (if it is capable of remedy) and to make reasonable compensation in money. These pre-conditions are set out in section 146(1) of the Law of Property Act 1925, which applies to both leases and agreements for leases and to High Court and county court cases.

The sub-section imposes on the landlord the obligation of serving a notice when he has a right to forfeit because of a breach of covenant or condition in the lease, except a covenant to pay rent and certain breaches of covenant in mining leases. It has no application, however, in relation to

[5] See, e.g. Peninsular Maritime Ltd. v. Padseal Ltd. (1981) 259 E.G. 860.
[6] s. 210 of the Common Law Procedure Act 1852.

6

certain instances of bankruptcy.[7] Section 146 cannot be excluded by contract and it expressly applies to a lease limited to continue so long as the tenant abstains from committing a breach of covenant. The purpose of the section 146 notice is, of course, to give the tenant an opportunity to remedy the breach complained of and thereby avoid a forfeiture of his lease.

Under section 146(1) the landlord must require the breach to be remedied if, but only if, it is "capable of remedy". The sub-section, therefore, draws a distinction between remediable and irremediable breaches of covenant. If the breach is incapable of remedy, as a matter of law, the section 146 notice need not require the tenant to remedy it and the landlord may proceed to forfeit with little delay. In this connection, the breach of a negative covenant which leaves a "stigma" on the demised premises is considered incapable of remedy.

In cases involving an illegal or immoral user of the premises (for example, where the premises have been used as a brothel or for unlawful gambling), the courts have looked at the effect of the breach and have concluded that the stigma attached to the premises by the wrongful user can only be erased if the tenant who brought the taint was no longer associated with the premises. In this sense, therefore, the breach is considered, as a matter of law, to be incapable of remedy within a reasonable period of time from the date of the landlord's notice. If, however, the breach of a negative covenant does not involve any lingering stigma or taint on the premises, then the breach may be capable of remedy. In this connection, the question whether a breach of a negative covenant is capable of remedy is dependent on whether the harm done to the landlord by the relevant breach is for practical purposes capable of being retrieved. In other words, a section 146 notice does not require the tenant to remedy the breach if it is not capable of remedy within a reasonable time after the service of the notice.

It has been held,[8] however, that a breach of a covenant not to assign, underlet or part with possession of the demised premises is not a breach capable of remedy within the meaning of section 146(1) of the 1925 Act. On the other hand, the breach of a positive covenant (for example, to repair) is ordinarily remediable within the meaning of the sub-section.

If the breach is classified as irremediable, it follows that the landlord need not require it to be remedied. However, the fact that the breach is irremediable will not prevent the tenant from applying for relief from forfeiture under section 146(2) of the 1925 Act (see later).

Special provisions apply where the landlord seeks to forfeit for breach of a covenant to repair. As a pre-requisite to forfeiture, the landlord must

[7] See, ss. 146(9) and (10) of the 1925 Act.
[8] *Scala House & District Property Co. Ltd.* v. *Forbes* [1974] Q.B. 575, (C.A.) and *Expert Clothing Service & Sales Ltd.* v. *Hillgate House Ltd.* [1986] Ch. 340, (C.A.).

serve a section 146 notice on the tenant specifying the particular breach complained of and requiring the tenant to remedy the same within a reasonable time. In addition, (where appropriate) the notice must refer to the landlord's claim for compensation. The notice need not itself specify the precise time within which the breach of covenant must be remedied and it is considered good practice simply to require the tenant to remedy within a "reasonable time" from the date of service of the notice. It will then be a matter for the landlord's surveyor to advise his client on what period of time can safely be allowed to elapse before the commencement of proceedings for forfeiture. His advice will, no doubt, take into account such matters as the extent and nature of the disrepair, the time of year and availability of builders. It is usual to particularise the breach or breaches complained of by means of annexing to the notice a schedule of dilapidations prepared by the landlord's surveyor.

Where the lease in question was granted for seven or more years and three years or more remain unexpired at the date of the section 146 notice, the landlord's remedies of forfeiture (and damages) for disrepair are further limited by the provisions of the Leasehold Property (Repairs) Act 1938. The Act applies in the case of a breach of any covenant or agreement to keep or put the whole or part of the premises in repair during the currency of the term. Where the Act applies, the landlord cannot proceed without first serving a section 146 notice, which must also inform the tenant of his right to serve a counter-notice claiming the benefit of the Act. If the tenant does serve such a counter-notice within 28 days, no further proceedings for possession by action or otherwise (*i.e.* by initiating proceedings for possession or by physically re-entering upon the demised premises) can be taken by the landlord without leave of the court establishing a case on the balance of probabilities that one or more of the five conditions[9] set out in the Act have been fulfilled. These conditions may conveniently be summarised as follows:

(a) the value of the reversion has been substantially diminished or will be if the breach is not immediately remedied;

(b) immediate remedying is required by any Act, bye-law, court order or local authority order;

(c) immediate remedying is required in the interests of an occupier (of the whole or part of the property) other than the tenant;

(d) the cost of immediate remedying is relatively small in comparison with the likely cost if the work is postponed;

(e) special circumstances exist which in the opinion of the court render it just and equitable that leave should be given;

In granting or refusing leave, the court may impose such terms and

[9] See, s. 1(5), grounds (*a*) to (*e*) of the 1938 Act.

conditions on the landlord or tenant as it thinks fit. Moreover, the landlord's right, under section 146(3) of the 1925 Act, to recover his costs and expenses of employing a solicitor and surveyor or valuer, does not arise unless he applies for leave to proceed under the 1938 Act.[10]

In cases not involving disrepair, the section 146 notice will be effectively served if the general provisions[11] governing the service of notices under the 1925 Act are complied with, and it is enough if the notice is sent by registered or recorded delivery[12] post provided it is not returned undelivered by the post office. In cases involving a breach of covenant to repair, however, section 18(2) of the Landlord and Tenant Act 1927 requires the landlord to prove that the service of the notice was actually *known* to the tenant or to a sub-tenant holding under a sub-tenancy, which reserved only a nominal reversion to the tenant, or to the person who last paid rent. Section 18(2) also provides, in effect, that the reasonable time which must be allowed to elapse for the repairs to be carried out is to run from the date when service became known to the tenant (or to the other persons mentioned above).

Where the landlord must do urgent repairs in order to preserve the premises, there is a danger of invalidating any subsequent notice served pursuant to section 146 of the 1925 Act. In *S.E.D.A.C. Investments Ltd.* v. *Tanner*[13] the landlord discovered that the stonework on the front wall of the demised premises was loose and falling on the pavement endangering passers-by. Remedial work was, therefore, undertaken by the landlord as a matter of urgency in the absence of any co-operation from the tenant who was responsible for the defects under its repairing covenant in the lease. Subsequently, the landlord served a section 146 notice on the tenant requiring compensation to which the tenant claimed the benefit of the 1938 Act. The court held that a section 146 notice to be effective had to be served *before* the breach complained of was remedied. Accordingly, when the landlord himself remedied the breach prior to attempting to serve the notice, he thereby put it out of his power to serve a valid section 146 notice thereafter, with the consequence that the court had no jurisdiction to give him leave to commence proceedings under the 1938 Act.

(6) *Waiver of forfeiture*

Instead of electing to forfeit the lease, the landlord may decide to treat the lease as continuing and waive the forfeiture. If, with knowledge of the breach, the landlord acknowledges to the tenant the continuance of the tenancy he will be taken to have elected not to forfeit. The consequences

[10] See, s. 2 of the 1938 Act.
[11] See, s. 196 of the Law of Property Act 1925.
[12] See, s. 1 of the Recorded Delivery Service Act 1962.
[13] [1982] 1 W.L.R. 1342.

of a waiver are a matter of law to be viewed objectively without regard to the intention of the landlord or the belief or understanding of the tenant. Thus, since it is irrelevant *quo animo* an act of waiver was made, knowledge of the breach by the landlord's agent will be sufficient even where the act of acknowledgment of the lease is that of another agent who is unaware of the breach. Moreover, because the consequence of a particular act relied on as a waiver is a matter of law and not of the parties' intention, the landlord cannot avoid a waiver by accepting or demanding rent "under protest" or "without prejudice" to his right of re-entry.

The knowledge required to put a landlord to his election to waive an act of forfeiture is knowledge of the basic facts that in law constitute a breach of covenant (or condition) entitling him to forfeit the lease. The fact, however, that the landlord is ignorant or has doubts as to whether the facts amount in law to a breach is immaterial.

The effect of a waiver will depend on the nature of the breach giving rise to the landlord's election to forfeit. If the breach is classified as being of a continuing nature (for example, a breach of a repairing or user covenant), a fresh right of forfeiture will arise after the act of waiver. This is because there is a continually recurring cause of forfeiture and the waiver will operate only in relation to past breaches, that is to say, breaches committed in the period prior to the landlord's act which constitutes the waiver. On the other hand, where the breach is classified not as continuing but as a "once and for all breach" (for example, breach of a covenant against assigning or subletting), the right to forfeit for that breach will be lost upon waiver.

The various acts on the part of the landlord which have (and have not) been held to constitute a waiver of forfeiture are considered in detail in Chapter 6. An obvious example of an act of waiver is the demand or acceptance of rent by the landlord accrued due after the breach.

(7) *Relief from forfeiture*

Even if a ground of forfeiture exists (and has not been waived), it does not necessarily follow that the landlord will be successful in his claim to recover possession of the demised premises. Both equity and statute law have intervened so as to provide the tenant with the right to apply for relief from forfeiture of his lease. The forms of relief differ depending on whether the landlord claims forfeiture for non-payment of rent or for breach of other covenants in the lease.

(a) *Relief from forfeiture for non-payment of rent*

From earliest times, equity recognised that it had jurisdiction to relieve against forfeiture where the object of the forfeiture clause was to secure payment of a definite sum of money. Accordingly, the Court of Chancery allowed a tenant to keep his lease provided that he paid the arrears of rent and the landlord's costs and expenses by a specified time.

This equitable jurisdiction remains intact to this day subject only to various statutory provisions which have merely modified equity's power to grant relief in certain procedural respects. Whilst these provisions differ as between the High Court and county court, the nature of relief in both jurisdictions continues to be rooted in equity's inherent power to relieve against forfeiture for non-payment of rent.

Under section 212 of the Common Law Procedure Act 1852, the tenant may avoid a forfeiture by paying all the arrears and costs to the landlord or into court before the trial. The effect of so doing will be to stay the landlord's action. In order, however, for the section to apply, there must be at least six months' rent in arrears. No such limitation is to be found in section 138(2) of the County Courts Act 1984, which governs actions in the county court. Under section 138(2), however, the payment of all arrears and costs must be made not less than five clear days before the return day.

Under section 210 of the 1852 Act, applicable to High Court cases, the tenant is also entitled to relief in equity at or after the trial of the landlord's action, if he pays all the arrears of rent and costs within six months of the execution of the order for possession. Where, however, there is less than six months' rent in arrears, the six months' limitation period has no application so as to confine the tenant to a period of six months after execution of the order for possession in which to bring his application for relief. In such circumstances, the court's inherent equitable jurisdiction will apply without strict statutory time-limit, although the six month time-limit prescribed under section 210 of the 1852 Act is usually taken as a guide in the exercise of the court's discretion whether to grant or refuse relief.

Although the common law courts were given jurisdiction, under section 212, to grant relief from forfeiture on payment by the tenant of the arrears of rent and costs *before* trial, relief *after* judgment for possession was only obtainable from the Court of Chancery until the coming into effect of section 1 of the Common Law Procedure Act 1860. This section was repealed and replaced by section 46 of the Supreme Court of Judicature (Consolidation) Act 1925, which empowered the High Court (in the case of any action for forfeiture for non-payment of rent) to give relief in a summary manner and subject to the same terms and conditions in all respects as to the payment of rent, costs and otherwise as could formerly have been enforced by the Court of Chancery. This provision is currently contained in section 38(1) of the Supreme Court Act 1981.

In practice, the court will invariably grant relief to the tenant upon payment of the rent due and the landlord's costs of the action. The court does, however, retain a discretion to refuse relief under the foregoing statutory provisions in exceptional circumstances where, for example, the landlord (and any other interested parties) cannot be put back into their original position.

The provisions of the 1852 and 1981 Acts will govern proceedings for the granting of equitable relief in cases where the landlord is enforcing his right of forfeiture by action through the courts. Where, therefore, the landlord proceeds to forfeit the lease for non-payment of rent by physically re-entering onto the premises without recourse to legal proceedings, these statutory provisions will have no application and the tenant will be entitled to rely upon equitable relief without any fixed (statutory) time limit. In such circumstances, however, relief may be refused on equitable grounds where, for example, the tenant has unduly delayed in bringing his application for relief.

In the county court, relief is based upon the making of a suspended order for possession. Under section 138(3) of the County Courts Act 1984, where the tenant seeks relief at the trial of the landlord's action, the court is obliged to order possession of the land to be given to the landlord at the expiration of such period, not being less than four weeks from the date of the order, as the court thinks fit, unless within that period the tenant pays into court all the rent in arrears and the costs of the action. The court has power, under section 138(4), to extend the period for payment at any time before possession of the land is recovered by the landlord. If the tenant pays the rent due and costs within the time limit fixed under the order (or any extension thereof), he will continue to hold under the lease but, if he fails to pay within the time limit, the order for possession will be enforced. Under sub-section (9A) of the 1984 Act (inserted by section 55(5) of the Administration of Justice Act 1985), the tenant has the right to apply for relief at any time within six months from the date on which the landlord recovers possession of the demised premises.

The foregoing county court provisions apply to cases where the landlord is proceeding *by action* to enforce a right of forfeiture for non-payment of rent. Where the landlord forfeits the lease by physically re-entering onto the demised premises, section 139(2) of the 1984 Act expressly confers on the county court the same power to relieve against forfeiture for non-payment of rent as the High Court could have granted, provided that the application for relief is made within six months from the date of the landlord's re-entry.

In addition to relief being available to the tenant, relief may be granted to sub-tenants and mortgagees who derive title from him. Thus, in the High Court, a sub-tenant or mortgagee may obtain relief under sections 210 and 212 of the Common Law Procedure Act 1852 and section 38(1) of the Supreme Court Act 1981. In addition, he may apply for relief under section 146(4) of the Law of Property Act 1925 at any time before the landlord has actually obtained possession of the premises pursuant to an order of the court. Under section 146(4), the court may make an order vesting a new lease in favour of the sub-tenant or mortgagee in which the covenants and conditions as to rent and otherwise will be entirely at the discretion of the court unfettered by any limitation except that contained in the latter part of the sub-section, namely, that a sub-tenant shall not be entitled to require a lease for a term longer than he had under his original sub-lease.

In the county court, the right of a sub-tenant or mortgagee to apply for relief from forfeiture for non-payment of rent under section 146(4) of the Law of Property Act 1925 is expressly preserved by section 138(10)(*b*) of the County Courts Act 1984. Moreover, where the landlord is proceeding by re-entry without action, an application under section 139(2) of the 1984 Act may be made by a person with an interest derived from the tenant (whether immediately or otherwise) and the court may make an order which (subject to such terms and conditions as it thinks fit) vests the land (or a part thereof) in such person for the remainder of the term of the lease or for any less term.[14]

(b) *Relief from forfeiture otherwise than for non-payment of rent*

Whilst equity's jurisdiction to grant relief against forfeiture for non-payment of rent is extensive, its jurisdiction to grant relief in cases involving other breaches of covenant is severely limited. This is because, historically, the underlying principle governing relief was whether the landlord could be adequately compensated for his loss occasioned by the tenant's breach. Thus, whilst there was no difficulty in compensating a landlord for a tenant's failure to pay rent by simply permitting the tenant to tender late payment with interest and costs, other breaches of covenant did not readily permit the placing of the landlord in the same position he would have been if no breach had occurred.

Coupled with this inherent difficulty, was the Court of Chancery's acceptance of the principle that equity would not relieve against a wilful breach of covenant other than one involving the non-payment of a specific sum of money. The result was the emergence of only a limited equitable jurisdiction to relieve from forfeitures of property, restricted essentially to two specific heads of relief, namely, (a) where the right to forfeit was inserted by way of security for the payment of a specific sum of money, (such as rent) and (b) where the breach had been occasioned by fraud, accident, mistake or surprise. The foregoing remained the position until the decision in *Shiloh Spinners Ltd.* v. *Harding*[15] in which the House of Lords took the opportunity to reiterate the scope of equity's jurisdiction to relieve against forfeitures of property. In that case, Lord Wilberforce, who

---

[14] See, s. 139(3) of the 1984 Act, inserted by s. 55(5) of the Administration of Justice Act 1985.
[15] [1973] A.C. 691.

gave the leading speech of the House, restated the basis for equitable relief in these expansive terms:[16]

> "... we should reaffirm the right of the courts of equity in appropriate and limited cases to relieve against forfeiture for breach of covenant or condition where the primary object of the bargain is to secure a stated result which can effectively be attained when the matter comes before the court, and where the forfeiture provision is added by way of security for the production of that result."

The majority[17] of the Court of Appeal in *Billson* v. *Residential Apartments Ltd.*[18] has recently held that equity's inherent jurisdiction to relieve against forfeiture from a wilful breach of covenant (other than non-payment of rent), which had been resurrected retrospectively by the House of Lords in the *Shiloh* case, was entirely extinguished in the landlord and tenant context by virtue of the provisions of section 146 of the Law of Property Act 1925. The upshot of the majority decision, therefore, is that relief against forfeiture in respect of breaches of covenant or condition other than non-payment of rent is now governed exclusively by statute in the landlord and tenant field, except in cases where there is some element of fraud, accident, surprise or mistake[19] or in circumstances where the statutory code does not apply.[20]

As mentioned earlier, the general statutory provisions relevant to relief against forfeiture from breaches of covenant other than non-payment of rent are contained in section 146 of the Law of Property Act 1925. Under section 146(2) of the 1925 Act, the tenant is entitled to apply to the court (in the landlord's action or in an action brought by himself) for relief against forfeiture of his lease. The court may grant or refuse relief, on terms, as it thinks fit and, in the case of a breach of a repairing covenant, the court will usually require the tenant to remedy the disrepair and make compensation to the landlord for any damage to the reversion before it grants such relief. It should be noted, in this connection, that a special form of relief is available to the tenant in respect of internal decorative repairs under section 147 of the 1925 Act, which provides that the court may relieve the tenant from liability for such repairs if "having regard to all the circumstances of the case (including in particular the length of the lessee's term or interest remaining unexpired), the court is satisfied that the [landlord's] notice is unreasonable." The court's power under section 147 is to

---

[16] *Ibid*, 723.
[17] Sir Nicholas Browne-Wilkinson V.-C. and Parker L.J., Nicholls L.J. dissenting.
[18] [1991] 3 W.L.R. 264. Although the case went on appeal to The House of Lords, the point now under discussion was not referred to by their Lordships.
[19] See, *e.g. Barrow* v. *Isaacs* [1891] 1 Q.B. 417.
[20] See, *Shiloh Spinners Ltd.* v. *Harding* [1973] A.C. 691, (H.L.), (where the relationship of landlord and tenant did not exist) and *Ladup Ltd.* v. *Williams & Glyn's Bank plc* [1985] 1 W.L.R. 851, (where relief was granted to an equitable chargee).

grant relief not merely from forfeiture but from the need to do the decorative repairs at all.

The tenant may apply for relief under section 146(2) where the landlord is proceeding to forfeit by action or by physical re-entry.[21] In the former case, the tenant will normally apply for relief after the writ or summons has been served and, in the latter case, after the landlord has physically re-entered. But, strictly speaking, a tenant may apply for relief as soon as a section 146 notice has been served on him. However, the tenant will be barred from seeking relief once the landlord has recovered judgment for possession and has re-entered in reliance on that judgment unless, of course, the judgment is set aside or successfully appealed. Section 146(2) provides that the court may grant or refuse relief, having regard to the proceedings and conduct of the parties and to all other circumstances, as it thinks fit. Moreover, in case of relief, the court may grant it on "such terms, if any, as to costs, expenses, damages, compensation, penalty, or otherwise, including the granting of an injunction to restrain any like breach in the future" as, in the circumstances of each case, it thinks fit. The court's discretion to grant or refuse relief is very wide and will usually depend on any one or more of the following factors:

(a) whether the tenant is able and willing to remedy and/or recompense the landlord for the breach;
(b) whether the breach was wilful;
(c) whether the breach involves an immoral/illegal user;
(d) the gravity of the breach;
(e) the extent of the diminution in the value of the landlord's reversionary interest as compared to the value of the leasehold interest threatened with forfeiture;
(f) the conduct of the landlord;
(g) the personal qualifications of the tenant;
(h) the financial position of the tenant.

Each of these factors is considered fully in Chapter 10.

If relief is granted by the court, the tenant will retain his lease as if it had never been forfeited but, under section 146(3), the landlord will be entitled to recover his reasonable costs and expenses incurred by him in the employment of a solicitor and surveyor or valuer if relief is granted or if the landlord waives the breach at the tenant's request.

Relief is also available, under section 146(4) of the 1925 Act, to holders of interests deriving from the tenant's lease including sub-tenants and their and his mortgagees. However, relief is not available after the landlord has recovered possession. If relief is granted, it takes the form of a new tenancy granted to the applicant.

---

[21] *Billson* v. *Residential Apartments Ltd.* [1992] 2 W.L.R. 15, (H.L.).

Special provisions apply in cases involving relief against forfeiture on the tenant's bankruptcy or the taking of his lease in execution. The provisions of section 146 do not apply to a condition of forfeiture on the tenant's bankruptcy,[22] or the taking in execution of his interest under the lease, if the premises fall into any one of the following categories:[23]

(a) agricultural or pastoral land;

(b) mines or minerals;

(c) a house used or intended to be used as a public-house or beer-shop;

(d) a house let as a dwelling-house, with the use of any furniture, books, works of art, or other chattels not being in the nature of fixtures;

(e) any property with respect to which the personal qualifications of the tenant are of importance for the preservation of the value or character of the property, or on the ground of neighbourhood to the landlord, or to any person holding under him.

If the premises do not fall within any of the above categories, section 146(10) of the 1925 Act provides that the protection of section 146 applies for one year from the date of the bankruptcy or taking in execution. If the tenant's interest is not sold within that year, the protection ceases and the section will no longer apply. If, however, the tenant's interest is sold during the year, the protection will continue indefinitely for the benefit of the new tenant. The effect of the provision is to encourage a sale within a year and to enable a sale within that period to be made at a price which is not depressed by the purchaser's fear of having to face an action for possession by the landlord without statutory protection.

(8) *Relief against forfeiture of options to renew leases*

In Chapter 11, the question whether equity has any jurisdiction to relieve a tenant from the consequences of his failure to comply with the pre-conditions for the exercise of an option to renew his lease is examined in some detail. Invariably, the consequences of such failure will involve the tenant in the loss of his interest in the demised premises arising under the option to renew. It is submitted that the loss of such an interest arising under the option may properly be characterised as a forfeiture of a proprietary interest in the subject premises.

In Australia and New Zealand, various statutes have given the courts power to grant relief to a tenant against the forfeiture of an option contained in a lease resulting from a breach of covenant. In England,

---

[22] Bankruptcy includes liquidation by arrangement and, in relation to a corporation, means its winding up: See, s. 205(1)(*i*) of the 1925 Act.

[23] These categories are listed in s. 146(9) of the 1925 Act.

whilst statute[24] provides for relief against forfeiture of a lease based on a tenant's failure to perform a covenant, this statutory jurisdiction has been held[25] to have no application where a landlord seeks to resist specific performance of a covenant to renew which is conditional on the performance of the tenant's covenants in the lease. In England, equitable relief will only be available to a tenant, who fails to comply strictly with the terms of a renewal covenant, where there has been some element of accident or misfortune which the tenant could not prevent by reasonable diligence or where, as a result of unconscionable conduct on the part of the landlord, the tenant has been misled to believe that strict compliance with the terms of the renewal/option covenant will not be insisted upon. Moreover, English authority has consistently denied relief to the tenant against the loss of a right of renewal in circumstances where the tenant is in breach of other covenants in the lease.

There is much to be said for the introduction of legislation on the lines of the Australian and New Zealand statutes into English law. At present, however, this area of law is governed by old authorities which have denied relief to the defaulting tenant regardless of the merits of the case.

A wider perspective

The law of forfeiture is not, of course, limited to the subject of leases. A forfeiture may also arise in the context of a contract of sale or hire-purchase, a building contract, and in relation to deposits, mortgages and the transfer of proprietary or possessory interests in property other than land. It also features significantly in the context of the criminal law. What follows is a brief discussion of these various subject areas so as to give the reader a wider perspective of the law of forfeiture both in its civil and criminal context.

(1) *Forfeiture of instalments paid under a contract of sale or hire-purchase*

Many contracts of sale and hire-purchase contain a clause entitling the seller, upon the purchaser's default in any of the instalments of the purchase price, to terminate the contract, forfeit the instalments already paid and retake possession of the subject-matter of the contract. Such a forfeiture clause is to be contrasted with a penalty, the latter representing a stipulated sum which will become payable upon breach of the contract and which, unlike liquidated damages, is inserted not as a genuine attempt to pre-estimate the likely loss to the innocent party but *in terrorem* of the party in breach with the intention of providing a strong incentive

---

[24] s. 146 of the Law of Property Act 1925.
[25] *Greville v. Parker* [1910] A.C. 335, (P.C.).

for the performance of the contract. In the case of a forfeiture, however, the seller is not seeking to exact a penalty but, on the contrary, wishes to keep money which already belongs to him since it has already been paid by the buyer in the form of instalments in part-payment of the purchase price.

It has long been settled that a court may grant equitable relief where the object of the right to forfeit is essentially to secure payment of a specific sum of money. In this connection, there is some judicial support[26] for the proposition that, in relation to a contract for the sale of land or goods, equity not only has jurisdiction to extend time for the payment of the outstanding instalments due under the contract but, in an appropriate case, will permit recovery by the buyer of instalments already paid to the seller by means of restitutionary relief. For this latter jurisdiction to operate, however, the sum forfeited must be out of all proportion to the damage suffered by the seller and it must be unconscionable for the seller to retain the money.[27]

In principle, similar reasoning should apply to a hirer seeking relief under a hire-purchase agreement but in *Galbraith* v. *Mitchenhall Estates*,[28] a case concerning the hire of a caravan, Sachs J. held[29] that there was no equitable right to the restitution of instalments already paid where the contract in question had been freely entered into in the absence of fraud, sharp practice or unconscionable conduct on the part of the seller. It is, however, implicit in Sachs J.'s judgment that a hirer may be entitled to invoke equity's more limited jurisdiction to grant an extension of time for payment in circumstances where the forfeiture clause is characterised as penal and where the hirer shows himself to be able and willing to perform the contract.

(2) *Forfeiture in the context of building contracts*

Building and engineering contracts frequently give the employer express power to determine the contract or the contractor's employment

---

[26] *In Re Dagenham (Thames) Dock Co.* (1873) L.R. 8 Ch. 1022, (C.A.); *Cornwall* v. *Henson* [1900] 2 Ch. 298, 302, (C.A.), *per* Collins L.J.; *Kilmer* v. *British Columbia Orchard Lands Ltd.* [1913] A.C. 319, (P.C.); *Steedman* v. *Drinkle* [1916] 1 A.C. 275, (P.C.); *Stockloser* v. *Johnson* [1954] 1 Q.B. 476, *per* Somervell and Denning L.JJ.; *Starside Properties Ltd.* v. *Mustapha* [1974] 2 All E.R. 567, (C.A.); *Scandinavian Trading Tanker Co. AB* v. *Flota Petrolera Ecuatoriana, The Scaptrade* [1983] 2 All E.R. 763, 768, (H.L.), *per* Lord Diplock. The weight of authority, however, is against positive relief in the form of a right of recovery of instalments already paid: see *Mussen* v. *Van Dieman's Land Co.* [1938] Ch. 253, *per* Farwell J.; *Stockloser* v. *Johnson* [1954] 1 Q.B. 476, (C.A.), *per* Romer L.J.; *Bridge* v. *Campbell Discount Co.* [1962] A.C. 600, 626, *per* Lord Radcliffe; *Galbraith* v. *Mitchenhall Estates* [1965] 2 Q.B. 473, *per* Sachs J. See, generally, *Relief Against Forfeiture of Leases*, M. Pawlowski, [1993] E.G., March 27, 1993, p. 122.
[27] See, *Stockloser* v. *Johnson* [1954] 1 Q.B. 476, *per* Somervell and Denning L.JJ.
[28] [1965] 2 Q.B. 473.
[29] Applying the minority view of Romer L.J. in *Stockloser* v. *Johnson* [1954] 1 Q.B. 476, (C.A.).

or to "forfeit"[30] the contract on the happening of some event (for example, the bankruptcy or liquidation of the contractor) or on some default by the contractor. Sometimes, a similar power may be conferred on the contractor.

The contract will also invariably provide for the rights and liabilities of the parties on the exercise of a power to determine. Typically, for example, the contract may provide that the property in the contractor's materials or plant on site should become forfeit and vest in the employer. A provision vesting the contractor's property absolutely in the employer may be unenforceable as being a penalty. Generally speaking, however, such a provision will be intended to operate by way of security for the completion of the works and will not be construed as a penalty.[31]

Where, however, the contract (or the contractor's employment under it) is determined by reason of the contractor's bankruptcy or insolvency, a provision passing the property in plant and materials to the employer will be void as against the trustee in bankruptcy or liquidator.[32] Such a provision will, however, be enforceable against the trustee in bankruptcy or liquidator if the contract is a personal contract.[33] Moreover, a transfer of property as between employer and contractor will, generally, be valid.[34]

(3) *Forfeiture of deposits*

The subject of forfeiture arises, perhaps, most vividly in the context of deposits. A contract of sale or hire-purchase will often call for the immediate payment of a specified sum by the buyer as a guarantee or security that the contract will be performed. Where the buyer defaults, a forfeiture will be implied, as a matter of law, from the mere fact that the sum is stated to be paid as a "deposit". This is to be contrasted with an express provision for forfeiture which takes the form of a forfeiture clause expressly providing that the money deposited shall become forfeited on the buyer's default.

At common law, a seller is entitled to retain money which he has received from the buyer by way of deposit[35] but, as a general rule, will be

---

[30] Although such provisions are still commonly referred to as forfeiture clauses in the context of engineering contracts, the term now in vogue is "determination clause".
[31] *Ranger* v. *Great Western Railway Co.* (1854) 5 H.L. Cas. 72, 108–109; 10 E.R. 824, 839, *per* Lord Cranworth. See also, *Marshall* v. *Mackintosh* (1898) 78 L.T. 750.
[32] s. 127 and 284 of the Insolvency Act 1986 (relating to bankruptcy and liquidation, respectively). See also, *Re Walker, ex p. Barter, ex p. Black* (1884) 26 Ch. D. 510, (C.A.); *Higinbotham* v. *Holme* (1812) 19 Ves. 88, 92; 34 E.R. 451, 452, *per* Lord Eldon; *Re Jeavons, ex p. Mackay, ex p. Brown* (1873) 8 Ch. App. 643; *Re Harrison, ex p. Jay* (1880) 14 Ch. D. 19, (C.A.).
[33] *Re Walker, ex p. Gould* (1884) 13 Q.B.D. 454.
[34] *Re Harrison, ex p. Jay* (1880) 14 Ch. D. 19, 26, (C.A.), *per* Cotton L.J.
[35] *Wallis* v. *Smith* (1882) 21 Ch. D. 243, 258, *per* Jessel M.R.; *Willson* v. *Love* (1896) 1 Q.B. 626, 633, *per* Rigby L.J.

obliged to return money which constitutes a part payment[36] of the purchase price where the contract contains no express provision for forfeiture. In each case, it will be a question of construction to determine into which category the sum payable falls and whether it is forfeitable.[37]

Since the common law denies any redress to the buyer who has agreed to pay money in the form of a deposit, the question arises whether there is any equitable jurisdiction to relieve from the effects of a forfeiture in this context. In this connection, despite the fact that, in many cases, there may be little or no practical distinction between a deposit and a penalty (particularly where the deposit has fallen due for payment under the contract but remains unpaid by the purchaser), the English courts[38] have shown a marked reluctance to apply the law of penalties to deposits even in circumstances where the sum deposited is wholly out of proportion to the actual or probable loss accruing to the seller. There is, however, sufficient English authority[39] to support the proposition that equity does have jurisdiction to grant positive relief (apart from a mere extension of time to pay[40]) against the forfeiture of a deposit in circumstances where the sum retained is out of all proportion to the damage sustained and where it would be unconscionable for the vendor to retain the money.

In the context of a contract for the sale of land, a vendor's right at law to forfeit the purchaser's deposit is mitigated by section 49(2) of the Law of Property Act 1925, which provides that: "Where the court refuses to grant specific performance of a contract, or in an action for the return of a deposit, the court may, if it thinks fit, order the repayment of any deposit". The court has a very wide discretion under the sub-section to grant relief dependent on a general consideration of the conduct of both parties (especially the purchaser), the gravity of the matters in question and the

---

[36] *Dies* v. *British and International Mining and Finance Corp.* [1939] 1 K.B. 724; *Mayson* v. *Clouet* [1924] A.C. 980. But whether a party has the right to retain a part payment will depend on the nature and terms of the contract: *Hyundai Shipbuilding and Heavy Industries Co. Ltd.* v. *Pournaras* [1978] 2 Lloyd's Rep. 502, (C.A.) and *Hyundai Shipbuilding and Heavy Industries Co. Ltd.* v. *Papadopoulos* [1980] 1 W.L.R. 1129, (H.L.).

[37] *Howe* v. *Smith* (1884) 27 Ch. D. 89; *Hinton* v. *Sparkes* (1868) L.R. 3 C.P. 161.

[38] *Wallis* v. *Smith* (1882) 21 Ch. D. 243, 258, *per* Jessel M.R.; *Hinton* v. *Sparkes* [1868] L.R. 3 C.P. 161; *Linggi Plantations Ltd.* v. *Jagatheesan* [1972] 1 Malayan L.J. 89, (P.C.); *Windsor Securities Ltd.* v. *Loreldal Ltd. and Lester, The Times*, September 9, 1975.

[39] For cases supportive of an equitable jurisdiction to relieve in this context: See, *Barton* v. *Capewell Continental Patents Co. Ltd.* (1893) 68 L.T. 857; *Pye* v. *British Automobile Commercial Syndicate Ltd.* [1906] 1 K.B. 425; *Public Works Commissioner* v. *Hills* [1906] A.C. 368; *Brickles* v. *Snell* [1916] 2 A.C. 599, 604, (P.C.); *Stockloser* v. *Johnson* [1954] 1 Q.B. 476, 487, 489, (C.A.), *per* Somervell and Denning L.JJ., respectively; *Bridge* v. *Campbell Discount Co. Ltd.* [1962] A.C. 600, 624, 631, (H.L.), *per* Lord Radcliffe and Denning L.JJ., respectively; *Workers Trust & Merchant Bank Ltd.* v. *Dojap Investments Ltd.* [1993] E.G.C.S. 38, (P.C.). See, generally, *Relief Against Forfeiture of Deposits*, M. Pawlowski, [1992] E.G. 9246, 76.

[40] See, *Starside Properties Ltd.* v. *Mustapha* [1974] 2 All E.R. 567, where the Court of Appeal accepted that equity had a limited jurisdiction to grant relief in the form of an extension of time to pay a deposit which was expressed in the contract to be payable in instalments. The Court, however, reserved its position on the question whether a purchaser could recover instalments of the deposit already paid: *ibid*, 575, *per* Edmund Davies L.J.

amount at stake.[41] Although the jurisdiction is statutory, nevertheless, its discretionary character has been held to be "at least akin to equitable relief against forfeiture".[42]

(4) *Forfeiture in the context of mortgages*[42a]

The essential nature of a mortgage is that it is a conveyance of a legal or equitable interest in property with a provision for redemption (*i.e.* that upon repayment of the loan or the performance of some other obligation the conveyance shall become void or the interest shall be reconveyed).[43]

By the beginning of the seventeenth century, the mortgage had fully evolved into the form of a conveyance[43a] of the land to the mortgagee in fee simple subject to a condition that the mortgagor might re-enter and determine the mortgagee's estate if the money lent was repaid on a specified date. This condition was construed strictly[43b] so that if the mortgagor was late in repaying the loan, he lost his land forever and still remained liable for the debt. In the seventeenth century, however, equity took the view that the property mortgaged was merely a security for the money lent and that it was unjust that the mortgagor should lose his property merely because he was late in repaying the loan. Initially, the Court of Chancery intervened only in cases of accident, mistake or special hardship but later relief was given in all cases. Thus, even if the legal repayment date had passed, equity would, nevertheless, compel the mortgagee to reconvey the land to the mortgagor on payment of the loan with interest and costs. This is the mortgagor's equitable right to redeem which arises on any date after the date fixed for redemption by the mortgage. It provides a further facet of equity's jurisdiction to relieve against the strictness of common law forfeitures of property.

The mortgagee has a number of remedies available to him for enforcing payment of the principal sum. Of these, the taking possession of the mortgaged property is commonly exercised today as a preliminary to the mortgagee's exercise of his power of sale. In this connection, the court has

---

[41] See, *Schindler* v. *Pigault* (1975) 30 P. & C.R. 328; *Universal Corporation* v. *Five Ways Properties Ltd.* [1979] 1 All E.R. 552, (C.A.); *Dimsdale Developments (South East) Ltd.* v. *De Haan* (1983) 47 P. & C.R. 1.

[42] *Schindler* v. *Pigault* (1975) 30 P. & C.R. 328, 336, *per* Megarry J.

[42a] Although "forfeiture" is commonly associated with the equity of redemption, the enforcement of a mortgage does not strictly involve a forfeiture of property: "By failing to pay the debt on the law day, the mortgagor technically does not lose a title which he had immediately before that day; he fails to acquire again by the happening of a condition subsequent a title which he had lost when he made the mortgage": *Williston on Contracts*, (3rd ed.), Vol. 5, p. 641.

[43] *Santley* v. *Widle* [1899] 2 Ch. 474, 474, *per* Lindley M.R.

[43a] Today, a legal mortgage of the freehold may take only one of two forms, namely a demise for a term of years absolute subject to a provision for cesser on redemption or a charge by way of legal mortgage: see s.85(1) of the Law of Property Act 1925.

[43b] See, for example, the explanation for equity's intervention given by Jessel M.R. in *Campbell* v. *Holyland* (1877) 7 Ch.D. 166, 171.

only a very limited inherent equitable jurisdiction[44] to adjourn an application or suspend an order for possession for a short period to allow the mortgagor the opportunity of paying off the loan (or otherwise remedying his default) assuming that there is a reasonable prospect of the opportunity being utilised. However, in *Quennell* v. *Maltby*[45] Lord Denning M.R. ventured to suggest that:[46]

"... in these modern times equity can step in so as to prevent a mortgagee, or a transferee from him, from getting possession of a house contrary to the justice of the case. A mortgagee will be restrained from getting possession except when it is sought bona fide and reasonably for the purpose of enforcing the security and then only subject to such conditions as the court thinks fit to impose. When the bank itself or a building society lends the money, then it may well be right to allow the mortgagee to obtain possession when the borrower is in default. But so long as the interest is paid and there is nothing outstanding, equity has ample power to restrain any unjust use of the right to possession."

In that case, a landlord let a house to the first defendant and another university student for one year expiring on December 31, 1974. In August 1974, the landlord mortgaged the house to his bank to secure a loan of £2,500. The mortgage contained a prohibition on any lettings without the consent of the bank during the continuance of the security. In December 1974, without the consent of the bank, the landlord relet the house for a further year to two other students and, on the expiration of that year, he again (without the bank's consent) let the house to the first and second defendants. Subsequently, the landlord wished to sell the house with vacant possession but the bank refused his request to take proceedings to evict the defendants. After receiving legal advice, the landlord's wife paid off the money owing to the bank who then transferred the benefit of the mortgage to her. She then claimed possession of the property against the defendants as the bank's successor in title. The trial judge gave effect to her absolute right to possession as mortgagee but, in the Court of Appeal, Lord Denning M.R. pointed out that this would open the way to widespread evasion of the Rent Act 1977 (to which the lettings were subject).

---

[44] *Birmingham Citizens Permanent Building Society* v. *Caunt* [1962] 1 Ch. 883. Because the court's discretion is so limited, statute has intervened to confer much wider discretionary powers in the case of dwelling-houses: See s. 36 of the Administration of Justice Act 1970, s. 8(1) of the Administration of Justice Act 1973 and *Town & Country Building Society* v. *Julien* (1991) 24 H.L.R. 312, (C.A.). See also s. 1(5) of the Matrimonial Homes Act 1967. The court also has a wide discretionary power to make time orders in respect of certain types of mortgage effecting commercial property: See ss.16 and 129 of the Consumer Credit Act 1974 and *First National Bank plc* v. *Syed* [1991] 2 All E.R. 250 (C.A.).

[45] [1979] 1 W.L.R. 318.

[46] *Ibid*, 322.

He, therefore, took the view that the landlord and his wife had the ulterior motive of obtaining possession to re-sell the house at a profit free from the tenancies and that, accordingly, equity could intervene to restrain them from getting possession.

Lord Denning's suggestion that the court has a wide equitable discretion to prevent a mortgagee from obtaining possession of the mortgaged property conflicts with authority[47] and renders largely unnecessary the protection accorded mortgagors under the Administration of Justice Acts 1970 and 1973. The better view,[48] therefore, is that, since the wife was not exercising her powers as a mortgagee in order to protect or enforce the security but in order to obtain possession on behalf of her husband (so that the house could be sold with vacant possession), she was to be treated as acting on his behalf with the result that, since the husband as landlord could not obtain an order for possession against the defendants (as they had a statutory tenancy protected under the Rent Act 1977), the wife was similarly not entitled to any such order.

(5) *Forfeiture of interests in property other than land*

Whilst equity's jurisdiction to relieve against forfeiture of property is normally associated with the grant of a lease of land, a number of recent decisions have extended the equitable principle of relief from forfeiture to other commercial transactions where a transfer of proprietary or possessory rights has taken place. Historically, equity has consistently refused to proclaim any general jurisdiction to relieve from men's bargains.[49] Consequently, the areas in which courts of equity have been prepared to grant relief against forfeiture have been limited, notably, relief against forfeiture of land (in the context of leases and mortgages) and relief against penalty and forfeiture clauses in contracts. A variety of considerations has led to equity's reluctance to interfere with contractual rights and obligations on a more general and robust basis. Prominent among such considerations has been the desirability that contractual promises should be observed and respected and the undesirability of the law appearing to condone flagrant disregard of such promises. Moreover, it has been questioned how far it is reasonable to require a party who is prima facie entitled to invoke a forfeiture clause to accept an alternative

---

[47] *Robertson* v. *Cilia* [1956] 1 W.L.R. 1502; *Birmingham Citizens Permanent Building Society* v. *Caunt* [1962] Ch. 883, 896, *per* Russell J.; *Alliance Perpetual Building Society* v. *Belrun Investments Ltd.* [1957] 1 W.L.R. 720, 723, *per* Harman J.; *Four-Maids Ltd.* v. *Dudley Marshall (Properties) Ltd.* [1957] Ch. 317, 320, 322, *per* Harman J.

[48] See, the judgments of Bridge and Templeman L.JJ. in *Quennell* v. *Maltby* [1979] 1 W.L.R. 318, 323–324, (C.A.).

[49] "The Chancery mends no man's bargain", *per* Lord Nottingham in *Maynard* v. *Moseley* (1676) 3 Swanst. 651. "The court of equity never undertook to serve as a general adjuster of men's bargains", *per* Lord Radcliffe in *Bridge* v. *Campbell Discount Co. Ltd.* [1962] A.C. 600, 626.

23

form of relief.[50] Against these considerations, is the underlying notion that the vindication of contractual rights may be grossly excessive and harsh in circumstances where the damage done to the innocent party is small and the moral culpability of the party in breach is negligible.

This underlying notion has prompted several judicial attempts to confer upon equity a more liberal and extensively based attitude towards relief against forfeitures and to apply such relief to subject matter other than interests in land. A strong protagonist of the expansive approach in recent years has been Lord Simon of Glaisdale who, in his speech in *Shiloh Spinners Limited* v. *Harding*,[51] put forward the view that: "equity has an unlimited and unfettered jurisdiction to relieve against contractual forfeitures and penalties".[52] In his view, the various considerations in favour of limiting equity's jurisdiction to relieve against forfeiture fall to be treated as no more than internal factors to be weighed by the court in deciding how to exercise its unfettered discretion as opposed to an external constraint on its jurisdiction. This view has received some measure of judicial support[53] but has been castigated by the House of Lords in *Scandinavian Trading Tanker Co. AB* v. *Flota Petrolera Ecuatoriana, The Scaptrade*,[54] a case involving a time charterparty which contained a clause permitting the owners to withdraw the vessel from the service of the charterers upon non-payment of the hire, as "beguiling heresy".[55]

In the *Scaptrade*, the House of Lords held that, since a time charter (as opposed to a charter by demise) transferred to the charterers no interest in or right to possession of the vessel in question, the shipowners could not be prohibited from exercising their right of withdrawal of the vessel by invoking an equitable jurisdiction to relieve from such forfeiture. The House of Lords' decision in the *Scaptrade* has been followed by the Court of Appeal[56] and House of Lords[57] in *Sport International Bussum BV* v.

---

[50] The relief will usually take the form of an extension of time to make payment or reinstatement of the subject matter.

[51] [1973] 1 All E.R. 90, (H.L.). See also, Lord Simon's views in *Mardorf Peach & Co. Ltd.* v. *Attica Sea Carriers Corporation of Liberia, The Laconia* [1977] 1 All E.R. 545, (H.L.).

[52] *Ibid*, 104.

[53] See, *e.g.* the judgments of Lloyd J. in *Afovos Shipping Co. SA* v. *R. Pagnan and F. Lli, The Afovos* [1980] 2 Lloyd's Rep. 469, 477 and *Scandinavian Trading Tanker Co. AB* v. *Flota Petrolera Ecuatoriana, The Scaptrade* [1981] 2 Lloyd's Rep. 425, (cases involving charterparties). See also, *Tankexpress A/S* v. *Compagnie Financiere Belge des Petroles SA, The Petrofina* [1949] A.C. 76, 100, *per* Lord Uthwatt who appears also to have envisaged the possibility of equitable relief in relation to a charterparty. In *Tropwood A.G. of Zug* v. *Jade Enterprises Ltd., The Tropwind* [1982] 1 Lloyd's Rep. 232, 234, Lord Denning had occasion to remark: "to my mind the withdrawal clause is nothing more nor less than a penalty or a forfeiture clause. I welcome the suggestion recently thrown out by Mr. Justice Lloyd that equity may in a proper case grant relief against it". See also his observations in *China National Foreign Trade Transportation Corp.* v. *Eulogia Shipping Co. SA, The Mihalios Xilas* [1978] 2 Lloyd's Rep. 397, 403–404.

[54] [1983] 2 All E.R. 763.

[55] *Ibid*, 766, *per* Lord Diplock.

[56] [1984] 1 All E.R. 376.

[57] [1984] 1 W.L.R. 776.

Inter-Footwear Limited, a case involving licences to use certain names and trade marks. Oliver L.J. (giving the judgment of the Court of Appeal) reiterated the view put forward by Lord Diplock in the *Scaptrade* case that where that which is forfeited is a right depending solely on a contract and where relief from that forfeiture would in effect mean that the court would be specifically enforcing the contract, relief would not be granted in cases where (apart from the forfeiture) the court would not, in any event, decree specific performance. However, unlike the view put forward in the *Scaptrade*, Oliver L.J. proceeded to hold that the availability of equitable relief was confined to cases where the subject-matter of the forfeiture was an interest in land. This is in contrast to the *Scaptrade*, where it was suggested that equity's jurisdiction would not extend beyond contracts "not involving any transfer of proprietary or possessory rights".[58] It was, however, this latter statement of principle which was accepted by the House of Lords in the *Sport International* case and, as such, it left open the possibility of equity's intervention in contracts creating interests in property other than land such as, for example, a lease of pure personalty.

The question of equity's jurisdiction to relieve from forfeiture of a proprietary right in relation to *personal* property under a commercial agreement was considered by the Court of Appeal in *BICC plc* v. *Burndy Corporation*,[59] where two companies, who had decided to dissolve their partnership, entered into a "commercial agreement" (which provided for the continued sale of goods between them) and an "assignment agreement" (regarding their joint patent rights) which provided that such rights were to be vested in the parties jointly with freedom for each to use and exploit them. The assignment agreement also provided that the plaintiff company was to be primarily responsible for paying the costs and fees relating to the parties' joint patent rights, subject to the defendant reimbursing the plaintiff for half such costs and fees. The agreement also contained a clause which provided that if the defendant failed to reimburse the plaintiff within 30 days of the plaintiff's written request to do so, the plaintiff was entitled to require the defendant to assign to the plaintiff all its interest in the patent rights concerned. The plaintiff incurred costs and fees in respect of the joint patents and served the defendant with ordinary commercial invoices for the defendant's half share of those expenses without insisting on payment within 30 days. When the defendant (who was under the impression that there was no urgency in the matter and at a time when the plaintiff's indebtedness to the defendant under the commercial agreement was well in excess of the amount of the invoices) failed to pay the invoices, the plaintiff invoked its right to

---

[58] [1983] 2 All E.R. 763, 767, *per* Lord Diplock.
[59] [1985] Ch. 232. See also, *Jobson* v. *Johnson* [1989] 1 W.L.R. 1026, (C.A.), (shares in a football club) and *Goker* v. *NSW Bank plc The Times*, May 23, 1990, 393, (purchase of car under a hire-purchase agreement).

require the defendant to assign its interest in the patent rights. The value of the defendant's interest in the rights greatly exceeded the amount due to the plaintiff under the invoices. The defendant, not surprisingly, refused to assign and the plaintiff brought an action seeking specific performance of the assignment.

One of the arguments raised by the defendant was that the provision entitling the plaintiff to require the defendant to assign was a forfeiture clause and that the defendant was entitled to seek relief against forfeiture. The Court of Appeal held that, although relief was only available in respect of proprietary or possessory rights, it was not restricted to interests in real property but extended to interests in personal property as well. In the instant case, the relevant provision was construed as a forfeiture clause invoking the forfeiture by the defendant of its proprietary rights in personal property (namely, the patent rights) and, accordingly, the Court had jurisdiction to grant the defendant relief. Moreover, in the circumstances of the case, the Court of Appeal considered it appropriate to grant relief by giving the defendant an extension of time to comply with its obligations as to payment of the costs and fees under the assignment agreement. In the course of his judgment,[60] Dillon L.J. referred to the earlier case of *Barton Thompson & Co. Ltd* v. *Stapling Machines Co.*,[61] in which Pennycuick J. was called upon to consider whether relief could be granted against forfeiture of a lease of chattels. That case involved a hiring agreement under which the defendants leased to the plaintiffs for a term of 25 years various machines for making wire-bound boxes. In case of breach of any term of the agreement, the defendants were entitled to serve a notice requiring the plaintiffs to remedy the breach within 30 days and, in default, to terminate the agreement. The plaintiffs failed to make payments due under the agreement and to comply with a notice requiring payment. The defendants then served a notice terminating the agreement and the plaintiffs took out a summons seeking relief from forfeiture. Pennycuick J., on the defendants' application to strike out the plaintiffs' summons on the ground that it disclosed no reasonable cause of action, held that it was arguable, as a matter of law, whether the court could (in the absence of unconscionable behaviour) grant relief from forfeiture in the case of a lease of chattels and, accordingly, permitted the plaintiffs to argue the case if it was maintainable on other grounds. In particular, he relied on the statements of principle enunciated by Lord Greene M.R. in *Chandless-Chandless* v. *Nicholson*[62] to the effect that a court of equity always regarded a forfeiture

---

[60] *Ibid*, 251–252.
[61] [1966] Ch. 499.
[62] [1942] 2 K.B. 321, 323. See also, *Re Dixon, Hayes* v. *Dixon* [1900] 2 Ch. 561, 576, *per* Rigby L.J.

clause for non-payment of rent as being merely security for the payment of the rent and provided the landlord was paid the arrears, relief was given.

In the latest decision on the subject, *Crittall Windows Ltd.* v. *Stormseal (UPVC) Window Systems Ltd.*,[62a] a case involving the infringement of a trade mark, Scott J. re-affirmed the principle that mere contractual rights were ineligible for relief from forfeiture. Here, the defendants' rights under various registered user agreements were purely contractual, and did not give rise to any proprietary or possessory rights. Moreover, the defendants' obligations under the agreements did not involve the payment of money nor could the case be described as one in which the primary object of the bargain was to secure a stated result which could effectively be attained when the matter came before the court and where the forfeiture provision was added by way of security for the production of that result.[62b] For all these reasons, therefore, relief from forfeiture was held to be unavailable.

It will be apparent from the foregoing analysis that equity's jurisdiction to relieve against forfeitures extends to cases where the failure to comply with an instalment obligation under a contract results in the repossession of some property other than land. In these cases, equity treats the forfeiture clause as a mere security for the performance of the buyer's principal obligation to meet the instalment payments on time. Accordingly, relief will take the form of the grant to the buyer of an extension of time within which to perform this principal obligation. However, such relief will only be granted on terms that the buyer pays interest on the amounts outstanding and bears the vendor's costs, thereby fully compensating the vendor for his loss occasioned by the breach. Where, however, the buyer is unable or unwilling to perform his principal obligation under the contract, relief will be denied as the object of giving this form of relief is not restitutionary. It also seems apparent that this form of relief will not be granted in every case where a forfeiture takes place and the buyer is willing and able to tender late performance. The exercise of the court's discretion whether or not to grant relief will depend on all the circumstances of the case,[63] including the conduct of the parties, the nature and gravity of the breach and its relation to the value of the property which might be forfeited.[64]

The unwillingness of the courts to extend equity's jurisdiction to commercial contracts creating purely contractual rights between the parties appears to be based on considerations of policy that, in these cases, the

---

[62a] [1991] R.P.C. 265.
[62b] See, *Shiloh Spinners Ltd.* v. *Harding* [1973] A.C. 691, 721–724, (H.L.), *per* Lord Wilberforce.
[63] See, *e.g. BICC plc* v. *Burndy Corporation* [1985] Ch. 232, 252, *per* Dillon L.J. and *Jobson* v. *Johnson* [1989] 1 W.L.R. 1026, 1043, *per* Nicholls L.J.
[64] See, *Shiloh Spinners Ltd.* v. *Harding* [1973] A.C. 691, 725, *per* Lord Wilberforce.

parties have bargained on equal terms and have contemplated a degree of certainty in their dealings with one another.[65] Quite apart from policy considerations, the courts have proceeded on the basis that, if relief against forfeiture would necessarily amount to specific performance of the contract, such relief must be refused unless the contract is one that falls within the category of contracts that are specifically enforceable.[66] Another apparent obstacle to relief in this context (to be deduced from the Court of Appeal's decision in *Sport International Bussum BV* v. *Inter-Footwear Ltd.*[67]) is the buyer's inability to obtain the remedy of specific performance in circumstances where he is in default in the performance of an essential term of the contract. This inability, it has been suggested, necessarily determines his equitable interest in the property with the consequence that he has no equitable interest to forfeit in respect of which equitable relief can be granted. This reasoning has been challenged[68] on various grounds and the alternative view,[69] that where the court grants relief from forfeiture it, in effect, absolves the defaulting party from his breach of contract as a preliminary to specific performance, has (it is submitted) much to recommend it. This view also accords with various decisions[70] which have upheld the right of a purchaser under an instalment contract to obtain relief if he is able and willing to perform the contract which has been rescinded by the vendor for breach of an essential term.

(6) *Forfeiture of a purchaser's interest in land under a contract of sale*[71]

Given that equity has jurisdiction to relieve from the forfeiture of a proprietary or possessory interest in appropriate cases, to what extent is it possible to invoke equity's jurisdiction to relieve a purchaser of land from the consequences of the vendor's rescission of the contract of sale resulting from the purchaser's failure to complete the purchase in due time?

A failure to comply with the vendor's notice to complete, served in

---

[65] See, *e.g.* the observations of Lord Bridge in *AS Awilco of Oslo* v. *Fulvia S.P.A. Di Navigazione of Cagliari, The Chikuma* [1981] 1 W.L.R. 314, 321–322, in the context of a time charterparty and *China National Foreign Trade Transportation Corporation* v. *Eulogia Shipping Co. SA, The Mihalios Xilas* [1978] 2 Lloyd's Rep. 397, 409, *per* Geoffrey Lane L.J. to the same effect.

[66] See *Sport International Bussum BV* v. *Inter-Footwear Ltd.* [1984] 1 All E.R. 376, (C.A.).

[67] [1984] 1 All E.R. 376.

[68] See, C. Harpum, (1984) 100 L.Q.R. 369.

[69] See, *e.g. Legione* v. *Hateley* (1983) 46 A.L.R. 1, 15–16, *per* Gibbs C.J. and Murphy J. In this case, the High Court of Australia held that specific performance could be decreed, following a purchaser's default in an essential term of the contract, if the exercise of the right of forfeiture by the vendor was unconscionable.

[70] See, *In Re Dagenham (Thames) Dock Co.* (1873) L.R. 8 Ch. 1022 and *Kilmer* v. *British Columbia Orchard Lands Ltd.* [1913] A.C. 319, (P.C.).

[71] See, generally, C. Harpum, [1984] C.L.J. 134 and A. Long, 100 L.Q.R. 427.

accordance with the terms of the contract, will invariably result in the forfeiture by the vendor of not only the purchaser's deposit payable under the contract but also his equitable proprietary interest arising thereunder as purchaser of the land. In this connection, the moment there is a valid contract of sale, the vendor becomes in equity a trustee for the purchaser of the estate sold and the beneficial ownership passes to the purchaser. The result is that, in the eyes of equity, the purchaser becomes the owner of the land and the vendor the owner of the purchase money just as if the contract had been completed by a conveyance or transfer.[72] In principle, therefore, since rescission of the contract necessarily involves the destruction of a proprietary interest in land, equity's power to relieve against forfeiture should be available in the type of case now under discussion.[73]

Various limitations, however, present themselves to the granting of equitable relief in this context. One apparent limitation has been the court's reluctance in some of the cases[74] to relieve against forfeiture of the purchaser's interest in the land if he was, for some reason, debarred from claiming specific performance of the contract. This is because the purchaser's equitable interest in the land is dependent upon the award of specific performance and, consequently, where time is made of the essence in the contract, default in prompt payment of the purchase price will deprive him of that remedy. The result is that the purchaser has no equitable interest to forfeit in respect of which equitable relief can be granted. A number of other cases,[75] however, have favoured the view that equity can relieve a defaulting purchaser against forfeiture of his interest in the land in circumstances where he had failed to comply with a condition making time of the essence.

A second limitation to a purchaser's right to be relieved from forfeiture of the land is that the forfeiture clause itself should be characterised as penal in nature.[76] This is in sharp contrast to the Australian[77] and

---

[72] See, e.g. Hillingdon Estates Co. v. Stonefield Estates Ltd. [1952] Ch. 627, 631, per Vaisey J. and Capital Finance Co. Ltd. v. Stokes [1968] 1 W.L.R. 1158, 1162–1163, per Pennycuick J.; on appeal [1969] 1 Ch. 261. Before the trust can arise, the contract must be specifically enforceable and the purchaser must have accepted the vendor's title: Howard v. Miller [1915] A.C. 318, 326, per Lord Parker of Waddington and Lysaght v. Edwards (1876) 2 Ch. D. 499, 506–507, per Jessel M.R.

[73] Indeed, it is submitted that the true theoretical basis for such jurisdiction ("unconscionability") is identical to that applicable to the loss of interest of a mortgagor or lessee: See, Weil v. Barthel (1955) 279 P. 2d. 544; Mussen v. Van Dieman's Land Co. [1938] Ch. 253, 261, per Farwell J. and Snell v. Brickles (1914) 49 S.C.R. 360, 371–372, per Duff J.

[74] Notably, Steedman v. Drinkle [1916] A.C. 275, (P.C.); Brickles v. Snell [1916] 2 A.C. 599, 604–605, (P.C.), per Lord Atkinson.

[75] Vernon v. Stephens (1722) 24 E.R. 642; In Re Dagenham (Thames) Dock Co. (1873) L.R. 8 Ch. App. 1022; Kilmer v. British Columbia Orchard Lands Ltd. [1913] A.C. 319, (P.C.).

[76] See, In Re Dagenham (Thames) Dock Co. (1873) L.R. 8 Ch. App. 1022, 1025, per Mellish L.J.; Kilmer v. British Columbia Orchard Lands Ltd. [1913] A.C. 319, 325, (P.C.), per Lord Macnaghten.

[77] Legione v. Hateley (1983) 46 A.L.R. 1; Ciavarella v. Balmer (1983) 57 A.L.J.R. 632.

American[78] experience where the concept of "unconscionability" has been applied as a basis for equity's jurisdiction to relieve from forfeitures in the context of cases involving the sale of land.

A third and final limitation to the grant of equitable relief revolves around the purchaser's willingness and ability to pay off the arrears of instalments due (together with interest and costs) within an agreed or stipulated time period.[79] Thus, in *In Re Dagenham (Thames) Dock Co.*[80] relief was granted on terms that the purchaser pay the residue of the purchase money (i.e. the outstanding instalment of £2,000 which had fallen due for payment) with interest. Similarly, in *Kilmer* v. *British Columbia Orchard Lands Ltd.*[81] the purchaser was relieved from forfeiture on payment of the purchase money then due to the vendor.[82] In *Steedman* v. *Drinkle*[83] the Privy Council granted relief "on proper terms" but there is no reference in the report as to what those terms may have been. In *Starside Properties Ltd.* v. *Mustapha*[84] the county court judge had suspended the vendor's order for possession of the house for three months to enable the purchaser to raise the money to acquire the property from the vendor at the original contract price. The purchaser was, in fact, unable to raise the money in time and applied for a further extension of time on the ground that she had contracted to sell the property at a figure which would bring her in a profit. The Court of Appeal held that the trial judge had jurisdiction to grant a further extension of time and remitted the case to him so that he could consider the purchaser's application on the merits.

(7) *Forfeiture in the context of the criminal law*

(a) *Rule of public policy*

There is a common law rule[85] of public policy which prevents a person

---

[78] *Cheney* v. *Libby* (1890) 134 U.S. 68; *Dependabilt Homes Inc.* v. *White* (1951) 117 NE 2d. 706, (Ohio Court of Appeal); *Peterson* v. *Richenour* (1955) 135 Cal. App. 2d. 720; *Ward* v. *Union Bond & Trust Company* (1957) 243 F. 2d. 476, (U.S.C.A., California); *Land Development Inc.* v. *Padgett* (1962) 369 P. 2d. 888, (Supreme Court of Alaska).

[79] According to Romer L.J. in *Stockloser* v. *Johnson* [1954] 1 Q.B. 476, 497, the purchaser need show no more than a "reasonable prospect" of being able to pay if extra time is given. See also *Jobson* v. *Johnson* [1989] 1 W.L.R. 1026, a case involving the purchase of shares in a football club, where Kerr L.J. intimated that relief against forfeiture would normally entail payment of the outstanding instalments in full together with interest and the vendor's costs: *ibid*, 1047. Relief was refused in *Barton Thompson & Co. Ltd.* v. *Stapling Machines Co.* [1966] Ch. 499, a case involving a lease of chattels, because the lessees had failed to show that they would ever be able to pay off the arrears of rent which had fallen due under the lease.

[80] (1873) L.R. 8 Ch. App. 1022.

[81] [1913] A.C. 319, (P.C.).

[82] In fact, the purchaser had paid the money that had fallen due for payment into court.

[83] [1916] 1 A.C. 275, (P.C.).

[84] [1974] 1 W.L.R. 816, (C.A.).

[85] The rule is expressed by the maxim *"ex turpi causa non oritur actio"*, (an action does not arise from a base cause).

30

who has unlawfully killed another from acquiring a benefit in consequence of that killing. This rule of forfeiture is intended to act as a disincentive to criminal activity and to reflect public conscience. One of the leading authorities on the subject is *Cleaver* v. *Mutual Rescue Fund Life Association*[86] in which Fry L.J. said[87]:

"It appears to me that no system of jurisprudence can with reason include amongst the rights which it enforces rights directly resulting to the person asserting them from the crime of that person."

In that case, a husband (James Maybrick) took out an insurance policy on his life with the defendants for £2,000 in favour of his wife (Florence Elizabeth Maybrick). He subsequently died from poison which had been intentionally administered by his wife who was later convicted of his wilful murder. The Court of Appeal held that the husband's executors could maintain an action on the policy to recover the sum insured for the benefit of the estate notwithstanding that the death of the insured had been caused by the felonious act of his wife. However, the wife herself could not lay any claim to the money as the trust created by the policy in her favour under section 11 of the Married Women's Property Act 1882 had become incapable of performance by reason of her crime.

The Forfeiture Act 1982[87a] gives the court power to grant relief to certain persons guilty of unlawful killing from forfeiture of inheritance and other similar rights. Under section 2(1), the court must first determine whether the rule of public policy precludes an offender (*i.e.* a person who has unlawfully killed another[88]) acquiring an interest in property. Once this has been established, it is then open to the court to make an order modifying the effect of the rule in the given case provided that it is satisfied that, having regard to the conduct of the offender and of the deceased and to such other circumstances as appear to be material, the justice of the case requires the effect of the rule to be so modified.[89] The interests in property in respect of which an order can be made are defined

---

[86] [1892] 1 Q.B. 147, (C.A.). See also, *In Re Peacock, Midland Bank Executor and Trustee Co. Ltd.* v. *Peacock* [1957] 1 Ch. 310; *In the Estate of Crippen* [1911] P. 108; *In Re Sigsworth, Bedworth* v. *Bedworth* [1935] 1 Ch. 89; *Beresford* v. *Royal Insurance Co. Ltd.* [1937] 2 K.B. 197, (C.A.); [1938] A.C. 586, (H.L.); *In Re Callaway, Callaway* v. *Treasury Solicitor* [1956] 1 Ch. 559; *Hall* v. *Knight and Baxter* [1914] P. 1, (C.A.); *Gray* v. *Barr* [1970] 2 Q.B. 626; *R.* v. *National Insurance Commissioner, ex p. Connor* [1981] 1 Q.B. 758; *In Re Giles, Giles* v. *Giles* [1972] 1 Ch. 544; *In Re Royse, Royse* v. *Royse* [1984] 3 W.L.R. 784, (C.A.); *Re H, Deceased* [1990] 1 F.L.R. 441; *Re K, Deceased* [1985] Ch. 85.

[87] *Ibid*, 156. His Lordship made reference to the House of Lords decision in *The Amicable Society for a Perpetual Life Assurance Office* v. *Bolland*, (*Fauntleroy's Case*) (1830) 4 Bli. (N.S.) 194; 5 E.R. 70, as proceeding on this principle of public policy, which in that case prevented the assignees of a forger from claiming the benefit of a policy on his death (by execution) by reason of his forgery.

[87a] See, generally, *Review of Forfeiture Act 1982*, M. Pawlowski, (1993) Litigation, Vol. 12/4.

[88] It is interesting to observe that the provision applies even if the offender is not convicted or even if he is not charged. The Act, however, does not affect the application of the forfeiture rule in the case of a person who stands convicted of murder: s. 5.

[89] s. 2(2).

in section 2(4) of the Act. For illustrations of the application of these provisions, the reader is referred to *In Re K, Deceased*[90] and *Re H, Deceased*.[91]

The Act also provides[92] that the forfeiture rule will not preclude a person from making an application under various statutory provisions, namely, any provision of the Inheritance (Provision for Family and Dependants) Act 1975,[93] sections 31(6) (variation etc. of periodical payments orders) and 36(1) (variation of maintenance agreements) of the Matrimonial Causes Act 1973 and section 5(4) of the Divorce (Scotland) Act 1976 (variation etc. of periodical allowances). Reference should also be made to section 4 of the 1982 Act, which provides, in respect of a variety of pension and social security benefits payable as a consequence of death, for the issue as to forfeiture to be decided by a Social Security Commissioner. Prior to the amendments made to this Section under section 76 of the Social Security Act 1986, a Commissioner had no power to modify the effect of the forfeiture rule as regards any social security entitlement. Accordingly, the effect of the (unamended) section was simply to give the Commissioner original jurisdiction to determine at first instance whether or not the forfeiture rule should apply to a given claim before him. The effect of section 76 of the 1986 Act is to amend section 4 to give the Commissioner the same powers to modify the effect of the forfeiture rule in relation to social security benefits as the courts already enjoy under section 2(1) in relation to interests in property. Consequently, the amendment enables a Commissioner to decide in cases where the forfeiture rule applies whether, and if so for how long, an offender should forfeit benefit.

(b) *Statutory powers of forfeiture*

There are various statutory provisions which empower a criminal court to make orders depriving offenders of property used in connection with the commission of an offence. The more important of these may be listed as follows:

    (a)   Section 43 of the Powers of Criminal Courts Act 1973 (deprivation of property used in the commission of certain offences);

    (b)   Sections 71–102 of the Criminal Justice Act 1988 (confiscation orders in respect of certain offences);

    (c)   Section 27 of the Misuse of Drugs Act 1971 (forfeiture of drugs etc.);

[90] [1985] Ch. 85.
[91] [1990] 1 F.L.R. 441.
[92] s. 3(1) and (2).
[93] See *In Re Royse, Royse* v. *Royse* [1984] 3 W.L.R. 784, (C.A.).

(d)   Section 1(1) of the Drug Trafficking Offences Act 1986 (confiscation of benefits arising from drug-trafficking);

(e)   Sections 25 and 26 of the Criminal Justice (International Co-operation) Act 1990 (forfeiture of cash representing proceeds of drug trafficking);

(f)   Sections 49(1), 53(4) and (8), 61(5), 66(2), 74(2), 78(4), 81(6) and (7), 88, 89(1), 90, 141(1)(a) of the Customs and Excise Management Act 1979 (forfeiture orders connected with the unlawful importation or exportation of goods);

(g)   Sections 7 and 24 of the Forgery and Counterfeiting Act 1981 (forfeiture of property used for the making of any false instrument etc.);

(h)   Section 13(2) of the Prevention of Terrorism (Temporary Provisions) Act 1989 (forfeiture of property solicited for terrorist purposes);

(i)   Section 5(7) of the Bail Act 1976 (forfeiture of security);

(j)   Section 3(3) of the Obscene Publications Act 1959 (forfeiture of obscene articles);

(k)   Section 5 of the Protection of Children Act 1978 (forfeiture of indecent photographs of children);

(l)   Section 25(6) of the Immigration Act 1971 (forfeiture of ships, aircraft, or vehicles used in connection with illegal entry or harbouring);

(m)   Section 46 of the Gaming Act 1968 (forfeiture of things related to unlawful gambling);

(n)   Section 1(3) of the Honours (Prevention of Abuses) Act 1925 (forfeiture of gift, money or other consideration as inducement or reward for procuring the grant of a dignity or title);

(o)   Section 2 of the Forfeiture Act 1870 (forfeiture of certain rights upon conviction for treason).

Part II: Elements of Forfeiture

Chapter Two

The right of forfeiture

When the right of forfeiture arises

The circumstances in which a landlord[1] has a right to forfeit the lease are limited and may be grouped under the following headings:

(1) Under a proviso for re-entry contained in the lease;
(2) Upon the happening of an event specified in an express condition subject to which the term of the lease was created;
(3) Where the tenant denies the landlord's title and
(4) Under section 35(2) of the Sexual Offences Act 1956.

(1) *Under a proviso for re-entry*

A lease will invariably contain a proviso for re-entry[2] (or forfeiture clause) entitling the landlord to terminate the lease and re-enter the demised premises upon the happening of certain specified events. These will invariably include non-payment of rent, the tenant's breach of any of his covenants in the lease, the tenant's bankruptcy or liquidation, where the tenant makes a composition with his creditors and where a judgment creditor has levied execution[3] against his goods to secure payment of a judgment debt. A landlord who purports to re-enter the tenant's premises otherwise than upon the events specified in the proviso will be treated as a trespasser and liable to pay damages to the tenant for any injury suffered as a result of the wrongful re-entry. Thus, in *Yelloly* v.

---

[1] Whilst there is nothing in theory to prevent the parties from incorporating terms in a lease making it terminable by the *tenant* for fault on the part of the landlord, this is very rarely done in practice.

[2] For forms of proviso for re-entry: See *Encyclopaedia of Forms and Precedents* (5th ed.) Vol. 23, paras. 1231–1235, Forms 473–475.

[3] *Davis* v. *Eyton* (1830) 7 Bing. 154; 131 E.R. 60 (landlord entitled to emblements upon re-entry); *Harvey* v. *Larkin* (1950) 66 T.L.R. 896 (proviso for re-entry will apply to distress levied by landlord himself); *Rees d. Powell* v. *King and Morris* (1800) Forr. 19 (in the case of a re-entry if no sufficient distress found, every part of the premises must be searched); *Shepherd* v. *Berger* (1891) 1 Q.B. 597.

Morley[4] the tenant, without committing any breach of covenant, affixed an election poster on the demised premises. The landlord entered upon the premises and removed the poster claiming he had a right to do so under the proviso for re-entry contained in the lease, which permitted re-entry upon non-performance of the covenants by the tenant or non-payment of rent. Since the tenant had committed no breach of covenant in affixing the poster, the landlord's re-entry was held to be unlawful.

In the absence of a proviso for re-entry contained in the lease, the landlord will have no right to forfeit for breach by the tenant of any term in the lease unless it is construed as a breach of condition.[5] A proviso will not be implied into the lease so that, if the lease contains no express forfeiture clause, the landlord will be limited to an action for damages or an injunction to restrain the tenant's breach of covenant.

It was once thought that the doctrine of repudiatory breach (to be found in the law of contract) had no application to leases. In the words of Lord Denning M.R. in *Total Oil Great Britain Ltd.* v. *Thompson Garages (Biggin Hill) Ltd.*[6]:

"A lease is a demise. It conveys an interest in land. It does not come to an end like an ordinary contract on repudiation and acceptance."

Lord Denning M.R. based this proposition on essentially two grounds, first, that a lease differed from other contracts in creating an estate in land and, secondly, that a lease could not be determined by frustration[7] and nor, therefore, by repudiation and acceptance. Both these grounds have now been destroyed by decisions of the House of Lords. The premise that a lease of land is in its essence different from other contracts has been overturned by the House of Lords in *United Scientific Holdings Ltd.* v. *Burnley Borough Council*[8] and the notion that a lease cannot be determined by frustration has been overset by the House of Lords in *National Carriers Ltd.* v. *Panalpina Northern Ltd.*[9] In the latter case, the House of Lords ruled that the doctrine of frustration was, in principle, applicable to leases although the actual circumstances in which a lease could be frustrated would be rare. The point has received recent judicial scrutiny in *Hussein* v. *Mehlman*,[10] in which Mr. Stephen Sedley Q.C. (sitting as an assistant recorder at the Wood Green Trial Centre) held that a lease or tenancy

---

[4] (1910) 27 T.L.R. 20.
[5] A proviso for re-entry is not required where the breach consists of a breach of condition in the lease: *Bashir* v. *Commissioner of Lands* [1960] A.C. 44, (P.C.).
[6] [1972] 1 Q.B. 318, 324.
[7] Relying on *Cricklewood Property and Investment Trust Ltd.* v. *Leighton's Investment Trust Ltd.* [1945] A.C. 221, (H.L.).
[8] [1978] A.C. 904, (H.L.), approving *C.H. Bailey Ltd.* v. *Memorial Enterprises Ltd.* [1974] 1 W.L.R. 728, (C.A.). See also, *Hammersmith and Fulham London Borough Council* v. *Monk* [1991] 3 W.L.R. 1144, (H.L.) and *Hussein* v. *Mehlman* [1992] 32 E.G. 59.
[9] [1981] A.C. 675, (H.L.).
[10] [1992] 32 E.G. 59.

could come to an end by the tenant's acceptance of his landlord's repudiatory conduct. In that case, the landlord had been in breach of his implied obligations to repair under section 11 of the Landlord and Tenant Act 1985. In the face of several refusals to carry out the repairs, the tenants returned the keys and vacated the premises which comprised a dwelling-house let on an assured shorthold tenancy. On the evidence, the learned assistant recorder held that the landlord had been guilty of a repudiatory breach and that the tenants, by vacating the house and returning the keys, had accepted that repudiation as putting an end to the tenancy. In the course of his judgment,[11] he also recognised that default in an obligation to pay rent, if sufficiently fundamental to the purpose of the contract of letting, would constitute a repudiatory act on the part of the tenant. However, he went on to observe[12] that any such conclusion would:

"... have effect subject not only to all the statutory provisions but also, I would think, to the provisions contained in the contract of letting itself in relation to forfeiture (where there is a term certain): in other words, the right to terminate by acceptance of repudiatory conduct may itself be modified by further contractual provisions which lay down conditions, supported by statute, for the exercise of the right."

Indeed, if the position were otherwise, the effect would presumably be that a repudiatory breach by the tenant, coupled with its acceptance by the landlord, would of itself terminate the tenancy and the law of forfeiture would thus be completely avoided.

A proviso for re-entry may also be found in an agreement for a lease[13] entitling the landlord to re-enter the subject premises for breach of any of the terms of the agreement. In *Doe* d. *Thompson* v. *Amey*,[14] the tenant was let into possession of land and paid rent as a yearly tenant under a written agreement for a future lease for 14 years. The agreement contained a tenant's covenant against growing two successive crops of corn on the land and a proviso for re-entry for breach of covenant. No actual lease was ever made or executed by the parties. Lord Denman C.J. said[15]:

"In this case, the defendant was let into possession under an agreement, which gave the parties a right to go into equity to compel the

---

[11] *Ibid*, 61.
[12] *Ibid*, 61.
[13] A proviso for re-entry on non-payment of rent (but not other breaches of covenant) is a "usual" covenant: *In Re Anderton and Milner's Contract* [1890] 45 Ch. D. 476. It has been held that it is not usual for a lease to be terminable upon the tenant's insolvency: *Hyde* v. *Warden* (1877) 3 Ex. D. 72. But see: *Chester* v. *Buckingham Travel Ltd.* [1981] 1 W.L.R. 96.
[14] (1840) 12 Ad. & E. 476; 113 E.R. 892.
[15] *Ibid*, 479; 893.

execution of it by making out a formal lease.[16] Under such circumstances it has long been the uniform opinion of Westminster Hall, that the tenant in possession holds upon the terms of the intended lease. One of these terms was, that the lessee should not take successive crops of corn, and that the lessor should have power to re-enter on the breach of any such agreement. This agreement and proviso apply to the yearly tenancy of the defendant."

In this case, although the yearly tenancy arose by operation of law, it had engrafted upon it the terms of the written agreement including the proviso for re-entry entitling the landlord to re-enter on breach of the tenant's covenant against taking successive crops. Similarly, in *Thomas* v. *Pacher*,[17] a proviso for re-entry on nonpayment of rent was held to attach to a yearly tenancy created by the tenant's holding over and paying rent after the expiration of his lease. The same principle will apply if the tenant goes into possession of the premises under a void lease at law.[18] But, apart from these circumstances, the proviso will only operate during the term of the lease.[19]

Conditions and covenants, the breach of which may lead to a forfeiture, will be construed[20] (like other contractual terms) by reference to the objective intentions of the parties to the lease to be gathered from the words used by them.[21] In *Doe* d. *Davis* v. *Elsam*,[22] Lord Tenterden C.J. said:

"I do not think provisos of this sort are to be construed with the strictness of conditions at common law. These are matters of contract between the parties, and should, in my opinion, be construed as

[16] See *Walsh* v. *Lonsdale* (1882) 21 Ch. D. 9, in which the Court of Appeal established the principle that, where a tenant holds premises under an agreement for a lease, he holds under the same terms in equity as if a lease had been granted to him on the basis that the agreement is specifically enforceable in equity.

[17] (1857) 1 H. & N. 669; 156 E.R. 1370. See also, *Hayne* v. *Cummings* (1864) 16 C.B. (N.S.) 421; 143 E.R. 1191.

[18] *per* Watson B. in *Thomas* v. *Pacher* (1857) 1 H. & N. 669, 672–673; 156 E.R. 1370, 1371–1372.

[19] *Johns* v. *Whitley* (1770) 3 Wils. 127; 95 E.R. 970.

[20] As to the nature of extrinsic evidence admissible for the purposes of construction: See *City and Westminster Properties (1934) Ltd.* v. *Mudd* [1959] Ch. 129. The surrounding circumstances with reference to which the lease was entered into (*i.e.* the nature of the property and the purpose for which it is suitable) are admissible but not the conduct of the parties or their statements of intention.

[21] *Croft* v. *Lumley* (1858) 6 H.L. Cas. 672, 693; 10 E.R. 1459, 1468, *per* Channell B.

[22] (1828) M. & M. 189; 173 E.R. 1126. See also, *Goodtitle* d. *Luxmore* v. *Saville* (1812) 16 East 87, 95; 104 E.R. 1022, 1025, *per* Lord Ellenborough C.J.; *Doe* d. *Muston* v. *Gladwin* (1845) 6 Q.B. 953, 961; 115 E.R. 359, 362, *per* Patteson J.; *Perry* v. *Davis* (1858) 3 C.B. (N.S.) 769 and *Bristol Corporation* v. *Westcott* (1879) 12 Ch. D. 461. In *Doe* d. *Lloyd* v. *Ingleby* (1846) 15 M. & W. 465, 470; 153 E.R. 933, 935, Platt J. took a stricter approach to the construction of the proviso before him: "Whenever there is a stipulation for a forfeiture the case must be clearly and strictly brought within the terms of the condition." As to re-entry under a statutory power: See, *Doe* d. *Bywater* v. *Brandling* (1828) 7 B. & C. 643: 108 E.R. 863.

other contracts. The parties agree to a tenancy on certain terms, and there is no hardship in binding them to those terms. In my view of the cases of this sort the provisos ought to be construed according to fair and obvious construction, without favour to either side."

In the case of a covenant with a proviso for re-entry, the court must first construe the covenant fairly, ascertaining its meaning without regard to the forfeiture, and then see, upon that ascertained meaning, whether a forfeiture has been incurred.[23] As to the proviso itself, the court leans towards a literal[24] or strict[25] construction against the landlord so that any ambiguity in wording will be resolved in favour of the tenant. Thus, in *Doe d. Abdy* v. *Stevens*,[26] the proviso gave the landlord power of re-entry if the tenant "shall do or cause to be done any act, matter or thing contrary to and in breach of any of the covenants" in the lease. This wording was held not to apply to a breach of the covenant to repair since an *omission* to repair was not to be construed as an "act done" within the meaning of the proviso. The position will be different if the proviso makes reference to covenants on the part of the tenant which are required to be "performed", "observed", "obeyed" or "kept" since negative as well as positive covenants may be performed, observed, obeyed or kept.[27] This is because the words "perform" etc. apply to the obligation or duty under the negative covenant so that the covenantor is said to perform his obligation by abstaining from doing the thing which he has covenanted not to do. Similar reasoning will apply if the re-entry is expressed to take effect "on breach" of any of the tenant's covenants in the lease.

The omission of the words "to re-enter" in a proviso for re-entry will not

---

[23] *Bristol Corporation* v. *Westcott* (1879) 12 Ch. D. 461, 467, (C.A.), *per* Cotton L.J.

[24] See, *e.g. Doe* d. *Spencer* v. *Godwin* (1815) 4 M. & S. 265; 105 E.R. 833.

[25] *Croft* v. *Lumley* (1858) 6 H.L. Cas. 672, 693; 10 E.R. 1459, 1468, *per* Channell B.

[26] (1823) 3 B. & Ad. 299; 110 E.R. 112.

[27] *Harman* v. *Ainslie* [1904] 1 K.B. 698, (C.A.); *Croft* v. *Lumley* (1858) 6 H.L. Cas. 672, 719; 10 E.R. 1459, 1478, *per* Martin B. (non-observance of a negative covenant entitled landlord to re-enter); *Timms* v. *Baker* (1883) 49 L.T. 106 (the words "perform and keep" held wide enough to cover a breach of a negative covenant); *Barrow* v. *Isaacs* [1891] 1 Q.B. 417, 419, 424, *per* Lord Esher M.R. and Kay L.J., respectively. In *Doe* d. *Palk* v. *Marchetti* (1831) 1 B. & Ad. 715; 109 E.R. 953, the proviso referred to the default in performance of the tenant's covenants after the space of 30 days' notice. The reference to notice made it applicable only to a positive covenant. In *West* v. *Dobb* (1870) L.R. 5 Q.B. 460, it was suggested that a clause for re-entry "if the lessees should fail in observance or performance of any of their covenants" did not apply to a negative covenant; *Hyde* v. *Warden* (1877) 3 Ex. D. 72, 82, *per* Brett L.J. (power of re-entry in the event of the lessee "wilfully failing or neglecting to perform any of the covenants" did not apply to a breach of a negative covenant); *Evans* v. *Davis* (1878) 10 Ch. D. 747, 761, *per* Fry J. (the word "perform" not applicable to negative covenants); *Wadham* v. *Postmaster General* (1871) L.R. 6 Q.B. 644, 648, *per* Blackburn J. (whether power of re-entry applied to negative as well as positive covenants will depend upon the particular wording of the proviso). Where the proviso entitles the landlord to forfeit on breach of "covenants and stipulations", it will apply to a provision against assignment albeit that the provision is not in the form of a covenant: *Brookes* v. *Drysdale* (1877) 3 C.P.D. 52.

deprive the landlord of his right to forfeit.[28] But where the wording of the proviso is grammatically unintelligible, the court will not rewrite the proviso so as to make sense of it.[29] In *Doe* d. *Spence* v. *Godwin*,[30] the proviso stipulated that "if all or any of the covenants *hereinafter* contained on the part of the lessee shall be broken", it should be lawful for the landlord to re-enter. There were no covenants on the part of the tenant after the proviso. The Court of King's Bench held that the landlord could not re-enter for breach of the covenant not to assign, which appeared before the proviso, because the proviso only comprehended subsequent covenants.

A proviso for re-entry which stipulates that the lease shall be *void* on non-payment of the rent or non-performance of the tenant's covenants gives only the landlord (and not the tenant) the option of determining the lease on the tenant's default. In the words of Lord Ellenborough C.J. in *Rede* v. *Farr*[31]:

> "If that be a principle of law, that a party shall not take advantage of his own wrong, then a lessee shall not avail himself of his own act to vacate his lease."

In *Doe* d. *Nash* v. *Birch*,[32] the proviso stipulated that the lease should be "null and void" in the event of the tenant's failure to erect a shop-front on the demised premises within three calendar months. The Court of Exchequer held that the wording of the proviso made the lease voidable only at the election of the landlord.

A proviso for re-entry on bankruptcy has been construed as referring to the bankruptcy of the person who is tenant at the relevant time and not to the bankruptcy of the original tenant following an assignment of the lease. In *Smith* v. *Gronow*,[33] the proviso stipulated that if the tenant, "his executors,[34] administrators or assigns shall become bankrupt", it should be lawful for the landlord to re-enter the demised premises. The original tenant assigned the lease and subsequently became bankrupt. Wright J. held that the proviso referred only to the bankruptcy of the person who for the time being was possessed of the leasehold estate and that, accord-

---

[28] *Hunt* v. *Bishop* (1853) 8 Ex. 675.

[29] *Doe* d. *Wyndham* v. *Carew* (1841) 2 Q.B. 317; 114 E.R. 124. In *Doe* d. *Darke* v. *Bowditch* (1846) 8 Q.B. 973; 115 E.R. 1140, the wording of the proviso was not so obscure as to be meaningless and effect was given to it.

[30] (1815) 4 M. & S. 265; 105 E.R. 833.

[31] (1817) 6 M. & S. 121, 125; 105 E.R. 1188, 1190.

[32] (1836) 1 M. & W. 402; 150 E.R. 490. See also, *Hayne* v. *Cummings* (1864) 16 C.B. (N.S.) 421, 426; 143 E.R. 1191, 1194, *per* Willes J. and *Arnsby* v. *Woodward* (1827) 6 B. & C. 519, 523; 108 E.R. 542, 544, *per* Lord Tenterden C.J.

[33] [1891] 2 Q.B. 394. An express right to forfeit on the insolvency of the tenant's surety is effective: *Halliard Property Co. Ltd.* v. *Jack Segal Ltd.* [1978] 1 W.L.R. 377.

[34] If the tenant's executor becomes bankrupt, the lease is subject to forfeiture: *Doe* d. *Bridgman* v. *David* (1834) 1 Cr. M. & R. 405; 149 E.R. 1137 and *Doe* d. *Williams* v. *Davies* (1834) 6 C. & P. 614; 172 E.R. 1388.

ingly, no act of forfeiture had occurred on the facts before him. His reasoning was based partly on the assumption that an assignee of the lease should take the same estate as that of his assignor, the original tenant. He said[35]:

"Upon the plaintiff's construction, the assignee ... would take a different estate and a more precarious one, because it would be determinable not merely on his own default, but also on the default of a stranger to the estate. Suppose the original lessee assigned part of the estate to one approved person, and the residue to another—on the plaintiff's construction, the bankruptcy of one of the assigns would give the lessor the right of re-entry on both parts of the estate. I do not think a construction involving such consequences ought to be adopted in the present case."

In *Doe* d. *Lloyd* v. *Ingleby*,[36] the Court of Exchequer held that a proviso for re-entry upon the tenant being "duly found and declared a bankrupt" did not apply to an invalid adjudication of bankruptcy. Where a re-entry is expressed to arise should the tenant company "enter into liquidation, whether compulsory or voluntary", it has been held[37] that the lease is forfeitable where the company goes into voluntary liquidation, not by reason of insolvency, but for the purpose of reconstruction or amalgamation. The determining event in such a case is the entering into liquidation and the cause which led to that event is immaterial. To construe the provision otherwise would involve the introduction into the proviso after the word "voluntary" of the words "in consequence of insolvency", which would not be justified on a plain reading of the provision.

Various attempts have been made by landlords to disguise a forfeiture clause as a contractual provision giving the landlord the right (upon notice to the tenant) to determine the lease on the happening of certain events including the tenant's default. If the clause is construed as an effective contractual right to terminate the lease (as opposed to a provision for forfeiture), this will have the effect of denying the tenant the right to apply for any relief[38] in the event of the right being exercised. The point was considered in *Richard Clarke & Co. Ltd.* v. *Widnall*,[39] where the landlords granted a yearly tenancy of licensed premises to the tenant determinable by 12 months' notice by either party. A clause in the tenancy

---

[35] [1891] 2 Q.B. 394, 397. But an express right of forfeiture upon the original tenant's bankruptcy will be valid.

[36] (1846) 15 M. & W. 465; 153 E.R. 933.

[37] *Horsey Estate Ltd.* v. *Steiger* [1899] 2 Q.B. 79; *Re Walker, ex p. Gould* (1884) 13 Q.B.D. 454. If the proviso stipulates for re-entry on the tenant's "insolvency", this will not justify forfeiture in the case of a solvent bankruptcy: *Doe* d. *Gatehouse* v. *Rees* (1838) 4 Bing. N.C. 384. See also, *Re Riggs, ex p. Lovell* [1901] 2 K.B. 16. In a compulsory liquidation, the right to forfeit arises on the making of the winding up order: *General Share and Trust Co.* v. *Wetley Brick and Pottery Co.* (1882) 20 Ch. D. 260.

[38] The right to relief being only available to a tenant in the event of the landlord's forfeiture of his lease.

[39] [1976] 1 W.L.R. 845.

agreement provided that, if the tenant committed *inter alia* a breach of the covenant to pay rent, the landlords would be entitled to obtain possession of the premises or, alternatively, give the tenant three months' notice to determine the tenancy. The tenant failed to pay the rent and the landlords served a three months' notice to quit in compliance with the clause. The Court of Appeal held that the operation of the notice to quit amounted to the exercise by the landlords of a right of re-entry and, since the tenant had paid all outstanding arrears of rent before trial, the tenant was entitled to relief from forfeiture. Megaw L.J. said[40]:

> "The inclusion of a period of notice before the lease terminates, being a period unilateral to the landlord and less than the general period of notice available to either party, does not deprive the tenant of his right to claim relief when, as here, the event on which the landlord relies as giving rise to his right to terminate is a breach by the tenant of his covenant to pay rent."

In *Clays Lane Housing Co-operative Ltd.* v. *Patrick*,[41] the tenancy agreement created a weekly tenancy in favour of the tenant terminable by either party by not less than four weeks' notice in writing. Clause 7 of the agreement provided that the landlord could terminate the tenancy, by giving four weeks' notice to quit, in the event of the tenant's non-payment of rent. The Court of Appeal held that, for a provision in a tenancy agreement to constitute a forfeiture clause, it was necessary that it brought the lease to an end earlier than the actual termination date of the tenancy (*i.e.* prior to the contractual expiry date of a fixed term or the date on which a periodic tenancy could be brought to an end by notice to quit). The Court, therefore, was able to distinguish the *Richard Clarke* case on the ground that in that case the landlords' right to terminate brought the lease to an end *before* its natural termination date. In *Richard Clarke*, the landlords could only determine the tenancy upon 12 months' notice after the first six months of the term had expired but, under the forfeiture clause, the landlords could, on the tenant's default, determine the tenancy prematurely on giving only three months' notice.

Although a covenant in the lease may expressly prescribe a particular remedy in case of its breach by the tenant, this will not preclude the landlord from exercising his right of forfeiture under the proviso for re-entry upon the tenant's default. Thus, in *Doe* d. *Antrobus* v. *Jepson*,[42] the lease contained a covenant that the tenant should not carry any hay off the premises under a penalty of £5 per ton. A clause followed which enumerated all the covenants (except the hay covenant) and provided

[40] *Ibid*, 851.
[41] (1985) 49 P. & C.R. 72, applied in *Underground (Civil Engineering) Ltd.* v. *Croydon London Borough Council* [1990] E.G.C.S. 48, (building agreement).
[42] (1832) 3 B. & Ad. 402; 110 E.R. 144.

that, upon breach of any of those covenants, the landlord could forfeit the lease. The Court of King's Bench held that the penalty contained in the covenant did not prevent the clause of re-entry from applying to the hay covenant, the words of the proviso being large enough to comprehend it. Similarly, in *Weston* v. *Metropolitan Asylums Board*,[43] the reddendum provided that additional rent was payable by the tenants in the event of their breach of a user covenant in the lease. The lease also contained a proviso for re-entry in case of non-payment of rent or breach of any of the tenants' covenants. The Court of Appeal held that the inclusion of a penalty in the reddendum did not preclude the landlords from re-entering the premises upon the tenants' breach of the user covenant. The lease gave the landlords the choice whether to avail themselves of the proviso for re-entry or, alternatively, claim the additional rent by way of penalty for the tenants' breach.

A right of forfeiture contained in a proviso cannot be exercised in circumstances where the tenant's breach of covenant is committed involuntary by act of law.[44] In *Doe* d. *Lord Grantley* v. *Butcher*,[45] land was demised for 1000 years for the purpose of erecting a poor-house thereon. The lease contained a proviso for re-entry if the tenants discontinued to adopt the provisions of a certain statute under which the poor-house was to be run. Subsequently, under the Poor Law Amendment Act, the tenants were directed to remove all the inmates of the poor-house to a neighbouring building. The Court of Queen's Bench held that, since the relevant condition had been broken under compulsion of a statutory authority, no act of forfeiture had arisen under the proviso.

Where land is let on a tenancy for use by the tenant as an allotment garden[45a] (or is let to any local authority or association for the purpose of being sub-let for such use) the tenancy of the land (or any part) may be terminated under a provision for re-entry for non-payment of rent or breach of any term or condition of the tenancy or on account of the tenant becoming bankrupt or compounding with his creditors, or where the tenant is an association, on account of its liquidation.[45b]

Finally, it should be noted that, in relation to a tenancy of an agricultural holding, the proviso for re-entry must include a provision stating that the landlord's right to forfeit is only exerciseable on the expiry of notice to the tenant of a sufficient duration (preferably, more than one month) to enable the tenant to serve certain notices under the Agricultural Holdings Act 1986 on the landlord.[46]

---

[43] (1882) 9 Q.B.D. 404. See also, *French* v. *Macale* (1842) 2 Dr. & W. 269.
[44] *Doe* d. *Marquis of Angelsea* v. *Churchwardens of Rugeley* (1844) 6 Q.B. 107, 114; 115 E.R. 41, 44, *per* Lord Denman C.J.
[45] (1840) 6 Q.B. 115n; 115 E.R. 44n.
[45a] For meaning of "allotment garden": See s. 22(1) of the Allotments Act 1922.
[45b] s. 1(1)(*e*) of the Allotments Act 1922. See also, s. 1(1)(*b*), (*c*) and (*d*).
[46] *Parry* v. *Million Pigs Ltd.* (1981) 260 E.G. 281.

(2) *Upon the happening of an event specified in an express condition in the lease*

Where the particular stipulation in the lease falls to be construed as a condition[47] (as opposed to a covenant), the landlord will be entitled to forfeit the lease upon the happening of the event(s) specified in the condition without recourse to a proviso for re-entry contained in the lease.[48] In *Doe* d. *Lockwood* v. *Clarke*,[49] for example, a farmhouse was leased to the tenant for 21 years if he should "so long continue to inhabit and dwell with his and their family and servants in the said farmhouse and he ... should so long continue actually to hold and occupy the said farm lands". The lease contained a proviso for re-entry if any of the tenant's covenants were broken. The tenant became bankrupt and ceased to occupy the premises. The Court of King's Bench held that the landlord could bring an action for ejectment without placing reliance upon the proviso for re-entry since the continuation of the term was made conditional on the tenant's actual occupation of the premises. In the words of Lawrence J.[50]:

"Here the lease in effect is for 21 years if [the tenant] shall so long live in the house. Then if he has ceased to live there, for whatever cause, the condition on which the term was made to determine has happened, and there is an end of his interest in the premises."

In *Doe* d. *Willson* v. *Phillips*,[51] however, the relevant provision in the tenancy agreement (which contained no proviso for re-entry) was held to constitute a covenant and not a condition operating in defeasance of the leasehold estate. Accordingly, the landlord's action for ejectment could not succeed.

It is always a matter of construction as to whether a particular term in the lease is a covenant or condition. In *Doe* d. *Henniker* v. *Watt*,[52] it was

---

[47] A condition should also be distinguished from a limitation. A condition exists when a landlord grants a lease for a specified period but includes a provision making it terminable upon the happening of a specified event (*e.g.* tenancy granted *upon condition* that planning permission is not given). In the case of a limitation, the specified event is built into the primary formula which fixes the period for which the lease is limited to last so that the happening of the event will automatically bring the tenancy to an end because its period has expired (*e.g.* tenancy granted *until* planning permission is granted). In the latter case, no question of forfeiture arises. See, "*Automatic Determination of Leases?*", F.R. Crane, (1963) 27 Conv. (N.S.) 111. See also s. 146(7) of the Law of Property Act 1925, which expressly extends the provisions of s. 146 relating to notice and relief to some limitations by deeming the event in question to be a breach of covenant. See further, *Plymouth Corportaion* v. *Harvey* [1971] 1 W.L.R. 549.

[48] *Freeman* v. *Boyle* (1788) 2 Ridg. Parl. Rep. 69, 79 and *Sexton* d. *Freeman* v. *Boyle* (1788) Vern. & Scr. 402, 414.

[49] (1807) 8 East 185; 103 E.R. 313.

[50] *Ibid*, 187, 314.

[51] (1824) 2 Bing. 13; 130 E.R. 208.

[52] (1828) 8 B. & C. 308; 108 E.R. 1057.

held that the words "it is stipulated and conditioned" that the tenant should not assign, transfer or underlet any part of the demised premises created a condition, upon breach of which the landlord could forfeit the lease regardless of the existence of an express proviso for re-entry in the lease. In *Simpson* v. *Titterell*,[53] it was held that a proviso[54] in a lease that the tenant shall perform or not perform an act, in the absence of any penalty annexed to it, operated so as to create a condition as opposed to a covenant. In *Maley* v. *Fearn*,[55] the terms of a weekly tenancy were contained in a rent book under the heading "Terms of Tenancy". The Court of Appeal held that this heading did not preclude the terms thereunder being construed as conditions giving the landlord a right of re-entry upon their breach.

The question of construction will be decided by looking at the intention of the parties to be gathered from the wording of the lease as a whole[56] and it is clear that no precise form of wording is necessary to create a condition. In the words of Bayley J. in *Doe* d. *Henniker* v. *Watt*[57]:

> "A party who demises land by an instrument not under seal may introduce a condition into it, provided he use apt and proper words for the purpose ... in a lease for years no precise form of words is necessary to make a condition. It is sufficient if it appears that the words used were intended to have the effect of creating a condition."

In *Shaw* v. *Coffin*,[58] however, the tenant *agreed* that he would not underlet the demised premises without consent in writing of the landlord. These words of contract were held not to create a condition and, accordingly, the landlord could not re-enter for breach of the agreement except under a proviso for re-entry.

In *Whitchcot* v. *Fox*,[59] the Court of King's Bench held that a covenant on the part of the tenant against assignment was capable of constituting a condition notwithstanding that the words were not expressed as those of the landlord but of the tenant.

It is possible for a term in the lease to have the dual characteristics of a covenant and a condition, in which case the only remedy available to the landlord for breach is apparently to forfeit the lease.[60]

---

[53] (1591) Cro. Eliz. 242; 78 E.R. 498. See also, *The Earl of Pembroke* v. *Berkeley*, Cro. Eliz. 384; 78 E.R. 630 (the words "provided also" held to give rise to a condition); *Harrington* v. *Wise*, Cro. Eliz. 486; 78 E.R. 737 ("provided always that" held to create both a covenant and condition) and *Marsh* v. *Curteys* (1596) Cro. Eliz. 528 ("upon condition that" assumed to create a condition).

[54] e.g. "provided always" or "provided that" or "provided also".

[55] [1947] 176 L.T. 203.

[56] *Bashir* v. *Crown Lands Commissioner* [1960] A.C. 44, (P.C.).

[57] (1828) 8 B. & C. 308, 315; 108 E.R. 1057, 1060.

[58] (1863) 14 C.B.(N.S.) 372; 143 E.R. 490, applied in *Crawley* v. *Price* (1875) L.R. 10 Q.B. 302.

[59] (1616) Cro. Jac. 398; 79 E.R. 340.

[60] *Bashir* v. *Crown Lands Commissioner* [1960] A.C. 44, (P.C.).

Today, the most common condition included amongst the terms of a lease is the condition which entitles the landlord to forfeit the lease if the tenant becomes bankrupt or goes into liquidation or permits other associated events[61] to occur during the currency of the term. Such a condition, however, is invariably to be found in the proviso for re-entry which is included in the lease in any event in order to permit forfeiture for breach of covenant. As such, it is not a typical condition in the classical sense because conditions of the latter kind are imposed independently of any forfeiture clause in the lease and give rise to an automatic right of forfeiture.

(3) *Where the tenant denies the landlord's title*

It will be apparent from the preceding section that a landlord may forfeit the lease on the happening of an event specified in a condition subject to which the term of the lease was created without placing any reliance upon a proviso for re-entry. A forfeiture may also be incurred (without recourse to a proviso for re-entry) by breach on the part of the tenant of an *implied* condition of the lease in three distinct circumstances:

(a)   denial by matter of record;
(b)   denial by act *in pais* and
(c)   disclaimer by a yearly or other periodic tenant.

(a) *Denial by matter of record*

A denial by matter of record[62] will arise when the tenant, in the course of his pleadings, expressly denies the landlord's title and is thereby estopped by the record from re-asserting his lease or tenancy. This form of denial (or disclaimer) was discussed in *Warner* v. *Sampson*,[63] in which the tenant's defence to a landlord's action for possession based on alleged breaches of covenant of the lease contained the following paragraph in the common form of a general traverse: "Save and except for the admissions herein contained this defendant denies each and every allegation in the statement of claim as if the same were specifically set out and traversed seriatim." The landlord's statement of claim *inter alia* referred to the lease, set out the landlord's title and specified the breaches of covenant alleged. The landlord contended that the tenant in his defence had disclaimed the landlord's title and that she was now entitled to claim

---

[61] *e.g.* when the tenant makes a composition with his creditors or when a judgment creditor levies execution against his goods.

[62] Historically, this meant the denial by a tenant in a court of record of his landlord's title.

[63] [1959] 1 Q.B. 297. Denial by matter of record can be traced back to the reign of Henry II and is founded on the Oath of Fealty given by a tenant of real property to his lord under the medieval system of tenure. The judgment of Lord Denning contains an interesting historical account of the subject.

forfeiture of the lease on this ground. The Court of Appeal held[64] that a general traverse did not involve the affirmative setting up by the tenant of a title adverse to that of the landlord as it merely put the landlord to proof of the allegations traversed.[65] In the words of Tindal C.J. in *Doe d. Williams and Jeffery v. Cooper*[66]:

> "To constitute a disclaimer, there must be a renunciation by the party of his character of tenant, either by setting up the title of a rival claimant, or by asserting a claim of ownership in himself."

In the same case, Coltman J. said[67]:

> "A disclaimer I understand to be the setting up of a title that is inconsistent with the title of the landlord."

Thus, a general denial of the landlord's title in the tenant's pleading (which does not amount to a positive averment) merely puts the landlord to proof of his title[68] and will not involve the affirmative setting up of an adverse title against him.[69] There may, however, be cases where, as a matter of construction, a mere denial in a pleading will give rise to an affirmative, contradictory allegation.[70]

It has recently been held[71] that a partial disclaimer of the landlord's title is not sufficient to constitute a disclaimer of the whole since it does not show that the tenant has evinced the necessary intention no longer to be bound by his relationship with the landlord. In *W.G. Clark (Properties) Ltd. v. Dupre Properties Ltd.*[72] the tenant of a basement flat wished to develop a

---

[64] Overruling *Kisch v. Hawes Brothers Ltd.* [1935] Ch. 102, in which Farwell J. held that a plea by the tenants that they were in possession of the premises was a cause of forfeiture on the ground that it amounted to a denial of the landlord's title. The decision had already been criticised by the Supreme Court of Eire in *Wallace v. Dalby & Co. Ltd.* [1949] I.R. 352.

[65] *per* Hodson and Ormerod L.JJ. Lord Denning, however, went further and suggested that the landlord's right to claim a forfeiture upon a tenant's disclaimer by matter of record had become obsolete with the abolition of the feudal system of tenure. On the assumption that the denial in the tenant's defence had created a forfeiture, The Court of Appeal held (in the alternative) that the landlord had not effectively elected to claim it either by peaceable re-entry or by proceedings for possession. It is essential, therefore for the landlord to exercise his right of forfeiture in the appropriate way if he is to rely on the tenant's denial. It seems also that a tenant could avoid forfeiture by retracting his denial of title before the landlord elected to forfeit the lease in reliance on it. Conversely, a disclaimer may be waived by the landlord by any act (for example, by a distress for subsequent rent) acknowledging the tenant as such: *Doe d. David v. Williams* (1835) 7 C. & P. 322.

[66] (1840) 1 Scott N.R. 36, 41.

[67] *Ibid*, 43.

[68] See also the earlier cases on the subject: *Doe d. Lewis v. Cawdor* (1834) 1 Cr. M. & R. 398; 149 E.R. 1134 and *Jones v. Mills* (1861) 10 C.B. (N.S.) 788; 142 E.R. 664.

[69] No apparent distinction lies between a non-admission and a denial of the landlord's title: *Warner v. Sampson* [1959] 1 Q.B. 297.

[70] See, *e.g. MacLulich v. MacLulich* [1920] P. 439, a case involving a petition for the restitution of conjugal rights.

[71] *W.G. Clark (Properties) Ltd. v. Dupre Properties Ltd.* [1991] 3 W.L.R. 579.

[72] [1991] 3 W.L.R. 579.

courtyard situated at the rear of the flat. Consequently, the landlord and the tenant entered into a deed of variation and licence whereby the tenant surrendered his existing lease of the flat and the landlord granted him a new lease of the flat and courtyard. The tenant then extended the flat into the courtyard. However, the registered proprietor of the courtyard was the owner of a neighbouring property and the Land Registry refused to register the deed of variation. The landlord then asserted ownership of the courtyard by adverse possession and the neighbour responded by bringing an action against the tenant seeking an order that the extension built by the tenant on the courtyard be pulled down. The tenant then brought a separate action against the landlord claiming damages for misrepresentation of title and also filed a defence in the neighbour's action claiming that the neighbour had lost its title to the courtyard by reason of the landlord's adverse possession and asserting title to the courtyard through the landlord. The landlord subsequently brought pro- ceedings against the tenant claiming possession of the flat on the ground that the tenant had denied the landlord's title by asserting in the tenant's action against the landlord that the freehold owner of the courtyard was the neighbour and not the landlord. Mr. T.R.A. Morison Q.C. (sitting as a deputy judge of the High Court) held that the tenant's pleading had only disclaimed the landlord's title to part of the property (*i.e.* the courtyard) and had asserted the landlord's title to the remainder (*i.e.* the flat) and such partial disclaimer was not sufficient to constitute a disclaimer of the whole since it did not show that the tenant had evinced an intention no longer to be bound by the landlord and tenant relationship.[73] In so holding, the learned Judge concluded that the doctrine of disclaimer of title was analogous to the doctrine of repudiation of contract and a tenant who repudiated the relationship of landlord and tenant ought not to be in a different position to a party to a contract who repudiated or renounced the contract. Thus, provided the renunciation of the landlord and tenant relationship by the tenant was clear and unambiguous, the landlord had the option of either ignoring the renunciation and enforcing the terms of the lease or accepting the renunciation by re-entry or by issuing proceed- ings for possession.

Once the landlord has commenced proceedings for possession based on disclaimer of his title in the tenant's pleading, the tenant cannot improve his position by amending his pleading to remove the disclaimer notwithstanding that the amendment of a pleading relates back to the date of the original pleading.[74] This is because the landlord's service of proceedings for possession is the equivalent to actual re-entry onto the

---

[73] This, however, does not rule out the possibility that a partial disclaimer might lead to forfeiture of part of the demised premises: *ibid*, 604, referring to *G.M.S. Syndicate Ltd.* v. *Gary Elliott Ltd.* [1982] Ch. 1.

[74] *W.G. Clark (Properties) Ltd.* v. *Dupre Properties Ltd.* [1991] 3 W.L.R. 579, 587–589.

demised premises which brings the landlord and tenant relationship to an end. The tenant may, however, avoid a forfeiture by retracting his denial of title *before* the landlord re-enters or takes effective proceedings for re-entry in reliance on the denial.[75]

(b) *Denial by act in pais*[76]

This will arise when the tenant deliberately attempts to set up an adverse (or hostile) title either in himself or in a stranger in the face of the landlord's title. An early case is *Read and Morpeth* v. *Errington*,[77] where a tenant's alienation of his landlord's estate was held to constitute a disclaimer giving the landlord a right to forfeit the lease. In *Doe* d. *Ellenbrock* v. *Flynn*,[78] the tenant delivered up possession of the demised premises and surrendered the lease, in fraud of his landlord, to a person who claimed under a hostile title, with the intention of enabling that person to set up a claim adverse to the title of the landlord. The Court of Exchequer held that the act of the tenant constituted a disclaimer entitling the landlord to re-enter. Lord Lyndhurst C.B. said[79]:

> "If the tenant sets up a title hostile to that of his landlord, it is a forfeiture of his term, and it is the same if he assists another person to set up such a claim. Whether he does the act himself, or only colludes with another to do it, it is equally a forfeiture."

The rule in *Ellenbrock* must, however, be cautiously applied, as illustrated by the case of *Doe* d. *Graves, Downe* v. *Wells*,[80] where it was held by the Court of Queen's Bench that a tenant for a term of years had not forfeited his term merely by *orally* refusing to pay his rent and claiming the landlord's estate as his own. Lord Denman C.J. said[81]:

> ". . . no case, I think, goes so far as the present: and I feel the danger of allowing an interest in law to be put to an end to by mere words."

And Patteson J. observed[82]:

> "No case has been cited where a lease for a definite term has been forfeited by mere words. We know that mere words cannot work a disseisin, although some acts have been held to work a disseisin at the election of the party disseised, which, as against him, would not

---

[75] *Warner* v. *Sampson* [1959] 1 Q.B. 297, 322, *per* Hodson L.J.
[76] The phrase "act *in pais*" means act in the country. In other words, an act or transaction done or made otherwise than in the course of proceedings.
[77] (1594) Cro. Eliz. 321; 78 E.R. 571.
[78] (1834) 1 C.M. & R. 137; 149 E.R. 1026.
[79] *Ibid*, 141, 1028.
[80] (1889) 10 Ad. & E. 426; 113 E.R. 162.
[81] *Ibid*, 435, 165.
[82] *Ibid*, 437, 166.

work a disseisin. An attornment again is an act. Here there is no act; and if we held that there was a forfeiture, we should be going much beyond any previous decision."

The principle that it is dangerous to allow an interest in law to be forfeited by mere words was applied in *Wisbech St. Mary Parish Council* v. *Lilley*,[83] where a yearly tenant of a cottage owned by the plaintiff Council agreed to sell the same to the defendant for the sum of £20. After the death of the tenant, the Council discovered that the defendant was occupying the cottage and brought proceedings against him to recover possession on the ground that the tenant had disclaimed his leasehold interest in the cottage by denying his landlord's title. It was alleged that the tenant had stated to the defendant that he was the absolute owner of the cottage for many years and that he had never paid rent for it. This evidence, it was argued, suggested that it had been the tenant's intention to let the defendant into possession with a view to enabling him to set up an adverse title to the Council. The Court of Appeal, however, rejected this contention, concluding that the landlords had failed to establish the requisite unequivocal intention on the part of the tenant to assert a hostile title against them. The tenant's denial of his landlord's title by mere words will, therefore, only give rise to a forfeiture if, on the facts, it is clearly proved.[84] In the words of Romer L.J.[85]:

"... the law on this subject is archaic in some degree and is founded upon feudal principles which certainly do not loom very large in modern life. But I accept ... that, even now, if a tenant does in fact deliberately assert a title in himself adverse to his landlord, or if he lets a stranger into possession with the intention of enabling him to set up a title adverse to the landlord, then this amounts to a repudiation of the landlord's title; and it would seem that when the tenancy in question is a yearly tenancy it is sufficient to constitute a repudiation if the assertion of title against the landlord is made orally."

The requisite criterion in all cases is whether an intended and deliberate assertion of an adverse title can be shown on the part of the tenant. Where, therefore, the acts of the tenant are equivocal, they will not amount to an act of forfeiture. Thus, in *Ackland* v. *Lutley*,[86] a house was demised for 21 years by a landlord who had devised the estate of which it formed part to trustees to receive the rent. The tenant gave up possession (before the term had come to an end) to the trustees, who by then no longer had title to the premises. Lord Denman C.J. held that the tenant's

---

[83] [1956] 1 W.L.R. 121.
[84] It is always a question of fact whether the tenant's acts or words amount to a denial of his landlord's title: *Doe* d. *Bennett* v. *Long* (1841) 9 C. & P. 773.
[85] *Ibid*, 126.
[86] (1839) 9 Ad. & E. 879; 112 E.R. 1446.

act was equivocal and did not necessarily import either a surrender or a forfeiture of the term.

(c) *Disclaimer by a yearly or other periodic tenant*

Disclaimer of the lease (whether by words or acts) by a yearly or other[87] periodic tenant will operate as a waiver by the tenant of the usual notice to quit. The effect of such disclaimer, therefore, is that the landlord may terminate the tenancy forthwith without serving the appropriate notice to quit on his tenant.[88] The principle appears to be founded on the doctrine of estoppel since the landlord is not obliged to determine the tenancy by notice to quit because the tenant has already asserted by words or conduct that it has no existence. In the words of Best C.J. in *Doe* d. *Calvert* v. *Frowd*[89]:

"... a notice to quit is only requisite where a tenancy is admitted on both sides, and if a defendant denies the tenancy, there can be no necessity for a notice to end that which he says has no existence."

Thus, strictly speaking, an act of disclaimer on the part of the periodic tenant does not give the landlord a right of forfeiture but merely operates to relieve him from serving the appropriate notice to quit to bring the tenancy to an end. This was made clear in *Doe* d. *Graves, Downe* v. *Wells*,[90] where Lord Denman C.J. said[91]:

"It may be fairly said, when a landlord brings an action to recover the possession from a defendant who has been his tenant from year to year, that evidence of a disclaimer of the landlord's title by the tenant is evidence of the determination of the will of both parties, by which the duration of the tenancy, from its particular nature, was limited."

Patteson J. also observed[92]:

"It is sometimes said that a tenancy from year to year is forfeited by

---

[87] See, *e.g. Jones* v. *Mills* (1861) 10 C.B. (N.S.) 789; 142 E.R. 664 (weekly tenant). A disclaimer of the landlord's title will also determine a tenancy at will: *Doe* d. *Price* v. *Price* (1832) 9 Bing. 356,358; 131 E.R. 649, 650.

[88] The earliest reported case on the subject appears to be *Throgmorton* v. *Whelpdale* (1769) Bull N.P. (7th ed.), 96, where it was said that a notice to quit was necessary unless the tenant had attorned to some other person, or done some other act, disclaiming to hold as tenant to the landlord. See also: *Saunders* v. *Freeman* 2 Dyer 209a; 73 E.R. 461; *Doe* d. *Foster* v. *Williams* (1777) 2 Cowp. 622; 98 E.R. 1273, *per* Lord Mansfield; *Bower* v. *Major* (1819) 1 Brod. & Bing. 4; 129 E.R. 624 (dealing with the analogous case of a composition of tithes); *Doe* d. *Grubb* v. *Grubb* (1830) 10 B. & C. 816; 109 E.R. 652; *Doe* d. *Lewis* v. *Lord Cawdor* (1834) 1 Cr. M. & R. 398; 149 E.R. 1134 and *Doe* d. *Davies* v. *Evans* (1841) 9 M. & W. 48; 152 E.R. 21.

[89] (1828) 4 Bing. 557, 559; 130 E.R. 883, 884.

[90] (1889) 10 Ad. & E. 426; 113 E.R. 162.

[91] *Ibid*, 435, 165.

[92] *Ibid*, 437, 166.

disclaimer: but it would be more correct to say that a disclaimer furnishes evidence in answer to the disclaiming party's assertion that he has had no notice to quit; inasmuch as it would be idle to prove such a notice where the tenant has asserted that there is no longer any tenancy."

A number of early authorities provide useful illustrations as to what will amount to a disclaimer in this context. Thus, in *Doe* d. *Whitehead* v. *Pittman*,[93] the words "I have no rent for you because A.B. has ordered me to pay none" were held to be evidence of a disclaimer of the tenancy. But mere payment of rent to a person not entitled to receive it, will not constitute a disclaimer of the title of the person who is actually entitled to recover it.[94] In *Doe* d. *Jefferies* v. *Whittick*,[95] the tenants claimed the landlord's lands as their own freehold. Holroyd J. held that such an assertion of rights operated as an effective disclaimer of the landlord's title. In *Doe* d. *Calvert* v. *Frowd*,[96] the tenant held premises under a tenant for life, on whose death possession was claimed and rent demanded by the heir at law of the devisor. The tenant wrote to the attorney of the heir at law stating that he held as tenant under the husband of the tenant for life, that he had never considered the claimant as the landlord and that he would be ready to pay the arrears of rent to any person who should be proved to be the heir at law. The tenant's letter was held to amount to an effective disclaimer of title of the heir at law.

Similarly, in *Doe* d. *Phillips* v. *Rollings*,[97] the tenant declined to pay rent to the plaintiff remainderman, after the death of the tenant for life who had made a voidable lease, until it was settled who was entitled to the demised premises. The tenant, in fact, placed the rent in a bank account with a view to paying it afterwards to the person who could establish title to it. Willes C.J.[98] held that the tenant's conduct amounted to a disclaimer of the remainderman's title. The last two-mentioned cases may be contrasted with *Doe* d. *Williams* v. *Pasquali*,[99] where Lord Kenyon held that a mere refusal to pay rent to a devisee under a contested will, accompanied by a declaration that the tenant was ready to pay to any person entitled, did not give rise to a disclaimer. Again, in *Doe* d. *Williams*, *Jeffery* v. *Cooper*,[1] the landlord let premises to the tenant at a yearly rent with an agreement to grant him a lease for seven years or a lease for lives under which the landlord held the property. The landlord told the tenant to pay

---

[93] 2 Nev. & M. 673.
[94] *Doe* d. *Dillon* v. *Parker* (1820) Gow. 180; 171 E.R. 879.
[95] (1820) Gow. 195; 171 E.R. 883.
[96] (1828) 4 Bing. 557; 130 E.R. 883.
[97] (1847) 4 C.B. 188; 136 E.R. 476.
[98] *Ibid*, 200–201, 481.
[99] (1793) Peake 259; 170 E.R. 149.
[1] (1840) 1 M. & G. 135; 133 E.R. 278.

his rent to one Kent (the headlessor) and, according to the agreement, he was not to be called upon to pay until the landlord himself paid his rent under the headlease to Kent. The landlord subsequently assigned his interest to the plaintiff who, being under the impression that the seven year lease had expired, demanded possession. The tenant then declared that he held under the lease for lives and refused to pay rent to the plaintiff on the ground that, under his agreement, he was obliged to pay rent only to Kent. This was held not to constitute a disclaimer of the plaintiff's title. Tindal C.J. said[2]:

"A disclaimer, as the word imports, must be a renunciation by the party of his character of tenant, either by setting up a title in another, or by claiming title in himself. The facts of this case support neither of these views."

Coltman J. said[3]:

"The defendant . . . certainly had a right to a further lease, and in asserting this right, he did not in reality deny the title of the lessor of the plaintiff. With respect to his refusing to pay rent, a refusal to do so, is not in itself a disclaimer, although it may be evidence of a disclaimer. Here the tenant wished to be secured from being called upon to pay his rent over again to the superior landlord."

Similarly, in *Jones* v. *Mills*,[4] the defendant had for several years occupied a cottage as a weekly tenant under one Mears. After the death of Mears, the defendant continued to pay his rent weekly to certain persons to whom Mears had devised the premises. The devise was later discovered to be void whereupon the heir at law of Mears demanded the rent. The defendant responded by stating that he had received notice from another party claiming title to the cottage and that he was not paying anymore rent until he knew who was the right owner. The Court of Common Pleas held that this did not constitute a repudiation of the title of the heir at law so as to entitle him to eject the defendant without any notice to quit. In essence, the defendant was entitled to pause to make enquiries and receive further information before he yielded to the demand for rent from a new claimant. A mere omission, therefore, to acknowledge the landlord by requesting further information as to proof of his title will not by itself be sufficient to amount to a disclaimer.[5]

Ultimately, the question will resolve itself into one of fact as to the true nature of the tenant's intention. Thus, in *Doe* d. *Bennett* v. *Long*,[6] several

---

[2] *Ibid*, 140, 280.
[3] *Ibid*, 142, 281.
[4] (1861) 10 C.B. (N.S.) 789; 142 E.R. 664.
[5] *Doe* d. *Gray* v. *Stanion* (1836) 1 M. & W. 695, 703; 150 E.R. 614, 617, *per* Parke B.
[6] (1841) 9 C. & P. 773.

persons joined in the letting of land to the tenant and it was agreed that the rent should be paid to their agent. Subsequently, one of the landlords (who alone, in fact, owned the land) demanded rent from the tenant. The tenant responded by saying: "You are not my landlord". In this case, it was left to the jury to decide, as a matter of fact, whether the tenant intended that the relation of landlord and tenant should not exist between them or merely that the rent was to be paid to the agent.

In *Hunt* v. *Allgood*,[7] certain parish lands were let to the inhabitants of the area at a rent of 4s. per acre. The lands were later inclosed and the church wardens of the parish increased the rent to 12s. per acre in order to raise a sufficient fund to pay for the expenses of the inclosure. When enough money had been raised to satisfy the inclosure expenses, the tenants believed (wrongly) that the rent ought to be reduced to the original figure of 4s. per acre. They, therefore, refused to pay the rent at the higher rate. Erle C.J. held that their refusal did not constitute a disclaimer so as to entitle the landlords to eject them without notice. He said:[8]

"... when we look at the circumstances under which the words were used, it appears to me that their more probable meaning was an assertion of a right to continue their tenancy under the plaintiffs at the rent of 4s. This is much more likely than that they meant to claim an estate in themselves adversely to and inconsistent with the rights of their landlords."

In *Doe* d. *Lansdell* v. *Gower*,[9] the tenant was let into possession of a cottage upon a weekly tenancy paying a rent of 1s. 6d. per week. The tenant occupied the cottage for 20 years (without paying rent) until he was served with a notice to quit the premises. The tenant refused to give up the cottage and claimed it as his own, continuing to occupy it for a further five years and, thereafter, he sold to a third party. Lord Campbell C.J. observed[10] that the tenant had effectively disclaimed the tenancy by his conduct and, therefore, no notice to quit was necessary as a pre-requisite to any action for ejectment.

In *Vivian* v. *Moat*,[11] the landlords gave notice to the tenants that their rents would be raised. The tenants responded by writing a letter stating that they disputed the landlord's alleged right to raise the rent, but were willing and offered to pay what was due in respect of a customary rent of 11s. a year for the property. Fry J. held that assertion of a right to hold the

[7] (1861) 10 C.B. (N.S.) 253; 142 E.R. 448.
[8] *Ibid*, 258, 451.
[9] (1851) 17 Q.B. 589; 117 E.R. 1406.
[10] *Ibid*, 592, 1408.
[11] (1881) 16 Ch. D. 730.

property upon payment of a customary rent amounted to a repudiation of the relationship of landlord and tenant between the parties. He held, accordingly, that the landlords were entitled to bring an action for eject-ment without proving the service of a notice to quit. In the course of his judgment, he referred to *Doe d. Gray* v. *Stanion*,[12] in which Parke B. enunciated the following principle:

> "In order to make a verbal or written disclaimer sufficient, it must amount to a direct repudiation of the relation of landlord and tenant; or to a distinct claim to hold possession of the estate upon a ground wholly inconsistent with the existence of this relation, which by necessary implication is a repudiation of it."

In the *Stanion* case itself, a yearly tenant had agreed to purchase the demised property and, upon the landlord claiming possession thereof, the tenant declared in a conversation that "he had bought the property, and would keep it". Parke B. held that these words did not constitute a disavowal of the yearly tenancy because the tenant did not claim to hold the estate on a ground necessarily inconsistent with the continuance of the tenancy. The tenant had, in effect, a double right to enforce his bargain for the purchase of the estate and to continue, in the meantime, to hold it as a yearly tenant.

(4) *Under section 35(2) of the Sexual Offences Act 1956*

Where the tenant[13] is convicted of knowingly permitting the whole or part of the demised premises to be used as a brothel,[14] the landlord has a statutory right to determine the lease if the tenant fails to assign it within three months of being required to do so by the landlord.[15] To exercise the right under the Act, the landlord must first require the tenant to assign to some person approved by the landlord (such approval not to be unrea-sonably withheld).[16] If the tenant fails to assign within the three month time period, the landlord can determine the lease and seek a summary order for the delivery up of possession of the premises from the criminal court.[17] If, with notice of the tenant's conviction, the landlord fails to exercise his statutory right or later grants another lease to or for the benefit of the tenant and the offence is repeated, the landlord will be

---

[12] (1836) 1 M. & W. 695; 150 E.R. 614.

[13] The word "tenant" refers to a tenant in occupation of the premises so that a landlord, who is himself a tenant, is not a tenant within the meaning of the section: *Siviour* v. *Napolitano* [1931] 1 K.B. 636.

[14] For the meaning of "brothel", see cases cited in *Halsbury's Statutes*, (4th ed.) Vol. 12, at p. 264.

[15] S. 35(2) and the First Sched. to the 1956 Act.

[16] paras 1 and 4 of the First Sched.

[17] paras 2 and 3 of the First Sched.

deemed to be a party to its commission, unless he can show that he has taken all reasonable steps to prevent its repetition.[18]

Section 35(2) of the 1956 Act gives the landlord a *statutory* right to forfeit in circumstances falling within the section. The landlord, may, therefore, rely additionally upon his contractual right of forfeiture arising under a proviso for re-entry or condition contained in the lease.[19] It seems, however, that the landlord may be at an advantage in relying upon the statutory provision since the doctrines of waiver of forfeiture and relief from forfeiture are not applicable to the 1956 Act.

Who may assert a right of forfeiture?

(1) *At common law*

At common law, the general principle is that: "a party in whom there is no reversion, cannot have the right to re-enter."[20] This means that the only person who can exercise a right of re-entry for a forfeiture is the person in whom the legal estate is then vested. Thus, in *Doe* d. *Barker* v. *Goldsmith*,[21] a testator bequeathed certain leasehold premises to his trustees on trust to permit his wife to receive the rents during her life. Later, the surviving trustee and the wife granted a lease of the premises, the rent to be paid to the wife. The lease contained a proviso for re-entry upon non-payment of rent in favour of the lessors. Following the death of the surviving trustee, the wife purported to forfeit the lease for non-payment of rent. The Court of Exchequer held that, being a stranger to the legal estate, the power of re-entry could not be reserved to the wife. In this case, the lease expressly stated that the wife's title was equitable. If, however, the lease had referred to her by name only, notwithstanding the nature of her right in the premises, her want of the legal estate would have been immaterial since, as against the tenant, she would have had a legal estate by estoppel.[22]

Similarly, in *Fenn* d. *Matthews* v. *Smart*,[23] the Court of King's Bench held that, once the reversioner had conveyed his legal estate to a third party absolutely, he could no longer maintain an action for forfeiture against the tenant.

---

[18] s. 35(3).

[19] See, *e.g. Rugby School Governors* v. *Tanahill* [1935] 1 K.B. 87 (use of house for immoral purposes) and *Egerton* v. *Esplanade Hotels* [1947] 2 All E.R. 88 (use of hotel as a brothel).

[20] *Doe* d. *Barney* v. *Adams* (1832) 2 C. & J. 232, 236; 149 E.R. 101, 102, *per* Bayley B. See also, *Doe* d. *Barber* v. *Lawrence* (1811) 4 Taunt 23; 128 E.R. 235.

[21] (1832) 2 C. & J. 674; 149 E.R. 283.

[22] *Ibid*, 676, 284, *per* Bayley B. See also, *Cuthbertson* v. *Irving* (1860) 6 H. & N. 135; 158 E.R. 58 (mortgagor in possession, who had no legal title to the demised premises, could nevertheless establish his title by way of estoppel binding on the tenant).

[23] (1810) 12 East 444; 104 E.R. 173.

In *Marriott* v. *Edwards*,[24] the landlord, after granting a lease, executed a mortgage whereby he assigned all his legal and equitable interest in the premises to the mortgagee. The Court of King's Bench held that he could not subsequently bring an action against the tenant for forfeiture of his lease.[25] At common law, the covenants in the lease were deemed to be incident to the reversion and passed with it by mortgage. Similarly, a reversioner whose interest has been merged (and thereby extinguished) cannot avail himself of a right of re-entry.[26] This may arise when a tenant grants a sub-lease and later assigns his reversionary interest thereunder to a third party, who also acquires the freehold estate in the premises. This will have the effect of merging the tenant's reversionary interest under the sub-lease with the freehold estate so that the former will be extinguished.

The principle that a right of re-entry cannot be enforced by a stranger to the legal estate will apply with equal force to someone who is a party to the lease but who is expressed in the lease to have only a limited (equit-able) interest in the demised premises.[27] However, the proviso for re-entry may expressly extend the right of forfeiture to persons other than the landlord, for example, his heirs, executors or administrators[28] or his assigns.[29] A right of re-entry can also be validly reserved on an assign-ment of the leasehold term when the assignor retains no reversion. Thus, in *Doe* d. *Freeman* v. *Bateman*,[30] the tenant assigned his whole leasehold interest subject to a right of re-entry on a breach of a condition in the lease. The Court of King's Bench held that the tenant could still exercise a right of forfeiture for breach of the condition even though he had no reversion-ary interest in the premises. In *Shiloh Spinners Ltd.* v. *Harding*,[31] the tenants of certain buildings assigned their interest in part thereof to a company who covenanted *inter alia* to fence the boundaries and to keep certain parts of the property in repair. The assignment contained a right to re-enter the assigned premises in the event of breach of the covenants. The House of Lords held that the right of re-entry had been validly

---

[24] (1834) 5 B. & Ad. 1065; 110 E.R. 1086.

[25] See also, *Doe* d. *Prior* v. *Ongley* (1850) 10 C.B. 25; 138 E.R. 11.

[26] *Webb* v. *Russell* (1789) 3 T.R. 393, 402; 100 E.R. 639, 644, *per* Lord Kenyon C.J.

[27] *Doe* d. *Barber* v. *Lawrence* (1811) 4 Taunt. 23; 128 E.R. 235; *Doe* d. *Barney* v. *Adams* (1832) 12 C. & T. 232; 149 E.R. 101; *Moore* v. *Earl of Plymouth* (1819) 3 B. & Ald. 66; 106 E.R. 587; *Saunders and Waine* v. *Merryweather* (1865) 3 H. & C. 902; 159 E.R. 790 and *Doe* d. *Barker* v. *Goldsmith* (1832) 2 C. & J. 674; 149 E.R. 283.

[28] *Doe* d. *Banford* v. *Hayley* (1810) 12 East 464; 104 E.R. 181 (devisee of landlord held entitled to determine the lease).

[29] *Greenway* v. *Hart* (1854) 14 C.B. 340 (owner of reversion under settlement held entitled to re-enter as assigns of the settlor).

[30] (1818) 2 B. & Ald. 168; 106 E.R. 328. The decision was approved in *Hyde* v. *Warden* (1877) 3 Ex. D. 72, 84, *per* Brett L.J. and *Shiloh Spinners Ltd.* v. *Harding* [1973] A.C. 691, 717, *per* Lord Wilberforce.

[31] [1973] A. C. 691.

reserved by the tenants as assignors even though they retained no reversion in the property assigned. The position is the same in respect of a
landlord who assigns the whole of his reversionary interest but expressly
reserves to himself a power of re-entry.[32]

A tenant cannot rely upon his own default in order to bring the lease to
an end. In *Rede* v. *Farr*,[33] the proviso for re-entry stipulated that, if the rent
should be unpaid for forty days after it fell due, the lease "shall be void".
Lord Ellenborough C.J. said[34]:

"... it would be contrary to an universal principle of law, that a party
shall never take advantage of his own wrong, if we were to hold that
a lease, which in terms is a lease for twelve years, should be a lease
determinable at the will and pleasure of the lessee; and that a lessee
by not paying his rent should be at liberty to say that the lease is
void."

Thus, the lease will only be voidable at the option of the landlord and
not the tenant in default.[35]

(2) *Under statute*

The common law principle that only the grantor of the lease or his
heirs[36] could effect a forfeiture of the lease was extended, under the
Grantees of Reversions Act 1540, to all grantees and assignees of the
reversionary interest. The current provisions are contained in section 141
of the Law of Property Act 1925. Under section 141(1), the benefit of every
condition of re-entry contained in a lease is deemed to be annexed and
incident to and go with the reversionary estate[37] in the land immediately
expectant on the term granted by the lease. Under section 141(2), any
tenant's covenant or provision having reference to the subject-matter of
the lease,[38] is deemed to be capable of being enforced and taken advantage of by the person for the time being entitled, subject to the term of the
lease, to the income of the land leased. The broad effect of section 141(2) is
that the right to enforce the terms of the lease is given not only to the legal
reversioner but to any person beneficially entitled to the income from the
demised premises to the exclusion of all others. A beneficiary under a

---

[32] *Shiloh Spinners Ltd.* v. *Harding* [1973] A.C. 691, 717, *per* Lord Wilberforce.
[33] (1817) 6 M. & S. 121; 105 E.R. 1188.
[34] *Ibid*, 124, 1189.
[35] *Hayne* v. *Cummings* (1864) 16 C. & B. (N.S.) 421, 426; 143 E.R. 1191, 1194, *per* Willes J.;
    Arnsby v. *Woodward* (1827) 6 B. & C. 519, 523; 108 E.R. 542, 544, *per* Lord Tenterden C.J. and
    Doe d. *Nash* v. *Birch* (1836) 1 M. & W. 402; 150 E.R. 490.
[36] *Re Evans's Contract* [1920] 2 Ch. 469.
[37] The grant of the reversion upon a lease is valid without attornment: s. 151(1) of the Law of
    Property Act 1925.
[38] These words are equivalent to the phrase "which touch and concern the land" as used in
    Spencer's Case (1583) 5 Co. Rep. 16a.

trust, however, is not entitled to the rent as such but only to an account from his trustee of the profits received from the demise and, therefore, cannot enforce a forfeiture under the section.[39]

Under section 141(3), the person entitled to the income of the land leased, whether by conveyance or otherwise, may take advantage of a tenant's covenant or provision having reference to the subject-matter of the lease notwithstanding that he became so entitled after the condition of re-entry or forfeiture had become enforceable. In *London and County (A.D.) Ltd. v. Wilfred Sportsman Ltd.*,[40] the Court of Appeal held[41] that, under section 141, an assignee of the reversion could sue and re-enter premises for rent that was in arrear at the date of the assignment when the right of re-entry had arisen before the assignment.[42] Section 141(3), however, does not render enforceable any condition of re-entry which has been waived or released by a previous reversioner.[43] Moreover, once the right of the reversioner to enforce breaches of the tenant's covenants in the lease has effectively passed to the assignee upon assignment of the reversionary estate, the assignor will no longer, after the date of the assignment, have any right to enforce a right of re-entry against the tenant. In the words of Upjohn L.J. in *Re King, Robinson v. Gray*[44]:

"... consider the case of a lease containing a covenant to build a house according to certain detailed specifications before a certain day. Let me suppose that after that certain day the then lessor assigns the benefit of the reversion to an assignee, and at the time of the assignment the lessee has failed to perform the covenant to build. Who can sue the lessee for breach of covenant? It seems to me clear that the assignee alone can sue. Upon the assignment the benefit of

[39] *Schalit v. Joseph Nadler Ltd.* [1933] 2 K.B. 79, where a tenant sub-let part of his premises to the plaintiff and then executed a declaration of trust by which he declared he held the property on trust for the defendant. The defendant was not entitled to distrain for rent which the plaintiff had allowed to fall into arrear. A person in whom the reversionary interest under a lease is vested by a private Act of Parliament is the person entitled to the income under s. 141(2) and is, therefore, empowered to enforce the covenants in the lease: *Sunderland Orphan Asylum v. River Wear Commissioners* [1912] 1 Ch. 191.

[40] [1971] Ch. 764.

[41] Overruling *Flight v. Bentley* (1835) 7 Sim. 149; 58 E.R. 793.

[42] See also, *Re King, Robinson v. Gray* [1963] Ch. 459 (s. 141 operated to confer upon an assignee of the reversion the right to damages for breach of covenant to build a factory which had already been breached by the tenant before the assignment); *Rickett v. Green* [1910] 1 K.B. 253 (under s. 10 of the Conveyancing and Law of Property Act 1881, right of re-entry for non-payment of rent, existing at the date of the assignment of the reversion, passed to and could be relied upon by the new reversioner) and *Ellis v. Torrington* [1920] 1 K.B. 399 (right to sue on breaches of covenant to repair committed before assignment may be transferred to the assignee of the reversion).

[43] *London and County (A.D.) Ltd. v. Wilfred Sportsman Ltd.* [1971] Ch. 764. (grant of reversionary lease by landlords "subject to and with" the benefit of existing lease no waiver of right to forfeit for non-payment of rent) overruling *Davenport v. Smith* [1921] 2 Ch. 270. See also, *Atkin v. Rose* [1923] 1 Ch. 522, 537–538.

[44] [1963] 1 Ch. 459, 487–488.

every covenant on the lessee's part to be observed and performed is annexed and incident to and goes with the reversionary estate. The benefit of that covenant to build, therefore, passed; as it had been broken, the right to sue also passed as part of the benefit of the covenant and, incidentally also the right to re-enter, if this has not been waived ... The assignor has by operation of section 141 assigned his right to the benefit of the covenant and so has lost his remedy against the lessee."

Thus, the effect of section 141(1) is that, after the assignment of the reversionary interest in a lease, the assignee alone will be entitled to sue the tenant for breaches of covenant contained in the lease, whether such breaches occurred before or after the date of the assignment to him. The same principle will apply to a continuing breach of covenant (such as a covenant to repair) which is broken before the date of the assignment. The rationale is that, under this principle, justice is done to all parties concerned in that (a) the assignor will suffer no loss by being unable to sue because the sale price of the reversionary estate will take account of the value of the right of action which is transferred to the assignee (b) the assignee will be able to enforce any remedy against the tenant and (c) the tenant will remain liable for any loss occasioned to the reversionary estate by his breach of covenant whenever committed.[45]

Reference may also be made to section 4(3) of the Law of Property Act 1925 under which all rights of entry affecting a legal estate which are exerciseable on condition broken or for any other reason may be made exerciseable by any person (and the person deriving title under him) but, in regard to an estate in fee simple (not being a rentcharge held for a legal estate), only within the period authorised by the rule relating to perpetuities.

By virtue of section 98(1) of the Law of Property Act 1925, a mortgagor for the time being entitled to the possession or receipt of the rents and profits of any land (as to which the mortgagee has not given notice of his intention to take possession or to enter into the receipt of the rents and profits thereof), may *inter alia* sue for such possession or for the recovery of such rents and profits. In *Matthews* v. *Usher*,[46] the Court of Appeal held that, under the predecessor to this section, a mortgagor in possession of the demised premises had no right to re-enter for breach of the covenants contained in the lease. Section 141(2) of the 1925 Act, however, does give to a mortgagor entitled to possession or to the receipt of rents and profits of the premises subject to the lease, whose mortgagee has neither taken

---

[45] *Ibid*, 497–498, *per* Diplock L.J.
[46] [1900] 2 K.B. 535.

possession nor given notice of his intention to take possession, the right to enforce the tenant's covenants in the lease.[47]

Burden of proof

Before a forfeiture is established, it must be clearly shown, in the case of a condition, that the event specified in the condition has happened and, in the case of a proviso for re-entry on breach of a covenant, that the proviso extends to the covenant[48] and that there has been a breach.[49] The burden of proof lies on the landlord to establish an act of forfeiture on the part of the tenant entitling him to determine the lease. Thus, in *Doe d. Bridger v. Whitehead*[50] the landlord brought an action in ejectment alleging a forfeiture by breach of a covenant to insure. It was held that the tenant's omission to insure had to be proved by the landlord and it was not sufficient proof of such omission that the tenant had failed to produce the policy at the hearing of the action. In order, therefore, to prove an omission to insure, it will invariably be necessary for the landlord to call an employee of the insurance office who enters policies and premiums and who has searched the records to give evidence.[51] In the words of Abbott C.J. in *Doe d. Chandless v. Robson*[52]:

"... in all cases of forfeiture, the lessor ... must give some negative evidence that the thing has not been done. If the covenant is to pay rent, it ought to be shewn that the rent has been demanded; and if the covenant be for the doing of any act, some evidence of the omission should be given before a remedy so highly penal can be put in force."

Thus, in *Toleman v. Portbury*[53] the landlord's action for ejectment for forfeiture alleging a breach of covenant not to permit a sale by auction on the demised premises without the landlord's consent was non-suited on the ground that the landlord had failed to produce any evidence that the sale had taken place and that consent was not obtained.

In the case of non-payment of rent, if the landlord's demand for the arrears is inaccurate, this will invalidate any subsequent forfeiture of the lease.[54] This is because no forfeiture of property can be made unless every

---

[47] *Turner v. Walsh* [1909] 2 K.B. 484. A mortgagee in possession can recover rent and enforce covenants in the lease of the mortgaged land whether the lease was made prior to the mortgage or under s. 99 of the Law of Property Act 1925: *Municipal Permanent Investment Building Society v. Smith* (1888) 22 Q.B.D. 70. The mortgagee in possession can recover arrears of rent falling due since the date of the mortgage and remaining unpaid: *Re Ind Coope & Co. Ltd.* [1911] 2 Ch. 223.

[48] *Croft v. Lumley* (1858) 6 H.L. Cas. 672, 693, *per* Channell B.

[49] *Bristol Corporation v. Westcott* (1879) 12 Ch. D. 461, (C.A.).

[50] (1838) 8 Ad. & El. 571; 112 E.R. 955.

[51] *Chaplin v. Reid* (1858) 1 F. & F. 315; 175 E.R. 743.

[52] (1826) 2 C. & P. 245; 172 E.R. 111.

[53] (1870) L.R. 5 Q.B. 288.

[54] *Jackson and Co. v. Northampton Street Tramways Co.* (1886) 55 L.T. 91.

condition precedent has been strictly and literally complied with by the landlord.[55]

The burden of proof remains on the landlord to establish an act of forfeiture even where the tenant has admitted the facts amounting to a breach of covenant. In *Duke's Court Estates Ltd.* v. *Associated British Engineering Ltd.*[56] the tenants covenanted to use the premises only as offices in connection with their business and/or other businesses in which they and their subsidiary or associated companies might be interested and not to assign, underlet or part with possession of the premises without the landlords' consent. The landlords brought an action for possession alleging *inter alia* that the tenants had allowed certain named persons and companies to use the premises and that those persons and companies were not subsidiaries or associates of the tenants and that their businesses were not businesses in which the tenants or their subsidiaries or associates were interested. The tenants admitted in their defence that they had allowed the companies named to use the premises but denied that they were not their subsidiaries or associates. The landlords then sought an order that the tenants give particulars of their defence, specifying which of the companies they alleged to be their subsidiaries or associates, and which of the businesses carried on by them were businesses in which the tenants and their subsidiaries and associated companies were alleged to be interested, and the nature and extent of those interests. Harman J., in refusing the landlords' application, held that— the action being for forfeiture and the onus of proof, notwithstanding the tenants' admissions, being on the landlords—the landlords had to prove affirmatively that the companies were not subsidiaries or associates of the tenants.[57]

In *Hagee (London) Ltd.* v. *Co-operative Insurance Society Ltd.*[58] the landlord's peaceable re-entry onto the premises was held unlawful on the ground that the installation of air-conditioning equipment (the subject of the alleged breaches of covenant) was carried out by an independent contractor and its sub-contractor without the tenant's knowledge and contrary to its instructions. In these circumstances, the tenant was held to have committed no breach of covenant entitling the landlord to forfeit the lease. Similarly, in *Doe* d. *Lloyd* v. *Powell*[59] a purported assignment of the lease by a bankrupt tenant to trustees for the benefit of his creditors was

---

[55] *Ibid*, 92, *per* Stirling J.
[56] [1948] 1 Ch. 458.
[57] It seems that the position might be different in the case of a covenant not to assign or underlet because in that case, if a tenant pleaded that he had assigned or underlet but had been permitted to do so, the burden would clearly be on him: *ibid*, 462, *per* Harman J.
[58] [1992] 07 E.G. 122.
[59] (1826) 5 B. & C. 308; 108 E.R. 115. See also, *Bowser* v. *Colby* 1 Hare 109, 138; 66 E.R. 969, 980, (creation of equitable charge no breach of condition against assignment).

held to be void as an act of bankruptcy and, consequently, incapable of giving rise to an act of forfeiture entitling the landlord to re-enter.

Prior to section 16(1) of the Civil Evidence Act 1968, a landlord could not seek discovery of documents from his tenant in order to prove a forfeiture. The rationale behind this rule was that an action for forfeiture was always regarded with great strictness because it was an action to destroy an estate which the landlord had himself created and, therefore, no assistance was given to him by way of discovery of documents or interrogatories, to help him in establishing his case.[60] Section 16(1)(a) of the 1968 Act now abrogates the rule whereby, in any legal proceedings, a person cannot be compelled to answer any question or produce any document or thing if to do so would tend to expose him to a forfeiture. The consequential effect of this sub-section upon the current rules of discovery is that a tenant may no longer claim privilege from disclosure of documents or refuse to answer interrogatories on the ground that the documents or answers may expose him to a forfeiture of his lease.[61]

Loss of the right of forfeiture by limitation

Section 15(1) of the Limitation Act 1980 provides that no action shall be brought by any person to recover any land after the expiration of 12 years from the date on which the right of action accrued to him. In relation to forfeiture, a right of action to recover the land will be deemed to have accrued on the date on which the forfeiture was incurred by the tenant.[62]

---

[60] *Duke's Court Estates Ltd.* v. *Associated British Engineering Ltd.* [1948] Ch. 458, 461, *per* Harman J. See also, *Earl of Mexborough* v. *Whitwood Urban District Council* [1897] 2 Q.B. 111, (C.A.).

[61] See, R.S.C. Ord. 24, r. 2.

[62] s. 8(1) of the 1980 Act and *Doe* d. *Tarrant* v. *Hellier* (1789) 3 T.R. 162, 172, 173; 100 E.R. 511, 516, 517, *per* Lord Kenyon C.J. and Bullen J.; *Doe* d. *Cook* v. *Danvers* (1806) 7 East 299; 103 E.R. 115; *Doe* d. *Allen* v. *Blakeway* (1833) 5 C. & P. 563.

Chapter Three

Exercise of the right of forfeiture

Act of forfeiture renders the lease voidable

An act of forfeiture on the part of the tenant only renders the lease voidable at the option of the landlord. In other words, a breach by the tenant giving rise to an act of forfeiture does not automatically discharge the lease. This will be the position even where the proviso for re-entry expressly stipulates that the lease shall be "void" or "cease to have effect" upon the tenant's default. For example, in *Rede* v. *Farr*,[1] the proviso stated that if the rent should be unpaid for forty days "the demise, and every article, clause and thing herein contained shall cease, determine and be utterly void to all intents and purposes . . ." This wording, despite being in emphatic terms, was held to render the lease only voidable at the election of the landlord. Similarly, in *Doe* d. *Nash* v. *Birch*,[2] where the proviso stipulated that the lease should be "null and void" in the event of the tenant's failure to erect a shop-front on the demised premises within a stipulated time. In *Davenport* v. *R.*[3] the principle was neatly summarised by Sir Montague E. Smith[4]:

> "In a long series of decisions the Courts have construed clauses of forfeiture in leases declaring in terms, however clear and strong, that they shall be void on breach of conditions by the lessees, to mean that they are voidable only at the option of the lessors."

---

[1] (1817) 6 M. & S. 121; 105 E.R. 1188.
[2] (1836) 1 M. & W. 402; 150 E.R. 490.
[3] (1877) 3 App. Cas. 115, (P.C.). See also, *Quesnel Forks Gold Mining Company Ltd.* v. *Ward* [1920] A.C. 222, (P.C.) and *Jardine* v. *Att.-Gen. for Newfoundland* [1932] A.C. 275, (P.C.).
[4] *Ibid*, 128.

Thus, the tenant in default cannot rely upon his own wrongdoing in order to treat the lease as at an end.[5]

In *Richard Clarke & Co. Ltd.* v. *Widnall*,[6] a yearly tenancy agreement contained a clause entitling the landlords to give the tenant three months' notice in writing to determine the tenancy upon the tenant's breach of the covenants in the agreement. This was held to constitute a forfeiture clause rendering the agreement voidable at the instance of the landlords. The fact that the clause provided for the right of re-entry to be effective only after a stated period of notice had expired did not alter the character and legal consequences of that right. The effect in law of such a clause did not differ from the effect of a clause which provided for a forfeiture operating immediately upon the landlord indicating his intention to act upon it.[7]

Since, therefore, the lease is only made voidable upon the tenant's default, the landlord may elect either to forfeit the lease or, alternatively, to treat the lease as still continuing by waiving the forfeiture.[8] Once, however, the landlord has made his election one way or the other, it will be irretractable.[9]

Election to forfeit

In order to bring about an effective forfeiture of the lease, the landlord must take some positive[10] and unequivocal[11] step to signify to the tenant his intention of treating the lease as at an end as a consequence of the tenant's breach of covenant or condition in the lease. This may be effected, under a proviso for re-entry, in one of two ways, namely, by the landlord either physically re-entering upon the demised premises or suing the tenant for possession (or a declaration[12] of title to possession) of the demised premises. It seems that these are the only two methods by which the landlord may signify his intention to determine the lease where the right to forfeit arises out of a proviso for re-entry contained in the lease. Thus, in *Bishop* v. *Trustee of the Bedford Charity*,[13] the landlords' act of

---

[5] *Hayne* v. *Cummings* (1864) 16 C.B. (N.S.) 421, 426; 143 E.R. 1191, 1194, *per* Willes J. (lease "shall cease and be void"); *Arnsby* v. *Woodward* (1827) 6 B. & C. 519, 523; 108 E.R. 542, 544, *per* Lord Tenterden C.J. (term should "cease, determine and be wholly void"); *Doe* d. *Bryan* v. *Bancks* (1821) 4 B. & A. 401; 106 E.R. 984 (lease should be "null and void to all intents and purposes") and *Roberts* v. *Davey* (1833) 4 B. & Ad. 664; 110 E.R. 606 (licence should "cease, determine and be utterly void and of no effect").

[6] [1976] 1 W.L.R. 845.

[7] See also, *Clays Lane Housing Co-operative Ltd.* v. *Patrick* (1985) 49 P. & C. R. 72.

[8] The subject of waiver of forfeiture is considered in Chap. 6.

[9] *Scarfe* v. *Jardine* (1882) 7 App. Cas. 345, 360–361, *per* Lord Blackburn and *Central Estates (Belgravia) Ltd.* v. *Woolgar (No. 2)* [1972] 1 W.L.R. 1048, 1054, *per* Buckley L.J.

[10] *Serjeant* v. *Nash, Field & Co.* [1903] 2 K.B. 304, 310, *per* Collins M.R. See also, *Roberts* v. *Davey* (1833) 4 B. & Ad. 664; 110 E.R. 606.

[11] *Jones* v. *Carter* (1846) 15 M. & W. 718; 153 E.R. 1040, *per* Parke B.

[12] *Cohen* v. *Donegal Tweed Co. Ltd.* (1935) 79 S.J. 592, (C.A.).

[13] (1859) 1 El. & El. 697, 714; 120 E.R. 1071, 1078.

giving notice to the tenants' lodgers to pay rent in future to them instead of to the tenants was held not to constitute an effective election to re-enter. In *Moore* v. *Ullcoats Mining Co. Ltd.*,[14] Warrington J. said[15]:

"I am of the opinion upon the authorities . . . that where the condition in the lease is that the landlord may re-enter he may actually re-enter, or he must do that which is in law equivalent to re-entry, namely, commence an action for the purpose of obtaining possession."

In that case, the landlords had merely given notice to the tenants of their intention to re-enter and this was held insufficient to constitute an effective election to forfeit the lease under the proviso for re-entry. Similarly, in *Warner* v. *Sampson*,[16] the landlord had counterclaimed in her reply to the tenant's defence alleging that, by that defence, the tenant had disclaimed the landlord's title and that, therefore, she was entitled to exercise her right to forfeit the lease. The Court of Appeal held that the landlord had not effectively elected to claim a forfeiture because her reply contained nothing equivalent to a physical re-entry or the bringing of proceedings for possession founded upon the alleged forfeiture.

Where, however, the right to forfeit does not arise out of a proviso for re-entry, the landlord may signify his intention to forfeit the lease by taking some positive step other than physical re-entry or the bringing of an action for possession. The distinction was made by Bayley J. in *Fenn* v. *Smart*[17] where he said[18]:

"Must not the necessity of an entry depend upon the wording of the condition? If the words be, that upon the doing of such an act, the reversioner may enter, there must be an entry to avoid the estate: but if the estate be granted upon condition that if the grantee do such an act, the estate shall thereupon immediately cease and determine, there no entry is necessary."

Thus, where the right to forfeit arises out of a proviso which renders the lease void upon the tenant's breach without reference to any pre-requisite of "re-entry" in order to bring about a forfeiture of the lease, the landlord may signify his intention to forfeit the lease by simply giving notice of his intention to the tenant.[19] In *Moore* v. *Ullcoats Mining Co. Ltd.*[20] a lease of a

---

[14] [1908] 1 Ch. 575. See also, *Serjeant* v. *Nash, Field & Co.* [1903] 2 K.B. 304, 310–311, *per* Collins M.R.

[15] [1908] 1 Ch. 575, 587–588.

[16] [1959] 1 Q.B. 297.

[17] (1810) 12 East 444; 104 E.R. 173. See also, *Moore* v. *Ullcoats Mining Co. Ltd.* [1908] 1 Ch. 575, 588, *per* Warrington J. and *Jones* v. *Carter* (1846) 15 M. & W. 718, 725; 153 E.R. 1040, 1043, *per* Parke B.

[18] *Ibid*, 448; 175.

[19] *Moore* v. *Ullcoats Mining Co. Ltd.* [1908] 1 Ch. 575, 588, *per* Warrington J. See also *Richard Clarke & Co. Ltd.* v. *Widnall* [1976] 1 W.L.R. 845 (landlord effected a forfeiture by serving short notice of termination of the lease).

[20] [1908] 1 Ch. 575.

mine contained a proviso that, on default by the tenants in performing any of the covenants in the lease, the landlord could re-enter and thereupon the lease would be determined. In breach of covenant, the tenants refused the landlords' agent to inspect the mine and the landlords gave the tenants written notice that they had determined the lease. Warrington J. held that, having regard to the form of the proviso for re-entry in the lease, actual re-entry or its equivalent (namely, the issue and service of a writ claiming possession) was necessary in order to effect a forfeiture and that the notice by itself was not sufficient for this purpose.

It is possible for a landlord, in certain circumstances, to forfeit in respect of part only of the demised premises. In *G.M.S. Syndicate Ltd.* v. *Gary Elliott Ltd.*[21] the demised property comprised the ground floor and basement of a building let to the first defendant for the purpose of a retail clothing business. The first defendant sub-let the basement to two sub-lessees for use as a sauna bath, gymnasium and health club. The sub-lessees, in turn, assigned the benefit of the sub-tenancy to a husband and wife who used the basement for immoral purposes. The landlord claimed forfeiture in respect of both the ground floor and basement but he was willing for the first defendant to continue to use the ground floor for the purposes of its business. Nourse J. held[22] that it was possible for the landlord to forfeit in respect of part only of the demised property (the basement) and for the court to grant relief against forfeiture in respect of the other part (the ground floor) where, as in the present case, the demised property was physically separated into two parts and not only could both parts be separately let and enjoyed but the immoral user had been confined to one part.

A related question is whether a landlord can bring a whole lease to an end because of a breach of covenant by one assignee to whom only a part of the premises has been assigned. Let us assume, for example, that a building is let as a single unit to one tenant. Subsequently, the tenant assigns half the premises to A and half to B. Suppose then, that B breaks an obligation of the tenancy. Can the landlord bring the whole tenancy to an end? The answer is, clearly, in the negative. In the Irish case of *Dooner* v. *Odlum*,[23] Cherry L.C.J. said[24]:

"The law is, I think, well settled that where a lessee of demised premises assigns a portion of these premises to a stranger, the assignee is liable to the lessor upon the covenants contained in the lease only in so far as those covenants affect the lands in his possession;

---

[21] [1982] 1 Ch. 1.
[22] Relying on *Dumpor's Case* (1603) 4 Co. Rep. 119b.
[23] [1914] 2 I.R. 411.
[24] *Ibid*, 425.

and, as regards rent, only for an apportioned part of the rent properly chargeable in respect of the lands actually vested in him."

The rationale behind this principle is that if the landlord had wanted to be able to recover the whole of the demised premises, he could (and should) have forbidden partial assignments. The position is, doubtless, the same if, in our example, the tenant (instead of assigning half of the building to A and half to B), assigned half to A and retained half for himself.

It is, perhaps, self-evident that if the landlord acts precipitously in forfeiting the lease before any right of forfeiture has arisen, he will be liable to the tenant in damages for any loss resulting from the wrongful forfeiture.[25]

It will now be convenient to consider the two primary modes of effecting a forfeiture, namely, physical re-entry and proceedings for possession, in more detail.

(1) *Physical re-entry*

The landlord may signify his intention to forfeit the lease by actually physically re-entering upon the demised premises. In *Thatcher v. C.H. Pearce & Sons (Contractors) Ltd.*,[26] the landlords peaceably re-entered the demised premises (comprising a scrap-yard), whilst the tenant was in prison, and changed the locks. This was held to be an effective re-entry for the purpose of determining the lease. The retention of a key to the main gates of the premises was considered to be of particular significance as evidencing an intention to re-enter. Re-entry may also be effected by the landlord letting a new tenant into occupation of the premises or by accepting an existing occupier as tenant. Thus, in *Edward H. Lewis & Son Ltd. v. Morelli*[27] the landlord let to an Italian certain restaurant premises which were occupied by a manager who ran the business as the tenant's partner. The tenant subsequently went to Italy and was resident there when war broke out between Great Britain and Italy. The landlord then let thè premises to the manager on a weekly tenancy. Denning J. held that, on the outbreak of war with Italy, the tenant had become an alien enemy and the contract between him and the manager was dissolved with the consequence that there was no one in this country authorised to pay the rent or perform the covenants on behalf of the tenant. The landlord was, therefore, in a position to forfeit the lease and his action in

---

[25] *South Tottenham Land Securities* v. *R & A Millett (Shops) Ltd.* (1983) 268 E.G. 703, 706, *per* Woolf J., upheld on appeal: [1984] 1 All E.R. 614, (C.A.).

[26] [1968] 1 W.L.R. 748. See also, *Billson* v. *Residential Apartments Ltd.* [1991] 3 W.L.R. 264, (C.A.), [1992] 2 W.L.R. 15, (H.L.), (change of locks).

[27] [1948] 1 All E.R. 433, reversed on appeal on other grounds: [1948] 2 All E.R. 1021, (C.A.).

granting and continuing a tenancy to the manager was in law a re-entry which effected a forfeiture.

Similarly, in *Baylis* v. *Le Gros*,[28] the landlord, intending to take advantage of the forfeiture clause in the lease, granted to a sub-tenant in possession of the premises a yearly tenancy of the same and subsequently received rent from him. These acts were held to amount to a sufficient election on the part of the landlord to determine the lease.[29] Cockburn C.J. said[30]:

> "Finding the premises in a dilapidated state, the landlord comes upon them and enters into an agreement with a man he finds in possession, to become his tenant—intending thereby to act upon the forfeiture and to oust the lessee. I think this was quite sufficient to constitute an entry by the landlord . . ."

Crowder J. observed[31]:

> "Then it is said there has been no re-entry. The landlord, however, is in and occupying the premises by a tenant who is paying him rent. I think this is the strongest possible case of re-entry."

The decision in *Baylis* was applied in *London and County (A.D.) Ltd.* v. *Wilfred Sportsman Ltd.*,[32] where the defendants, who occupied adjoining premises, entered into possession of the demised premises as trespassers, at the invitation of the tenant's guarantor, in anticipation of the grant by the head landlords of a reversionary lease to the guarantor. The head landlords subsequently granted the reversionary lease to the guarantor and this was held to perfect the guarantor's peaceable re-entry. The mere continuance of the defendants' possession of the premises following the grant of the reversionary lease was sufficient to operate as a re-entry since their trespass did not need to be discontinued before there could be an effective forfeiture. In the *Baylis* case, the position was very much the same since there was a sufficient re-entry by the mere acceptance of the sub-tenant already in occupation as tenant of the forfeiting landlord. In neither case, therefore, was it necessary for the parties to go through the "idle ceremony"[33] of withdrawing from the demised premises and then re-entering physically shortly thereafter in order to

---

[28] (1858) 4 C.B. (N.S.) 537; 140 E.R. 1201.

[29] The fact that the tenant was unaware of the acts of the landlord did not preclude a valid re-entry in these circumstances. The current statutory requirement of notice to the tenant before the landlord may enforce a right of re-entry by action or otherwise, contained in s. 146 of the Law of Property Act 1925, will not necessarily prevent such acts from being held to amount to a re-entry, although the tenant is not aware of the acts when they were done: See *Capital & City Holdings Ltd.* v. *Dean Warburg Ltd.* [1989] 25 E.G. 97, *per* Ralph Gibson L.J.

[30] *Ibid*, 554, 1208.

[31] *Ibid*, 555, 1209.

[32] [1971] Ch. 764.

[33] *Baylis* v. *Le Gros* (1858) 4 C.B. (N.S.) 537, 555; 140 E.R. 1201, 1208, *per* Williams J.

achieve a forfeiture. In *Ashton* v. *Sobelman*,[34] however, the landlords' act of changing the locks on the premises, in the absence of any intention to exclude the sub-tenant from possession under the terms of his existing tenancy, was held not to give rise to an effectual exercise of the landlords' right of forfeiture of the tenants' lease. In that case, the tenants had defaulted in the payment of rent and the landlords wrote to the sub-tenant explaining that they intended to forfeit the premises and re-take possession by changing the locks on the front door and instructed the sub-tenant to pay all future rent directly to them as their direct tenant. On the landlords' assurance that his rights of occupation under the sub-tenancy would in no way be affected, the sub-tenant agreed to the change of the locks and to the arrangement regarding the payment of rent. In this case, therefore, the landlords had sought to effect a re-entry against their tenant by an arrangement with an existing sub-tenant under which the latter was to remain in occupation of the premises as tenant of the landlords upon the terms not of a new tenancy and for a different term, as in the *Baylis* case, but upon the terms of his existing sub-lease. Accordingly, there could be no effective re-entry since the continuance of the sub-tenancy was entirely inconsistent with the forfeiture of the headlease. The *Ashton* case was applied in *Hammersmith and Fulham London Borough Council* v. *Top Shop Centres Ltd.*[35] where Warner J. held[36] that, once a headlease had been forfeited, a sub-tenant was in relation to the freeholder a trespasser against whom the freeholder's right of re-entry could be effectively asserted by compelling the sub-tenant to take a new lease or give up possession but not by merely receiving rent payable under the erstwhile underlease.

There will be no sufficient re-entry to avoid the lease where the landlord relets to a stranger to whose entry the sub-tenant objects. In *Parker* v. *Jones*,[37] the tenant of a field, in breach of covenant not to underlet without licence, sublet the land to the plaintiff on a yearly tenancy. The tenant subsequently surrendered his lease to the landlord, who accepted the surrender in ignorance of the subletting and of the plaintiff's occupation. The landlord then relet the land to the defendant who entered into possession and removed the plaintiff's cattle. The plaintiff brought an action to recover possession of the land and damages for trespass. Darling J.[38] held that the reletting to the defendant did not operate as a re-entry by the landlord so as to effect a forfeiture of the tenant's lease and that, accordingly, the plaintiff's interest in the land was still subsisting. He said[39]:

---

[34] [1987] 1 W.L.R. 171.
[35] [1990] Ch. 237.
[36] *Ibid*, 260–261.
[37] [1910] 2 K.B. 32.
[38] See also the judgment of Bucknill J.
[39] *Ibid*, 37.

" . . . I think the plaintiff's term must be treated as still subsisting at the date of the trespass complained of. It was not put an end to by [the tenant's] surrender, and I do not think it could be got rid of merely by the landlord granting over his head another tenancy incompatible with his."

It is essential for the landlord to point to some unequivocal act evidencing a physical re-entry. Thus, where the landlord wears two hats, that of a landlord and also that of a mortgagee in possession of the demised premises by assignment, it is important for him to make clear to the tenant by unequivocal acts or words that the lease was being forfeited and not simply that he was re-entering in his capacity as mortgagee.[40] In *Revlok Properties Ltd.* v. *Dixon*,[41] the tenant vacated the premises without informing the landlords. When this was discovered by the landlords, they changed the locks but only with the intention of securing the premises (and the tenant's interest therein) but not to shut him out. The Court of Appeal held that the landlords could still maintain an action for the rent as their act of taking possession did not constitute either a re-entry or an acceptance of a surrender offered by the abandonment of the premises by the tenant. The onus in such cases is on the tenant to prove that the landlord had done more than just protected his interest and effected a termination of the lease.

When the landlord effects a physical re-entry, he will be taken to have elected to forfeit the lease from the moment he physically takes possession of the demised premises. However, the landlord must ensure that his re-entry is peaceable and does not contravene the provisions of section 6 of the Criminal Law Act 1977.[42] If the landlord uses or threatens violence[43] for the purpose of securing entry into the premises,[44] he will be

---

[40] *Hone* v. *Daejan Properties Ltd.* (1976) 120 S.J. 488, (C.A.).

[41] (1973) 25 P. & C.R. 1. See also, *Oastler* v. *Henderson* (1877) 2 Q.B.D. 575, (C.A.) (possession of house by landlord not inconsistent with the continuance of the tenant's term so as to estop the landlord from alleging the continuance of it and effecting a surrender of the term by operation of law).

[42] The landlord no longer commits an offence under the Forcible Entry Acts of 1381 to 1623 since these were repealed by s. 13 of the 1977 Act.

[43] The word "violence" covers any application of force to the person but, in relation to property, carries a more restricted meaning. For example, splintering a door or window would be violence but forcing a window catch with a thin piece of metal would not: See Law Com. Report, *Conspiracy and Criminal Law Reform*, (Law Com. No. 76), para. 2.61.

[44] See s. 12(1)(*a*) for the meaning of "premises". A person already in lawful occupation of a building may commit the offence by using or threatening violence to secure entry to another part of the same building (e.g. a particular flat) under separate occupation. "Premises" will include "any movable structure, vehicle, or vessel designed or adapted for use for residential purposes": See s. 12(2). Land, however, is not "premises" unless it is "ancillary to a building": See s.12(2) (*b*).

guilty of a criminal offence[45] provided that (a) there is someone present on the premises at the time who is opposed to the entry and (b) the landlord knows that this is the case.[46] It is immaterial whether the violence is directed against the person or against the premises and whether the entry is for the purpose of acquiring possession of the premises or for any other purpose.[47] It should also be noted that physical re-entry is not available to a landlord where the premises are let as a dwelling and whilst any person[48] is lawfully residing therein.[49]

In *Billson* v. *Residential Apartments Ltd.*[50] the House of Lords held that a tenant has the right to apply for relief from forfeiture under section 146(2) of the Law of Property Act 1925[51] even after the landlord has forfeited the lease by physically re-entering on the premises. The effect of this decision, together with the provisions of section 6 of the Criminal Law Act 199, is that it is unlikely that landlords will opt to exercise their right of forfeiture by physical re-entry as opposed to recovering possession by court action. Prior to the House of Lords' decision in *Billson*, the major attraction to landlords of physical re-entry was that it was inexpensive, fast and avoided prolonged litigation. That attraction has now been largely removed and, except in cases where there is little chance of the tenant applying for relief, a landlord may be better advised to forfeit by issuing and serving proceedings for possession of the premises. A landlord who physically re-enters may well find that the tenant will simply re-possess the premises following re-entry or, alternatively, apply to the court for an order entitling him to resume possession pending the outcome of his application for relief. Moreover, since the landlord will remain vulnerable to a tenant's application for relief for some time after

---

[45] The landlord will be liable on summary conviction to imprisonment for a term not exceeding six months or to a fine not exceeding 2,000 or both: See s. 6(5) as amended by s. 37(2) of the Criminal Justice Act 1982. A constable in uniform has the power to arrest without warrant anyone who is, or whom he, with reasonable cause, suspects to be, guilty of an offence under s. 6: See s. 6(6).

[46] s. 6(1) of the 1977 Act.

[47] See s. 6(4) of the 1977 Act.

[48] Not just the tenant under the forfeited lease. See, *e.g.*, *Iperion Investments Corporation* v. *Broadwalk House Residents Ltd.*, [1992] 2 E.G.L.R. 235, where the tenant's housekeeper was resident in the premises.

[49] s. 2 of the Protection from Eviction Act 1977 (replacing s. 31 of the Rent Act 1965), declaring that it shall not be lawful to enforce a right of re-entry or forfeiture in such circumstances otherwise than by proceedings in court. The only apparent penalty for the offence is contained in s. 1 of the 1977 Act, which provides for the offence of unlawful eviction and harrassment. In addition, an injunction or damages for trespass, breach of the covenant for quiet enjoyment and unlawful eviction may be claimed either at common law or under statute: See s. 27(3) of the Housing Act 1988, and *Tagro* v. *Cafane* [1991] 1 W.L.R. 378 and *Jones* v. *Miah* [1992] 33 E.G. 59, (C.A.) as to the measure of damages recoverable under s. 28(1) of the 1988 Act.

[50] [1992] 2 W.L.R. 15.

[51] s. 146(2) is discussed in Chap. 10.

re-entry,[52] his safest course will be to obtain a final judgment for posses-sion by court action thereby debarring the tenant from seeking relief in the future.[53]

If the landlord is a company, it can by its directors appoint[54] an agent to re-enter onto the demised premises and thereby effect a forfeiture of the lease.[55] Where, however, an administration order under Part II of the Insolvency Act 1986 is in force, no proceedings or other legal process and no other step may be taken to enforce any security over a company's property except with the consent of the administrator or leave of the court.[56] In *Exchange Travel Agency Ltd.* v. *Triton Property Trust plc*[57] Harman J. held that a peaceable re-entry was either the enforcement of a "security" or some "other legal process" within the meaning of section 11 of the 1986 Act and that, accordingly, such a step required the consent of an administrator or leave of the court.[58]

If the landlord commences court proceedings to effect a re-entry, he is obliged[59] to serve notice of those proceedings on any known under-lessee (including a mortgagee) but there is no such corresponding obligation where the landlord seeks to forfeit by peaceable re-entry. Indeed, the landlord is not even obliged to inform the sub-tenant or mortgagee that he has served a notice under section 146 of the Law of Property Act 1925.

(2) *Suing for possession/declaration of title to possession*

The issue and service of a writ[60] or summons[61] against the tenant claiming possession (or a declaration[62] of title to possession) of the demised premises will operate as a final and conclusive election by the landlord to forfeit the lease.[63] In the words of Willes J. in *Grimwood* v. *Moss*[64]:

---

[52] The tenant's application will, of course, be ultimately barred by undue delay: *ibid*, 23–24, 26, *per* Lords Templeman and Oliver.

[53] See further, Chap. 10.

[54] Such an appointment can be made by parol: s. 36 of the Companies Act 1985.

[55] See, Table A art. 71 of the Companies (Tables A to F) Regulations 1985, (S.I. 1985 No. 805).

[56] See, s. 11 of the 1986 Act. As to the exercise of the court's discretion to grant leave: See *Re Atlantic Computer Systems plc* [1992] 2 W.L.R. 367, (C.A.).

[57] [1991] 35 E.G. 120. See also, *Re Memco Engineering Ltd.* [1986] Ch. 86.

[58] The same principle applies under s. 130(3) of the Insolvency Act 1986 in the context of a winding-up or voluntary liquidation: *ibid*, 121. See, *General Share and Trust Co.* v. *Wetley Brick and Pottery Co.* (1882) 20 Ch. D. 260, (C.A.); *Re David Lloyd & Co. Ltd.* (1877) 6 Ch. D. 339, (C.A.).

[59] See R.S.C. Ord. 6, r. 2 and C.C.R. Ord. 6, r. 3.

[60] In the High Court, the landlord may apply for judgment under R.S.C. Ord. 14, r. 1.

[61] In the county court, there is no corresponding right to apply for summary judgment.

[62] *Cohen* v. *Donegal Tweed Co. Ltd.* (1935) 79 S.J. 592, (C.A.).

[63] *Jones* v. *Carter* (1846) 15 M. & W. 718; 153 E.R. 1040; *Serjeant* v. *Nash, Field & Co.* [1903] 2 K.B. 304 and *Woolwich Equitable Building Society* v. *Preston* [1938] 1 Ch. 129.

[64] (1872) L.R. 7 C.P. 360, 364.

"... the bringing of the action of ejectment is equivalent to the ancient entry. It is an act unequivocal in the sense that it asserts the right of possession upon every ground that may turn out to be available to the party claiming to re-enter."

More recently, Lord Templeman in *Billson* v. *Residential Apartments Ltd.*[65] observed[66]:

"In order to exercise his option to determine the lease the landlord must either re-enter the premises in conformity with the proviso or must issue and serve a writ claiming possession. The bringing of an action to recover possession is equivalent to an entry for the forfeiture."

Under the old practice in an action for ejectment, the tenant admitted the landlord's entry onto the premises and evidence of an actual entry was not, therefore, required in most cases.[67] The practice was rendered obsolete with the enactment of the Common Law Procedure Act 1852 and the landlord may now maintain an action to recover possession of the premises without proof of actual re-entry in order to bring about a forfeiture of the lease.[68]

To effect a conclusive election to forfeit, the landlord must not only issue but also *serve* his writ/summons on the tenant. Thus, it is the *service* of the proceedings which constitute, as a matter of law, the notional physical re-entry in proceedings for forfeiture of a lease.[69] If the tenant consists of several persons under a partnership firm or joint tenants, service of the proceedings on one of them will be sufficient.[70] Since the landlord's election takes effect from the date of service of the proceedings, he can only claim arrears of rent under the lease which fell due before this date. Thereafter, his claim will be for mesne profits for the tenant's use

---

[65] [1992] 2 W.L.R. 15, (H.L.).

[66] *Ibid*, 18.

[67] See *Doe* d. *Phillips* v. *Rollings* (1847) 4 C.B. 188, 197–200; 136 E.R. 476, 480–481, for a discussion of the consent rule which admitted entry. See also, *Goodright* d. *Hare* v. *Cator* (1780) 2 Doug. 477, 485; 99 E.R. 304, 309, *per* Lord Mansfield.

[68] *Ware* v. *Booth* (1894) 10 T.L.R. 446 and *Re Morrish, ex p. Sir W. Hart Dyke* (1882) 22 Ch. D. 410.

[69] *Canas Property Co. Ltd.* v. *K.L. Television Services Ltd.* [1970] 2 Q.B. 433 (C.A.) not following *Elliott* v. *Boynton* [1924] 1 Ch. 236 on this point. See also, *Jones* v. *Carter* (1846) 15 M. & W. 718, 726; 153 E.R. 1040, 1043, *per* Parke B. and *Scarf* v. *Jardine* (1882) 7 App. Cas. 345, 360–361, *per* Lord Blackburn (an election of two inconsistent remedies not final until it is communicated to the party concerned); *Car and Universal Finance Co. Ltd.* v. *Caldwell* [1965] 1 Q.B. 525, 556, *per* Upjohn L.J.

[70] *Doe* d. *Bennet* v. *Roe* (1849) 7 C.B. 127; 137 E.R. 52. But, in order to obtain an effective judgment for possession against two joint tenants, judgment must be obtained against both of them: *Gill* v. *Lewis* [1956] 2 Q.B. 1.

and occupation of the premises *qua* trespasser.[71] Moreover, if the rent is payable quarterly in advance (say, on March 25) and the writ is issued and served during the currency of a quarter (say, on April 25), the writ should claim for the whole rent due in advance for that quarter (on March 25) and mesne profits from the next quarter day (June 24) to the date of delivery up of possession of the premises.[72] If, however, the rent is payable in arrear, the writ should claim the last quarter's rent due (on March 25) and for the rent from that date to the date of service of the writ and mesne profits from that date (*i.e.* the date of service) until the date of delivery up of possession of the premises.[73]

Although it is the service (and not issue) of the writ on the tenant which is treated as the notional re-entry which completes the landlord's forfeiture of the lease, there is no *locus poenitentiae* between the issue of the writ and its service entitling the tenant to tender arrears of rent and avoid the forfeiture. In *Richards* v. *De Freitas*,[74] the landlords issued a writ for possession of factory premises alleging forfeiture on the ground of non-payment of rent. Before the writ was served on the tenant company, the receiver forwarded a cheque for the amount due. May J. held that, by issuing the writ, the landlord had made his election to forfeit the lease and there was no obligation upon him, during the period between its issue and service, to accept tender of the rent from the receiver. He said[75]:

> "[The landlord] was entitled to say to the defendant lessee that he had so conducted himself as to incur a liability to forfeiture which he, the lessor, proposed to enforce. To accept rent thereafter would, as I have indicated, have negatived his clear election. Once the right of forfeiture has accrued no lessor is bound to give up that right ..."

The issue and service of the proceedings must amount to an unequivocal declaration by the landlord of his intention to forfeit the lease. In *Commissioners of Works* v. *Hull*,[76] the tenant assigned his tenancy, in breach of covenant, to the defendant and subsequently absconded from

---

[71] *Associated Deliveries Ltd.* v. *Harrison* (1984) 272 E.G. 321, (C.A.), applying *Canas Property Co. Ltd.* v. *K.L. Television Services Ltd.* [1970] 2 Q.B. 433, (C.A.). The Court has jurisdiction, in an action for possession of land, to order the tenant to make interim payments to the landlord for use and occupation: R.S.C. Ord. 29, r. 10, 12 (High Court), C.C.R. Ord. 13, r. 2 (county court). The jurisdiction is not, however, exercisable where the tenant has a *bona fide* counterclaim which may exceed the amount of the claim for mesne profits: *Old Grovebury Manor Farm Ltd.* v. *Seymour Plant Sales and Hire Ltd.* [1979] 1 W.L.R. 263.

[72] It is not necessary for the landlord to bring a second action for the amount due after the writ: *Southport Tramways Co.* v. *Gandy* [1897] 2 Q.B. 66.

[73] *Ellis* v. *Rowbotham* [1900] 1 Q.B. 740; *Canas Property Co. Ltd.* v. *K.L. Television Services Ltd.* [1970] 2 Q.B. 433, 442, *per* Denning L.J. and *Capital & City Holdings Ltd.* v. *Dean Warburg Ltd.* [1989] 25 E.G. 97.

[74] (1974) 29 P. & C.R. 1.

[75] *Ibid*, 10.

[76] [1922] 1 K.B. 205. The case is referred to with approval by Denning L.J. in *Canas Property Co. Ltd.* v. *K.L. Television Services Ltd.* [1970] 2 Q.B. 433, 441.

the premises. On discovering the position, the landlords brought an action against the assignee to eject him as trespasser. The landlords' action, although brought against the assignee of the lease and not the original tenant, was held a sufficient indication by the landlords of their intention to exercise their option to forfeit the tenancy for breach of covenant. The case proceeded on the basis that, on the disappearance of the tenant, the bringing of proceedings against the person actually in possession of the premises (being the assignee of the tenant) was equivalent to a physical re-entry onto the premises. However, in *Capital & City Holdings Ltd.* v. *Dean Warburg,*[77] Ralph Gibson L.J. doubted whether the principle of the *Hull* case could be applied to a situation where the landlords had served proceedings for possession against a trespassing company, which had been allowed into occupation of the premises by the tenant in breach of covenant in the lease. In his view, the position of a person in occupation of the premises, with the consent of the original tenant, was different from that of an assignee when considering the effect of the service of a writ to which the original tenant had not been made a defendant.

In order to constitute an effective election to forfeit, the writ/summons must contain an unequivocal demand for possession and this will not be so if it claims relief consistent with the continuation of the lease, for example, an injunction to restrain future breaches of covenant. Thus, in *Evans* v. *Davis,*[78] the landlord's writ was indorsed with a claim for an injunction to restrain the tenant from committing a breach of the covenants contained in an agreement for a lease and to recover possession of the premises comprised in the agreement. Fry J. held that the claim for an injunction, which was founded on the continuation of the agreement, was inconsistent with the claim to recover possession and that, accordingly, the landlord was not entitled to recover possession. He said[79]:

> "[The] writ was, in my opinion, not unequivocal; on the contrary, it asked, as I think, for relief which could only be had in the alternative, and as the plaintiff did not disclose by the writ which of the two alternatives he desired to pursue, he left the matter open and ambiguous."

In *Moore* v. *Ullcoats Mining Co. Ltd.,*[80] the landlords issued a writ against the tenants claiming (a) possession of the demised premises (an iron ore mine) (b) mesne profits (c) an injunction to restrain the tenants from working the mine (d) an order permitting the landlord to inspect the mine and its workings (e) a receiver and (f) damages. Warrington J. held that

[77] [1989] 25 E.G. 97.
[78] [1878] 10 Ch. 747.
[79] *Ibid,* 763.
[80] [1908] 1 Ch. 575.

the claim in the writ for possession of the mine was inconsistent with the claim for an injunction and, accordingly, the writ did not constitute an unequivocal demand for possession so as to operate as a final election to determine the lease. In *Wheeler* v. *Keeble (1914) Ltd.*,[81] however, the landlords by their writ claimed (a) possession of the premises comprised in the lease (b) damages for breach of covenants contained in the lease and (c) an interim injunction. The landlords also served a notice of motion for an injunction to restrain the tenants from erecting certain lettering on the front of the premises in breach of covenant in the lease. Younger J. held that the writ to recover possession constituted an unequivocal determination of the lease on the part of the landlords and that it was not open to them to move for an injunction on the footing that the lease was still subsisting. Accordingly, the motion for an interlocutory injunction was dismissed. Younger J. said[82]:

> " . . . there can be no question that the writ on its true construction amounts to an unqualified election on the part of the plaintiffs to determine the lease. All the relief claimed by the writ subsequent to the claim for possession is subsidiary to that relief and claim for possession."

In this case, therefore, the interim injunction was treated, as a matter of construction of the writ, as being only ancillary and incidental to the claim for possession and, therefore, not inconsistent with it. The *Wheeler* case was distinguished in *Calabar Properties Ltd.* v. *Seagull Autos Ltd.*,[83] where the landlords, by their writ, claimed possession of the premises, alleging breach of the user covenant in the lease, and "without prejudice to the claim for possession" various injunctions to enforce the covenant. Buckley J. held that the writ was equivocal on the ground that the landlords had not sought relief solely on the footing that the lease had come to an end. He said[84]:

> "The injunctions which are claimed are injunctions of a permanent nature. They are injunctions founded upon breach of covenants contained in the lease. They are claimed, it is true, without prejudice to the claim for possession but that makes it clear to me that the claim for injunctions is not ancillary to the claim for possession. On the contrary, it is an alternative claim put forward in such a way as not to prejudice the claim for possession."

In the *Calabar* case, therefore, it would have been open to the landlords at the trial of the action to abandon their claim for possession and proceed

[81] [1920] 1 Ch. 57.
[82] *Ibid*, 62.
[83] [1969] 1 Ch. 451.
[84] *Ibid*, 456.

with their alternative claim for relief upon the footing that the lease was still in existence. On this basis, Buckley J. distinguished the *Wheeler* case and concluded that the case before him fell within the reasoning of the *Moore* decision.

Conversely, it seems that the making of an equivocal demand for possession in the writ will not operate as a waiver of the forfeiture on the part of the landlord. Thus, so long as the landlord has not conclusively elected to treat the lease as continuing (for example, by pursuing an injunction to enforce the covenants in the lease),[85] he will not be precluded from bringing a subsequent action claiming forfeiture of the lease.

A writ in a forfeiture action must be indorsed with the name and address of, and be sent to, any person whom the landlord knows to be entitled to claim relief against forfeiture, under section 146(4) of the Law of Property Act 1925 or in accordance with section 38 of the Supreme Court Act 1981, as underlessee or mortgagee.[86]

The effect of forfeiture

Although the issue and service of proceedings will constitute a final election on the part of the landlord to treat the lease as forfeited (subject to proof that there has, in fact, been a breach of covenant or condition), the rights of the parties will not determine until the final outcome of the landlord's action.[87] The conceptual nature of a lease during the "twilight period"[88] between its forfeiture and the determination of the tenant's application for relief from forfeiture was referred to in *Meadows* v. *Clerical, Medical and General Life Assurance Society*[89] by Sir Robert Megarry V.–C. where he said[90]:

"There are, of course, curiosities in the status of a forfeited lease which is the subject of an application for relief against forfeiture. Until the application has been decided, it will not be known whether the lease will remain forfeited or whether it will be restored as if it had never been forfeited. But there are many other instances of such uncertainties. When the validity of a notice to quit is in dispute, until that issue is resolved it will not be known whether the tenancy has ended or whether it still exists. The tenancy has a trance-like existence pendent lite; none can assert with assurance whether it is alive

---

[85] In *Evans* v. *Davis* [1878] 10 Ch. 747, Fry J. held that the landlord had waived his right to claim possession of the premises by stating in his pleadings that he was ready and willing to grant a new lease to the tenant.

[86] R.S.C. Ord. 6, rr. 2(1)(c)(iii) and (2) and C.C.R. Ord. 6, rr. (3)(1)(f) and (2).

[87] *Serjeant* v. *Nash, Field & Co.* [1903] 2 K.B. 304, 311–312, *per* Collins M.R.

[88] *Meadows* v. *Clerical, Medical and General Life Assurance Society* [1981] Ch. 70, 78, *per* Sir Robert Megarry V.–C.

[89] [1981] Ch. 70.

[90] *Ibid*, 75.

or dead. The status of a forfeited underlease which is the subject of an application for relief seems to me to be not dissimilar; at least it cannot be said to be dead beyond hope of resurrection."

Similarly, Parker L.J. in *Liverpool Properties Ltd.* v. *Oldbridge Investments Ltd.*[91] observed[92]:

"The position of a tenant under a lease subject to forfeiture for breach of covenant, when there is no issue but that the breach has taken place, is somewhat obscure. There is a period of limbo during which it cannot be predicated for a certainty whether the lease will ever truly come to an end, for if there is a counterclaim for relief in an action for forfeiture and that counterclaim for relief succeeds and any conditions are complied with, the original lease continues."

In *Driscoll* v. *Church Commissioners For England*,[93] the tenant of a number of houses applied to the Lands Tribunal, under section 84 of the Law of Property Act 1925, for an order modifying various covenants which prohibited the use of the houses for any trade or business. Subsequently, the landlords issued a number of writs against the tenant claiming forfeiture for breaches of the covenants. The tenant responded by counterclaiming for relief from forfeiture and was granted relief subject to certain conditions. The landlords then raised a preliminary issue as to whether they had, by issuing and serving the writs, unequivocally determined the leases of the houses so that, at the date of the Tribunal hearing, there were no subsisting covenants to be modified under the 1925 Act. On this point, the Court of Appeal held that the tenant had retained *locus standi* to apply to the Tribunal as a "person interested" under section 84 of the 1925 Act, notwithstanding the service of the writs, as the effect of any order for relief from forfeiture would be to re-establish the leases. Denning L.J. observed[94]:

" . . . although a writ is an unequivocal election, nevertheless, until the action is finally determined in favour of the landlord, the covenant does not cease to be potentially good. For instance, the forfeiture may not be established; or relief may be granted, in which case the lease is re-established as from the beginning."

The effect of treating the covenants in the lease as "potentially good",

[91] (1985) 276 E.G. 1352, (C.A.).
[92] *Ibid*, 1352.
[93] [1957] 1 Q.B. 330.
[94] *Ibid*, 340.

notwithstanding a forfeiture, is that the tenant[95] may continue to enforce the landlord's covenants pending the outcome of his application for relief from forfeiture. Thus, in *Peninsular Maritime Ltd.* v. *Padseal Ltd.*,[96] the Court of Appeal held that the tenants were entitled to an interlocutory mandatory injunction requiring the landlords, in compliance with their covenants in the lease, to use their best endeavours to put a lift in good working order in circumstances where the tenants had applied for relief against forfeiture in an action brought against them by the landlords. Despite the fact that the landlords had elected to forfeit the lease, the covenants remained in existence and were still enforceable pending a decision on the tenants' application for relief. The decision, however, does not support a general principle that a tenant can rely on the land-lord's covenants for all purposes.[97]

Moreover, a tenancy of business premises, in respect of which there is a judgment for forfeiture coupled with a subsisting application for relief, is not a tenancy which has "come to an end . . . by forfeiture" within the meaning of section 24(2) of the Landlord and Tenant Act 1954. The right to apply for relief is merely part of the process of forfeiture and that process will not be completed until the application for relief has been finally determined. Until that time, the tenancy is capable of being restored by the grant of relief and does not come to an end. Thus, Part II of the 1954 Act will continue to apply to the business tenancy and the tenant will be entitled to apply to the court for the grant of a new tenancy under the Act.[98] In *Meadows* v. *Clerical, Medical and General Life Assurance Society*,[99] Sir Robert Megarry V.–C. opined[1] that it did not appear to matter whether the form that the relief would take would be the restoration of the old lease or the grant of a new lease on terms of the old. In either case, in his view, the relief would simply relate back to the date of the forfeiture and produce a tenancy within Part II of the 1954 Act which would then form the basis of the tenant's application under section 24(1) of the Act. In *Cadogan* v. *Dimovic*,[2] however, this view was questioned by Robert Goff L.J. who concluded that the effect of a vesting order under section 146(4) of the Law of Property Act 1925 Act was to create a new lease in favour of a sub-tenant and not to create an interest in the premises subsisting before

---

[95] The landlord, of course, cannot rely upon any covenant in the lease because he has unequivocally elected to determine the lease by issuing and serving proceedings. He is, in effect, estopped from treating the covenants in the lease as still on foot: *Associated Deliveries Ltd.* v. *Harrison* (1984) 272 E.G. 321, (C.A.) and *Jones* v. *Carter* (1846) 15 M. & W. 718; 153 E.R. 1040.

[96] (1981) 259 E.G. 860.

[97] *Associated Deliveries Ltd.* v. *Harrison* (1984) 272 E.G. 321, 325, *per* Dillon L.J.

[98] *Meadows* v. *Clerical, Medical and General Life Assurance Society* [1981] Ch. 70.

[99] [1981] Ch. 70.

[1] *Ibid*, 77.

[2] [1984] 1 W.L.R. 609, (C.A.).

the date on which the vesting order was made. Moreover, a tenant who unduly delays in seeking relief may find that his claim will be disregarded in any event as not being genuine.[3]

The bringing of proceedings by the landlord will not, therefore, by itself operate so as to bring about a termination of the lease. The matter must go a stage further and a judgment obtained by the landlord for possession of the premises before the lease is finally treated as determined.[4] However, once judgment has been obtained, the determination of the lease will relate back to the date of the forfeiture.[5] Moreover, the effect of the forfeiture will be to determine not only the lease but any sub-leases, mortgages or other interests derived from it.[6] In the words of Mellish L.J. in *Great Western Railway Co.* v. *Smith*[7]:

> "It is a rule of law that if there is a lessee, and he has created an underlease, or any other legal interest, if the lease is forfeited, then the under-lessee, or the person who claims under the lessee, loses his estate as well as the lessee himself."

This principle has been held[8] to apply where two properties are comprised in one lease containing covenants which are common to both. In such circumstances, a sub-tenant of one property is liable to have his underlease determined by re-entry by the landlord for breach of any covenant relating to the other property.[9] The principle will apply with equal force to a business tenancy falling within the provisions of Part II of the Landlord and Tenant Act 1954, since section 24(2) of the 1954 Act expressly preserves various common law methods of ending the tenancy including termination by way of "forfeiture of a superior tenancy".[10]

If the landlord, having obtained a judgment for possession on the ground of forfeiture of the lease, goes into possession of the premises, he will not be liable to the tenant for damages for trespass (or breach of covenant for quiet enjoyment) if the judgment is subsequently reversed

---

[3] *Meadows* v. *Clerical, Medical and General Life Assurance Society* [1981] Ch. 70, 78, *per* Sir Robert Megarry V.–C.

[4] *Borczak* v. *Ahmed* [1965] 2 Q.B. 320. See, generally, *Termination of Leaser by Forfeiture. Writ or Judgment?*, D. G. Barnsley, (1965) 29 Conv. 267.

[5] *Elliott* v. *Boynton* [1924] 1 Ch. 236; *City of Westminster Assurance Co. Ltd.* v. *Ainis* (1975) 29 P. & C.R. 469, 471, *per* Cairns L.J. and *Meadows* v. *Clerical, Medical and General Life Assurance Society* [1981] Ch. 70, 77, *per* Sir Robert Megarry V.–C.

[6] But see the exception contained in s. 137 of the Rent Act 1977 in respect of certain sub-tenants of residential premises. In *Fleming* v. *House* (1972) 224 E.G. 2020, the interest of a service licensee was determined by the forfeiture of an agricultural tenancy.

[7] (1876) 2 Ch. D. 235, 253, (C.A.). See also, *Official Custodian For Charities* v. *Mackey* [1985] Ch. 168.

[8] *Darlington* v. *Hamilton* (1854) Kay 550; 69 E.R. 233 and *Creswell* v. *Davidson* (1887) 56 L.T. 811.

[9] The sub-tenant will, however, be entitled to claim relief from forfeiture under s. 146(4) of the Law of Property Act 1925. See further, Chap. 10.

[10] *Cadogan* v. *Dimovic* [1984] 1 W.L.R. 609 and *Hill* v. *Griffin* [1987] 1 E.G.L.R. 81.

84

on appeal.[11] This is because acts done pursuant to a valid order of the court cannot, as a matter of public policy, be treated as wrongful.

It may be that a tenant will seek relief *after* a landlord has obtained judgment and an order for relief is granted upon the fulfilment of certain conditions by the tenant. This is the situation which arose in *City of Westminster Assurance Co. Ltd.* v. *Ainis*.[12] In that case, the tenants brought forfeiture proceedings against their sub-tenants for non-payment of rent and breach of other covenants in the sub-lease and obtained judgment in default of appearance. The sub-tenants then applied for relief from forfeiture and obtained an order that, if they complied with certain conditions, they should be relieved. In default of compliance with any of the conditions, the order provided that the sub-tenants's application for relief should be dismissed. The tenants then brought summary proceedings for possession against some squatters who had unlawfully occupied the premises. At that time, the sub-tenants had complied with only one of the conditions specified in the order. The majority[13] of the Court of Appeal held that, since the order for relief was made conditional on terms to be complied with in the future, the sub-tenants (pending performance of the order) did not hold under the sub-tenancy but as tenants at will or sufferance[14] and that, accordingly, it was the tenants who could maintain the action for possession against the squatters. At first glance, this decision appears to be at variance with the principle that a lease will not determine pending the existence of the tenant's claim for relief from forfeiture. The decision, however, may be reconciled on the basis that the order giving rise to relief was construed as being one which did not restore to the sub-tenants the rights of a landlord under the forfeited sub-lease until the conditions had been fully complied with.[15]

In *Pips (Leisure Productions) Ltd.* v. *Walton*,[16] the landlords served a writ against the tenants claiming forfeiture of the lease for non-payment of rent. The tenants then contracted to sell their leasehold interest and issued a summons claiming relief against forfeiture and a stay of execution of the landlords' judgment for possession which they (the landlords) had obtained in default of defence. Sir Robert Megarry V.–C. held that the tenants had no title to compel a conveyance of the leasehold interest notwithstanding that they had a subsisting claim for relief from forfeiture of their lease. He said[17]:

---

[11] *Hillgate House Ltd.* v. *Expert Clothing Service & Sales Ltd.* [1987] 1 E.G.L.R. 65. See also, *Isaacs* v. *Robertson* [1985] A.C. 97.
[12] (1975) 29 P. & C.R. 469.
[13] Cairns and Lawton L.JJ., Mackenna J. dissenting.
[14] See also, *Talbot* v. *Blindell* [1908] 2 K.B. 114, 115–116.
[15] See the explanation of the decision given by Sir Robert Megarry V.–C. in *Meadows* v. *Clerical, Medical and General Life Assurance Society* [1981] Ch. 70, 77.
[16] (1982) 43 P. & C.R. 415.
[17] *Ibid*, 425.

"A vendor who has no more than the benefit of an unenforceable promise to give him the land, or a claim to relief against forfeiture, has no right which supports his contract, however well-founded his expectations."

Once the landlord has effectively elected to forfeit the lease, he will be precluded from enforcing any subsequent breach of covenant[18] against the tenant unless the conduct complained of is also tortious. The leading case is *Jones* v. *Carter*,[19] where it was held that the service of proceedings for possession of the demised premises operated as a final and conclusive election by the landlord to determine the lease so that he could not afterwards (notwithstanding that there had been no judgment in the action) sue for rent due or covenants broken after the date of service. Parke B. said[20]:

" . . . after [an ejectment], by which the lessor treats the lessee as a trespasser, the lessee would know that he was no longer to consider himself as holding under the lease, and bound to perform the covenants contained in it; and it would be unjust to permit the landlord again to change his mind, and hold the tenant responsible for the breach of duty, after this time."

The landlord cannot rely upon any subsequent breach of covenant in the lease because, having elected to forfeit the lease, he is effectively estopped from treating the lease and the covenants in the lease as still on foot.[21] Moreover, the landlord cannot seek interlocutory relief to restrain breaches of covenant once he has unequivocally elected to forfeit the lease. Thus, in *Wheeler* v. *Keeble (1914) Ltd.*,[22] the landlords by their writ claimed possession of the premises and an interim injunction. They also served a notice of motion for an injunction to restrain the tenants from erecting certain lettering on the front of the premises in breach of the covenant contained in the lease. Younger J. held that the writ was an unequivocal election on the part of the landlords to determine the lease so that it was not open to them to move for an injunction against the tenants on the footing that the lease was still subsisting. In the course of his

---

[18] Regardless whether the breach is a continuing breach or a once and for all breach: *Wheeler* v. *Keeble (1914) Ltd.* [1920] 1 Ch. 57, 64–65.

[19] (1846) 15 M. & W. 718; 153 E.R. 1040. See also the earlier case of *Bridges* v. *Smyth* (1829) 5 Bing. 410; 130 E.R. 1119.

[20] *Ibid*, 726; 1043.

[21] *Associated Deliveries Ltd.* v. *Harrison* (1984) 272 E.G. 321, 325, *per* Dillon L.J. (tenant's obligation to deliver up the demised premises in repair held not to survive during the twilight period between the service of the writ and the enforcement of the order for possession).

[22] [1920] 1 Ch. 57.

judgment, he referred *inter alia* to *Birch* v. *Wright*[23] where Ashurst J. observed[24]:

" . . . the plaintiff is precluded from recovering in this form of action; for that would be blowing both hot and cold at the same time, by treating the possession of the defendant as that of a trespasser, and that of a lawful tenant, during the same period."

A landlord will not, however, be precluded from seeking interlocutory relief where the writ is construed as being equivocal. Thus, in *Calabar Properties Ltd.* v. *Seagull Autos Ltd.*,[25] Buckley J. held that the landlords' claim for injunctive relief was not ancillary to their claim for possession but an alternative claim which rendered the writ equivocal. It was, therefore, open to the landlords at the trial of the action to abandon their claim for possession and proceed with their claim for this alternative relief on the basis that the lease was still in existence.

It is important to re-iterate that a landlord will be entitled to seek an injunction against the tenant based on a proprietary right operating *outside* the lease, regardless of his election to treat the lease as forfeited. For example, the landlord may be able to seek an injunction or claim damages founded on a cause of action in tort.[26] Moreover, a landlord is not, of course, precluded from recovering rent which accrued due *prior* to re-entry, even where the landlord under such re-entry is expressed to hold the premises as if no lease had ever been made.[27] It should also be pointed out that where the tenant obtains a court order granting him unconditional relief from forfeiture, the effect of the order will be to restore the original lease as if it had never become forfeited. Thus, the lease will continue in existence and the landlord will be entitled to sue upon the covenants contained in it notwithstanding his earlier election to treat the lease as at an end.[28]

Once the landlord has conclusively elected to forfeit the lease, the right of forfeiture ceases to be capable of waiver. Thus, in *Grimwood* v. *Moss*[29] the landlords brought an action for ejectment against the tenant of a farm for breaches of various covenants. After commencement of their proceedings but before trial, the landlords distrained for rent due prior to the action. The Court of Common Pleas held that the landlords had not

---

[23] (1786) 1 T.R. 378; 99 E.R. 1148.
[24] *Ibid*, 379, 1149.
[25] [1969] 1 Ch. 451. See also, *Moore* v. *Ullcoats Mining Co. Ltd.* [1908] 1 Ch. 575.
[26] *Wheeler* v. *Keeble (1914) Ltd.* [1920] 1 Ch. 57, 64.
[27] *Hartshorne* v. *Watson* (1838) 4 Bing. (N.S.) 178; 132 E.R. 756, applied in *Blore* v. *Giulini* [1903] 1 K.B. 356.
[28] *Dendy* v. *Evans* [1910] 1 K.B. 263, (C.A.), concerning s. 14(2) of the Conveyancing and Law of Property Act 1881, predecessor to the current provision contained in s. 146(2) of the Law of Property Act 1925, under which the effect of the granting of relief is that the original lease is deemed to continue for all purposes.
[29] (1871) L.R. 7 C.P. 360.

waived the forfeiture by distraining for the rent after the date of the service of the proceedings. In the words of Keating J.[30]:

> "The bringing of the action . . . was an unequivocal election to treat the tenant as a trespasser and the effect of it could not be varied by anything that subsequently took place. Taking the distress afterwards could not affirm the tenancy and waive the breaches . . . in respect of which the election to determine the tenancy had been irrevocably made."

In *Doe* d. *Morecraft* v. *Meux*[31] Lord Tenterden opined that the receipt of rent after an action was brought for forfeiture of the lease could not amount to a waiver of the forfeiture. In *Toleman* v. *Portbury*,[32] the landlord brought an action for ejectment and subsequently, in compliance with an order for particulars obtained by the tenant, gave as the alleged breaches the permitting of a sale by auction on the premises without the landlord's consent and also the non-payment of several quarters' rent which had accrued due after the date of the sale by auction. The tenant then obtained an order staying the landlord's action as to the breach for non-payment of rent on payment of the outstanding rent to the landlord or into court if he refused. The landlord, in fact, refused the rent and the money was paid into court. The Court of Exchequer Chamber, affirming the judgment of the Court of Queen's Bench, held that the inclusion in the particulars of breaches of the non-payment of rent accrued due after the sale by auction did not preclude the landlord from relying on the previous forfeiture by reason of the sale by auction.

In *Evans* v. *Enever*,[33] the lease contained a proviso for re-entry in the event of the tenant becoming bankrupt or if the rent should be in arrear for twenty-one days. The tenant was adjudicated bankrupt and two quarters' rent were in arrear. The landlords brought proceedings claiming possession of the premises on the ground only that the lease was liable to forfeiture for non-payment of rent. The tenant, pursuant to the provisions of section 212 of the Common Law Procedure Act 1852, paid the outstanding rent and costs to the landlord and the landlords' proceedings came to an end. Subsequently, the landlords brought a second action for possession claiming that the lease was forfeited by reason of the tenant's bankruptcy. Lord Coleridge J. held that the acceptance of the rent fol-

---

[30] *Ibid*, 365.
[31] (1824) 1 C. & P. 848. See also, *Jones* v. *Carter* (1846) 15 M. & W. 718, 725–726; 153 E.R. 1040, 1043, *per* Parke B. and *Civil Service Co-operative Society Ltd.* v. *McGrigor's Trustee* [1923] 2 Ch. 347.
[32] (1870) Law Rep. 6 Q.B. 245; (1871) Law Rep. 7 Q.B. 344.
[33] [1920] 2 K.B. 315.

lowing the landlords' first action did not operate as a waiver of the forfeiture in respect of the tenant's act of bankruptcy. Since the landlords had unequivocally elected to forfeit the lease by bringing their first action, the subsequent acceptance of rent could not prejudice their legal position.

Chapter Four

Forfeiture for non-payment of rent

Proviso for re-entry or condition necessary

A landlord cannot forfeit[1] a lease for non-payment of rent in the absence of a proviso[2] for re-entry or condition[3] contained in the lease giving the landlord the right so to do.

Where a proviso for re-entry entitles the landlord to forfeit the lease "if and whenever" any one quarter's rent should be in arrears for 21 days and no sufficient distress can be levied on the premises, the effect of the words "if and whenever" will be to give the landlord a right of forfeiture as often as at any moment in time the two pre-conditions specified in the proviso exist. Thus, in *Shepherd* v. *Berger*[4] the tenant was in arrears with three quarters' rent and the landlord distrained for the amount due, leaving more than one quarter's rent still outstanding. The Court of Appeal held that the landlord was entitled to recover possession of the premises because the two pre-conditions specified in the proviso existed at the time when he brought his proceedings.

A landlord is entitled to bring his action for possession for non-payment of rent without showing that he has made an actual physical re-entry upon the demised premises before the commencement of his proceedings.[5]

---

[1] For useful precedents, see Atkin's Court Forms, (2nd ed., 1990) Vol. 24, p. 285, Form 49; p. 287, Form 51; pp. 300–301, Forms 73–74. See also Pt. VI of this work.

[2] See, *e.g. Doe* d. *Dixon* v. *Roe* (1849) 7 C.B. 134; 137 E.R. 55 (proviso for re-entry for "non-payment of rent within 21 days next after any of the days whereon the same ought to be paid").

[3] See, *e.g. Hill* v. *Kempshall* (1849) 7 C.B. 975; 137 E.R. 386 (condition that, if default should be made in payment of rent, it should be lawful for the landlord, within 21 days, to enter into and take possession of the dwelling-house).

[4] [1891] 1 Q.B. 597.

[5] *Ware* v. *Booth* (1894) 10 T.L.R. 446.

Pre-condition of formal demand at common law[6]

At common law, in the absence of express words in the lease dispensing with a formal demand, the landlord can only forfeit for non-payment of rent if he has made a formal demand for the rent.[7] The purpose of the formal demand is to ensure that the tenant is given an opportunity to settle the outstanding arrears before the landlord proceeds to forfeit the lease for non-payment. The demand must be for the precise rent due[8] and be made by the landlord (or his duly authorised agent[9]) at the place specified by the lease[10] on the last day when payment became due.[11] Thus, a demand made before or after the last day for payment will not be sufficient.[12] Moreover, the demand must be made at a convenient time before sunset on the last day payment is due and continued till sunset.[13] In *Acocks* v. *Phillips*,[14] the landlord visited the premises and made his demand for the rent at ten-thirty on the morning of the last day for payment of the rent. It was held that this was not a convenient time before sunset in compliance with the common law rules.

As regards the place of demand, if the lease fails to specify the place at which the rent is to be paid, the demand must be made upon the demised premises and at the most notorious place of it. In this connection, it has been said[15]:

> "It must be made upon the land and at the most notorious place of it. Therefore, if there be a dwelling-house upon the land, the demand must be made at the front or fore door, though it is not necessary to enter the house notwithstanding the door be open . . . A demand of

---

[6] See, generally, *Cole on Ejectment*, (1857), pp. 410–414.

[7] *Molineux* v. *Molineux* (1605) Cro. Jac. 144; 79 E.R. 126; *Doe d. Forster* v. *Wandlass* (1797) 7 T.R. 117; 101 E.R. 885; *Acocks* v. *Phillips* (1860) 5 H. & N. 183; 157 E.R. 1149; *Duppa* v. *Mayo* (1668) 1 Wms. Saund. 275, 287; 85 E.R. 336, 366; *Doe d. Chandless* v. *Robson* (1826) 2 C. & P. 245.

[8] *Fabian and Windsor's Case* (1589) 1 Leo. 305; 74 E.R. 278 ("not one penny more or less than is due"). See also *Jackson and Co.* v. *Northampton Street Tramways Company* (1886) 55 L.T. 91 (no forfeiture of property unless every pre-condition has been strictly and literally complied with).

[9] *Toms* v. *Wilson* (1862) 32 L.J. Q.B. 382.

[10] *Buskin* v. *Edmunds* (1595) Cro. Eliz. 415; 78 E.R. 657 and *Burrough's Case* (1596) 4 Co. Rep. 72b.

[11] *Doe d. Dixon* v. *Roe* (1849) 7 C.B. 134; 137 E.R. 55 (21 day period specified in proviso for re-entry had not elapsed before landlord had affixed notice of possession on the demised premises); *Doe d. Forster* v. *Wandlass* (1797) 7 T.R. 117; 101 E.R. 885 and *Smith and Bustard's Case* (1589) 1 Leo. 141; 74 E.R. 131.

[12] The pre-requisites of a formal demand at common law are fully explored in *Duppa* v. *Mayo* (1668) 1 Wms. Saund. 275, 287 n. 16; 85 E.R. 336, 374 n. 16.

[13] *Duppa* v. *Mayo* (1668) 1 Wms. Saund. 275, 287 n. 16; 85 E.R. 336, 374 n. 16.

[14] (1860) 5 H. & N. 183; 157 E.R. 1149. See also, *Wood and Chiver's Case* (1573) 4 Leo. 141; 74 E.R. 806 and *Doe d. Wheeldon* v. *Paul* (1829) 3 C. & P. 613.

[15] *Duppa* v. *Mayo* (1668) 1 Wms. Saund. 275, 287 n. 16; 85 E.R. 336, 374 n. 16.

the rent must be made in fact . . . although there should be no person on the land ready to pay it."

If the tenant is absent from the demised premises, the demand may be made on a sub-tenant in occupation of the premises.[16] If the premises consist of a wood only, the demand must be made at the gate of the wood, or at some highway leading through it or other more notorious place.[17]

The landlord can only forfeit for non-payment of two or more instalments of rent if he has made a formal demand in respect of each at the due date.[18]

The pre-condition of a formal demand can be and, in practice, invariably is dispensed with by agreement between the parties by the use of appropriate words of exception contained in the proviso for re-entry or condition in the lease. Thus, in *Doe d. Harris* v. *Masters*[19] the lease contained a proviso that, if the rent was in arrears for 21 days, the landlord might re-enter "although no legal or formal demand should be made." This wording was held sufficient to dispense with the pre-requisite of a demand for rent prior to forfeiture of the lease. In *Goodright d. Hare* v. *Cator*[20] a proviso for re-entry for non-payment of rent "although no demand thereof should be lawfully made" was also held to exempt the landlord from the pre-condition of any demand for the rent. In modern leases, the pre-condition of a formal demand is usually dispensed with by the insertion of the words "whether formally demanded or not." In *Doe* d. *Scholefield* v. *Alexander*[21] the lease reserved a quarterly rent with a proviso that, if the rent should be in arrears 21 days next after any of the days of payment, "being lawfully demanded", the landlord should have a right to re-enter the demised premises. There were four quarters' rent in arrear and the landlord re-entered onto the premises without any formal demand for the rent unpaid. It was held[22] that the words "being lawfully demanded" did not absolve the landlord from the requirement of a common law demand.[23] However, in *Manser* v. *Dix*[24] the words "being first lawfully demanded" were held sufficient to dispense with the technicality of a formal demand. Similarly, in *Phillips* v. *Bridge*[25] a tenancy

[16] *Doe* d. *Brook* v. *Brydges* (1822) 2 D. & R. 29. See also, *Kidwelly* v. *Brand* (1551) Plow. 70a, 70b.
[17] Co. Lit. 201b, 202a. If one place be as notorious as another, the landlord may elect at which place to make his demand.
[18] *Scot* v. *Scot* (1587) Cro. Eliz. 773; 78 E.R. 333; *Thomkins* v. *Pincent* (1702) 7 Mod. 96; 87 E.R. 1118 and *Doe* d. *Wheeldon* v. *Paul* (1829) 3 C. & P. 613; *Fabian* v. *Winston* (1589) Cro. Eliz. 209; 78 E.R. 465.
[19] (1824) 2 B. & C. 490; 107 E.R. 466.
[20] (1780) 2 Doug. 468; 99 E.R. 304.
[21] (1814) 2 M. & S. 525; 105 E.R. 477.
[22] Ellenborough C.J. dissenting.
[23] In this case, however, the demand was dispensed with by statute under s. 210 of the Common Law Procedure Act 1852.
[24] (1857) 8 De G.M. & G 703; 44 E.R. 561.
[25] (1873) L.R. 9 C.P. 48.

agreement contained a condition which provided that, if the tenant should make default in payment of the rent within 21 days after the same should become due, "being demanded", it should be lawful for the landlord to re-enter upon the premises. The Court of Common Pleas held that, to entitle the landlord to avail himself of the right of re-entry, the rent had to be 21 days in arrear and a demand made by the landlord following the expiry of the 21 day period. However, the Court[26] also concluded that the words "being demanded" were inserted into the condition with the intention of dispensing with the strictness of the *common law* requirement of a formal demand for the rent.

Statutory exception to formal demand[27]

By section 210 of the Common Law Procedure Act 1852,[28] the common law requirement of a formal demand is rendered unnecessary where at least six months' rent is in arrear before the date of service of the writ and no sufficient distress is to be found on the demised premises countervailing the arrears then due. In the words of Lord Denman C.J. in *Doe* d. *Darke* v. *Bowditch*[29]:

> "The object of the section[30] ... appears, by the preamble, to have been to remove the inconvenience to landlords from the niceties attending re-entries at common law ... "

The primary effect, therefore, of the section is to enable the landlord to bring proceedings for possession without formal demand even though such a demand is not expressly dispensed with in the proviso for re-entry or condition in the lease. The section achieves this result by treating the service of the landlord's proceedings for possession as equivalent to a formal demand of the rent under common law. In this connection, the section specifically states that the landlord may "without any formal demand or re-entry serve a writ in ejectment for the recovery of the demised premises ... which service ... shall stand in the place and stead of a demand and re-entry ... " It is important, however, to note that the section merely authorises the bringing of proceedings in those cases to which it applies and will not, therefore, apply to a landlord who is seeking to forfeit for non-payment of rent by actual physical re-entry onto the premises. It should also, perhaps be stressed that the section is of limited

---

[26] *Per* Keating and Brett JJ.

[27] See, generally, *Cole on Ejectment*, (1857), pp. 414–418.

[28] Formerly, s. 2 of the Landlord and Tenant Act 1730. In the county court, the relevant provision is contained in s. 139(1) of the County Courts Acts 1984, replacing s. 191(2) of the County Courts Act 1959.

[29] (1846) 8 Q.B. 973; 115 E.R. 1140, 1143.

[30] Referring to s. 2 of the Landlord and Tenant Act 1730, being the predecessor to s. 210 of the 1852 Act.

importance today since it is now, of course, the normal practice to include a form of wording dispensing with the requirement of a formal demand[31] in the lease.

The section only applies to "cases between landlord and tenant" but the word "tenant" in this context has been given a broad and generous meaning. Thus, in *Doe* d. *Whitfield* v. *Roe*[32] it was held that the assignee of the lease by way of mortgage was a "tenant" within the meaning of the section. Similarly, a sub-tenant[33] will qualify, as will a person in possession of the premises but who cannot prove his title either as underlessee or assignee of the original lease.[34]

In order to fall within section 210, the landlord must show that at least six months' rent is in arrear at the date of service of the proceedings. Thus, in *Cotesworth* v. *Spokes*[35] three quarters' rent was in arrear under a lease containing a proviso for re-entry on non-payment of rent within 21 days after each quarter day. The landlords distrained for the rent and, after a sale of the distrained goods, there remained less than a half-years' rent due. It was held that, in these circumstances, the landlords' action for possession was not maintainable in the absence of a formal demand for the rent at common law. In *Doe* d. *Scholefield* v. *Alexander*[36] the lease reserved a rent payable quarterly with a proviso that, if the rent was 21 days in arrear next after the day of payment, being lawfully demanded, the landlord could re-enter. In this case, five quarters' rent were in arrear prior to the service of the proceedings and no sufficient distress had been levied on the premises. The Court[37] held that the landlord could rely on the statute and re-enter without any prior demand for the rent. In the course of his judgment, Le Blanc J. said[38]:

> "The Act of Parliament meant to remedy the difficulties which landlords were under in making a re-entry according to the formalities of the common law. For this purpose it meant to allow them, under certain circumstances, to serve a declaration or ejectment, and where there was no sufficient distress on the premises to recover possession without a previous formal demand. If the party had stipulated that the landlord should have a right to re-enter in case of non-payment of rent, it is clear that before the statute the landlord must have made a common law demand, in order to entitle himself to re-enter. And

---

[31] The phrase "whether formally demanded or not" is commonly used in modern leases.
[32] (1811) 3 Taunt. 402; 128 E.R. 160. See also, *Williams* v. *Bosanquet* (1819) 1 Brod. & B. 238; 129 E.R. 714.
[33] *Doe* d. *Wyatt* v. *Byron* (1845) 1 C.B. 623; 135 E.R. 685.
[34] *Moore* v. *Smee and Cornish* [1907] 2 K.B. 8.
[35] (1861) 10 C.B. (N.S.) 103; 142 E.R. 389.
[36] (1814) 2 M. & S. 525; 105 E.R. 477.
[37] Ellenborough C.J. dissenting.
[38] *Ibid*, 529–530; 479.

where the statute meant to remedy that, it applies as well to cases where the party has expressed that the landlord shall re-enter after the rent has been lawfully demanded, as where it is omitted. The inclination, therefore, of my opinion is that this is a case within the provision of the Act, more than half a year's rent being in arrear, and there being no sufficient distress on the premises, notwithstanding the introduction of the words lawfully demanded, and therefore the plaintiff is entitled to recover."

In this case, therefore, the landlord did not lose the benefit of the statute (despite the fact that he had omitted to comply with a demand for the rent as required by the lease), since no demand of any kind was necessary provided that at least six months' rent was due before the service of the action and no sufficient distress could be found on the premises.

In addition to there being at least six months' rent in arrear, the landlord must show that no sufficient distress is to be found on the demised premises (or any part thereof) countervailing the arrears due at the date of the service of the proceedings. Thus, in *Doe* d. *Forster* v. *Wandlass*[39] the landlord could not rely upon the statute since it was conceded that there was a sufficient distress on the premises for the half-year's rent due under the lease. It was at one time thought that, in order to comply with the statute, the landlord had only to show that there was insufficient distress in respect of a half-year's rent notwithstanding that, in fact, more than six months' rent was due from the tenant.[40] The correct view, however, is that no sufficient distress must be found on the premises countervailing *all* the arrears due at the date of the service of the writ and not merely six months' arrears when, in fact, more is due.[41]

Where a distress is made on the premises which satisfies only part of the arrears of rent, leaving a residue in excess of six months' rent outstanding, the landlord is entitled to pursue an action for forfeiture for such residue provided that no sufficient distress can be found for such residue.[42] If, however, the distress reduces the arrears to less than six months' rent, then the landlord will not be entitled to rely upon the statute and will have to comply with the requirement of a formal demand for the rent at common law.[43] By virtue of section 19 of the Limitation Act 1980, a distress under section 210 of the 1852 Act cannot be relied upon for more than six years' arrears of rent.

In order to constitute a "sufficient distress" under the statute, the

---

[39] (1797) 7 T.R. 117; 101 E.R. 885.
[40] *Doe* d. *Powell* v. *Roe* (1841) 9 Dowl. 548.
[41] *Cross* v. *Jordan* (1853) 8 Ex. 149; 155 E.R. 1297.
[42] *Brewer* d. *Onslow* v. *Eaton* (1783) 3 Doug. 230; 99 E.R. 627.
[43] *Cotesworth* v. *Spokes* (1861) 10 C.B. (N.S.) 103; 142 E.R. 389.

landlord must make a strict search of the demised premises and look into every part thereof.[44] But the tenant's goods must be so visibly on the premises that a broker going to distrain would, using reasonable diligence, find them.[45] Moreover, a distress "cannot be found" if the demised premises are locked up and the landlord cannot gain entry. Thus, in these circumstances, the statute will be satisfied and the landlord will be entitled to forfeit without proof of a formal demand. In *Doe* d. *Chippendale* v. *Dyson*,[46] the tenant had locked the outer door of the premises thereby preventing the landlord from entering in order to distrain for unpaid rent. It was held that the landlord was entitled to recover under the statute, without showing that there was, in fact, no sufficient distress on the premises. Lord Tenterden C.J. said:

> "The words 'no sufficient distress was to be found upon the premises', must mean no sufficient distress which can be got at. In this case the doors are locked up, so that the landlord cannot get at the premises to distrain: there is, consequently no sufficient distress, for there is no available distress at all."

In *Rickett* v. *Green*,[47] it was held that the landlord was not obliged under the statute to go through the formality of actually levying distress in order to prove that no sufficient distress could be found on the premises. The statute does not, in terms, require the landlord to actually levy distress and the fact that there is no sufficient distress on the premises may be proved by other evidence. Darling J. said[48]:

> "The landlord may be able to tell without distraining: for instance, he may be able by looking in at the window to see what goods are there ... the tenant may ask him to come in and look for himself."

In addition to showing that at least six months' rent is due before the writ is served and that there is no sufficient distress to be found on the premises, section 210 of the 1852 Act also requires the landlord to show that he has a right of re-entry for non-payment of the rent reserved in the lease.[49] In *Doe* d. *Darke* v. *Bowditch*,[50] a clause in the lease gave the landlord a right to re-enter upon the demised premises but only during the period whilst the rent remained unpaid. It was held that the landlord could not

---

[44] *Rees* d. *Powell* v. *King* (1800) Forr. 19; 145 E.R. 1100, (cottage forming part of the demised premises not searched).

[45] *Doe* d. *Haverson* v. *Franks* (1847) 2 C. & K. 678; 175 E.R. 284; *Wheeler* v. *Stevenson* (1860) 6 H. & N. 155; 158 E.R. 64.

[46] (1827) Mood. & M. 77; 173 E.R. 1087. See also, *Doe* d. *Cox* v. *Roe* (1847) 5 D. & L. 272 and *Hammond* v. *Matther* (1862) 3 F. & F. 151; 176 E.R. 68.

[47] [1910] 1 K.B. 253. The case was concerned with s. 139 of the County Courts Act 1888. The current provision is to be found in s. 139(1) of the County Courts Act 1984.

[48] *Ibid*, 261.

[49] *Brewer* d. *Onslow* v. *Eaton* (1783) 3 Doug. 230; 99 E.R. 627.

[50] (1846) 8 Q.B. 973; 115 E.R. 1140.

rely upon the statute since the clause did not give him an absolute right to re-enter and determine the lease. Moreover, the landlord must await the expiry of the period (usually 21 days) specified in the proviso for re-entry before his right of forfeiture will accrue for non-payment of the rent. Thus, in *Doe* d. *Dixon* v. *Roe*,[51] the lease contained a proviso for re-entry for non-payment of rent "within 21 days next after any of the days whereon the same ought to be paid" and for other breaches of covenant. Before the 21 days had elapsed, the landlord purported to re-enter the premises. Wilde C.J. held that the landlord could not bring himself within the statute because the right of re-entry had not accrued prior to the expiry of the 21 day period.

Finally, it may be mentioned that, whereas in an ordinary case, the landlord's act of distraining upon the premises will operate as a waiver of forfeiture,[52] there will be no waiver in cases falling within the statute. In the words of Lord Mansfield in *Brewer* d. *Onslow* v. *Eaton*[53]:

> "At common law, the distress operated as a waiver of the forfeiture which incurred on the non-payment of rent; but here the distress affords no presumption that the landlord has waived the forfeiture, because, as the statute requires him to prove at the trial that no sufficient distress was to be found on the premises countervailing the arrears due, he has distrained in order to complete the title given him by the statute."

In *Thomas* v. *Lulham*,[54] the landlord demised a house to the tenant for a term of 21 years at a rent of £130 per annum payable on the usual quarter days. The lease contained a proviso for re-entry if the rent remained unpaid for 21 days after it became due, whether demanded or not. The tenant failed to pay three quarters' rent and the landlord distrained on the premises but was only able to realise such an amount as left more than half a year's rent still outstanding. He then issued proceedings against the tenant seeking forfeiture of the lease. The Court of Appeal, applying the *Brewer* case, held that the distress for rent levied by the landlord did not operate as a waiver of his right of re-entry so as to prevent him from maintaining an action for possession of the premises under section 210 of the 1852 Act. Kay L.J. said[55]:

> "The statute evidently contemplates an actual distress, and expressly

---

[51] (1849) 7 C.B. 134; 137 E.R. 55.
[52] See, Chap. 6.
[53] (1783) 3 Doug. 230, 230–231; 99 E.R. 627, 628.
[54] [1895] 2 Q.B. 400. See also, *London & County (A. & D.)* v. *Wilfred Sportsman* [1971] Ch. 764, 786, where Russell L.J., referring to *Shepherd* v. *Berger* [1891] 1 Q.B. 597, said: "There was no right of re-entry at all unless and until it was shown that distress was an insufficient remedy, and it could not be said that the very pre-requisite of the right destroyed the right."
[55] [1895] 2 Q.B. 400, 402.

authorises the ejectment under the proviso for re-entry, notwith-standing such distress, if half a year's rent remains due."

Residential tenancies

(1) *Under the Rent Act 1977*

It is important to bear in mind that in the case of a dwelling-house let on a protected tenancy or subject to a statutory tenancy within the meaning of the Rent Act 1977, the power of the court to grant possession is restricted by section 98 of that Act. In this connection, the landlord must, in addition to showing that the contractual tenancy has determined by forfeiture (or any other common law method of termination), establish the relevant ground for possession[56] under the 1977 Act.[57] The landlord's action for possession should be brought in the county court notwith-standing that the High Court also has jurisdiction.[58]

Although, at common law, a sub-tenancy will come to an end automat-ically on the forfeiture of the tenancy out of which it was created,[59] the security of tenure of certain sub-tenants of residential premises may be preserved under section 137 of the 1977 Act.

(2) *Under the Housing Act 1988*

A landlord who wishes to forfeit an assured tenancy under the Housing Act 1988 for non-payment of rent must initiate possession proceedings in accordance with the procedure laid down by that Act.[60] This is because the statement contained in section 5(1) of the Act, that a fixed term tenancy can be brought to an end by a landlord who exercises a power contained in the lease to determine it in certain circumstances, has no application to a right of re-entry or proviso for forfeiture.[61] Moreover, in relation to an assured fixed term tenancy, the terms of the tenancy must make provision for it to be brought to an end on the ground for possession relied on[62] (whether that provision takes the form of a provision for re-entry, forfeiture or for determination of the tenancy by notice or

---

[56] See, Case 1 of Sched. 15 to the Rent Act 1977, (rent lawfully due from the tenant has not been paid).

[57] See, *Atkin's Court Forms* (2nd ed., 1990) Vol. 24, p. 313, Form 89.

[58] *Peachey Property Corporation Ltd.* v. *Robinson* [1967] 2 Q.B. 543, (C.A.).

[59] *Great Western Railway Co.* v. *Smith* (1876) 2 Ch. D. 235, 253, *per* Mellish L.J.; *Parker* v. *Jones* [1910] 2 K.B. 32.

[60] Essentially, this involves serving on the assured tenant a notice of proceedings for possession prior to commencing an action for possession: See, s. 8 of the 1988 Act.

[61] See, s. 45(4) of the 1988 Act.

[62] In relation to non-payment of rent, Ground 8 (mandatory), Ground 10 (discretionary) and Ground 11 (discretionary) will be relevant: See, Sched. 2 to the 1988 Act.

otherwise).[63] The upshot of the foregoing is that an action for forfeiture of an assured tenancy must be combined with a claim for possession under the 1988 Act.

Where the tenancy is an assured shorthold tenancy under the 1988 Act, the right of the landlord to recover possession before the expiry of the fixed term under the provisions applicable to assured tenancies generally is expressly preserved under section 21(1) of the Act.

Business tenancies

The landlord's common law right to terminate a business tenancy[64] on the ground of forfeiture is expressly preserved by section 24(2) of the Landlord and Tenant Act 1954.

Agricultural tenancies

(1) *Under the Agricultural Holdings Act 1986*

Forfeiture of an agricultural holding is not excluded by the Agricultural Holdings Act 1986.

(2) *Under the Rent Agriculture Act 1976*

The reader is referred to Chapter 5, p. 135.

---

[63] See, s. 7(6)(*b*) of the 1988 Act.
[64] *i.e.* a tenancy falling within the provisions of Pt. II of the Landlord and Tenant Act 1954: See, ss. 23 and 43 of the Act.

Chapter Five

Forfeiture for other breaches of covenant

Pre-condition of section 146 notice

Before a landlord can forfeit[1] the lease for a breach of covenant or condition in the lease (other than non-payment of rent[2]), he must serve a notice[3] on the tenant (a) specifying the particular breach complained of (b) if the breach is capable of remedy, requiring the tenant to remedy the breach and (c) in any case, requiring the tenant to make compensation in money for the breach. Further, the landlord cannot enforce his right of forfeiture (whether by action for possession or by physical re-entry[4]) until the tenant has failed within a reasonable time after service of the notice to remedy the breach (if it is capable of remedy) and to make reasonable compensation in money to the satisfaction of the landlord for the breach.[5] These pre-conditions are set forth in section 146(1) of the Law of Property Act 1925.[6] The underlying philosophy of this provision is summarised by Kay J. in *Creswell* v. *Davidson*[7] in the following terms[8]:

"In spite of the contract between the parties, the Legislature[9] . . .

---

[1] For useful precedents, see Atkin's Court Forms (2nd ed. 1990) Vol. 24, pp. 360–363, Forms 152–154 and Pt VI of this work.
[2] Forfeiture for non-payment of rent is considered in Chap. 4.
[3] For forms of notice: See *Encyclopaedia of Forms and Precedents* (5th ed.) Vol. 22, paras. 1158–1166, Forms 167–174 and Pt VI of this work.
[4] *In Re Riggs, ex p. Lovell* [1901] 2 K.B. 16, 20, *per* Wright J.
[5] *Fox* v. *Jolly* [1916] 1 A.C. 1, 8–9, where Lord Buckmaster L.C. sets out the various pre-conditions which must be satisfied by the landlord under s. 14 of the Conveyancing and Law of Property Act 1881, predecessor to s. 146 of the Law of Property Act 1925.
[6] The Crown as landlord is subject to the provisions of the section: s. 208(3) of the Law of Property Act 1925.
[7] (1887) 56 L.T. 811.
[8] *Ibid*, 812.
[9] The learned Judge was referring to s. 14 of the Conveyancing and Law of Property Act 1881, predecessor to s. 146 of the Law of Property Act 1925.

interposes so as to counteract the exceeding folly displayed by lessees in the mode in which they have been accustomed to allow themselves to contract. The Legislature has interfered, and says although a lessee has contracted to allow the lessor a right of re-entry or forfeiture for a breach of any covenant or condition in the lease, yet a *locus poenitentiae* shall be afforded to the lessee; and the Legislature thus requires the lessor to give the lessee an opportunity of repairing and making good any breach of covenant. But it does not actually take away any right of re-entry or forfeiture which the lessor may have."

Accordingly, the effect of section 146(1) is to postpone the landlord's exercise of his right of forfeiture until a reasonable time has expired from the date of the service of the notice so as to afford the tenant the opportunity to remedy the breach and make compensation to the landlord for his default.

(1) *Application of section 146*

Section 146 applies to both leases[10] and agreements for leases where the tenant has become entitled to have his lease granted to him[11] and to High Court and county court cases. It imposes on the landlord[12] the obligation of serving a notice when he has a right to forfeit[13] because of a breach of covenant or condition in the lease, except a covenant to pay rent[14] and, in the case of a mining lease, a covenant or condition for allowing the landlord to have access to or inspect books, accounts, records, weighing

---

[10] See s. 146(5) for the meaning of "lease", which includes an original or derivative underlease. "Lessor" and "Lessee" have corresponding meanings and also include persons deriving title under a lessee or lessor: s. 205(1)(xxiii). See also, s. 154 which provides that "lease" includes an underlease or other tenancy. But s. 146 has no application to a statutory tenancy under the Rent Act 1977: *Brewer* v. *Jacobs* [1923] 1 K.B. 528.

[11] s. 146(5). As to the application of s. 146 to equitable leases: see, *Charrington & Co. Ltd.* v. *Camp* [1902] 1 Ch. 386; *Greville* v. *Parker* [1910] A.C. 335, (P.C.) and *Sport International Bussman BV* v. *Inter-Footwear Ltd.* [1984] 1 W.L.R. 776, 789–790, (C.A.), *per* Oliver L. J. For a full discussion of the point, see *Forfeiture of Equitable Leases*, P. Sparkes (1987) 16 Anglo-American L. Rev. 160, at pp. 169–171 and *The Tenant under an Agreement and section 146 of the Law of Property Act 1925*, P. H. Pettit, (1960) 24 Conv. 125. The orthodox view is that the breach of a term in an agreement for a lease involves the loss of the right to specific performance needed to create the equitable term and not the forfeiture of the equitable term: See *Coatsworth* v. *Johnson* (1886) 55 L.J.Q.B. 220, (C.A.); *Swain* v. *Ayres* (1888) 21 Q.B.D. 289, (C.A.) and *Strong* v. *Stringer* (1889) 61 L.T. 470. Equity, however, may grant specific performance despite breaches of covenant, if they were caused by accident, surprise or other excuse: *Swain* v. *Ayres* (1888) 21 Q.B.D. 289, 294, *per* Lord Esher M.R.

[12] Where there is a legal mortgage of the reversion, the mortgagor in possession, being entitled to enforce the right of re-entry, is the proper person to give the notice.

[13] In the absence of such notice, the right of forfeiture will fail: *Greenfield* v. *Hanson* (1886) 2 T.L.R. 876 and *Jacques* v. *Harrison* (1884) 12 Q.B.D. 165. The absence of a notice will also be fatal to an action for a declaration of forfeiture: *Wilson* v. *Rosenthal* (1906) 22 T.L.R. 233.

[14] s. 146(11) and *Scott* v. *Matthew & Co. Ltd.* (1884) 51 L.T. 746.

machines or other things, or to enter or inspect the mines or the workings thereof.[15]

The reason for this exception in the case of mines is that the amount of rent payable under a mining lease usually depends upon the amount of minerals produced and it is, therefore, of particular importance that the tenant should comply with obligations to let the landlord inspect books, accounts etc.

A notice is not necessary where the landlord's action is for the appointment of a receiver.[16]

Further, section 146 has no application in relation to certain instances of the tenant's bankruptcy.[17] Under section 146(9), on the occurrence of the forfeiture of the lease on the tenant's bankruptcy or the taking in execution of the tenant's interest in the lease, the landlord's right to forfeit is unaffected by section 146 if the lease is of (a) agricultural[18] or pastoral land; (b) mines[19] or minerals[20]; (c) a house used or intended to be used as a public-house or beershop; (d) a house let as a dwelling-house, with the use of any furniture, books, works of art, or other chattels not being in the nature of fixtures; or (e) any property with respect to which the personal qualifications of the tenant are of importance for the preservation of the value or character of the property, or on the ground of neighbourhood to the landlord or to any person holding under him.[20a] In the case of leases falling outside section 146(9), the landlord's right to forfeit on bankruptcy or taking in execution is fettered by section 146 if the tenant's interest is sold within one year from the date of bankruptcy or taking in execution.[21] If, however, the tenant's interest is not sold before the expiration of that year, section 146 only applies to the forfeiture condition in the lease during the first year from the date of the bankruptcy or taking in execution.[22] In *Horsey Estate Ltd.* v. *Steiger*[23] the lease contained a proviso for re-entry if the tenant company should enter into liquidation, whether

---

[15] s. 146(8)(ii).

[16] *Leney & Sons Ltd.* v. *Callingham and Thompson* [1908] 1 K.B. 79, (C.A.), applying *Charrington & Co. Ltd.* v. *Camp* [1902] 1 Ch. 386.

[17] "Bankruptcy" includes the liquidation of a company: s. 205(1)(i) of the Law of Property Act 1925. See also, *Horsey Estate Ltd.* v. *Steiger* [1899] 2 Q.B. 79, (C.A.) and *Fryer* v. *Ewart* [1902] A.C. 187, (H.L.), where it was held that a voluntary liquidation for the purpose of reconstruction or amalgamation came within the meaning of "bankruptcy" for the purpose of (what is now) s. 146(9) and (10) of the 1925 Act.

[18] For the meaning of "agricultural land", see s. 1 of the Agricultural Holdings Act 1986. See also, *Ferguson* v. *Ferguson* [1924] Ir. R. 22, (lease of 37.5 acres of land including a factory and other buildings held to be "agricultural land" and, therefore, excluded from s. 146).

[19] For the meaning of "mining lease", see s. 205(1)(xiv) of the 1925 Act.

[20] See, *Gee* v. *Harwood* (1932) 48 T.L.R. 606, (lease of premises used as a mineral water spa at a rent which varied with the amount of mineral water produced held not to be a lease of mines and minerals).

[20a] *Hockley Engineering Co. Ltd.* v. *V. & P. Midlands Ltd.* [1993] 18 E.G. 129.

[21] s. 146(10)(a).

[22] s. 146(10)(b).

[23] [1899] 2 Q.B. 79, (C.A.).

compulsory or voluntary. The tenant passed a resolution for a voluntary winding-up, not by reason of insolvency, but for the purpose of reconstruction with additional capital. The Court of Appeal held that a sufficient notice under (what is now) section 146(1) of the 1925 Act was a condition precedent to enforcing the forfeiture on the tenant's liquidation where the landlord's action was brought within a year from the resolution for winding-up.

If a receiving order in bankruptcy is made against the tenant, leave of the court under section 285(3) of the Insolvency Act 1986 is not required before an action for possession on the ground of forfeiture of the lease is commenced against him.[24]

Where a lease provides that the landlord shall have the right to re-enter on the bankruptcy of a surety who has guaranteed the obligations of the tenant under the lease, the surety's bankruptcy is a "breach of . . . condition" within the meaning of section 146(1) and, accordingly, the landlord is required to serve on the tenant a section 146 notice specifying the bankruptcy of the surety as the breach of condition complained of before exercising his right of forfeiture.[25]

It may be that the pre-requisite of the service of a notice under section 146(1) is necessary where the landlord claims forfeiture in cases where the tenant has denied the landlord's title.[26]

The landlord cannot exclude the operation of section 146 which will have effect notwithstanding any stipulation to the contrary.[27] Moreover, the section will apply to a lease which is expressly limited to continue so long as the tenant abstains from committing a breach of covenant.[28] In *Plymouth Corporation* v. *Harvey*[29] the tenant executed a deed of surrender which he delivered in escrow to a third party on terms that the latter would deliver the deed to the landlord in the event of the tenant failing to remedy a breach of covenant in the lease. Plowman J. held that the deed of surrender was void as being a device intended to circumvent the provisions of section 146(1) of the 1925 Act. He said[30]:

"Section 146 prevents a lessor from putting an end to a lease for breach of covenant without serving the appropriate notice, and he

[24] *Ezekiel* v. *Orakpo* [1977] 1 Q.B. 260, (C.A.). Section 285 of the 1985 Act essentially re-enacts ss. 7 and 9 of the Bankruptcy Act 1914 which are now repealed.
[25] *Halliard Property Co. Ltd.* v. *Jack Segal Ltd.* [1978] 1 W.L.R. 377. *Quaere*, whether a s. 146 notice would be required in the case of a proviso for re-entry on the death of a third party: *ibid*, 381. It would, clearly, not be required in the case of a right to re-enter a specified time after the service of a notice.
[26] *W.G. Clark (Properties) Ltd.* v. *Dupre Properties Ltd.* [1991] 3 W.L.R. 579, 589–591, *per* Mr. T.R.A. Morison Q.C. Contrast *Warner* v. *Sampson* [1958] 1 Q.B. 404, 424–425, *per* Ashworth J.
[27] s. 146(12).
[28] s. 146(7).
[29] [1971] 1 W.L.R. 549.
[30] *Ibid*, 554.

cannot avoid this result by attempting to change the mechanics of the operation. A forfeiture in the guise of a surrender in my judgment remains a forfeiture for the purposes of section 146."

It is, perhaps, important to note that section 146(7), which expressly extends the provisions of notice and relief to some limitations, only contemplates the case where the landlord protects himself against the happening of the event in question by means of a covenant. In this connection, the sub-section makes the breach of a covenant an event upon which the limitation turns. Where, therefore, the event in question (for example, the grant of planning permission) is not made the subject of a covenant at all but merely of a limitation,[31] the sub-section will have no application.

The provisions of section 146 will also apply to a lease permitting the landlord to serve a notice to quit on breach of covenant by the tenant. In *Richard Clarke & Co. Ltd.* v. *Widnall*[32] a clause in the tenancy agreement provided that, if the tenant committed *inter alia* a breach of the covenant to pay rent, the landlords would be entitled to give the tenant three months' notice to determine the tenancy. The tenant failed to pay the rent and the landlords served a three months' notice in compliance with the clause. The Court of Appeal held that the operation of the notice to quit amounted to the exercise by the landlords of a right of re-entry for breach of covenant. The fact that the clause provided for the right of forfeiture to be effective only after a stated period of notice had expired did not alter the nature and legal consequences of this right. The decision may be contrasted with *Clays Lane Housing Co-operative Ltd.* v. *Patrick*[33] where the tenancy agreement created a weekly tenancy in favour of the tenant terminable by either party by not less than four weeks' notice in writing. Clause 7 of the agreement provided that the landlord could terminate the tenancy by giving four weeks' notice to quit in the event of the tenant's non-payment of rent. The Court of Appeal held that, for a provision in the tenancy agreement to constitute a forfeiture clause, it was necessary that it brought the lease to an end earlier than the actual termination date of the tenancy (*i.e.* prior to the contractual expiry date of a fixed term or the date on which a periodic tenancy could be brought to an end by notice to quit). The Court, therefore, was able to distinguish the *Richard Clarke* case on the ground that in that case the landlords' right to terminate brought the lease to an end before its natural termination date. In *Richard Clarke*, the landlords could only determine the tenancy upon twelve months'

---

[31] *e.g.* the grant of a lease until planning permission is given would end automatically on the happening of the specified event and no question of forfeiture would arise.
[32] [1976] 1 W.L.R. 845.
[33] (1985) 49 P. & C.R. 72.

notice after the first six months of the term had expired but, under the forfeiture clause, the landlords could, on the tenant's default, determine the tenancy prematurely on giving only three months' notice.

It is to be observed that the provisions of section 146 which deal with notice (and relief) apply to a "right of re-entry or forfeiture under any proviso or stipulation in a lease for a breach of *any* covenant or *condition* in the lease"[34] (emphasis supplied). It is submitted that the section does not apply to conditions under which the lease becomes terminable upon the happening of an entirely neutral event (for example, the grant of planning permission) which does not connote any fault on the part of the tenant. Indeed, the service of a notice (and the exercise of the court's relief-giving discretion) under the section seem wholly inappropriate in the case of neutral events and the actual provisions of the section go some way to make this clear. In *Halliard Property Co. Ltd.* v. *Jack Segal Ltd.*[35] Goulding J. held that the words "breach of condition" in section 146(1) applied not only to voluntary but involuntary acts by the tenant so that the bankruptcy of the tenant's surety was to be considered a breach of condition within the meaning of the section. The decision is, perhaps, not surprising in view of the fact that (subject to certain exceptions[36]) a condition for forfeiture on the bankruptcy of the tenant is, clearly, contemplated by the statutory provisions. In the words of the learned Judge[37]:

> "The surety is a person put forward by the lessee in support of his own obligations under the lease and the common sense of the matter seems to me to require the bankruptcy of the surety to be within the section if the bankruptcy of the lessee is prima facie included."

In the course of his judgment, Goulding J. also alluded to several examples of cases in which, under the provisions, of a lease a landlord may have the right to re-enter. One such case involves a landlord's right to re-enter a specified time after the service of a notice. A good example is a proviso under which the landlord is entitled to re-enter after say, the seventh year of the term, if he serves six months' prior notice. Another example is a proviso under which he may re-enter if he serves a notice of specified length certifying his desire to use the land for some specified purpose such as building. In such a case, it would be absurd to think that the landlord was seeking to exercise a right of re-entry for breach of a covenant or condition. A more difficult case, however, involves a condition in a lease entitling the landlord to re-enter upon the death of a third party during the currency of the term. This, it is submitted, is like the first

[34] See, s. 146(1).
[35] [1978] 1 W.L.R. 377.
[36] See, s. 146(9) and (10).
[37] [1978] 1 W.L.R. 377, 381.

case referred to above, because it is something outside the voluntary sphere of the tenant's influence and, moreover, does not involve any unjustifiable violation or transgression of his tenancy obligations. Accordingly, the words "breach of condition" in section 146(1) would appear to be equally inapposite. It is regrettable, however, that Goulding J. did not take the opportunity to express any opinion on the point.[38]

(2) *Validity of notice*

The notice served by the landlord "specifying the particular breach complained of"[39] must provide sufficient detail of the breach as would enable the tenant to understand with reasonable certainty what it is he is required to do so that he has an opportunity of remedying the breach before the landlord proceeds to forfeit the lease.[40] Thus, a mere general notice of breach of a specified covenant will not be sufficient. In *Fletcher* v. *Nokes*[41] a landlord's notice stating that "you have broken the covenant for repairing the inside and outside of the houses" was held invalid on the ground that it failed to sufficiently particularise the breaches complained of by the landlord. There was nothing in the notice to indicate in which of the houses the default had been made or whether it had been made in all of them. North J. said[42]:

> "I do not mean that the landlord need go through every room in the house and point out every defect. But the notice ought to be so distinct as to direct the attention of the tenant to the particular things of which the landlord complains . . ."

Similarly, in *In Re Serle, Gregory* v. *Serle*[43] the landlord's notice informing the tenant that "he has not kept the said premises well and sufficiently repaired, and the party and other walls thereof" was held to constitute a bad notice in so far as it did not direct the tenant's attention to the particular breaches complained of by the landlord. Moreover, the fact that the notice sufficiently specified other alleged breaches of covenant did not

---

[38] *Ibid*, 382.
[39] s. 146(1).
[40] *Fox* v. *Jolly* [1916] 1 A.C. 1, recently applied in *Cardigan Properties Ltd.* v. *Consolidated Property Investments Ltd.* [1991] 07 E.G. 132, (notice calling upon tenant to insure the premises in accordance with the covenant in the lease held valid).
[41] [1897] 1 Ch. 271. See also, *Penton* v. *Barnett* [1898] 1 Q.B. 276, 281, *per* Collins L.J.: "the tenant should be informed of the particular condition of the premises which he was required to remedy . . . the tenant is to have full notice of what he is required to do"; *Horsey Estate Limited* v. *Steiger* [1899] 2 Q.B. 79, 91, *per* Lord Russell C.J. (notice must be such as to give the tenant precise information of what is alleged against him and what is demanded from him).
[42] [1897] 1 Ch. 271, 274.
[43] [1898] 1 Ch. 652. See also, *Davenport* v. *Smith* [1921] 2 Ch. 270, (notice requiring tenant to remedy the breach but not specifying clearly what required to be done held invalid).

save it from invalidity.[44] In *Jolly* v. *Brown*[45] the landlord of six small houses served notice on the tenant stating that the repairing covenants in the lease had been broken and that the particular breaches which were complained of were the committing or allowing the dilapidations mentioned in a schedule annexed to the notice. The schedule indicated under general headings repairs which were required to be done to all of the houses and, in a few instances only, specified repairs to be done to particular houses. The schedule concluded with the words: "and note that the completion of the items mentioned in this schedule does not excuse the execution of other repairs if found necessary." The Court of Appeal held[46] that the notice was a good notice and was not vitiated by the addition of the general clause at the end which merely reserved the landlord's rights if he later discovered a further breach. Buckley L.J. said[47]:

> "The notice must be one which calls the tenant's attention to the particular condition of the premises which is alleged to be defective. It need not identify every defect in the condition to which attention is called . . . it is no objection that [the landlord] leaves it to the tenant to find the particular defects in that condition of the premises to which the tenant's attention is called."

Thus, the tenant is entitled to know how he is alleged to have broken the covenant to repair, for example, that he has broken it by not keeping the roof in proper repair. However, the landlord is not obliged to go further and identify, say, the particular slates on the roof in which the alleged defect occurs since that is a matter for the tenant to find out himself.

The fact that the notice contains allegations of breach of covenant which cannot be substantiated will not affect the validity of the notice.[48] Thus, the landlord will not be prejudiced by inserting in the notice matters of complaint which subsequently he fails to establish at the trial of the

---

[44] "The notice cannot be saved as a whole simply because a part of it is good", [1898] 1 Ch. 652, 657, *per* Kekewich J. But see *Fox* v. *Jolly* [1916] 1 A.C. 1, 14–15, *per* Lord Buckmaster L.C.: ". . . it does not necessarily follow that imperfect description of the breach of one covenant would take away from him the right to re-enter for breach of the other covenants which had been sufficiently described", and *ibid*, 18, *per* Lord Atkinson: "The breach cannot, in my view, be taken in globo, nor can the several statements contained in the notice be taken in globo. Each breach working a forfeiture must be taken by itself, and the statement in the notice dealing with it be taken by itself".

[45] [1914] 2 K.B. 109, (C.A.).

[46] Vaughan Williams L.J. dissenting. The majority view of the Court of Appeal was affirmed by the House of Lords: *Fox* v. *Jolly* [1916] 1 A.C. 1.

[47] [1914] 2 K.B. 109, 127–128.

[48] *Jolly* v. *Brown* [1914] 2 K.B. 109, 130, *per* Kennedy L.J. See also, *Fox* v. *Jolly* [1916] 1 A.C. 1, 12, 22, *per* Lord Buckmaster L.C. and Lord Parmoor, respectively and *Lock* v. *Pearce* [1893] 2 Ch. 271, (C.A.), (notice containing claim in respect of surveyors' fees and solicitors' charges which were not justified in law held valid).

action. In *Pannell* v. *City of London Brewery Co.*[49] it was held that the landlord's notice referring to several distinct alleged breaches of covenant was not invalidated because it turned out at the trial that, although some of the alleged breaches had occurred, the others had never been committed or the landlord was not entitled to rely on them.

The notice does not require the landlord to inform the tenant what it is he ought to do in order to remedy the breach of which complaint is made. In the words of Lord Buckmaster L.C. in *Fox* v. *Jolly*[50]:

"All that the landlord is bound to do is to state particulars of the breaches of covenants of which he complains and call upon the lessee to remedy them. The means by which the breach is to be remedied is a matter for the lessee and not for the lessor."

In *Matthews* v. *Usher*[51] the landlord's notice did not specify the repairs required in each particular house demised but it gave (in great detail) every repair that might be required according to the condition of each house. It, therefore, did not inform the tenant what precise work was to be done but it told him what work was to be done if required. Ridley J. held that the notice was sufficient on the ground that the onus lay on the tenant, upon the receipt of such a notice, to apply it to the premises where appropriate: "he must, on knowing what sort of work is required, do it where wanted."[52]

In *Silvester* v. *Ostrowska*[53] the landlord served notice on the tenant alleging various breaches of the repairing covenant contained in the lease and a breach of the covenant against sub-letting of the premises into three dwellings and a shop. The schedule of dilapidations accompanying the notice particularised the breaches of covenant to repair but contained no reference to any breach of covenant not to sub-let. In fact, the lease did not contain a covenant against sub-letting. It was held that the reference to a non-existent covenant did not destroy the efficacy of the notice for the purposes of section 146(1) of the 1925 Act. Thus, a section 146 notice will be valid if it refers to alleged breaches of non-existent covenants provided that it is possible to uphold the notice so far as the alleged breach of the covenant to repair is concerned. However, in *Guillemard* v. *Silverthorne*[54] the notice was held ineffective where it set out the general covenant to repair contained in the lease and also two further special painting covenants which were not contained in the lease at all. The accompanying

---

[49] [1900] 1 Ch. 496, followed in *McIlveny* v. *McKeever* [1931] N.I. 161, (C.A.) and *Blewett* v. *Blewett* [1936] 2 All E.R. 188, (C.A.).
[50] [1916] 1 A.C. 1, 11. See also, *Piggott* v. *Middlesex County Council* [1909] 1 Ch. 134, 147, *per* Eve J.
[51] (1899) 81 L.T. 542.
[52] *Ibid*, 545.
[53] [1959] 1 W.L.R. 1060.
[54] (1908) 99 L.T. 584.

schedule of works lumped all the dilapidations together, including items which were not attributable to the general covenant to repair but referred to the other covenants which had wrongly been included in the notice. The basis of the decision was that the notice did not agree with the terms of the lease and the work required to be done under the notice was not the same as the work which would have been required if the covenants in the lease had been properly set out in the notice. The case is, therefore, distinguishable from the decision in *Silvester* on the ground that the schedule of works included matters not referable to the general covenant to repair but referable to the particular covenants which, in fact, did not appear in the lease.[55]

In *Jacob* v. *Down*[56] the tenants were in breach of a covenant to erect certain buildings on the demised premises within 12 months and in breach of a further covenant to keep the premises so to be erected in good and substantial repair. The landlord's notice made reference to the building covenant (as to the breach of which there was a waiver by acceptance of rent by the landlords) but made no mention of the breach of the repairing covenant which was unaffected by the waiver since it constituted a continuing breach of covenant. Stirling J. held that the notice was insufficient in so far as it made no reference to the continuing breach of the repairing covenant and, consequently, the landlords' action for possession of the premises based on that covenant failed.

In *Van Haarlam* v. *Kasner*[56a] Harman J. held that a landlord's notice which failed to refer specifically to section 146 of the Law of Property Act 1925 and to the tenant's covenants by number or other indication but which, nevertheless, contained general words indicating that the tenant's user of the premises for illegal purposes was for acts preparatory to the commission of offences under the Official Secrets Acts, fell within the necessary requirements of a valid section 146 notice. The words used were almost identical to those appearing in the indictment and were, therefore, considered sufficiently specific for the tenant to know the matters of complaint against him.

A reference in the schedule of dilapidations accompanying the landlord's notice to the effect that the schedule is an interim one and does not represent the full extent of the tenant's liability will not render the notice insufficiently specific for the purpose of section 146(1) of the 1925 Act.[57]

A defect in the landlord's notice may be waived by the service of a

[55] *Silvester* v. *Ostrowska* [1959] 1 W.L.R. 1060, 1063, *per* H.H. Percy Lamb, Q.C.
[56] [1900] 2 Ch. 156.
[56a] [1992] 36 E.G. 135.
[57] *Greenwich London Borough Council* v. *Discreet Selling Estates Ltd.* [1990] 2 E.G.L.R. 65, where the Court of Appeal held that the "interim" note on the schedule of works was merely a reservation of possible rights and threw no doubt on the specific nature of the defects relied on as a ground of forfeiture. In so holding, the Court of Appeal followed the observations of Lord Sumner in *Fox* v. *Jolly* [1916] 1 A.C. 1, 20.

tenant's counter-notice pursuant to the Leasehold Property (Repairs) Act 1938.[58] In *Sidnell* v. *Wilson*[59] the landlord served a section 146 notice which omitted to contain a statement that the tenants were entitled to serve a counter-notice claiming the benefit of the 1938 Act. By a subsequent letter, the landlord rectified that omission and the tenants duly served a counter-notice under the 1938 Act, which obliged the landlord to apply to the court for leave to bring proceedings for forfeiture. The Court of Appeal[60] held that the landlord's letter, either alone or when read together with the defective notice, constituted a valid notice for the purpose of section 1(3) of the 1938 Act and that, in any event, any defect in the notice had been waived by the tenants giving the counter-notice.

The landlord's notice under section 146(1) requiring the tenant to remedy a breach of covenant will be good even though it does not require payment of compensation in money for the breach. In other words, if the landlord does not want compensation in money from the tenant, his notice need not stipulate it.[61] The same principle will apply *a fortiori* to a case where not only does the landlord not want compensation but where, in fact, no compensation for the breach is possible.[62]

Where the breach of covenant is incapable of remedy, as a matter of law,[63] the notice need not require the tenant to remedy it[64] and the landlord may proceed with his action (or physical re-entry) with little delay. In such circumstances, it has been held that 14 days is a sufficient time to elapse between the service of the section 146 notice and the date of the writ of summons claiming forfeiture of the lease.[65] Further, since the breach is technically incapable of remedy, the tenant's only recourse is to seek relief from forfeiture under the provisions of section 146(2) of the 1925 Act.

Where the breach of covenant is capable of remedy, the notice itself need not specify the time within which the breach is to be remedied since section 146(1) merely precludes the landlord from enforcing his right of forfeiture until the expiry of a reasonable period of time from the date of

---

[58] The 1938 Act is discussed at pp. 124–132.

[59] [1966] 2 Q.B. 67.

[60] *Ibid*, 77, *per* Denning L.J.

[61] *Lock* v. *Pearce* [1893] 2 Ch. 271, (C.A.).

[62] *Civil Service Co-operative Society Ltd.* v. *McGrigor's Trustee* [1923] 2 Ch. 347, (a case involving the tenant's bankruptcy). See also, *Governors of Rugby School* v. *Tannahill* [1935] 1 K.B. 87, (C.A.), (where the breach was incapable of remedy).

[63] The question of remediable and irremediable breaches of covenant is discussed at pp. 116–124.

[64] s. 146(1) specifically provides that the landlord need only require the lessee to remedy the breach "if the breach is capable of remedy."

[65] *Scala House & District Property Co. Ltd.* v. *Forbes* [1974] Q.B. 575, (C.A.), involving a breach of covenant not to assign, underlet or part with possession of the demised premises. See also, *Fuller* v. *Judy Properties Ltd.* [1992] 14 E.G. 106, (C.A.), (involving a breach of covenant against assignment where seven days was held a reasonable time) and *Van Haarlam* v. *Kasner Charitable Trust* [1992] 36 E.G. 135, (involving a breach of covenant not to use the premises for any illegal or immoral purposes, where 30 days' notice was held reasonable).

the service of his notice.[66] Thus, even where the notice does set out a stated time within which the breach is required to be remedied, the landlord will be precluded from effecting a forfeiture after the expiration of that stated period unless the time allowed is, in fact, reasonable in all the circumstances of the case.

The reason for giving the tenant "reasonable" notice is not limited to giving him the opportunity to remedy the breach. In *Horsey Estate Ltd.* v. *Steiger*,[67] Lord Russell L.J. observed[68]:

> "... he ought to have the opportunity of considering whether he can admit the breach alleged; whether it is capable of remedy; whether he ought to offer any, and, if so, what, compensation and finally, if the case is one for relief, whether he ought or ought not promptly to apply for such relief. In short, the notice is intended to give to the person whose interest it is sought to forfeit the opportunity of considering his position before an action is brought against him."

In that case, the landlords served notice on the tenant company alleging (as a ground of forfeiture) the tenant's voluntary liquidation and breaches of the covenant to repair and requiring it to remedy the same within a reasonable time. Two days later, the landlords commenced proceedings for forfeiture of the lease. The Court of Appeal held *inter alia* that the notice was bad in that the landlords had only allowed two days to elapse after the service of the notice and before their action for possession.

A number of other cases provide useful guidance as to the length of the period of time which should be allowed the tenant to remedy the particular breach before the right of forfeiture is exercised. For example, in *Civil Service Co-operative Society* v. *McGrigor's Trustee*[69] the landlords served notice on the tenant's trustee in bankruptcy stating that they intended to enforce their right of forfeiture on the bankruptcy of the tenant on the expiry of 14 days from the date of the notice. Russell J. held that 14 days was a sufficient time to enable the trustee to consider his position and to take appropriate action before the commencement of forfeiture proceedings. In *Cardigan Properties Ltd.* v. *Consolidated Property Investments Ltd.*[70] the landlord had made a physical re-entry onto the demised premises only 10 days after serving a section 146 notice alleging a breach of the

---

[66] It is considered good practice for the notice simply to require the tenant to remedy the breach within a "reasonable time" from the date of the service of the notice. It will then be a matter for the landlord to determine what period of time can safely be allowed to elapse before exercising his right of forfeiture. In the case of the breach of a repairing covenant, no doubt the landlord would take into account such matters as the extent and nature of the disrepair, the time of year and availability of builders.

[67] [1899] 2 Q.B. 79.

[68] *Ibid*, 91.

[69] [1923] 2 Ch. 347.

[70] [1991] 07 E.G. 132.

insurance covenant in the lease. It was held that, since compliance with the covenant involved the securing of agreement between the landlord and the head-tenant as to the full replacement value of the premises (requiring, in turn, a survey of the premises), the period of 10 days allowed by the landlord was not sufficient time to enable the tenant to comply with the notice. In *Billson v. Residential Apartments Ltd.*[71] the tenants, in breach of covenant not to make alterations to the demised premises without previous consent in writing, proceeded to make such alterations without seeking the landlords' consent. The landlords peaceably re-entered on the premises only 14 days after the service of their section 146 notice. The Court of Appeal held that the landlords had allowed sufficient time for the tenants to remedy the breach since, as soon as a tenant made it clear that he was not proposing to remedy the breach, the landlord had, by definition, allowed a reasonable time to elapse and could then proceed to forfeit. To hold otherwise would be to deprive the landlord of any effective remedy in so far as the taking of any step to restrain further breaches by injunction might amount to a waiver of the forfeiture.[72] In the instant case, the tenants had continued to press on with the unauthorised works in defiance of the landlords' notice and this merely demonstrated that the tenants had no intention to remedy the breach at all. In the words of Sir Nicolas Browne-Wilkinson V.-C.[73]:

> "If the actions of the lessee make it clear that he is not proposing to remedy the breaches within a reasonable time, or indeed any time, in my judgment a reasonable time must have elapsed for remedying the breaches once it is clear that they are not proposing to take the necessary steps to remedy the breach but are committing further breaches ... The only effective remedy of a landlord, faced with intransigent behaviour such as that of the defendants in the present case, must be to forfeit the lease on the grounds that whatever time was allowed the defendant was showing no intention of remedying the breach at all."

In *Penton v. Barnett*[74] the landlords served notice on the tenant to execute certain repairs to the premises within three months of the date of the notice. After more than three months had elapsed, the landlord commenced proceedings for forfeiture of the lease. The Court of Appeal held that the notice was good. A.L. Smith L.J. said[75]:

> "... a right of re-entry for breach of covenant is not enforceable

---

[71] [1991] 3 W.L.R. 264, (C.A.). See also, *Grosvenor Estate Belgravia v. Cochran* [1991] 44 E.G. 169, (six days was a reasonable period).
[72] *Ibid*, 275, *per* Nicolas Browne-Wilkinson V.-C.
[73] *Ibid*, 275.
[74] [1898] 1 Q.B. 276, (C.A.).
[75] *Ibid*, 279–280.

unless the lessor serves on the tenant a notice specifying the particular breach complained of, so that the tenant may have a reasonable time to remedy the breach and make reasonable compensation to the lessor."

Again, in *Gulliver Investments Ltd.* v. *Abbott*[76] three months' notice was considered reasonable to carry out repairs to the premises and the fact that the writ was issued two weeks after the expiry of the notice did not make the time unreasonable.

The last two-mentioned cases may be contrasted with *Bhojwani* v. *Kingsley Investment Trust Ltd.*[76a] where the amount of time that had elapsed between the service of the section 146 notice (requiring extensive underpinning works) and peaceable re-entry was only two months. Mr T. Morison Q.C. (sitting as a deputy judge of the High Court) observed:[76b]

"Generally, a period of three months is thought to be adequate but there are no hard-and-fast rules and all will depend upon what is required to be done."

In cases involving disrepair to the premises, the court will, no doubt, take into account all the circumstances of the case, including such matters as the extent and nature of the disrepair, the time of year and availability of builders, in determining whether or not the landlord had allowed a reasonable time to elapse before commencing his proceedings for forfeiture.[77] In cases of disrepair, the question is whether the time given in the notice is reasonable for doing *all* the remedial work and not for doing only some part of it.[78] Thus, the landlord will be precluded from exercising his right of forfeiture in respect of any of the breaches until a reasonable time for remedying all of them has elapsed.

A section 146 notice will be valid even if served by a landlord who is already in possession of the demised premises by reason of an earlier re-entry in respect of an irremediable breach of covenant.[79] In the case of an irremediable breach, the tenant will not be prejudiced by being out of possession of the premises since he does not require any opportunity to remedy the breach of covenant.

(3) *Service of notice*

Under section 196 of the Law of Property Act 1925, a notice served

---

[76] [1966] E.G.D. 299.

[76a] [1992] 39 E.G. 138.

[76b] *Ibid*, 141. In this case, the s. 146 notice had been served on March 16, 1990 although the schedule of dilapidations had been with the tenants since the beginning of February 1990.

[77] See, *e.g. Myers* v. *Oldschool* [1928] E.G.D. 167, (three months' notice held valid).

[78] *Hopley* v. *Tarvin Parish Council* (1910) 74 J.P. 196, (notice requiring local authority to clean up a number of allotments not divisible).

[79] *Fuller* v. *Judy Properties Ltd.* [1992] 14 E.G. 106, (C.A.), (covenant against assignment).

under the Act is sufficiently served if left at the last known abode or place of business in the United Kingdom of the lessee or is affixed[80] or left for him on the land[81] or any house or building comprised in the lease[82] or if sent by registered letter or recorded delivery[83] addressed to the lessee to his last known abode or place of business and not returned by the post office undelivered.[84] If it is not so returned, it is immaterial that the notice was never, in fact, received by the lessee[85] and service will be deemed to have been effected at the time at which in the ordinary course of post the letter would have been delivered.[86]

The "lessee" for the purpose of service is the lessee who is in possession of the premises or who has a subsisting lease at the time the notice comes to be served.[87] The notice may be addressed to "the lessee" by that designation without his name or generally to the persons interested without any name and notwithstanding that any person to be affected by the notice is absent, under disability, unborn, or unascertained.[88] Where there is more than one lessee, all joint lessees must be served with the notice.[89]

[80] *Cusack-Smith* v. *Gold* [1958] 1 W.L.R. 611 (affixing notice to the door of the demised premises good service).
[81] The notice may be left with some person, *e.g.* an employee, on the premises provided there is reasonable ground for believing that that person will pass it on to the lessee if possible: *Cannon Brewery Co.* v. *Signal Press Ltd.* (1928) 139 L.T. 384. A notice will be properly served if pushed under the door and accidentally concealed under the linoleum: *Newborough (Lord)* v. *Jones* [1975] Ch. 90, (C.A.). In *Van Haarlam* v. *Kasner Charitable Trust* [1992] 36 E.G. 135, it was held that a s. 146 notice was validly served by posting it through the flat's letter box even though it was known that the tenant was in prison and unlikely to receive it.
[82] s. 196(3).
[83] The recorded delivery service may be used as an alternative to registered post: see Recorded Delivery Service Act 1962.
[84] s. 196(4).
[85] *In Re 88 Berkeley Road, NW9, Rickwood* v. *Turnsek* [1971] 1 Ch. 648, concerning a notice of severance under s. 36(2) of the 1925 Act.
[86] s. 196(4). See also, s. 18(2) of the Landlord and Tenant Act 1927, which provides that where the landlord is forfeiting for breach of covenant to repair, he must show that the fact of service of the notice was known either to the lessee or an underlessee or to the person who last paid rent under the lease. Notification is, however, presumed (unless the contrary is proved) where the notice is sent by registered letter or recorded delivery to the last known abode in the United Kingdom of such person. Moreover, the landlord is not required to allege specifically in his pleadings that the notice has been served on the lessee: *Gates* v. *W.A. & R.J. Jacobs Ltd.* [1920] 1 Ch. 567.
[87] *Church Commissioners for England* v. *Ve-Ri-Best Manufacturing Co. Ltd.* [1957] 1 Q.B. 238, (no obligation to serve s. 146 notice on tenant's mortgagee by legal charge). Similarly, there is no obligation to serve notice on a mortgagee by sub-demise: *Egerton* v. *Jones* [1939] 2 K.B. 702. A notice served upon an equitable assignee of a lease by name is not an effective service on the lessee: *Gentle* v. *Faulkner* [1900] 2 Q.B. 267. A notice addressed to the original lessee and "all others whom it doth or may concern" and served on the persons in occupation of the demised premises is sufficiently served on the assignee of the lease: *Cronin* v. *Rogers* (1884) 1 Cab. & El. 348.
[88] s. 196(2).
[89] *Blewett* v. *Blewett* [1936] 2 All E.R. 188, (where lease vested in the Public Trustee, s. 146 notice should be served on him); *Wilson* v. *Hagon* (1958) 109 L.J. 204.

If the tenant assigns his leasehold interest in breach of a covenant not to assign without consent of the landlord, the assignee is the "lessee" for the purpose of section 146(1) and the landlord's notice must be served on him.[90] An assignment made in breach of covenant is not void but only voidable at the instance of the landlord so that it is the assignee who will be concerned to avoid a forfeiture and not the original tenant. The assignment is an effective assignment despite the breach and, consequently, the original tenant, although remaining liable to fulfil the covenants under the lease after assignment, ceases to be the lessee of the landlord.[91] Equally, a former assignee of the lease, who has parted with his interest in the demised premises, is not a "lessee" within the meaning of section 146(1).[92]

Where, however, the lease is assigned *after* notice has been served on the tenant, the landlord is not required to serve a new notice on the assignee of the lease before exercising his right of forfeiture as against the assignee. In these circumstances, it is sufficient that the notice was served on the tenant, who was the "lessee" at the time when the notice was given.[93]

In *Gentle* v. *Faulkner*,[94] the tenant declared that he would stand possessed of all his leasehold property upon trust for a trustee for the benefit of his creditors. The trustee entered into possession of the demised premises but no legal assignment of them was executed in his favour. The Court of Appeal held that the service of a notice of forfeiture on the trustee, who only had an equitable interest in the premises, was not a sufficient compliance with section 146.

A landlord must serve notice on his tenant where he seeks to re-enter in reliance on a condition for forfeiture on the bankruptcy of the tenant's surety.[95]

Remediable and irremediable breaches of covenant

The question whether a breach of covenant is remediable or irremediable will be of vital importance to both the landlord and tenant in the context of proceedings for forfeiture.[96] This is because a landlord is pre-

---

[90] *Old Grovebury Manor Farm Ltd.* v. *Seymour Plant Sales & Hire Ltd. (No. 2)* [1979] 1 W.L.R. 1397, (C.A.), applied in *Fuller* v. *Judy Properties Ltd.* [1992] 14 E.G. 106, (C.A.). At first instance, it was submitted that the landlords were estopped from denying that the original tenant was the lessee for the purpose of the service of the notice: [1991] 31 E.G. 63.

[91] *Ibid*, 505, *per* Lord Russell of Killowen.

[92] *Cusack-Smith* v. *Gold* [1958] 1 W.L.R. 611.

[93] *Church Commissioners For England* v. *Kanda* [1958] 1 Q.B. 332, (C.A.).

[94] [1900] 2 Q.B. 267, (C.A.).

[95] *Halliard Property Co. Ltd.* v. *Jack Segal Ltd.* [1978] 1 W.L.R. 377.

[96] For a case concerning an irremediable breach in the context of a landlord's application for leave to enforce its right of re-entry under paragraph 4(1) of Sched. 3 to the Leasehold Reform Act 1967, see *Central Estates* v. *Woolgar* [1972] 1 Q.B. 48.

cluded by section 146(1) from enforcing a right of forfeiture for breach of a covenant or condition in the lease (other than non-payment of rent) unless he has first served a notice complying with the sub-section. The notice must *inter alia* specify the particular breach complained of and, "if the breach is capable of remedy", require the tenant to remedy it.[97] Thus, where the breach falls to be classified as remediable, the landlord must in his section 146 notice formally require it to be remedied and then give the tenant a reasonable period of time within which to remedy the breach. Where, however, the tenant's breach falls to be treated, as a matter of law, as irremediable, the landlord does not have to stipulate in his section 146 notice that the breach be remedied and may proceed to execute his right of forfeiture (whether by action or physical re-entry) without further delay.[98] Further, since the breach is categorised as being irremediable, the tenant is not in a position to avoid the forfeiture by ceasing the action which constitutes the alleged breach or by performing the obligation which he has failed to fulfil. In such circumstances, his only recourse is to seek relief from forfeiture under section 146(2) of the 1925 Act.[99]

The question whether a breach of covenant is remediable or irremediable may be considered under two separate headings, namely, (1) negative covenants and (2) positive covenants.

(1) *Negative covenants*

It is now well established that a breach of a negative covenant which leaves a "stigma" on the demised premises is generally incapable of remedy. In cases involving an illegal or immoral user of the premises, the courts have looked at the effect of the breach and have concluded that the stigma attached to the premises by the wrongful user can only be erased if the tenant who brought the taint about was no longer associated with the premises. In this sense, therefore, the breach is considered, as a matter of law, to be incapable of remedy within a reasonable period of time from the date of the landlord's notice.

In *Governors of Rugby School* v. *Tannahill*[1] the tenant permitted the premises to be used for prostitution in breach of her covenant in the lease not to use the premises for an illegal or immoral purpose. The landlords served her with a section 146 notice which did not request her to remedy the breach. The Court of Appeal held that, since the breach was not one capable of remedy, the omission to request it to be remedied did not invalidate the notice. Maugham L.J. said[2]:

---

[97] *North London Freehold Land and House Co.* v. *Jacques* (1883) 49 L.T. 659, (notice stating the breach but failing to require the tenant to remedy it held invalid).
[98] See, p. 111.
[99] See, Chap. 10.
[1] [1935] 1 K.B. 87.
[2] *Ibid*, 93–94.

"The use of the premises for a long period for an immoral purpose seriously tends to damage their value and to give them a bad name, as indeed is shown by the common designation of such premises – namely, a house of ill-fame; and merely ceasing for a reasonable time, perhaps a few weeks or a month, to use the premises for an immoral purpose would be no remedy for the breach of covenant which had been committed over a long period."

In *Egerton* v. *Esplanade Hotels, London Ltd.*[3] the tenants allowed hotel premises to be used as a brothel in breach of covenant in the lease. The landlords served a section 146 notice on the tenants which did not contain any requirement that the breach should be remedied. Morris J. held that the breach was incapable of remedy and that, therefore, there was no necessity for the landlords to have called on the tenants to remedy it in their notice. He said[4]:

"There are, of course, always the beneficial effects of time in effacing the memory of unhappy and unpleasant things, but this was not, in my opinion, a breach which was capable of remedy within a reasonable time."

In *Hoffman* v. *Fineberg*[5] the illegality consisted of unlawful gambling on club premises. Here again, the omission to ask that the breach be remedied was held not to invalidate the landlord's section 146 notice. Whilst no diminution in the landlord's reversionary interest was involved, nevertheless, the landlord was entitled to be protected against the "slur"[6] which was involved in being labelled as a landlord of a gaming house, even though no monetary damage ensued from it.

In *Glass* v. *Kencakes Ltd.*[7] the sub-tenant of residential flats permitted the premises to be used for the purposes of prostitution in breach of covenant in the lease. In consequence of the immoral user of the premises, the

---

[3] [1947] 2 All E.R. 88. See also, *Borthwick-Norton* v. *Romney Warwick Estates Ltd.* [1950] 1 All E.R. 798, (C.A.), where a sub-tenant was convicted of using a top-floor flat as a brothel and *Central Estates (Belgravia) Ltd.* v. *Woolgar* [1972] 1 Q.B. 48, (tenant, who was convicted of unlawfully keeping a brothel at the premises, seeking enfranchisement under the Leasehold Reform Act 1967).

[4] *Ibid*, 91.

[5] [1949] Ch. 245. See also, *Bickerton's Aerodromes* v. *Young* [1958] 108 L.J. 217, (failure to observe licensing laws); *Dunraven Securities Ltd.* v. *Holloway* (1982) 264 E.G. 709 and *D.R. Evans & Co.* v. *Chandler* (1969) 211 E.G. 1381, (use of premises for the sale of pornographic material); *Ali* v. *Booth* [1966] 110 S.J. 708, (conviction for breach of food regulations); *Van Haarlam* v. *Kasner Charitable Trust* [1992] 36 E.G. 135, (conviction under the Official Secrets Act 1920).

[6] *Ibid*, 257, *per* Harman J.

[7] [1966] 1 Q.B. 611. The decision has been explained on the basis that the head-tenants had no knowledge of the immoral user: *Dunraven Securities Ltd.* v. *Holloway* (1982) 264 E.G. 709, 711, *per* Stephenson L.J. Contrast *Borthwick-Norton* v. *Romney Warwick Estates Ltd.* [1950] 1 All E.R. 798, (tenants had deliberately shut their eyes to the premises being used as a brothel despite receipt of various complaints).

landlord served a section 146 notice on the head-tenants stating *inter alia* that the breach was incapable of remedy. The sub-tenant, as soon as he learnt of the notice, caused the prostitutes to leave the flats. Three weeks later, the head-tenants served a section 146 notice on the sub-tenant. Before notice was served on the head-tenants, they had no cause to suspect the immoral user and there was no evidence that the premises had acquired a bad reputation or declined in value. Paull J. held that the breach was capable of remedy and was, in fact, remediable within a reasonable period of time from the date of the landlord's notice. The decision lays down the following propositions in relation to the liability of a head-tenant for the immoral user of the premises by an offending sub-tenant: (a) the mere fact that the breach complained of was a user by a sub-tenant contrary to the covenants in the lease did not render it incapable of remedy; (b) the fact that the user involved immorality did not of itself render a breach of covenant incapable of remedy, provided that the tenant neither knew nor had reason to know of the user, and, if and when he knew of it, took immediate steps to stop it, starting, if necessary, within a reasonable time an action to forfeit the sub-lease and (c) before such a breach could be held to be capable of remedy, all the circumstances had to be taken into consideration and, in some cases, the damage to the premises might be so great that it could not be remedied.

A more restrictive approach, however, is to be found in *British Petroleum Pension Trust Ltd.* v. *Behrendt*[8] where a flat had been used for prostitution over a period of years. The tenant spent much of his time abroad and, when in England, lived in other premises from where he conducted his business. The flat had been occupied by a prostitute whom the tenant had evicted after receiving a section 146 notice from the landlords alleging that the flat was being used for immoral purposes. Despite assurances by the tenant, the regular use of the premises for prostitution continued and the landlords once again served a section 146 notice. The tenant responded to this second notice by promptly evicting the offending occupant. The evidence also showed that the tenant either knew or deliberately shut his eyes to the immoral user throughout the period in question. The Court of Appeal, in holding that the breach was irremediable, rejected the tenant's submission that a more liberal approach could be discerned from the authorities towards irremediable breaches and that even the use of premises for immoral purposes would not be treated as irremediable where no damage could be established to the landlord's reversion. Thus, the continuing presence of a tenant who *knowingly* suffers prostitution to take place on his premises (even if he himself has not actively participated in or permitted it) will have the effect of continuing the stigma resulting from

---

[8] [1985] 2 E.G.L.R. 97. See also, *Borthwick-Norton* v. *Romney Warwick Estates Ltd.* [1950] 1 All E.R. 798, (C.A.).

the immoral user. In such cases, therefore, the mere cesser of the offending use will not remedy the breach because the stigma will continue to attach to the premises so long as the tenant remains associated with them. Purchase L.J. was, however, prepared to concede that there might be a case for arguing that immoral user was a breach capable of remedy when the breach was committed by a sub-tenant and the tenant was completely innocent of the circumstances.[9]

In *Scala House & District Property Co. Ltd.* v. *Forbes*[10] the Court of Appeal had occasion to review the earlier authorities and held[11] that a breach of covenant not to assign underlet or part with possession of the demised premises was not a breach capable of remedy within the meaning of section 146(1) of the 1925 Act. Russell L.J., who gave the leading judgment of the Court, expressed the view that the "stigma" cases could be explained on the shorter ground that a breach of a negative covenant could never be capable of remedy. Any other view would, he felt, lead to anomalies where the tenant had ceased the wrongful user before the service of the section 146 notice. To hold such a breach to be "remedied" by the cessation of the wrongful user would mean that the landlord could never forfeit where the breach had stopped. On the other hand, to hold that such cessation alone rendered the breach irremediable would leave a tenant who had stopped the wrongful user before the landlord's notice in a worse position than a tenant who stopped after the notice. In the words of Russell L.J.[12]:

> "If a user in breach has ceased before the section 146 notice (quite apart from the stigma cases) then either it is incapable of remedy and after notice there is nothing in the way of a writ: or the cesser of use has somehow deprived the lessor of his ability to seek to forfeit though he has done nothing to waive the breach, a situation in law which I find extremely difficult to spell out of section 146."

On the authority of *Scala*, therefore, it seemed that the only breaches capable of remedy for the purpose of section 146 were breaches of repairing and similar positive obligations in the lease and, in view of the uncertainties raised by the decision, it became common practice for the landlord's notice to require the tenant to remedy the breach adding the words, "if capable of remedy".[13] The decision in *Scala* has been criticised

---

[9] *British Petroleum Pension Trust Ltd.* v. *Behrendt* [1985] 2 E.G.L.R. 97. See also, *Scala House & District Property Co. Ltd.* v. *Forbes* [1974] Q.B. 575, 587, *per* Russell L.J. (referring to the position of a tenant of a large block of flats) and *Glass* v. *Kencakes Ltd.* [1966] 1 Q.B. 611, Paull J.

[10] [1974] Q.B. 575. See also, *Troop* v. *Gibson* [1986] 1 E.G.L.R. 1, (C.A.), (assignment of agricultural tenancy in breach of restriction on assignment held irremediable).

[11] Overruling *Capital & Counties Property Co. Ltd.* v. *Mills* [1966] E.G.D. 96.

[12] *Ibid*, 588.

[13] The use of these words was approved by Harman J. in *Hoffman* v. *Fineberg* [1949] Ch. 245, 252 and by Paull J. in *Glass* v. *Kencakes Ltd.* [1966] 1 Q.B. 611, 629.

by a differently constituted Court of Appeal in *Expert Clothing Service & Sales Ltd.* v. *Hillgate House Ltd.*[14] In that case, the leading judgment was given by Slade L.J. who took the opportunity to analyse in some depth the distinction drawn in the authorities between positive and negative covenants. This distinction was first drawn by MacKinnon J. in *Governors of Rugby School* v. *Tannahill*[15] where he said[16]:

"A promise to do a thing, if broken, can be remedied by the thing being done. But breach of a promise not to do a thing cannot in any true sense be remedied; that which was done cannot be undone. There cannot truly be a remedy; there can only be abstention, perhaps accompanied with apology."

Thus, MacKinnon J. held that the breach of a negative covenant not to use the premises for an illegal or immoral purpose was not capable of remedy within the meaning of section 146. On appeal, however, the Court of Appeal[17] did not accept this broad test for distinguishing between remediable and irremediable breaches of covenant. Greer L.J., for example, commented[18] that MacKinnon J. had gone further than was necessary for the decision of the case in holding that a breach of a negative covenant could never be capable of remedy and suggested that, in some cases, the breach of a negative covenant could be remedied by the immediate ceasing of that which was complained of coupled with an undertaking against any further breach taking place in the future. Maugham L.J.,[19] on the other hand, came to two conclusions upon the effect of section 146, namely, that (a) the remedy must be a complete remedy and (b) the breach must be capable of remedy within a reasonable period of time.

In the *Hillgate* case, the Court of Appeal took the opportunity to confine the remarks of Russell L.J. in the *Scala* case to a "once and for all" breach of a negative covenant (*i.e.* a covenant not to assign, underlet or part with possession of the demised premises). The Court also concluded that the question whether a breach of covenant was capable of remedy was dependent on whether the harm done to the landlord by the relevant breach was for practical purposes capable of being retrieved.[20] In addition, the Court accepted that a section 146 notice would not require the tenant to remedy the breach if it was not capable of remedy within a reasonable time after the service of the notice. The breach of a negative user covenant, particularly where the breach amounted to an illegal or

---

[14] [1986] Ch. 340.
[15] [1934] 1 K.B. 695.
[16] *Ibid*, 701.
[17] [1935] 1 K.B. 87.
[18] *Ibid*, 90–91.
[19] *Ibid*, 93.
[20] *Expert Clothing Service & Sales Ltd.* v. *Hillgate House Ltd.* [1986] Ch. 340, 355, *per* Slade L.J.

immoral user of the premises, fell within this category even where compliance with the covenant could be restored within a reasonable period of time. This is because the effect of such a breach (*i.e.* the stigma or taint attached to the premises) could not be erased within a reasonable time. Such a breach, therefore, could only be classified as irremediable. In the words of Slade L.J.[21]:

> "On the facts of cases such as those, mere cesser by the tenant of the offending use within a reasonable period and for a reasonable period of time could not have remedied the breaches because it could not have removed the stigma which they had caused to attach to the premises. The harm had been irretrievably done."

The decision in *Hillgate* appears to leave open the argument that if a breach of a negative covenant does not involve any lingering stigma or taint on the premises then the breach may be capable of remedy. In the course of his judgment, O'Connor L.J. observed[22]:

> "To stop doing what is forbidden by a negative covenant may or may not remedy the breach even if accompanied by compensation in money. Thus to remove the window boxes and pay for the repair of any damage done will remedy the breach but to stop using the house as a brothel will not, because the taint lingers on and will not dissipate within a reasonable time".

In *Hartley* v. *Larkin*[23] the lease contained a proviso for re-entry if the rent should be unpaid for 21 days after becoming payable or if the tenant should suffer any distress or execution to be levied on his goods. The landlord levied distress on the premises in respect of arrears of rent and then served notice of forfeiture. On the following day, the tenant paid the arrears of rent due and the costs of the distress. Jones J. held that, in the particular circumstances, as the landlord had sustained no undue injury and no undue notoriety had attached to the premises as a result of the distress, the breach of the negative covenant not to suffer a distress was capable of being remedied and had been remedied by payment of the arrears and costs. It was accepted, however, that there might be other circumstances where the tenant had suffered a distress by a landlord and where the mere payment of what was due would not be sufficient to remedy that breach.[24] Similarly, in *Van Haarlam* v. *Kasner*[24a] Harman J. was not prepared to hold that all negative covenants (including those involving illegal or immoral user) were always incapable of remedy. He said[24b]:

---

[21] *Ibid*, 357.
[22] *Ibid*, 362.
[23] (1950) 66 (Pt I) T.L.R. 896.
[24] *Ibid*, 899.
[24a] [1992] 36 E.G. 135.
[24b] *Ibid*, 142.

"There are trivial breaches of what many people would call regulations rather than law where there is technically a criminal offence committed and possibly a breach of some negative covenant, but the court would not pay a great deal of heed to it and would hold that it was remediable."

In *Billson* v. *Residential Apartments Ltd.*[25] Sir Nicolas Browne-Wilkinson V.-C. expressed some doubt[26] as to whether the trial judge had been right in holding that a breach of a covenant not to make alterations to the demised premises without previous consent in writing of the landlord was an irremediable breach.

The bankruptcy of the tenant constitutes an irremediable breach.[27]

(2) *Positive covenants*

In *Expert Clothing Service & Sales Ltd.* v. *Hillgate House Ltd.*[28] the Court of Appeal held that the breach of a positive covenant (regardless whether continuous or once and for all) would ordinarily be remediable provided such remedy was carried out within a reasonable period of time which, in turn, depended on the particular circumstances of the case. In that case, the tenants had failed to comply with an obligation to reconstruct the premises by a certain date. The landlords duly served a section 146 notice alleging *inter alia* that the tenants were in breach of covenant to reconstruct and that the breach was incapable of remedy. The landlords argued that, because the breach was a once and for all breach, it should, by definition, be treated as irremediable or, alternatively, if that was not the case, that it could not be remedied within a reasonable time. In support of the first argument, the landlords relied on the observations of Russell L.J. in *Scala House & District Property Co. Ltd.* v. *Forbes,*[29] who concluded that the breach of a covenant against assignment or sub-letting was a once and for all breach which was irremediable. The Court of Appeal in *Hillgate,* however, had no difficulty in confining the observations of Russell L.J. to a once and for all breach of a *negative* covenant only, leaving it free to conclude that a once and for all breach of a *positive* covenant was ordinarily[30] capable of remedy. As to the second argument raised by the landlord (*i.e.* that the breach must be capable of remedy within a reasonable time),

[25] [1991] 3 W.L.R. 264, (C.A.).
[26] *Ibid,* 272.
[27] *Civil Service Co-operative Society Ltd.* v. *McGrigor's Trustee* [1923] 2 Ch. 347, 356, *per* Russell J.; *Fryer* v. *Ewart* [1902] A.C. 187, (liquidation).
[28] [1986] Ch. 340.
[29] [1974] Q.B. 575.
[30] The judgment of Slade L.J. does refer to some examples of a breach of a positive covenant which would not be capable of remedy. He cites the breach of a covenant to insure which might be incapable of remedy at the time when the premises had already burnt down and the breach of a positive covenant which could only be capable of being fully performed, if at all, after the expiration of the term of the lease: [1986] Ch. 340, 355.

the Court of Appeal concluded that, in relation to the breach of a positive covenant, the crucial question was whether performance of the obligation, albeit out of time, could effectively remedy the harm suffered by the landlord. Thus, in normal circumstances, the breach of a positive covenant to do some act by a certain time was, for practicable purposes, capable of being remedied by the act being done, even out of time. In the words of Slade L.J.[31]:

> "... the breach of a positive covenant to do something (such as to decorate or build) can ordinarily, for practical purposes, be remedied by the thing being actually done if a reasonable time for its performance (running from the service of the section 146 notice) is duly allowed by the landlord following such service and the tenant duly does it within such time."[32]

On the facts, therefore, the tenants' failure to reconstruct the premises was treated as being capable of remedy without permanent harm being done to the landlords on the basis that the tenants could carry out the work within a reasonable period and pay such compensation as was appropriate. Although the tenants had had 18 months from the date when they had covenanted to reconstruct in which to do the work, the landlords would not have suffered additional harm by requiring in their notice that the tenants should remedy the breach. In this connection, whilst the tenants had enjoyed 18 months in which to comply with their obligations (and that period could be taken into account in considering what reasonable time to allow them after the service of the notice), nevertheless, the landlords were not entitled to deny the tenants any further time at all in which to remedy the breach because they had so long to do the work already. Accordingly, the landlords were required to afford the tenants that opportunity and, in so far as they had failed to do this, their notice was invalid.[33]

Breach of covenant to repair

Where the landlord seeks to forfeit the lease for breach of a covenant to

---

[31] *Ibid*, 357.

[32] It is evident that, where a breach is capable of remedy, the main purpose of the s. 146 notice is to afford the tenant one last chance to comply with his obligations under the lease.

[33] The tenants' failure to notify the landlords of the fact that they had charged the premises to a bank, in breach of covenant to give notice of any charges, was also held to be remediable.

repair[34] and the lease in question was granted for seven or more years[35] and three years or more remain unexpired[36] at the date of the section 146 notice, the landlord's remedy of forfeiture (or damages[37]) is further limited by the provisions of the Leasehold Property (Repairs) Act 1938.[38] In *National Real Estate and Finance Co. Ltd.* v. *Hassan*,[39] Goddard L.J. stated the mischief that the 1938 Act was designed to remedy, namely[40]:

" . . . speculators buying up small property in an indifferent state of repair, and then serving a schedule of dilapidations upon the tenants, which the tenants cannot comply with . . . this is the general mischief, that the speculator buys at a very low price, turns out the tenants, and gets the reversion which he has never paid for, which is a great hardship to the tenants."

Where the Act applies,[41] the landlord cannot proceed without serving a

---

[34] The Leasehold Property (Repairs) Act 1938 applies to the breach of a covenant or agreement to keep or put in repair all or any part of the demised premises during the currency of the lease: s. 1(1). The breach of an obligation to lay out insurance monies in rebuilding or repairing the premises, as opposed to reinstating the same, following a fire is not a breach of a repairing covenant falling within the 1938 Act: *Farimani* v. *Gates* (1984) 271 E.G. 887, (C.A.). See also, *Starrokate Ltd.* v. *Burry* (1982) 265 E.G. 871.

[35] s. 7(1) of the 1938 Act. The Act does not apply to a lease of an agricultural holding within the meaning of the Agricultural Holdings Act 1986.

[36] The 1938 Act will not apply where there is less than three years of the term to run or where the lease has been surrendered at the date of the commencement of proceedings: *Baker* v. *Sims* [1959] 1 Q.B. 114, (C.A.).

[37] s. 1(2) of the 1938 Act. In this case, the notice under the Act must be served on the tenant not less than one month before the commencement of the action. A landlord will not require leave under s. 1(3) to bring an action for the cost of repairs where a tenant fails to comply with a covenant which expressly confers on the landlord the right to carry out the repairs and claim the cost from the tenant as a debt or rent in arrears: *Colchester Estates (Cardiff)* v. *Carlton Industries Inc.* [1984] 3 W.L.R. 693; *Hamilton* v. *Martell Securities Ltd.* [1984] Ch. 266. Contrast *Swallow Securities* v. *Brand* (1981) 45 P. & C.R. 328.

[38] As amended by s. 51(1) of the Landlord and Tenant Act 1954. See generally, "The Leasehold Property (Repairs) Act 1938", A. Blundell, (1938/9) 3 Conv. (N.S.) 10 and "A Review of the Operation of the Leasehold Property (Repairs) Act 1938", P.F. Smith, [1986] Conv. 85.

[39] [1939] 2 K.B. 61.

[40] *Ibid*, 78. See also, *Sidnell* v. *Wilson* [1966] 2 Q.B. 67, 76, *per* Lord Denning M.R. The 1938 Act was originally limited to tenants of long leases of small houses but, by virtue of s. 51(3) of the Landlord and Tenant Act 1954, the Act was extended to tenants of all properties, except agricultural property.

[41] The Act does not apply to a breach of covenant to put the premises in repair on taking possession or within a reasonable period thereafter: s. 3.

section 146 notice,[42] which must inform[43] the tenant[44] of his right to serve a counter-notice[45] within 28 days of the date of the service of the landlord's notice claiming the benefit of section 1(3) of the 1938 Act.[46] The landlord's notice must also specify the manner in which a counter-notice may be served and the name and address for service of the landlord.[47] If the landlord's notice fails to comply with these requirements, such failure will not preclude the landlord from serving a fresh notice complying with the 1938 Act. Further, there is authority for the view that a notice invalidated as regards alleged breaches of repairing covenants by the 1938 Act is, nevertheless, effective in relation to other alleged breaches not covered by the Act.[48]

The provisions of section 196 of the Law of Property Act 1925[49] and section 23(2) of the Landlord and Tenant Act 1927[50] (which authorises a tenant to serve documents on the person to whom he has been paying rent) apply to the service of counter-notices under the 1938 Act.

If the tenant does serve such a counter-notice within 28 days,[51] no further proceedings by action or otherwise (*i.e.* by initiating proceedings

---

[42] For forms of notice: See *Encyclopaedia of Forms and Precedents*, (5th ed.), Vol. 22, paras. 1162–1164, Forms 170–171 and Pt VI of this work.

[43] A notice which fails to inform the tenant of his right to claim the benefit of the 1938 Act may be validated by a subsequent letter complying with that requirement: *Sidnell* v. *Wilson* [1966] 2 Q.B. 67. The statement informing the tenant of his right to claim the benefit of the Act must be in characters no less conspicuous than those used in any other part of the notice: s. 1(4). The words "no less conspicuous" mean "equally readable" or "equally sufficient": *Middlegate Properties Ltd.* v. *Messimeris* [1973] 1 W.L.R. 168, (C.A.), (fact that print size of characters in question different from that used in rest of notice did not invalid same).

[44] Only a tenant who is in possession or has a subsisting lease at the time when proceedings are taken is entitled to the benefit of s. 1(3) of the 1938 Act: *Cusack-Smith* v. *Gold* [1958] 1 W.L.R. 611 (assignee who had assigned all his leasehold interest in the premises not entitled to benefit of 1938 Act).

[45] For form of counter-notice: See *Encyclopaedia of Forms and Precedents*, (5th ed.), Vol. 22, para. 1164, Form 172 and Pt VI of this work.

[46] Where the landlord alleges that there are breaches of covenant to repair falling within the 1938 Act as well as alleged breaches of other covenants under the same lease, it is good practice to serve two notices, namely, the first specifying the breaches of the repairing covenants with the additional notice under the 1938 Act and the other specifying the remaining breaches without any such notice: *Starrokate Ltd.* v. *Burry* (1982) 265 E.G. 871, (C.A.), 872, *per* May L.J. A notice specifying both breaches of covenant to repair and other breaches may be severed and held good in part and bad in part: *ibid*, 872, *per* May L.J.

[47] The statement to this effect must also be in characters no less conspicuous than those used in any other part of the landlord's notice: s. 1(4). It is sufficient if the notice specifies one good manner of service and an appropriate name and address for service, such as that of the landlord's solicitor: *Middlegate Properties Ltd.* v. *Messimeris* [1973] 1 W.L.R. 168, (C.A.).

[48] *Starrokate Ltd.* v. *Burry* (1984) 265 E.G. 871, 872, *per* May L.J., (severance of notice permissible) and *Pannell* v. *City of London Brewery Company* [1900] 1 Ch. 496.

[49] See s. 7(2) of the 1938 Act. S. 196 is discussed under the heading "Service of notice", at p. 114.

[50] See s. 51(4) of the Landlord and Tenant Act 1954.

[51] If no counter-notice is served by the tenant, the landlord may proceed to exercise his right of forfeiture without obtaining leave of the court.

for possession or by physically re-entering upon the demised premises) can be taken by the landlord without leave[52] of the court establishing a case, on the balance of probabilities,[53] that one or more[54] of the five grounds set out in section 1(5) of the Act have been fulfilled. The court to which application for leave should be made is the county court, except where the action for which leave may be given would have to be taken in another court.[55] In the county court, the application for leave is by originating application[56] which must state (a) the order applied for and sufficient particulars to show the grounds on which the landlord claims to be entitled to leave under the 1938 Act (b) the names and addresses of the persons (if any) intended to be served or that no person is intended to be served and (c) the landlord's address for service. In the High Court, the application for leave is made by originating summons[57] supported by an affidavit made by, or on behalf of, the landlord setting out the grounds on which leave to institute proceedings is sought and any facts necessary to substantiate those grounds.[58] The application will be heard by a master in chambers either in the Queen's Bench Division or in the Chancery Division but application may be made to a district registrar if it relates to premises situated in the district of his registry, notwithstanding that the proceedings are assigned to the Chancery Division.[59] Prior to the House of Lords' decision in *Associated British Ports* v. *C.H. Bailey plc*,[60] applications under the 1938 Act were usually determined solely by reference to affidavit evidence but contested applications will now inevitably require the attendance of witnesses for cross-examination.

The five grounds upon which leave may be given are summarised below:

[52] See, s. 1(3). Leave may be given although the actual identity of the lessee has not been ascertained: *Pascall* v. *Galinski* [1970] 1 Q.B. 38, (C.A.).

[53] *Associated British Ports* v. *C.H. Bailey plc* [1990] 2 W.L.R. 812, (H.L.), overruling the *prima facie* or arguable case test put forward in *Sidnell* v. *Wilson* [1966] 2 Q.B. 67, (C.A.). The earlier cases of *Charles A. Pilgrim* v. *Jackson* (1975) 29 P. & C.R. 328; *Metropolitan Film Studios Ltd.* v. *Twickenham Film Studios Ltd.* [1962] 1 W.L.R. 1315 and *Land Securities plc* v. *Receiver for Metropolitan Police District* (1983) 267 E.G. 675, are no longer good law on this point.

[54] The grounds specified in s. 1(5)(a) to (e) are alternatives and leave to proceed may be given on proof of any one of them: *Phillips* v. *Price* [1959] 1 Ch. 181.

[55] s. 6(1). The parties may, however, by written memorandum agree that a specified county court shall have jurisdiction to hear the application notwithstanding the limits in jurisdiction contained in s. 6(1) of the 1938 Act: s. 24(1) of the County Courts Act 1984.

[56] C.C.R. Ord. 3, r. 4. For a form of originating application: See Atkin's Court Forms, (2nd ed., 1990), Vol. 24, p. 356, Form 147 and Pt VI of this work.

[57] R.S.C. Ord. 32, r. 9(2). The originating summons should be in Form 10 in Appendix A to the Supreme Court Practice: R.S.C. Ord. 32, r. 9(3). For a form of originating summons: See Atkin's Court Forms, (2nd ed., 1990), Vol. 24, p. 353, Form 144 and Pt VI of this work.

[58] R.S.C. Ord. 32, r. 9(4). For a form of affidavit; See Atkin's Court Forms (2nd ed., 1990), Vol. 24, p. 354, Form 145 and Pt VI of this work.

[59] R.S.C. Ord. 32, r. 9(2).

[60] [1990] 2 W.L.R. 812.

(a) The value of the landlord's reversion has been substantially diminished or will be if the breach is not immediately remedied;[61]

(b) The immediate remedying is required by any Act, bylaw, court order or local authority order;[62]

(c) The cost of immediate remedying is required in the interest of an occupier of the whole or part of the premises other than the tenant;[63]

(d) The cost of immediate remedying is relatively small in comparison with the likely cost if the work is postponed;[64]

(e) Special circumstances exist which, in the opinion of the court, render it just and equitable that leave should be given.[65]

The relevant time at which compliance with section 1(5)(*a*) to (*d*) falls to be tested is the time when proof under the section is sought to be established, namely, the date of the hearing, but the section will not be construed so as to subject the landlord's vested rights to being barred by the action of the tenant subsequent to the issue of the landlord's application under the Act.[66]

It appears that the court has a discretion, and is not bound, to grant the landlord leave to bring an action on the alleged breaches of covenant, even where one or more of the grounds set out in section 1(5) are satisfied.[67] For example, in *Land Securities plc* v. *Receiver for the Metropolitan Police District*[68] the court, in its discretion, refused the landlord leave to proceed with his claim for forfeiture and damages so as to enable all the matters in dispute between the parties to be resolved at the same time in existing proceedings begun by the tenant, under the Landlord and Tenant Act 1987, seeking declarations that the landlord had unreasonably withheld consent to certain remedial work proposed by the tenant. The discretion is, however, not one that should be exercised to exclude the

---

[61] *Re Metropolitan Film Studios Ltd.* v. *Twickenham Film Studios Ltd.* [1962] 1 W.L.R. 1315; *Sidnell* v. *Wilson* [1966] 2 Q.B. 67; *Parker* v. *O'Connor* [1974] 1 W.L.R. 1160.

[62] *Parker* v. *O'Connor* [1974] 1 W.L.R. 1160.

[63] *Phillips* v. *Price* [1959] Ch. 181.

[64] *Re Metropolitan Film Studios Ltd.* v. *Twickenham Film Studios Ltd.* [1962] 1 W.L.R. 1315; *Parker* v. *O'Connor* [1974] 1 W.L.R. 1160.

[65] *Sidnell* v. *Wilson* [1966] 2 Q.B. 67.

[66] *Re Metropolitan Film Studios Ltd.* v. *Twickenham Film Studios Ltd.* [1962] 1 W.L.R. 1315, 1320, *per* Ungoed-Thomas J.

[67] *Re Metropolitan Film Studios Ltd.* v. *Twickenham Film Studios Ltd.* [1962] 1 W.L.R. 1315.

[68] (1983) 267 E.G. 675.

landlord from his rights unless the court is clearly convinced that, despite compliance with section 1(5), leave ought not to be granted.[69]

The court may, in granting or refusing leave, impose such terms and conditions on the landlord or tenant as it may think fit.[70] In an appropriate case, the court can itself specify the breaches which must be remedied by the tenant and may adjourn or dismiss the landlord's application on condition that certain repairs are carried out.[71]

The question whether the landlord has satisfied one or more of the grounds (and that the tenant is in breach) will be determined at a full hearing of the section 1(3) application, leaving only the question of the tenant's claim (if any) for relief from forfeiture as the sole matter to be determined at the trial of the forfeiture action in the event that the landlord is successful in obtaining leave.[72] If, however, the landlord fails to prove any one or more of the specified grounds (or that the tenant is in breach), then the tenant will be entitled, as of right, to a dismissal of the landlord's application under section 1(3) and will thereby be relieved from the threat of forfeiture. It is possible for the parties to postpone the determination of the main issues until the hearing of the forfeiture action, in which case leave to proceed under the 1938 Act will be granted by consent without the landlord adducing detailed evidence at that stage.[73] It has been held that an application, under section 1(3) of the 1938 Act, for leave to commence an action for forfeiture of a lease is a "pending land action" within the meaning of section 17(1) of the Land Charges Act 1972 and, consequently, is registrable as a pending action under section 5(1) of the 1972 Act.[74]

Where the landlord must do urgent repairs in order to preserve the premises, there is a danger of invalidating any subsequent notice served pursuant to section 146 of the 1925 Act. In *SEDAC Investments Ltd.* v. *Tanner*[75] the landlord discovered that the stonework on the front wall of the demised premises was loose and falling on the pavement endangering passers-by. Remedial work was, therefore, undertaken by the landlord as a matter of urgency in the absence of any co-operation from the tenant who was responsible for the defect under its repairing covenant in

---

[69] *Re Metropolitan Film Studios Ltd.* v. *Twickenham Film Studios Ltd.* [1962] 1 W.L.R. 1315, 1323–1324, *per* Ungoed-Thomas J. But note the *dictum* of Megarry V.-C. in *Land Securities plc* v. *Receiver for Metropolitan Police District* (1983) 267 E.G. 675, 678: "... the discretion of the court was much less fettered than is suggested by subjecting it to the words 'clearly convinced' ". See also, *Associated British Ports* v. *C.H. Bailey plc* [1990] 2 W.L.R. 812, 820, *per* Lord Templeman.

[70] s. 1(6)

[71] *Associated British Ports* v. *C.H. Bailey plc* [1990] 2 W.L.R. 812, 820, *per* Lord Templeman.

[72] *Associated British Ports* v. *C.H. Bailey plc* [1990] 2 W.L.R. 812, (H.L.), overruling *Sidnell* v. *Wilson* [1966] 2 Q.B. 67, (C.A.).

[73] *Ibid*, 821, *per* Lord Templeman.

[74] *Selim Ltd.* v. *Bickenhall Engineering Ltd.* [1981] 3 W.L.R. 1318.

[75] [1982] 1 W.L.R. 1342.

the lease. Subsequently, the landlord served a section 146 notice on the tenant requiring compensation to which the tenant claimed the benefit of the 1938 Act. The court held that a section 146 notice to be effective had to be served *before* the breach complained of was remedied. Accordingly, when the landlord himself remedied the breach prior to attempting to serve a valid section 146 notice, he thereby put it out of his power to serve a valid section 146 notice thereafter, with the consequence that the court had no jurisdiction to give him leave to commence proceedings under the 1938 Act. In such circumstances, the landlord may protect himself in other ways, for example, by seeking a mandatory injunction to compel the tenant to undertake the necessary remedial work in compliance with his covenant,[76] or by serving a section 146 notice requiring the tenant, in view of the urgency of the repairs, to commence remedial work within a matter of a few days.[77] In addition, there may be an express clause in the lease entitling the landlord (on giving prior notice) to enter the demised premises and execute the repairs and then claim the cost from the tenant as either a debt or rent in arrear. In such a case, the landlord does not require leave, under section 1(3) of the 1938 Act, to bring his action for recovery of the cost of the repairs.[78] The Act is limited in its wording to claims for contract damages and, hence, has no application to a covenant by the tenant to repay the landlord's costs of carrying out the tenant's repairs, which sum is expressed to be recoverable as a contract debt.[79]

In forfeiture cases involving a breach of covenant to repair, the landlord must also show that the fact of service of the section 146 notice on the tenant was known either to the tenant or an underlessee or to the person who last paid the rent due under the lease and that a time reasonably sufficient to enable the repairs to be executed has elapsed since the time when the fact of the service of the notice had come to the knowledge of any such person.[80] Notification is presumed, unless the contrary is proved, where the notice is sent by registered letter or recorded delivery[81]

---

[76] A mandatory injunction would be available without the landlord going through the 1938 Act procedure. See further, Blundell, (1938/39) 3 Conv. (N.S.), 10, 13.

[77] *Ibid*, 1349, *per* Mr. Michael Wheeler, Q.C.

[78] *Hamilton* v. *Martell Securities Ltd.* [1984] Ch. 266 applied in *Colchester Estates (Cardiff)* v. *Carlton Industries plc* [1984] 3 W.L.R. 693. Contrast *Swallow Securities Ltd.* v. *Brand* (1981) 260 E.G. 63. See further, "A Review of the Operation of the Leasehold Property (Repairs) Act 1938", P.F. Smith, [1986] Conv. 85.

[79] *Bader Properties Ltd.* v. *Linley Property Investments Ltd.* (1968) 19 P. & C.R. 620, 642–643, *per* Roskill J. and *Middlegate Properties Ltd.* v. *Gidlow-Jackson* (1977) 34 P. & C.R. 4, (C.A.), (landlords' claim to recover costs of s. 146 notice under a clause in the lease held not subject to the 1938 Act, as such a claim was for a debt, not damages).

[80] s. 18(2) of the Landlord and Tenant Act 1927.

[81] Recorded Delivery Service Act 1962.

to the last known place of abode[82] in the United Kingdom of such person.[83]

In *Church Commissioners For England* v. *Ve-Ri-Best Manufacturing Co. Ltd.*[84] the landlords served on the tenants and on the mortgagees of the demised premises a section 146 notice complying with the requirements of the 1938 Act. The mortgagees served a counter-notice claiming the benefit of the Act but no such counter-notice was served by the tenants. The landlords then issued proceedings, without first obtaining leave of the court, against the tenants claiming damages for breach of covenant to repair and possession. It was held that the landlords did not require leave of the court before commencing their action because the tenants had not served a counter-notice and could not rely on the counter-notice served by the mortgagees upon whom there was no obligation, under either section 146 of the 1925 Act or section 1(1) of the 1938 Act, to serve notice of a breach of covenant.[85] Where, however, the landlord has obtained leave to commence proceedings against the tenant, and the tenant subsequently assigns the lease, the landlord cannot bring an action against the assignee without fresh leave. Thus, in *Church Commissioners For England* v. *Kanda*[86] the landlord served notice on the tenant requiring that various breaches of the covenant to repair be remedied. The tenant duly served a counter-notice under the 1938 Act and the landlord obtained leave of the court to commence proceedings against the tenant to enforce his right of forfeiture. The tenant then assigned the lease to an assignee. The landlord's proceedings, which were initially brought against the tenant, were later amended so as to join the assignee as a defendant but no application was made by the landlord under the 1938 Act to commence proceedings against the assignee. The Court of Appeal held that (a) it was not necessary for the landlord to serve on the assignee a fresh section 146 notice, since service of the notice on the tenant who was the "lessee" at the time when the notice was served, was sufficient compliance with section 146(1) but (b) since the tenant had served a counter-notice on the landlord, the action could not lawfully be brought against the assignee without further leave being obtained pursuant to section 1(3) of the 1938 Act.

The landlord's action for forfeiture will invariably be coupled with a

---

[82] The term "place of abode" may include the tenant's business address: *Price* v. *West London Investment Building Society* [1964] 1 W.L.R. 616, (C.A.).

[83] s. 18(2) of the 1927 Act. The person is deemed to have knowledge of the fact that the notice has been served as from the time at which the letter would have been delivered in the ordinary course of post.

[84] [1957] 1 Q.B. 238.

[85] There is, no doubt, however, that a mortgagee may have a substantial interest in the outcome of the proceedings. Contrast *Grand Junction Co. Ltd.* v. *Bates* [1954] 2 Q.B. 160, where it was held that s. 146(4) of the 1925 Act is wide enough to cover a legal mortgagee or chargee including an underlessee-mortgagee.

[86] [1958] 1 Q.B. 332.

claim for damages. Here again, the landlord's claim is restricted by statute, namely, section 18(1) of the Landlord and Tenant Act 1927, which limits any damages to the diminution in value of the reversion and which specifically provides that no damages can be recovered where, at the end of the lease, the premises will either be demolished or altered in such a way that would render any repairs valueless.[87-88]

Finally, it may be mentioned that, under section 2 of the 1938 Act, a landlord on whom a counter-notice is served under the Act is not entitled to the benefit of section 146(3) of the Law of Property Act 1925 (relating to solicitors' and surveyors' costs incurred by the landlord in reference to breaches of covenant) so far as regards any costs or expenses incurred in reference to the breach in question, unless he makes an application for leave to take proceedings. On such application, the court has power to direct whether, and to what extent, the landlord is to be entitled to the benefit thereof.[89-90] If, however, the landlord waives the forfeiture at the instance of the tenant, he will lose the benefit of section 146(3) but the landlord will still be entitled to rely in such circumstances on any express covenant in the lease requiring the tenant to pay the expenses incurred by the landlord in, or in contemplation of, proceedings under section 146 of the 1925 Act.

Residential tenancies

(1) *Under the Rent Act 1977*

It should be mentioned that in the case of a dwelling-house let on a protected tenancy or subject to a statutory tenancy within the meaning of the Rent Act 1977, the power of the court to grant possession is restricted by section 98 of that Act. In this connection, the landlord must, in addition to showing that the contractual tenancy has determined at common law (*e.g.* by forfeiture), establish that his case falls within one or more of the grounds for possession listed in Schedule 15 to the Act. Moreover, the court will not make an order for possession in relation to any of the discretionary grounds for possession listed in Part I of Schedule 15 unless it considers it would be reasonable to make such an order.[91]

Although, at common law, a sub-tenancy will come to an end automatically on the forfeiture of the tenancy out of which it was created,[92] the

---

[87-88] See further, "Construction and Enforcement of Repairing Obligations in Leases", M. Pawlowski, Construction Law Journal, (1990) Vol. 6/2 113.

[89-90] See, *e.g.* the directions made in *Phillips* v. *Price* [1959] Ch. 181, 191, and *Re Metropolitan Film Studios Ltd.* v. *Twickenham Film Studios Ltd.* [1962] 1 W.L.R. 1315, 1325.

[91] s. 98(1) of the 1977 Act.

[92] *Great Western Railway Co.* v. *Smith* (1876) 2 Ch.D. 235, 253, *per* Mellish L.J.; *Parker* v. *Jones* [1910] 2 K.B. 32.

security of tenure of certain sub-tenants of residential premises may in that event be preserved by section 137 of the Rent Act 1977.

(2) *Under the Housing Act 1988*

In relation to an assured tenancy under the Housing Act 1988, the statement contained in section 5(1) of the Act that a fixed term tenancy can be brought to an end by a landlord who exercises a power contained in the lease to determine it in certain circumstances has no application to a right of re-entry or proviso for forfeiture for breach of any term or condition of the tenancy.[93] Accordingly, a landlord who discovers that his tenant is in breach of covenant and who wishes to forfeit the tenancy must initiate possession proceedings in accordance with the procedure[94] laid down by the 1988 Act. Moreover, the landlord must be entitled under the terms of the tenancy to bring the tenancy to an end on the ground for possession in question[95] by forfeiture, re-entry or notice.[96]

Where the tenancy is an assured shorthold tenancy under the 1988 Act, the right of the landlord to recover possession before the expiry of the fixed term under the provisions applicable to assured tenancies generally, is expressly preserved under section 21(1) of the Act.

(3) *Under Part I of the Landlord and Tenant Act 1954*

The reader is referred to Chapter 10, p. 281.

(4) *Under the Leasehold Reform Act 1967*

Paragraph 4(1) of Schedule 3 to the Leasehold Reform Act 1967[97] provides as follows:

> "Where a tenant makes a claim to acquire the freehold or an extended lease of any property, then during the currency of the claim no proceedings to enforce any right of re-entry or forfeiture terminating the tenancy shall be brought in any court without the leave of that court, and leave shall not be granted unless the court is satisfied that the claim was not made in good faith; but where leave is granted, the claim shall cease to have effect."

---

[93] See s. 45(4) of the 1988 Act.
[94] Essentially, this involves the service of a notice of proceedings for possession on the assured tenant prior to commencing an action for possession: See s. 8 of the 1988 Act.
[95] As to the grounds for possession of premises subject to an assured tenancy: See Sched. 2 to the 1988 Act.
[96] See s. 7(6)(*b*) of the 1988 Act.
[97] The 1967 Act (and the Leasehold Reform Act 1979) enable tenants of houses held on long leases at low rents to acquire the freehold or an extended lease.

In *Central Estates (Belgravia) Ltd.* v. *Woolgar, Liverpool Corporation* v. *Husan*[98] two tenants holding long leases at low rents claimed under the 1967 Act to acquire the freehold and an extended lease of two respective properties. In the first case, the tenant had been convicted in the previous month of unlawfully keeping a brothel at the premises and, in the second case, the tenant had allowed the premises to fall into a very poor state of repair and there was no prospect of his complying with the repairing covenants in the lease. The respective landlords applied for leave to enforce their rights of forfeiture under paragraph 4(1) of Schedule 3 to the 1967 Act. The Court of Appeal held that the landlords had rightly been granted leave since, in the first case, the tenant by his conviction had exposed himself to forfeiture for which relief would not be granted[99] and, in the second case, the tenant simply wanted to avoid the just consequences of his breaches of covenant to repair. In each case, therefore, the tenants' claims had not been made "in good faith" within the meaning of paragraph 4(1). In the course of his judgment, Lord Denning M.R. said[1]:

> "To my mind, under this statute a claim is made 'in good faith' when it is made honestly and with no ulterior motive. It must be made by the tenant honestly in the belief that he has a lawful right to acquire the freehold or an extended lease, and it must be made without any ulterior motive, such as to avoid the just consequences of his own misdeeds or failures. If the landlord asserts that the tenant's claim is not made in good faith, the burden is on the landlord to satisfy the court that the tenant, in making the claim, was acting dishonestly or with an ulterior motive."

The Court of Appeal[2] stressed that a tenant would not be debarred from enfranchisement simply because the premises were out of repair since a tenant would normally be granted relief against forfeiture on his undertaking to do the repairs within a reasonable period of time. In the present case, however, the tenant had not done the repairs and had no prospect of doing them in the future. In the words of Megaw L.J.[3]:

> "... if a tenant makes a claim for an extended lease under the Act, knowing of his inability, or recklessly disregarding the question of his ability, to perform essential obligations of the extended lease, the claim is not made honestly."

---

[98] [1972] 1 Q.B. 48, (C.A.).
[99] Relief from forfeiture is very rarely given for a breach which casts a "stigma" on the premises.
[1] *Ibid*, 55.
[2] *Ibid*, 59.
[3] *Ibid*, 60.

Business tenancies

The landlord's common law right to terminate a business tenancy on the ground of forfeiture is expressly preserved by section 24(2) of the Landlord and Tenant Act 1954.

Agricultural tenancies

(1) *Under the Agricultural Holdings Act 1986*

Forfeiture of an agricultural holding is not excluded by the Agricultural Holdings Act 1986 but the proviso for re-entry must include a provision stating that the landlord's right to forfeit is only exercisable on the expiry of notice to the tenant of a sufficient duration (of more than one month) to enable the tenant to serve certain notices claiming compensation under the Act. Moreover, the landlord's section 146 notice must (where the breach is capable of remedy) give the tenant a reasonable time to remedy the breach. Thus, in *Parry* v. *Million Pigs Ltd.*[4] a forfeiture clause was held void as providing for re-entry without notice thereby frustrating the possible rights of the tenant to give the necessary notices under section 34(2) and section 56 of the Agricultural Holdings Act 1948.[5] In addition, the landlord's section 146 notice was held invalid as the time of six months allowed to remedy the breaches of covenant was too short to be reasonable.

(2) *Under the Rent Agriculture Act 1976*

The Rent Agriculture Act 1976 gives security of tenure (broadly similar to that enjoyed by Rent Act tenants) to agricultural workers provided with tied cottages or other residential accommodation by their employers. In order to obtain possession of such accommodation, the landlord must establish that the contractual tenancy has come to an end (*e.g.* by expiry, notice to quit, surrender, forfeiture, etc.) and that one or more of the grounds for possession contained in Schedule 4 to the Act apply.[6] The grounds available are based on those applicable to an ordinary Rent Act tenant.

Abandoned premises

Abandonment of the demised premises by the tenant does not of itself

---

[4] (1981) 260 E.G. 281.
[5] See now, ss. 60(6) and 70(2) of the Agricultural Holdings Act 1986.
[6] See s. 6 of the 1976 Act.

entitle the landlord to forfeit the lease unless it amounts to a breach of covenant (and the lease contains a proviso for re-entry) or condition. Invariably, in such circumstances, the tenant will have absconded without paying rent so that the landlord will have a ground for forfeiture based on non-payment of rent which will entitle him (assuming that formal demand has been dispensed with or statutorily excepted) to physically re-enter the premises without the necessity of a formal notice under section 146. Moreover, assuming the premises have been abandoned, there will be no statutory restrictions[7] on his right to exercise actual re-entry.

In the case of any breach (other than non-payment of rent), the landlord will be obliged to serve a section 146 notice on the tenant although, except where the breach is of a repairing covenant,[8] there will be no necessity to show that the notice actually reached the tenant.[9]

Apart from relying on the law of forfeiture, the landlord may have resort to section 16 of the Distress for Rent Act 1737 which provides a means by which a landlord may, in certain circumstances, recover possession of premises left uncultivated or unoccupied. The section,[10] however, only applies where the premises were let at a rack rent or at a rent of three-quarters of their yearly value and half a year's rent is in arrear and where the tenant has deserted the premises and left them uncultivated or unoccupied "so as no sufficient distress can be had to countervail the arrears of rent". The landlord's application must be made to the local magistrates and two or more of them[11] will then be obliged to visit the demised premises and affix a notice of a second visit to take place in not less than 14 day's time. If, on the second visit, the rent arrears have not been paid (or there is no sufficient distress on the premises), the magistrates may give the landlord possession.

There is no doubt that, in view of the cumbersome nature of this procedure, the landlord's remedy of actual re-entry is to be preferred.

For the sake of completeness, mention should also be made of section 54 of the Landlord and Tenant Act 1954, which provides:

> "Where a landlord, having power to serve a notice to quit, on an application to the county court satisfies the court –
>
> (a) that he has taken all reasonable steps to communicate with the person last known to him to be the tenant, and has failed to do so,

---

[7] See, s. 6 of the Criminal Law Act 1977 and s. 2 of the Protection from Eviction Act 1977.
[8] See, s. 18(2) of the Landlord and Tenant Act 1927.
[9] See, s. 196 of the Law of Property Act 1925 and s. 1 of the Recorded Delivery Service Act 1962.
[10] As amended by the Deserted Tenements Act 1817.
[11] Or, in the Metropolitan Police District, a police constable: s. 13 of the Metropolitan Police Courts Act 1839.

(b) that during the period of six months ending with the date of the application neither the tenant nor any person claiming under him has been in occupation of the property comprised in the tenancy or any part thereof, and

(c) that during the said period either no rent was payable by the tenant or the rent payable has not been paid,

the court may if it thinks fit by order determine the tenancy as from the date of the order."

This provision is, clearly, of limited application since it applies only where the landlord has power to give a notice to quit and merely enables the court to terminate the tenancy despite the fact that such a notice cannot be served on the tenant.

Chapter Six

Waiver of forfeiture

Introduction

In an early case,[1] Lord Mansfield observed[2]:

> "Cases of forfeiture are not favoured in law; and where the forfeiture is once waived, the Court will not assist."

Whenever a landlord wishes to forfeit a lease[2a] for breach of a tenant's covenant or condition in the lease, he must take care not to do anything which may constitute, as a matter of law, an unequivocal election to treat the lease as continuing and so operate as a waiver of the tenant's act of forfeiture.[3] It has already been mentioned elsewhere[4] that an act of forfeiture on the part of the tenant only renders the lease voidable (and not void) at the option of the landlord. The landlord is, therefore, obliged to make an election[5] as soon as he becomes aware of the tenant's default either to forfeit the lease or, alternatively, to treat the lease as still continuing by waiving the act of forfeiture. Further, once the landlord has elected

---

[1] *Goodright* d. *Walter* v. *Davids* (1778) 2 Cowp. 804; 98 E.R. 1371. The common law doctrine of waiver was from early times viewed as a means of mitigating the harshness of the remedy of forfeiture.

[2] *Ibid.* p. 804; p. 1371.

[2a] As to the application of the doctrine of waiver to equitable leases: See *Forfeiture of Equitable Leases*, P. Sparkes, (1987) 16 Anglo-American L.Rev. 160, pp. 166–167.

[3] The reader may wish to contemplate the following remarks of Sachs J. in *Segal Securities Ltd.* v. *Thoseby* [1963] 1 Q.B. 887, 889: "When one approaches the law relating to waiver of forfeiture, one comes upon a field—one might say a minefield—in which it is necessary to tread with diffidence and warily. That is to no small degree due to the number of points in that field that are of a highly technical nature, originating in the days before the court was able to grant relief, if at all, with such freedom as it can nowadays." Early cases on waiver are collected in the note to *Dumpor's Case* (1603) 4 Co. Rep. 119 (*b*) in Smith, *Leading Cases In Equity* (13th. ed., 1929) Vol 1, pp. 38–44.

[4] See Chap. 3, pp. 67–68.

[5] The waiver of a right to forfeit falls to be treated as an aspect of the wider doctrine of election: *Kammins Ballrooms Co. Ltd.* v. *Zenith Investments (Torquay) Ltd.* [1971] A.C. 850, 883, *per* Lord Diplock. Essentially, the rule is designed to prevent the landlord from taking up two inconsistent positions. He cannot be allowed to both approbate and reprobate.

one way or the other, he will be irrevocably bound by that election. In the words of Buckley L.J. in *Central Estates (Belgravia) Ltd.* v. *Woolgar (No. 2)*[6]:

> "If the landlord by word or deed manifests to the tenant by an unequivocal act a concluded decision to elect in a particular manner, he will be bound by such an election. If he chooses to do something such as demanding or receiving rent which can only be done consistently with the existence of a certain state of affairs, *viz.*, the continuance of the lease or tenancy in operation, he cannot thereafter be heard to say that that state of affairs did not then exist."

Acknowledgment of lease with knowledge of the breach

If, with knowledge of the breach, a landlord acknowledges to his tenant the continued existence of the tenancy,[7] he will be taken to have elected not to forfeit the lease. As Parker J. said in *Matthews* v. *Smallwood*[8]:

> "Waiver of a right of re-entry can only occur where the lessor, with knowledge of the facts upon which his right to re-enter arises, does some unequivocal act recognising the continued existence of the lease."

It is also clear that whether a particular act, coupled with the requisite knowledge of the breach, constitutes a waiver is a question of law to be considered objectively without regard to the intention of the landlord or the belief or understanding of the tenant.[9] In *Expert Clothing Service & Sales Ltd.* v. *Hillgate House Ltd.*,[10] the Court of Appeal drew a distinction between cases involving the acceptance of (or demand for) rent where the legal effect of the acceptance or demand was clear, and other cases not involving the acceptance of or demand for rent. In the latter category, the court is free to look at all the circumstances of the case to consider whether the act relied on as amounting to a waiver was so unequivocal that, when considered objectively, it could only be regarded as having been done consistently with the continued existence of the tenancy.[11]

---

[6] [1972] 1 W.L.R. 1045, 1054. See also, *Scarfe* v. *Jardine* (1882) 7 App. Cas. 345, 360–361, *per* Lord Blackburn.

[7] *Ward* v. *Day* (1864) 5 B. & S. 359, 362; *Re Garrud, ex p. Newitt* (1881) 16 Ch. D. 522, 533, *per* Cotton L.J.

[8] [1910] 1 Ch. 777, 786.

[9] *Matthews* v. *Smallwood* [1910] 1 Ch. 777, 786, *per* Parker J. cited with approval in *Oak Property Co. Ltd.* v. *Chapman* [1947] K.B. 886, 898, *per* Somervell L.J., (C.A.). See also, *Croft* v. *Lumley* (1858) 6 H.L.C. 672; 10 E.R. 1459; *Windmill Investments (London) Ltd.* v. *Milano Restaurants Ltd.* [1962] 2 Q.B. 373, *per* Megaw L.J. and *Segal Securities Ltd.* v. *Thoseby* [1963] 1 Q.B. 887, 898, *per* Sachs J. The contrary view put forward by Harman J. in *Creery* v. *Summersell and Flowerdew & Co. Ltd.* [1949] 1 Ch. 751, no longer represents the law.

[10] [1985] 3 W.L.R. 359.

[11] *Ibid.* p. 376, *per* Slade L.J.

Since it is irrelevant *quo animo* an act of waiver was made,[12] knowledge of the breach by the landlord's agent will be sufficient even where the act of acknowledgment of the lease is that of another agent who is unaware of the breach. Thus, in *Central Estates (Belgravia) Ltd.* v. *Woolgar (No. 2)*,[13] the landlords' managing agents instructed their staff to refuse all rent from the tenant, who had been convicted of unlawfully keeping a brothel at the demised premises. The instructions failed to reach one of the clerks who sent out a routine demand for the quarter's rent and a subsequent receipt. The Court of Appeal held that the landlords' demand for and acceptance of the rent through their agents, with knowledge of the breach, effected a waiver of the forfeiture. Lord Denning M.R. said[14]:

> "The principal cannot escape the doctrine of waiver by saying that one clerk had the knowledge and the other received the rent. They must be regarded as one for this purpose. The landlords' agents knew the position and they accepted the rent with knowledge. That is a waiver."

The fact that in this case the landlords' agents did not intend to waive the forfeiture made no difference to the result.

The knowledge required to put a landlord to his election whether to waive an act of forfeiture is knowledge of the basic facts that in law constitute a breach of covenant (or condition) entitling him to forfeit the lease. In the classic words of Parker J. in *Matthews* v. *Smallwood*[15]:

> "It is not enough that [the landlord] should do the act which recognizes, or appears to recognize, the continued existence of the lease, unless, at the time when the act is done, he has knowledge of the facts under which, or from which, his right of entry arose."

A landlord must be fully aware of the facts establishing a breach of

---

[12] Contrast the position where a new tenancy is sought to be set up by acceptance of rent: *Doe d. Cheny* v. *Batten* (1775) 1 Cowp. 243, 245; 98 E.R. 1066, 1067, *per* Lord Mansfield; *Maconochie Bros. Ltd.* v. *Brand* [1946] 2 All E.R. 778; *Clarke* v. *Grant* [1950] 1 K.B. 104; *Longrigg Burrough & Trounson* v. *Smith* (1979) 251 E.G. 847; *Cardiothoracic Institute* v. *Shrewdcrest Ltd.* [1986] 2 E.G.L.R. 57; *Javad* v. *Aqil* [1991] 1 E.G.L.R. 82 and *Land* v. *Sykes* [1991] 1 E.G.L.R. 18. For a review of the relevant caselaw: See, "*When is it Safe to Accept Rent?*", (Blunden Memorial Lecture), J. Brock, [1992] E.G. 9248, p. 108.

[13] [1972] 1 W.L.R. 1048. For an interesting note on the case: See, *Forfeiture—Waiver and Relief*, Eric C.H. Owen, (1972) 122 N.L.J. 719.

[14] *Ibid.* p. 1052.

[15] [1910] 1 Ch. 777, 786, referred to in *Peyman* v. *Lanjani* [1985] 2 W.L.R. 154, 177, where the Court of Appeal held that where a party was faced with the option whether to affirm or rescind a contract, that party should not be held to have made an irrevocable election unless he/she had knowledge not only of the facts which give rise to the election but also of the right to elect itself. It is submitted, however, that a landlord, who has acted with knowledge of the facts giving rise to the right to forfeit, will be unable to successfully contend that he has not waived the right to forfeit because he did not know of its existence: See, *ibid*, 177 and 181, *per* Stephenson L.J. See also, *Kammins Ballrooms Co. Ltd.* v. *Zenith Investments (Torquay) Ltd.* [1971] A.C. 850, 883, *per* Lord Diplock.

covenant before he will be held to have waived the breach.[16] Thus, in *Chrisdell Ltd.* v. *Johnson*,[17] the tenant left his flat to go abroad and engaged a housekeeper to supervise the premises in his absence. The landlords' agents discovered that the housekeeper was in occupation of the flat but were assured by the tenant that no sub-letting or assignment of the tenancy into her name had taken place. Subsequently, the freehold reversion was acquired by the plaintiffs, who commenced proceedings for possession of the premises alleging that the tenant had sub-let the flat in breach of covenant. The Court of Appeal held that the landlords had not waived the breach since, in the light of the tenant's representation that he was still in occupation of the premises, it could not be said that they knew all the necessary facts to establish that the tenant had sub-let to the housekeeper and so was in breach of his tenancy agreement. Glidewell L.J. said[18]:

> "If a landlord receives a representation from his tenant which, if true, means that there has been no breach and if the landlord, not being sufficiently confident of the untruth of what the tenant says, decides not to take proceedings but proceeds on the basis that what the tenant says is true, then, in my judgment, it cannot later be said that he knew all the necessary facts to establish a breach."

In essence, the reasoning of the *Chrisdell* case is that where a landlord suspects that a tenant might be in breach of the terms of his lease but is not sufficiently confident that the court would disbelieve the tenant's denial of that allegation, a failure to take any action against the tenant and a continued acceptance of rent will not amount to a waiver of the breach. In order, however, to bring the *Chrisdell* principle into play, there must be a mere suspicion that a breach has been committed by the tenant coupled with a clear explanation and denial on the other side. These ingredients were found to be lacking in *Van Haarlam* v. *Kasner Charitable Trust*[18a] where Harman J. distinguished the *Chrisdell* case and held that the demand and receipt of rent, with knowledge that the tenant had been arrested for offences under the Official Secrets Acts, were sufficient acts which amounted to an affirmation of the tenancy and waived the right of forfeiture. In the instant case, there was clear evidence that the landlords believed that the tenant had committed various spying activities on the premises which amounted to an illegal user in breach of covenant.

The fact, however, that the landlord is ignorant or has doubts as to whether the facts amount in law to a breach is immaterial. In *David*

---

[16] See, *e.g. Atkin* v. *Rose* [1923] 1 Ch. 522, 537, *per* P.O. Lawrence J.
[17] (1987) 54 P. & C.R. 257.
[18] *Ibid.* p. 264.
[18a] [1992] 36 E.G. 135.

Blackstone Ltd. v. *Burnetts (West End) Ltd.*,[19] the lease contained a qualified covenant against subletting. The landlords consented to a subletting to a Mr. Atkins and a Mr. Davis on the misunderstanding that they were trading in partnership. The underlease, however, was executed to Flat Finders Ltd., a company of which Mr. Atkins was the managing director and Mr. Davis the secretary. The tenant informed the landlords' solicitors that the subletting had been executed to the company. Ten days later, while the solicitors were considering the legal implications of the subletting, an employee of the landlords' associated company in Leeds sent out a routine demand for rent. Swanwick J. held that once the landlords' agents knew the basic facts which in law constituted the breach, an appropriate act by the landlords or their agents would effect a waiver, their knowledge or ignorance of the law being irrelevant. The learned Judge, therefore, concluded that the landlords had sufficient knowledge of the breach to render the demand for rent a waiver of forfeiture. As to the moment in time when knowledge of the breach was to be assessed, Swanwick J. said[20]:

> ". . . for there to be a valid election to waive a breach, the landlord or his agent must have sufficient knowledge of the breach before despatching the document making the election, but . . . such election does not become effective until it is communicated to the tenant."

It appears that constructive knowledge of the basic facts that in law constitute a breach is not sufficient to put a landlord to his election whether to waive an act of forfeiture. In *Official Custodian of Charities* v. *Parway Estates Developments Ltd.*,[21] the Court of Appeal held that the landlords had not waived their right to forfeit the lease by accepting rent after the tenant had gone into liquidation because, at the time they accepted the rent, they did not know of the winding-up proceedings. The landlords had, in fact, no actual knowledge of the proceedings and official notification in the London Gazette of the making of the winding-up order and the appointment of the liquidator were held not to constitute constructive notice of these events. On the latter point, the Court held that, on the true construction of section 9(3) and (4) of the European Communities Act 1972, official notification of these various matters did not impute knowledge or notice of the same to the whole world.

On the other hand, in *Metropolitan Properties Co. Ltd.* v. *Cordery*,[22] a breach consisting of an unlawful subletting was held by the Court of

---

[19] [1973] 1 W.L.R. 1487. See also, *Bader Properties Ltd.* v. *Linley Property Investments Ltd.* (1968) 19 P. & C.R. 620 (landlords held to have knowledge of a breach of covenant against underletting, albeit that they did not know the precise terms on which the unlawful underletting had been effected).
[20] *Ibid.*, p. 1499.
[21] (1984) 270 E.G. 1077.
[22] (1980) 39 P. & C.R. 10.

Appeal to be waived where rent was accepted after the landlords' employee (a porter in a block of flats) learned of the facts, it being his duty to report them to the landlords. In this case, the landlords were held to have imputed knowledge of the basic facts through their agent having notice of them.

The onus is on the tenant to give evidence of (a) an act on the part of the landlord unequivocally recognising the subsistence of the lease and (b) the landlord's knowledge of the breach at the time when that act is performed.[23] Thus, mere proof of an act showing recognition of the tenancy will not throw the onus of proving want of knowledge on the landlord.[24]

Because the consequence of a particular act relied on as a waiver is a matter of law and not of the parties' intention, the landlord cannot avoid a waiver by accepting or demanding rent "under protest" or "without prejudice" to his right of re-entry.[25] In the words of Parker J. in *Matthews v. Smallwood*[26]:

> "If, knowing of the breach, he does distrain, or does receive the rent, then by law he waives the breach, and nothing which he can say by way of protest against the law will avail him anything."

Thus, in *Windmill Investments (London) Ltd.* v. *Milano Restaurants Ltd.*,[27] the landlords' acceptance of rent expressly "without prejudice" to the tenant's breach of covenant against parting with possession of the premises was held to constitute a waiver in law. Megaw J. said[28]:

> "Once it is decided as a fact that the money was tendered and accepted as rent, the question of its consequences as a waiver is a matter of law."

In *Segal Securities Ltd.* v. *Thoseby*,[29] the landlords had served the tenant with a notice, under section 146 of the Law of Property Act 1925, requiring him to remedy a breach of covenant as to the user of the demised premises. Subsequently, the landlords by a letter headed "without prejudice" demanded a quarter's rent payable in advance, the letter stating

---

[23] *Matthews* v. *Smallwood* [1910] 1 Ch. 777, 787, *per* Parker J. and *Atkin* v. *Rose* [1923] 1 Ch. 522, 537, *per* P. O. Lawrence J. See also, *Pennant's Case* (1596) 3 Co. Rep. 64a; 76 E.R. 775; *Harvey* v. *Oswald* (1597) Cro. Eliz. 553; 78 E.R. 798 and *Roe d. Gregson* v. *Harrison* (1788) 2 T.R. 425; 100 E.R. 229.

[24] *Fuller's Theatre and Vaudeville Company Ltd.* v. *Rofe* [1923] A.C. 435, 443.

[25] *Croft* v. *Lumley* (1858) 6 H.L.C. 672, 725; 10 E.R. 1459, 1480, *per* Williams J.; *Davenport* v. *The Queen* (1877) 3 App. Cas. 115, 131–132, *per* Sir Montague E. Smith; *Oak Property Co. Ltd.* v. *Chapman* [1947] K.B. 886, 898, *per* Somervell L.J. and *Central Estates (Belgravia) Ltd.* v. *Woolgar (No. 2)* [1972] 1 W.L.R. 1048, 1054, *per* Buckley L.J.

[26] (1910) 1 Ch. 777, 786–787.

[27] [1962] 2 Q.B. 373.

[28] *Ibid.*, p. 376.

[29] [1963] 1 Q.B. 887.

that the "demand and receipt for rent is made or given without prejudice to the service of the notice . . . and to any breaches of covenant in respect of user". Sachs J. held that a demand (or acceptance) of rent "without prejudice" operated as a waiver of the tenant's act of forfeiture. In this respect, the landlord's act of waiver is deemed to "speak louder than his words"[30] because it is the *act* (for example, of demanding or accepting rent) which unequivocally demonstrates the landlord's election to affirm the lease. The principle will also apply to a situation where the landlord waives the forfeiture by conduct even though the lease requires a waiver to be expressed in writing. Thus, in *R. v. Paulson*,[31] the Crown granted a mining lease of land in Canada, which provided that no waiver of any breach should take effect unless it was expressed in writing. The tenant failed to commence mining operations within the time-period stipulated in the lease. The Judicial Committee of the Privy Council held that the Crown had elected to treat the lease as subsisting by accepting rent from the tenant, with knowledge of the breach, despite the fact that such act did not constitute a waiver in writing as required under the terms of the lease.

Where rent is received by the landlord's agent who has no authority to accept it, the receipt may not constitute a waiver by the landlord if he rejects the payment as quickly as the circumstances permit it. In such case, the acceptance of rent by the agent may be treated as provisional upon the landlord's decision whether to accept or reject it.[32]

Effect of waiver depends on the nature of the breach

The effect of a waiver will depend upon the nature of the breach giving rise to the landlord's election to forfeit. In this connection, the tenant's breach will be classified either as a "continuing" breach or, alternatively, as a "once and for all" breach. It will be convenient to consider these two categories of breach separately.

(1) *Continuing breach*

If the breach is of a continuing nature, there is a continually recurring

---

[30] *Central Estates (Belgravia) Ltd. v. Woolgar (No. 2)* [1972] 1 W.L.R. 1048, 1054, *per* Buckley L.J.
[31] [1921] 1 A.C. 271. See also, *Inner City Businessmen's Club* v. *James Kirkpatrick Ltd.* [1975] 2 N.Z.L.R. 636. It is submitted that a clause in the lease purporting to contract out of the doctrine of waiver is wholly ineffectual: See, *R. v. Paulson* [1921] 1 A.C. 271, 283 and *Expert Clothing Services & Sales Ltd.* v. *Hillgate House Ltd.* [1985] 3 W.L.R. 359, *per* Slade L.J.
[32] *Mardorf Peach & Co. Ltd.* v. *Attica Sea Carriers Corporation of Liberia, The Laconia* [1977] A.C. 850 (no waiver of right to withdraw from charterparty by acceptance of hire instalment by owners' bank). Contrast *Central Estates (Belgravia) Ltd.* v. *Woolgar (No. 2)* [1972] 1 W.L.R. 1048, where the landlords' agents had full authority to manage the premises and accept rent on behalf of the landlord.

cause of forfeiture and the waiver will operate only in relation to past breaches, that is to say, breaches committed in the period prior to the landlord's act which constitutes the waiver.[33] Thus, a landlord who has waived a continuing breach for a period of time will not be precluded from subsequently ending his waiver and enforcing the covenant in the lease.[34]

Because the breach is continuing, a fresh right of forfeiture will arise after the act of waiver, but the landlord may lose his right to forfeit if he becomes estopped by his conduct from relying on the tenant's non-performance of the covenant. Thus, in *City and Westminster Properties (1934) Ltd.* v. *Mudd*,[35] the landlords' agent verbally informed the tenant, prior to the execution of a new lease of the premises, that if he signed the lease the landlord would not seek to enforce against him the covenants in the lease requiring him to use the premises as a shop only. The tenant, having signed the lease on the faith of this assurance, was held entitled to rely on the same so long as he was in occupation of the premises and the landlords' action for forfeiture on the ground of breach of the user covenants was dismissed.

Apart from estoppel, the landlord's right of forfeiture may be barred by evidence of acts of waiver which are so continuous or prolonged as to amount to a new agreement for letting or a licence or release of the tenant's covenant. In order, however, to preclude a landlord from forfeiting a lease for a continuing breach of covenant, acquiescence in the breach for a very long period of time must be shown. For example, in *Gibson* v. *Doeg*,[36] the tenant converted the premises into a public-house and grocery shop in breach of covenant and the landlord, with full knowledge of the breach for more than 20 years, continued to receive rent from the tenant. It was held that the user of the premises in their altered state during this period, with the landlord's knowledge, was evidence from which a jury might presume that the landlord had licensed the use of the premises in breach of covenant. In *Gibbon* v. *Payne*,[37] the tenant of a plot of land covenanted with the landlord to complete a coach-house and stable on the land within six months to the satisfaction of the landlord and to keep in repair the demised buildings. No coach-house or stable was ever built, the landlord accepting rent from the tenant for a period of nearly 40 years. An assignee of the landlord then sought to forfeit the lease for the continuing breach of covenant. A.T. Lawrence J. held that the true in-

---

[33] *Doe* d. *Rankin* v. *Brindley* (1832) 4 B. & Ad. 84; 110 E.R. 387 (receipt of rent due pending a notice to repair held no waiver of subsequent forfeiture occasioned by continuing breach of covenant to repair) and *Doe* d. *Baker* v. *Jones* (1850) 5 Exch. 498; 155 E.R. 218 (receipt of rent no waiver of continuing breach of covenant to repair).

[34] See, *e.g. Cooper* v. *Henderson* (1982) 263 E.G. 592 (C.A.), where the landlord withdrew his waiver after a period of one year.

[35] [1959] 1 Ch. 129.

[36] (1858) 2 H. & N. 623; 157 E.R. 253.

[37] (1905) 22 T.L.R. 54.

ference from the facts was that the parties intended to release the covenant to repair as regards the coach-house and stable. In *Hepworth v. Pickles*,[38] the period of acquiescence amounted to over 24 years and this was held to constitute a waiver or release of the covenant in question. Farwell J. said[39]:

> ". . . if you find a long course of usage, such as in the present case for twenty-four years, which is wholly inconsistent with the continuance of the covenant relied upon, the Court infers some legal proceeding which has put an end to that covenant, in order to show that the usage has been and is now lawful, and not wrongful."

In *In Re Summerson*,[40] a lease gave the landlord a right of re-entry if the premises should at any time be used as an inn, alehouse or spirit shop. The evidence showed that the premises had, with knowledge of the landlords, been uninterruptedly used as a public-house for upwards of 30 years. Romer J. held that this long period of acquiescence by the landlords amounted to either a licence or, alternatively, a release of the covenant. However, by contrast, in *Lloyds Bank v. Jones*,[41] the landlord's conduct in standing by for a period of 17 years without protest at the non-residence of one of two joint tenants on the premises was held not to constitute a release of or acquiescence in the tenant's breach of covenant in the lease. In this case, the facts did not raise any inference of a release of the covenant and in the words of Morris L.J.[42]:

> "It may well be that if [the landlords] accepted rent with knowledge they waived the breaches of covenant from time to time, but I can see no reason why they should be prevented from demanding proper compliance as from the date they required it."

In *Wolfe v. Hogan*,[43] Denning L.J. summarised the position as follows[44]:

> "A breach of covenant not to use premises in a particular way is a continuing breach. Any acceptance of rent by the landlord, after knowledge, only waives the breaches up to the time of the acceptance of rent. It does not waive the continuance of the breach thereafter and, notwithstanding his previous acceptance of rent, the landlord can still proceed for forfeiture on this account. Indeed in the case of a continuing breach, the acceptance of rent, after knowledge, is only a bar to a claim for forfeiture if it goes on for so long, or is

---

[38] [1900] 1 Ch. 108.
[39] *Ibid.* p. 110.
[40] Originally unreported but later appended as a note to *Hepworth v. Pickles* [1900] 1 Ch. 108, 112–113.
[41] [1955] 2 Q.B. 298.
[42] *Ibid.* p. 326.
[43] [1949] 2 K.B. 194.
[44] *Ibid.* p. 205.

accepted in such circumstances, that it can be inferred that the landlord has not merely waived the breach, but has affirmatively consented to the tenant continuing to use the premises as he has done."

In the case of a breach of a repairing covenant (which is of a continuing nature), no new notice under section 146 of the Law of Property Act 1925 will be required in respect of the non-repair after the expiration of the time specified in the notice. Moreover, any subsequent demand or acceptance of rent by the landlord will not affect his right to forfeit in respect of the continuing state of disrepair after the date when the rent fell due.[45] The position may be different if the physical condition of the premises has substantially altered during the period when the notice was given and the action for forfeiture was brought.[46] The point was considered in *New River Company* v. *Crumpton*,[47] where the landlords served a notice, pursuant to section 14 of the Conveyancing and Property Act 1881,[48] requesting the tenant to remedy various breaches of the covenant to repair. Subsequently, the landlords accepted rent from the tenant which had accrued due since the date when the notice expired. Rowlatt J. held that no new notice was necessary to support the landlords' action to recover possession of the premises in respect of the continuing breach of covenant to repair, even though a period of 12 months had elapsed between the date of the expiry of the notice and the commencement of the action and despite the fact that the tenant had done a portion of the repairs in this period so that the physical condition of the premises was no longer the same when the action was brought as when the notice was given. In this case, however, the condition of the premises at the time when the action was brought had not changed materially so as to render the landlord's notice no longer applicable. The tenant had, in fact, only remedied three items out of a long list of required repairs. In this connection, Rowlatt J. said[49]:

"I cannot think that the fact of the tenant doing a small portion of the required repairs makes the notice any the less applicable to the residue which has not been done . . ."

This case may be distinguished from *Guillemard* v. *Silverthorne*,[50] where

---

[45] *Penton* v. *Barnett* [1898] 1 Q.B. 276, (C.A.), applied in *Farimani* v. *Gates* (1984) 271 E.G. 887, (C.A.). See also, *Fryett* d. *Harris* v. *Jeffreys* (1795) 1 Esp. 393; 170 E.R. 395.
[46] *Penton* v. *Barnett* [1898] 1 Q.B. 276, 281–282, *per* Collins L.J. who stressed that "the physical condition of the premises which the tenant was required to make good was the same when the action was brought as when the notice was given."
[47] [1917] 1 K.B. 762.
[48] Predecessor to s. 146 of the Law of Property Act 1925.
[49] *Ibid.* p. 766.
[50] (1908) 99 L.T. 584.

Ridley J. held that, because some repairs had been done by the tenant, this precluded the landlords from relying upon their original notice of non-repair and obliged them, after the lapse of a period of six months, to serve a fresh notice under section 14 of the 1881 Act to support their action for forfeiture based on a continuing breach of the covenant to repair.

The question whether a fresh section 146 notice must be served following the landlord's waiver of a continuing breach of covenant to repair, was recently considered by the Court of Appeal in *Greenwich London Borough Council* v. *Discreet Selling Estates Ltd.*[51] In that case, the landlords had accepted rent after they had served various notices of disrepair under section 146(1) of the Law of Property Act 1925. The Court of Appeal, following *Penton* v. *Barnett*,[52] held that, in the case of a continuing breach, no further notice under section 146 was necessary if there had been no change in the condition of the demised premises since the date of the service of the notice. Staughton L.J., who gave the leading judgment of the Court, thought that no fresh notice was probably necessary where the only change in the condition of the premises was by way of deterioration. In the instant case, however, it was accepted that any deterioration had been minimal and that no improvement in the condition of the premises had taken place between the date of the notices and the commencement of proceedings. Accordingly, no fresh notice was necessary to maintain the landlord's action for possession.

Examples of breaches which are of a continuing nature include (a) breach of a user covenant,[53] (b) breach of a covenant to keep in repair,[54] (c) breach of a covenant to insure[55] and (d) breach of a covenant to work coal mines.[56]

(2) *Once and for all breach*

Where the breach is classified, not as a continuing one, but as a "once and for all breach", the right to forfeit for that breach will be lost upon waiver. The authorities do not provide any clear set of principles to distinguish between a continuing breach on the one hand and a once and

---

[51] [1990] 2 E.G.L.R. 65.

[52] [1898] 1 Q.B. 276, (C.A.).

[53] *Doe* d. *Ambler* v. *Woodbridge* (1829) 9 B. & C. 376; 109 E.R. 140 (covenant not to use rooms for certain purposes) and *Segal Securities Ltd.* v. *Thoseby* [1963] 1 Q.B. 887 (covenant to use premises for the purpose of a private residence in the occupation of one household only); *Creery* v. *Summersell and Flowerdew & Co. Ltd.* [1949] Ch. 751. See also, *Lawrie* v. *Lees* (1880) 14 Ch. D. 249, 262, *per* Bramwell L.J. (user of premises by subtenant contrary to covenant in the headlease). Contrast *Griffin* v. *Tomkins* (1880) 42 L.T. 359.

[54] *Penton* v. *Barnett* [1898] 1 Q.B. 276; *Doe* d. *Baker* v. *Jones* (1850) 5 Ex. 498; 155 E.R. 216 and *Coward* v. *Gregory* (1866) L.R. 2 C.P. 153, 169–170, *per* Erle C.J. (covenant to keep in repair).

[55] *Doe* d. *Flower* v. *Peck* (1830) 1 B. & Ad. 428; 109 E.R. 847 and *Doe* d. *Muston* v. *Gladwin* (1845) 6 Q.B. 953; 115 E.R. 359.

[56] *Doe* d. *Bryan* v. *Bancks* (1821) 4 B. & Ald. 401; 106 E.R. 984.

for all breach, on the other. In *Farimani* v. *Gates*[57] a breach of the obligation to lay out insurance moneys in rebuilding or repairing the demised premises was held to amount to a breach of a single obligation which could only be broken once. The Court of Appeal rejected a suggestion contained in *Emmett On Title*[58] that "if the lessee has it in his power to remedy the breach, it is a continuing breach but if he has not, then it will not be a continuing breach". Griffiths L.J. said[59]:

> "If an obligation is to perform an act by a given time, once that time has elapsed and the act has not been performed, there is a breach of a single obligation and not of a continuing one. The fact that it still lies within the power of the lessee to perform the act cannot affect the nature of his obligation. In this field of law a reference to a continuing breach is a way of referring to breaches of a continuing obligation and does not refer to the ability to remedy a single breach."

Generally speaking, therefore, if the relevant obligation is to perform an act by a given date or within a reasonable period of time, it will fall to be classified as an obligation that can only be broken once. Thus, if the particular act has not been performed by that date or within a reasonable time (as the case may be), there is a single breach of covenant.[60]

Examples of covenants which can only be broken once include (a) a covenant to put premises into repair,[61] (b) a covenant to build before a stated date,[62] (c) a covenant against assigning, subletting and prohibiting any other person from occupying,[63] (d) a covenant to pay rent,[64] (e) covenant to lay out insurance monies[65] and (f) covenant to re-instate premises within a reasonable time[66] and (g) covenant not to make alterations.[66a] It has also been held that the tenant's act of bankruptcy or

---

[57] (1984) 271 E.G. 887, (C.A.).

[58] (18th ed.), pp. 940–941.

[59] (1984) 217 E.G. 887, 888. See also, *Downie* v. *Turner* [1951] 2 K.B. 112, (C.A.) (test whether breach of covenant is continuous or not does not depend solely upon whether it remains in the tenant's power to discontinue it).

[60] *Re King Deceased, Robinson* v. *Gray* [1963] 1 Ch. 459, 478, *per* Lord Denning M.R., referring to a covenant to re-instate premises within a reasonable time after a fire.

[61] *Coward* v. *Gregory* (1866) L.R. 2 C.P. 153, 169–170, *per* Erle C.J.

[62] *Stephens* v. *Junior Army and Navy Stores Ltd.* [1914] 2 Ch. 516, 523, *per* Lord Cozens-Hardy M.R.; *Jardine* v. *Attorney-General for Newfoundland* [1932] A.C. 275, 292, (P.C.) and *Hubbard* v. *Stone* (1961) 180 E.G. 513.

[63] *Walrond* v. *Hawkins* (1875) L.R. 10 C.P. 342; *Scala House & District Property Co. Ltd.* v. *Forbes* [1974] 1 Q.B. 575.

[64] *London & County (A.& D.) Ltd.* v. *Wilfred Sportsman Ltd.* [1969] 1 W.L.R. 1215, 1224, *per* Buckley J., followed in *Church Commissioners for England* v. *Nodjoumi* (1986) 51 P. & C.R. 155, *per* Hirst J.

[65] *Farimani* v. *Gates* (1984) 271 E.G. 887.

[66] *Re King Deceased, Robinson* v. *Gray* [1963] 1 Ch. 459.

[66a] *Iperion Investments Corporation* v. *Broadwalk House Residents Ltd.*, [1992] 2 E.G.L.R. 235, Mr. Recorder Mauleverer Q.C., noted in [1992] E.G. 9236, p. 147 and [1992] E.G. 9237, p. 135.

insolvency constitutes a breach of a single obligation in the lease and not a continuing one.[67]

It is important to bear in mind that an act of waiver will only extend to the breach to which it relates and will not, therefore, operate as a general waiver of the benefit of the covenant unless a contrary intention appears.[68] However, an act of waiver by the landlord may have the effect of barring his right to forfeit not only in respect of a once and for all breach but also in respect of a continuing breach in circumstances where the latter breach is consequential upon and forms an integral part of the former. Thus, in *Griffin* v. *Tomkins*,[69] the tenants converted the premises into a shop and began to carry on a plumber's business thereon in breach of the covenants contained in the lease. It was held that the acceptance of rent by the landlord, with knowledge of the breaches, amounted to a waiver of both acts of forfeiture (*i.e.* the unlawful conversion and user), notwithstanding that the carrying on the business constituted a continuing breach of a user covenant. Similarly, in *Downie* v. *Turner*,[70] the lease contained a covenant against (a) subletting the demised premises without previous consent of the landlord and (b) user of the premises otherwise than as a private dwelling-house. The tenant sublet part of the premises without consent (in breach of the first covenant) for non-residential purposes (in breach of the second covenant). The Court of Appeal held that the landlord's acceptance of rent effected a waiver of both breaches of covenant, notwithstanding that the second breach was of a continuing nature, since both the subletting and the wrongful user of the premises arose out of the same unlawful subtenancy. Since the subletting and the wrongful user formed one indivisible act of forfeiture (as opposed to two separate and distinct breaches of covenant), it was impossible to distinguish the one from the other. In the words of Jenkins L.J.[71]:

> "The truth is that the two breaches are no more than different aspects of one and the same act. If the act in one aspect of it is waived as an available breach of covenant, it seems to me it is necessarily waived as an available breach in its other aspect also."

A waiver of forfeiture for not erecting buildings by a certain date, in accordance with a covenant to build, carries with it a waiver of forfeiture for breach of a covenant to repair the buildings if and when erected.[72]

---

[67] *Doe d. Gatehouse* v. *Rees* (1838) 4 Bing. N.C. 384; 132 E.R. 835.
[68] Section 148 of the Law of Property Act 1925, replacing s. 6 of the Law of Property Amendment Act 1860. Although the section refers to an "actual waiver", it is not limited to an express waiver by a formal written document: *Mills* v. *Griffiths* (1876) 45 L.J.Q.B. 771. See also s. 143(3) of the 1925 Act, (effect of licence on right of re-entry).
[69] (1880) 42 L.T. 359.
[70] [1951] 2 K.B. 112.
[71] *Ibid.* p. 119.
[72] *Stephens* v. *Junior Army and Navy Stores Ltd..* [1914] 2 Ch. 516.

Conduct amounting to waiver (where landlord has knowledge of the breach)

The various acts on the part of the landlord which have been held to constitute a waiver of forfeiture may conveniently be grouped under the following subject headings[73]:

(1) *Demand for rent due after breach*

An unambiguous demand for rent accruing due *after* the breach of covenant will constitute a waiver of forfeiture.[74] In *Doe* d. *Nash* v. *Birch*,[75] the landlord's son demanded rent after a breach of covenant whilst his father was sick. It was held that the son had no authority to waive the breach but Parke B. suggested[76] *obiter* that, if the son had had the requisite authority, his demand of the rent would have amounted to a waiver of the forfeiture. This view has been consistently followed in subsequent case law.[77] In *Welch* v. *Birrane*[78] the landlords refused the tenant permission to assign his lease to sitting sub-tenants in the demised premises on the ground that the proposed assignee might become entitled to enfranchisement under the Leasehold Reform Act 1967. The tenant, nevertheless, assigned the lease as originally intended. The landlords continued to demand rent from the tenant despite the breach of covenant and claimed forfeiture. Lawson J., following the decision of Swanwick J. in *David Blackstone Ltd.* v. *Burnetts (West End) Ltd.*,[79] held that the landlords, by demanding rent accruing due *after* the breach of covenant, had effectively waived the forfeiture. In *Van Haarlam* v. *Kasner Charitable Trust*[80] a lease of a flat provided for re-entry if the flat was used for an illegal purpose. The tenant was convicted of an offence under the Official Secrets Act 1920 and the landlord attempted to forfeit the lease having demanded and accepted rent during the period between the tenant's arrest and conviction. Harman J. held that the right to forfeiture had been waived.

There is, also, little doubt that a demand for rent qualified by such

---

[73] In each case, the reader should assume that the act of waiver is accompanied by the requisite knowledge of the breach on the part of the landlord.
[74] *David Blackstone Ltd.* v. *Burnetts (West End) Ltd.* [1973] 1 W.L.R. 1487, Swanwick J.
[75] (1836) 1 M. & W. 402, 408; 150 E.R. 490.
[76] *Ibid.* p. 408; p. 493.
[77] *Croft* v. *Lumley* (1858) 6 H.L.C. 672, 705; 10 E.R. 1459, 1472, *per* Bramwell B.; *Creery* v. *Summersell and Flowerdew & Co. Ltd.* [1949] Ch. 751, 761, *per* Harman J.; *Segal Securities Ltd.* v. *Thoseby* [1963] 1 Q.B. 887, 899, *per* Sachs J.; *Central Estates (Belgravia) Ltd.* v. *Woolgar (No. 2)* [1972] 1 W.L.R. 1048, 1054, *per* Buckley L.J.; *David Blackstone Ltd.* v. *Burnetts (West End) Ltd.* [1973] 1 W.L.R. 1487, *per* Swanwick J.; *Expert Clothing Service & Sales Ltd.* v. *Hillgate House Ltd.* [1985] 3 W.L.R. 359, 375, *per* Slade L.J.; *Van Haarlam* v. *Kasner Charitable Trust* [1992] 36 E.G. 135, 142, *per* Harman J.
[78] (1975) 29 P. & C.R. 102.
[79] [1973] 1 W.L.R. 1487.
[80] [1992] 36 E.G. 135.

words as "without prejudice" or "under protest" will operate as an effective waiver. In *Segal Securities Ltd.* v. *Thoseby*[81] Sachs J. said[82]:

> "As both demand and acceptance respectively are in law merely different forms of a notification by a landlord of election not to avoid or forfeit the lease, to my mind no distinction can nowadays be drawn between them in relation to a question whether the label 'without prejudice' affects their quality as an election ... Thus, whatever the origin and history of the use of the word 'unqualified' it seems to me that since 1910[83] it should not be so construed as to cause a 'without prejudice' demand to be a qualified demand."

In order to constitute a waiver, the demand must have been communicated to the tenant. Thus, there will be no waiver if the demand has been prepared and sent by the landlord but never received by the tenant.[84] In these circumstances, the uncommunicated rent demand can be withdrawn by the landlord at any time before it is received by the tenant.

Needless to say, the bringing of an *action* for rent accruing due after the breach will also amount to a waiver of the forfeiture. Thus, in *Dendy* v. *Nicholl*,[85] Crowder J. said[86]:

> "Here, the landlord, by bringing an action for rent accruing subsequently to the accrual of the forfeiture, and obtaining payment of the rent by means of that action, has clearly made his election to treat the lessee as still being his tenant. Surely this as unequivocally shows the landlord's determination to treat the lease as an existing lease, as the bringing of an ejectment demonstrates an intention to treat the tenant as trespasser."

(2) *Acceptance of rent due after breach*[87]

An acceptance of rent accruing due *after* the breach of covenant will constitute a waiver of forfeiture.[88] Moreover, an acceptance of rent will

[81] [1963] 1 Q.B. 887.

[82] *Ibid.* p. 899. In *Expert Clothing Service & Sales Ltd.* v. *Hillgate House Ltd.* [1985] 3 W.L.R. 359, 375, Slade L.J. said: "Though we have been referred to no authority binding on this court to this effect, I am also content for present purposes to assume, without finally deciding, that ... a demand for rent will, by itself, have the like effect [of operating as a waiver]."

[83] This is a reference to the dictum of Parker J. in *Matthews* v. *Smallwood* [1910] 1 Ch. 777, 786.

[84] *Trustees of Henry Smith's Charity* v. *Willson* [1983] Q.B. 316 and *David Blackstone Ltd.* v. *Burnetts (West End) Ltd.* [1973] 1 W.L.R. 1487, 1499, *per* Swanwick J.

[85] (1858) 4 C.B. (N.S.) 376; 140 E.R. 1130.

[86] *Ibid.* p. 385; p. 1134.

[87] See, generally, "*When is it Safe to Accept Rent?*", (Blundell Memorial Lecture), S. Copland, [1992] E.G. 9249, p. 74.

[88] *Central Estates (Belgravia) Ltd.* v. *Woolgar (No. 2)* [1972] 1 W.L.R. 1048; *Goodright* d. *Walter* v. *Davids* (1778) 2 Cowp. 803; 98 E.R. 371 and *Arnsby* v. *Woodward* (1827) 6 B. & C. 519; 108 E.R. 542; *Doe* d. *Griffiths* v. *Pritchard* (1833) 5 B. & Ad. 765; 110 E.R. 973; *Miles* v. *Tobin* (1867) 17 L.T. 432.

amount to waiver where it is accepted subject to the rubric "without prejudice."[89] Buckley L.J. in *Central Estates (Belgravia) Ltd.* v. *Woolgar (No. 2)*[90] put the matter succinctly in this way[91]:

> "If at the time of the act he had a right to elect whether to forfeit the lease or tenancy or to affirm it, his act will unequivocally demonstrate that he has decided to affirm it. He cannot contradict that by saying that his act was without prejudice to his right of election continuing or anything to that effect. In this respect, his act speaks louder than his words, because the act is unequivocal: it can only be explained on the basis that he has exercised his right to elect."

The same principle will apply in relation to an acceptance of rent "under protest" or as "payment for use and occupation" on the ground that the act of accepting rent speaks louder than words. Thus, in *Croft* v. *Lumley*[92] the landlord's acceptance of a tender of rent from the tenant was held to constitute a waiver of the forfeiture despite the fact that it was accepted on the basis that it represented compensation for past occupation of the premises and not as rent. An acceptance of rent will also amount to a waiver even where the lease requires a waiver to be expressed in writing and there has been no express waiver in writing complying with the terms of the lease.[93]

It is sufficient if payment is accepted from a sub-tenant[94] or other person on behalf of the tenant in satisfaction of the rent under the lease[95] but acceptance of money paid by a guarantor of the rent does not necessarily amount to a waiver.[96] Moreover, acceptance of rent from an assignee of the lease prior to the completion of the assignment will not render the assignor's title good when he has failed to comply with a notice of disrepair rendering the lease liable to forfeiture.[97]

It would appear that payment of rent into the landlord's bank account,

---

[89] *Davenport* v. *R.* (1877) 3 App. Cas. 115, 131–132, *per* Sir Montague E. Smith; *Strong* v. *Stringer* (1889) 61 L.T. 470, 472, *per* Kekewich J.; *Oak Property Co. Ltd.* v. *Chapman* [1947] K.B. 886, 898, *per* Somervell L.J.; *Carter* v. *Green* [1950] 2 K.B. 76, *per* Cohen L.J.; *Segal Securities Ltd.* v. *Thoseby* [1963] 1 Q.B. 887, 898, *per* Sachs J.; *Matthews* v. *Smallwood* [1910] 1 Ch. 777, 786, *per* Parker J.; *Windmill Investments (London) Ltd.* v. *Milano Restaurants Ltd.* [1952] 2 Q.B. 373, Megaw J.

[90] [1972] 1 W.L.R. 1048.

[91] *Ibid.* p. 1054.

[92] (1858) 6 H.L.C. 672; 10 E.R. 1459. See, in particular, the judgment of Bramwell B. at pp. 705–707; pp. 1472–1473 and that of Williams J. at p. 725; p. 1480.

[93] *R* v. *Paulson* [1921] 1 A.C. 271, (P.C.).

[94] *Price* v. *Worwood* (1859) 4 H. & N. 512; 157 E.R. 941.

[95] *Pellatt* v. *Boosey* (1862) 31 L.J.C.P. 281. *Quaere*, whether a landlord's notice under s. 6 of the Law of Distress (Amendment) Act 1908 will operate as a waiver of the right to forfeit for arrears of head rent.

[96] *London & County (A. & D.) Ltd.* v. *Wilfred Sportsman Ltd.* [1971] Ch. 764, (C.A.) (payments made by guarantor of the rent were merely payments made in discharge of its contractual obligation contained in a licence to assign and did not constitute payments of rent by or on behalf of the tenant).

[97] *Re Martin, ex p. Dixon (Trustee)* v. *Tucker* (1912) 106 L.T. 381. Contrast *Butler* v. *Mountview Estates Ltd.* [1951] 2 K.B. 563 (acceptance of rent by landlord cured defect of title).

if usual, will operate as a waiver even though the landlord has instructed the bank not to receive it. In *Pierson* v. *Harvey*[98] the tenant had sublet the premises in breach of covenant in the lease. He had been in the habit of paying his rent into the landlord's bank account but the landlord, on discovering the tenant's breach, gave instructions to his bank not to receive any further rent from the tenant. The tenant subsequently paid rent into the landlord's bank account and the landlord, who did not know of the payment for several months, failed to take any steps to repay it nor did he give the tenant any notice that he was refusing payment of rent. It was held that the landlord had waived the forfeiture by the receipt of rent, albeit through his bankers. The decision highlights the importance of the landlord taking appropriate steps to repay the moneys as soon as they are paid into his account and of giving appropriate notice to the tenant (as opposed to merely his bank) that the rent would not be received.

A further point to bear in mind relates to the demand (or acceptance) of rent (a) in arrear and (b) in advance as regards continuing breaches of covenant. Demand (or acceptance) of rent payable in arrear will only amount to a waiver of the forfeiture for the period up to the date when the rent falls due and the landlord will not be precluded from taking advantage of the continuing breach after such date.[99] On the other hand, a demand (or acceptance) of rent payable in advance will operate as a waiver of past and continuing breaches known to the landlord at the time of acceptance of the rent and for such period as the landlord knows they will continue.[1] The point was fully discussed by Sachs J. in *Segal Securities Ltd.* v. *Thoseby*,[2] who held that the landlord, in that case, who could not be taken to have had definite knowledge that the tenant's breach would continue after the expiry of his notice requiring the tenant to remedy the breach, had not waived the continuing breach which occurred between the date of the demand for rent and the commencement of proceedings. The following example may help to explain the principles involved: Assuming a breach of covenant to repair (that is to say, a continuing breach) which comes to the knowledge of the landlord in December, an acceptance of rent in advance on March quarter day would result in a waiver of the breach before that date and, if the landlord's knowledge was such that he knew definitely that the breach would continue throughout the ensuing quarter, then there would also be a waiver as regards that breach up to the next quarter day (June 24). If rent is again accepted on that day, following (say) the service of a notice under section 146 of the Law of Property Act 1925, this would waive the breach for the next

---

[98] (1885) 1 T.L.R. 430.
[99] *Penton* v. *Barnett* [1898] 1 Q.B. 276, (C.A.).
[1] But it, clearly, cannot constitute a waiver of future breaches of which the landlord has no advance knowledge.
[2] [1963] 1 Q.B. 887, 901–902.

ensuing quarter, so that the landlord could not rely on that breach as constituting a foundation for bringing his action. Assuming, however, that the landlord does not have definite knowledge that the breach will continue after the expiration of the section 146 notice, he will be entitled to rely on the breach for the period from September 29 (the next quarter day) up to the date (say, in November) of the issue and service of his writ claiming forfeiture.

Where a lease contains a proviso as to forfeiture on the tenant's bankruptcy and on his assigning without the landlord's consent, and, after the tenant's bankruptcy, the landlord accepts rent from the trustee in bankruptcy and treats him as tenant, the right of forfeiture will effectively be gone.[2a] It is not clear, however, whether in such a case the landlord may insist on the proviso as to forfeiture for assigning without consent.

The doctrine of waiver (by acceptance of rent accrued due after the breach) will apply to a Crown lease.[3]

(3) Distraining for rent whenever due

It is well settled that a forfeiture is waived by the landlord distraining for rent, whether accrued due before or after the breach.[4] The distress will waive any forfeiture not only up to the day on which the rent was due but up to the day of the distress itself.[5] In other words, a distress is only an acknowledgment of the tenancy up to the day of the distress and a waiver of forfeiture only to that time.[6]

A landlord who continues in possession of the distress upon the premises which was levied before the forfeiture will not thereby waive his right of re-entry.[7] Further, a distress for rent levied by the landlord, pursuant to section 210 of the Common Law Procedure Act 1852, will not operate as a waiver of his right of forfeiture so as to prevent him from maintaining an action for possession of the premises for non-payment of rent under the section.[8]

(4) Exercising a right to re-enter and effect tenant's repairs

It is common for a clause in the lease to give the landlord the right to

---

[2a] Dyke v. Taylor (1861) 30 L.J. Ch. 281.

[3] Bridges v. Longman (1857) 24 Beav. 27; 53 E.R. 267.

[4] Green's Case (1582) Cro. Eliz. 3; 78 E.R. 269; Doe d. Flower v. Peck (1830) 1 B. & Ad. 428; 109 E.R. 847 and Cotesworth v. Spokes (1861) 10 C.B. (N.S.) 103; 142 E.R. 389.

[5] Ward v. Day (1863–64) 4 B. & S. 337 and Doe d. Flower v. Peck (1830) 1 B. & Ad. 428; 109 E.R. 847.

[6] Doe d. Hemmings v. Durnford (1832) 2 Cr. & J. 667.

[7] Doe d. Taylor v. Johnson (1816) 1 Stark 411; 171 E.R. 513.

[8] Brewer d. Onslow v. Eaton (1783) 3 Doug. 230; 99 E.R. 627; Shepherd v. Berger [1891] 1 Q.B. 597.; Thomas v. Lulham [1895] 2 Q.B. 400 and London & County (A.& D.) v. Wilfred Sportsman [1971] Ch. 764, 786, per Russell L.J.

enter upon the demised premises in order to execute repairs which the tenant has covenanted to carry out after due notice, and then to charge the tenant with the costs of such repairs as a debt or rent in arrears. When the landlord exercises his right under such a clause and gives notice that he intends to enter upon the premises and executes the repairs himself, he will thereby be deemed to have waived his right of forfeiture for the tenant's disrepair. Thus, in *Doe* d. *Rutzen* v. *Lewis*[9] the landlord gave notice, under a clause in the lease, to effect repairs on the tenant's default and to distrain for the cost. It was held that the landlord had thereby waived his right to forfeit the lease for the tenant's failure to repair.

Where, however, the landlord serves notice on the tenant, under a proviso for re-entry, to repair within a stated period, an agreement between the parties whereby the landlord gives the tenant further time to repair will not amount to a waiver of the forfeiture but will simply have the effect of suspending the right of forfeiture until the expiry of the extended period.[10]

A landlord will waive his right of forfeiture for breach of covenant to repair during the period he keeps the tenant out of possession of the demised premises.[11] In such circumstances, although the tenant may be liable in an action on the covenant to repair, nevertheless, the landlord cannot take advantage of his own wrong and claim that the lease has been forfeited.

(5) *Express waiver*

A breach of covenant may be expressly waived by deed or oral agreement, whether or not there is consideration for the waiver. A landlord may be bound by an an oral promise to waive the forfeiture if he intends it to affect the rights of the tenant and to be acted upon by the tenant and it is, in fact, acted upon by him. In such circumstances, the landlord may be estopped from treating the lease as forfeited on the basis of a promissory estoppel.[12] In *Brikom Investments Ltd.* v. *Carr*[13] the landlords of a block of flats granted a 99 year lease of the flats and, at the same time, sought planning permission to build more flats on the roof of the block. The leases contained a stipulation that the tenants would contribute towards the maintenance of the roof. The roof was in a poor state of disrepair and

---

[9] (1836) 5 Ad & El. 277; 111 E.R. 1170. See also, *Doe* d. *Morecraft* v. *Meux* (1825) 4 B. & C. 606; 107 E.R. 1185, where the landlord had given notice to the tenant to effect repairs, pursuant to a covenant to repair within three months' after notice, and was thereby precluded from bringing proceedings for forfeiture until after expiry of the three month period. The service of notice under this specific covenant constituted a waiver of the general covenant to repair in the lease.

[10] *Doe* d. *Rankin* v. *Brindley* (1832) 4 B. & Ad. 84; 110 E.R. 387.

[11] *Pellatt* v. *Boosey* (1862) 31 L.J.C.P. 281.

[12] *Central London Property Trust Ltd.* v. *High Trees House Ltd.* [1947] K.B. 130; *Mitas* v. *Hyams* [1951] 2 T.L.R. 1215; *Hughes* v. *Metropolitan Railway Co.* (1877) 2 App. Cas. 439. See also, *Troop* v. *Gibson* [1986] 1 E.G.L.R. 1, (C.A.), (estoppel by convention).

[13] [1979] Q.B. 467.

the landlords gave an oral assurance to the tenants that they would carry out those repairs at their own expense. Some of the tenants obtained this assurance in writing whilst others executed their leases relying only on the oral assurance of the landlords. The landlords carried out the repair work and then sought to recover contributions from the tenants and their assignees. The Court of Appeal[14] held *inter alia* that the landlords' assurance operated as a waiver of their legal right to claim the contributions for the cost of the roof repairs. Moreover, this waiver subsisted so that, on any subsequent assignment of the leases, what was then assigned and re-assigned were the leases free of the waived obligation.

(6) *Electing to pursue a claim consistent with the continuation of the lease*

In *Calabar Properties Ltd.* v. *Seagull Autos Ltd.*,[15] the landlords brought an action for forfeiture and "without prejudice to the claim for possession" sought injunctive relief to enforce the user covenant in the lease, the subject of the claim for forfeiture. Buckley L.J. held that the writ was equivocal and, therefore, the landlords were free, at or before trial, to abandon the claim for possession and proceed on the alternative claim for an injunction on the footing that the lease was still in existence.[16] If, in these circumstances, the landlord conclusively elects to treat the lease as continuing (for example, by pursuing injunctive relief to enforce a covenant in the lease), he will thereby waive the right to forfeit for breach of that covenant thereafter. Thus, in *Evans* v. *Davies*,[17] the landlord's writ was indorsed with a claim for an injunction to restrain the tenant from committing a breach of the covenants contained in an agreement for a lease and to recover possession of the premises comprised in the agreement. The landlord had also (in his Statement of Claim) pleaded that, although no lease had actually been granted, he was at all material times ready and willing to grant a new lease to the tenant in conformity with the agreement. Fry J. held that the claim for an injunction, which was founded on the continuation of the agreement, was inconsistent with the claim to recover possession and that the landlord had waived his claim for possession by stating in his pleadings his willingness to grant a new lease to the tenant.

In the recent case of *Cardigan Properties Ltd.* v. *Consolidated Property*

---

[14] *per* Roskill and Cumming-Bruce L.JJ. Lord Denning M.R. preferred to base his judgment on the doctrine of promissory estoppel.

[15] [1969] 1 Ch. 451.

[16] See also, *Moore* v. *Ullcoats Mining Co. Ltd.* [1908] 1 Ch. 575, where Warrington J. held that the writ was equivocal in so far as it sought both possession of the demised premises and an injunction to restrain the tenants' breach of covenant in the lease.

[17] [1878] 10 Ch. 747.

Investments Ltd.,[18] the landlord's continuation of an action claiming a mandatory injunction for the production of policies of insurance relating to the demised premises was held to constitute a waiver of its right of forfeiture for breach of the tenant's covenant to insure. In this case, the action for an injunction was commenced prior to the forfeiture proceedings and it was the landlord's unequivocal act of not discontinuing that action which was held to give rise to the waiver of the forfeiture.

In *Billson* v. *Residential Apartments Ltd.*,[19] the landlord's letter requesting that the tenants cease carrying out unauthorised works, in breach of covenant not to make alterations to the premises without previous consent of the landlords, on penalty of the landlord issuing a summons for an injunction against the tenants, was held not to amount to a waiver of forfeiture. The Court of Appeal accepted the trial judge's finding that "the alterations to the property were being made as part of a continuing programme of process of alteration" which spanned the interval between the date of the landlord's letter and the service of their section 146 notice. Thus, even if the letter constituted a waiver of any past breaches, the landlord was entitled to rely upon further works which had been done subsequently, as to which there was no possibility of waiver.

In the case of a building lease, a landlord does not necessarily waive the forfeiture by allowing the tenant to proceed with the building works.[19a]

(7) *Service of a notice to quit*

A notice to quit served by the landlord after he has knowledge of a breach of covenant will waive the forfeiture but only if the notice affirms the existence of the tenancy. Thus, in *Marche* v. *Christodoulakis*,[20] the landlord let a maisonette on condition that, should the tenant sub-let the premises without his consent, he should have a right of re-entry. The tenant sub-let the maisonette without consent and the landlord, instead of exercising his right of re-entry under the lease, served a notice to quit on the tenant. Pritchard J. held that, by serving the notice to quit, the landlord had affirmed the tenancy with the consequence that the sub-tenancy was lawful.

---

[18] [1991] 07 E.G. 132. See also: *Iperion Investments Corporation* v. *Broadwalk House Residents Ltd.*, [1992] 2 E.G.L.R. 255, Mr Recorder Mauleverer, Q.C. noted in [1992] E.G. 9236, p. 147 and [1992] E.G. 9237, p. 135.

[19] [1991] 3 All E.R. 265, (C.A.).

[19a] *Doe* d. *Lord Kensington* v. *Brindley* (1826) 12 Moore C.P. 37.

[20] (1984) 64 T.L.R. 466 following *Norman* v. *Simpson* [1946] K.B. 158. See also, dictum of Denning J. in *Loewenthal* v. *Vanhoute* [1947] 1 All E.R. 116, 117. Presumably, the same result will follow if the landlord operates a break-clause in the lease.

(8) *Offer to purchase tenant's interest*

In *Bader Properties Ltd.* v. *Linley Property Investment Ltd.,*[21] Roskill J. expressed the opinion *obiter* that a landlord's offer, subject to contract, to purchase the tenant's leasehold interest in the demised premises was an unequivocal affirmation of the existence of the lease and, consequently, amounted to a waiver of the tenant's breach of covenant against assigning, subletting and parting with possession of the premises. He said[22]:

> "I am unable to understand how it can be said that the [landlords] by their solicitors could offer £2,500 to purchase the defendant's interest in the premises save on the basis that that interest was a subsisting interest and was no longer liable to forfeiture."

However, in *Expert Clothing Service & Sales Ltd.* v. *Hillgate House Ltd.*[23] the Court of Appeal drew a distinction between cases involving the acceptance (and demand) for rent where the legal effect of the acceptance (or demand) was clear, and other cases in which no acceptance (or demand) for rent was involved. In the latter category, the court was free to look at all the circumstances of the case to consider whether the act of the landlord relied on as constituting a waiver was so unequivocal that, when considered objectively, it could only be regarded as having been done consistently with the continued existence of the tenancy. Thus, the landlord's act of proffering a deed of variation of the terms of the lease for execution by the tenants was held not to amount to an unequivocal act of waiver against the background of the parties indicating their intentions to bring an action for possession of the premises and claim relief against forfeiture. It was accepted, however, that the proffering of a mere negotiating document could be capable of amounting to an unequivocal recognition of the existence of a subsisting tenancy, having regard to the background and the particular circumstances surrounding each individual case.

It has been held[24] that the mere entering into and continuation of negotiations between landlord and tenant will not, by itself, constitute a waiver of forfeiture.

(9) *Assignment of mortgage*

In *Hone* v. *Daejan Properties Ltd.*[25] the landlords granted a 99 year lease to

---

[21] (1968) 19 P. & C.R. 620. See also, *Doe* d. *Weatherhed* v. *Curwood* (1835) 1 Har. & W. 140. A landlord will not waive a forfeiture by agreeing to a voluntary arrangement under s. 260 of the Insolvency Act 1986, although this may involve the continuance of the lease: *Re Mohammed Naeem (A Bankrupt)* [1990] 1 W.L.R. 48.

[22] (1968) 19 P. & C.R. 620, 641.

[23] [1985] 3 W.L.R. 359.

[24] *Re National Jazz Centre Ltd.* [1988] 38 E.G. 142.

[25] (1976) 120 S.J. 488.

a tenant of a maisonette for a premium of £3,650 and at a ground rent of £15 per annum. The tenant obtained a mortgage from a building society and lived in the maisonette until he was evicted by the building society for arrears of mortgage instalments, the society taking possession of the premises. Subsequently, unknown to the tenant, the mortgage was assigned to the landlords. The tenant then sought to redeem the mortgage and the landlords claimed that, by reason of the tenant's non-payment of the ground rent, they had exercised their right to re-enter the premises and forfeit the lease. The Court of Appeal held *inter alia* that the assignment of the mortgage constituted an act of recognition that the lease was still in being and a waiver of any previous forfeiture which might have occurred.

(10) *Acceptance of surrender of head lease*

The acceptance of a surrender by the landlord of his tenant's interest in the premises will operate as a waiver of his right of forfeiture for breach of a covenant against subletting. The reasoning behind this principle is that the tenant cannot, by his own voluntary act of surrender, prejudice the estate of his sub-tenant or any other person who claims under him. In *Great Western Railway Co.* v. *Smith*,[26] Mellish L.J. said[27]:

"If the question arose between an under-lessee and the landlord, the moment the surrender was produced, and it appeared in Court that there was a surrender of the estate, I have no doubt that the landlord had waived all right to forfeiture by accepting a surrender."

It appears that a surrender will operate as a waiver of the breach of covenant notwithstanding that the landlord has no knowledge of the unlawful sub-letting. In *Parker* v. *Jones*,[28] the tenant of a field sublet the land in breach of covenant not to sublet without previous licence from the landlord. Later, the tenant surrendered his term to the landlord, who accepted the surrender in ignorance of the sub-letting and of the sub-tenant's occupation of the premises. Bucknill J. held that the acceptance of the surrender by the landlord precluded him from subsequently forfeiting the sub-tenant's interest regardless whether at the time of the surrender he had notice of that interest or not. Darling J., however, was not prepared to go this far and his judgment proceeded on the basis that the landlord had not waived his right of forfeiture by accepting a surrender of the tenant's lease because he had no knowledge of the unlawful sub-letting. The judgment of Darling J. is (it is submitted) to be preferred.

[26] (1876) 2 Ch. D. 235. See also, *Mellor* v. *Watkins* (1874) L.R. 9 Q.B. 400.
[27] (1876) 2 Ch. D. 235, 253.
[28] [1910] 2 K.B. 32.

Conduct not amounting to waiver

It will be convenient to list the various acts which have been held *not* to amount to a waiver under the following subject-headings:

(1) *Receipt of rent due prior to the breach*

It is well established that a receipt of rent accrued due *prior* to the breach of covenant does not amount to a waiver of forfeiture.[29]

In *Price* v. *Worwood*[30] Martin B. said[31]:

> "A receipt of rent, to operate as a waiver of a forfeiture, must be a receipt of rent due on a day after the forfeiture was incurred. The mere receipt of the money, the rent having become due previously, is of no consequence, and for the very plain reason that the entry for a condition broken does not at all affect the right to receive payment of a pre-existing debt."

Where the landlord, pursuant to a covenant in the lease, gives the tenant notice to repair within a specified period of time, the receipt of rent after the expiration of the notice which accrued due before will not amount to a waiver.[32]

(2) *Acceptance of rent or levying distress after service of the writ/summons*

Once the landlord has taken some positive step to signify his intention to forfeit (by actually physically re-entering upon the demised premises or by serving a writ/summons containing an unequivocal demand for or declaration of title to possession), the right of re-entry ceases to be capable of waiver and the landlord cannot elect to treat the lease as still subsisting. Thus, in *Grimwood* v. *Moss*[33] it was held that there was no waiver where the landlords had distrained for rent *after* the date of the service of their proceedings for possession. Similarly, in *Civil Service Co-operative Society Ltd.* v. *McGrigor's Trustee*[34] the demand for and acceptance of rent accrued due after the issue and service of the landlord's writ was held not to operate as a waiver of forfeiture.

---

[29] *Marsh* v. *Curteys* (1596) Cro. Eliz. 528; 78 E.R. 775; *Green's Case* (1582) Cro. Eliz. 3; 78 E.R. 269.

[30] (1859) 4 H. & N. 512; 157 E.R. 941.

[31] *Ibid.* 516; 942.

[32] *Cronin* v. *Rogers* (1884) Cab. & El. 348.

[33] (1871) L.R. 7 C. P. 360.

[34] [1923] 2 Ch. 347. See also, *Doe* d. *Morecraft* v. *Meux* (1824) 1 C. & P. 346; 171 E.R. 1225, *per* Abbot C.J.; *Jones* v. *Carter* (1846) 15 M. & W. 718, 725–726; 153 E.R. 1040, 1043, *per* Parke B. and *Toleman* v. *Portbury* (1870) Law Rep. 6 Q.B. 245; (1871) Law Rep. 7 Q.B. 344.

It is, perhaps, self-evident that a landlord's reliance upon two (or more) breaches of covenant in his pleadings as affording him grounds for forfeiture will not amount to a waiver so as to preclude him from seeking forfeiture upon all those breaches except the last. Thus, in *Toleman* v. *Portbury*[35] the landlord's claim for forfeiture by reason of non-payment of rent was held not to preclude the landlord from relying on a previous forfeiture pleaded in his writ notwithstanding that the former had come to an end by reason of the tenant's payment of the arrears into court. In *Evans* v. *Enevers*[36] the lease contained a proviso for re-entry in the event of the tenant's bankruptcy or if the rent should be in arrear for 21 days. The tenant was adjudicated bankrupt and two quarter's rent were in arrear. The landlords brought proceedings against the tenant claiming possession of the premises on the ground only of forfeiture for non-payment of rent. The tenant remedied the breach by paying the outstanding rent and costs to the landlords and the proceedings came to an end. Subsequently, the landlords brought a second action for possession claiming that the lease was forfeited by reason of the tenant's bankruptcy. Lord Coleridge J. held that the acceptance of the rent, following the landlord's first action, did not operate as a waiver of the forfeiture despite the fact that the rent had accrued due after the date of the tenant's adjudication of bankruptcy. He said[37]:

"... there is a series of cases which establish that if an action is brought for recovery of possession for breaches of covenants in the lease that is an irrevocable election to determine the lease, and that no subsequent acts of the plaintiff can be relied on as qualifying that position."

However, the acceptance of rent may be construed as an acknowledgment that there is, in fact, a new tenancy of the premises.[38] In these circumstances, the receipt of rent by the landlord may be treated as evidence from which the grant of a new tenancy can be inferred, having regard to the question *quo animo* the rent was received and what had been the real intention of the parties.[39] Thus, in *Evans* v. *Wyatt*,[40] for example, the acceptance of rent by the landlord after the bringing of an action for ejectment was held, on the facts, to amount to an agreement for a new tenancy from year to year on the same terms as the old lease.

[35] (1870) Law Rep. 6 Q.B. 245; (1871) Law Rep. 7 Q.B. 344.
[36] [1920] 2 K.B. 315.
[37] *Ibid.* p. 320.
[38] See, *e.g. Legal & General Assurance Society Ltd.* v. *General Metal Agencies Ltd.* (1969) 20 P. & C.R. 953.
[39] *Clarke* v. *Grant* [1950] 1 K.B. 104; *Doe* d. *Cheny* v. *Batten* (1775) 1 Cowp. 243; 98 E.R. 1066;, *Maconochie Bros. Ltd.* v. *Brand* [1946] 2 All E.R. 778 and *Blyth* v. *Dennett* (1853) 13 C.B. 178; 138 E.R. 1165.
[40] (1880) 43 L.T. 176.

(3) *Assignment of the reversion expressed to be subject to the lease*

In *London & County (A.D.) Ltd.* v. *Wilfred Sportsman Ltd.*[41] the Court of Appeal held[42] that the grant of a reversionary lease by a head landlord to the assignee "subject to and with the benefit of" the tenant's lease did not waive the right to forfeit the tenant's lease for non-payment of rent even though the assignee had knowledge of the breach, since it was not an unequivocal act of recognition of the pre-existing lease. A statement or act by a landlord which was neither communicated to a tenant, nor could have any impact on his tenancy was not an election to waive a forfeiture.

(4) *Service of a notice under section 146 of the Law of Property Act 1925*

The service of a notice under section 146 of the Law of Property Act 1925 will not amount to a waiver of forfeiture. In *Church Commissioners for England* v. *Nodjoumi*[43] the landlords served a section 146 notice on the tenant alleging that he had assigned the lease to his wife in breach of covenant. They subsequently brought proceedings claiming forfeiture of the lease on the ground of arrears of rent which dated back to a time prior to the service of the section 146 notice. Hirst J. held that, whilst the failures to pay rent had each been once and for all breaches capable of waiver, the purpose and effect of a section 146 notice was to operate as a preliminary to actual forfeiture and, therefore, it could not amount to an unequivocal affirmation of the existence of the lease. He said[44]

"... the section 146 notice ... was the very prerequisite of the right to forfeit, and it cannot therefore be said, in my judgment, that the service of that notice destroyed the very right that it was served for the purpose of achieving."

(5) *Entering into without prejudice negotiations*

The mere entering into and continuation of "without prejudice" negotiations between the landlord and the tenant will not, by itself, constitute a waiver of forfeiture. In *Re National Jazz Centre Ltd.*,[45] Peter Gibson J. put the matter in this way:

---

[41] [1971] Ch. 764.
[42] Overruling *Davenport* v. *Smith* [1921] 2 Ch. 270. In *Rickett* v. *Green* [1910] 1 K.B. 253, the mortgagee of the head lease assigned the premises to the plaintiff "subject to" the defendant's tenancy at a time when a quarter's rent was in arrear. It was assumed that the right of re-entry was not waived by the reference in the assignment to the tenancy or its benefit. See also, *Atkin* v. *Rose* [1923] 1 Ch. 522, 538–539, *per* P.O. Lawrence J.
[43] (1986) 51 P. & C.R. 155.
[44] *Ibid.* p. 159.
[45] [1988] 38 E.G. 142.

"It is impossible, in my judgment, to reach a conclusion that there has been an unequivocal acceptance of the existence of a lease by the entering into of negotiations, without looking at what occurred in the negotiations themselves, and that, it is quite clear . . . is something which the court cannot do."

In *Expert Clothing Service and Sales Ltd.* v. *Hillgate House Ltd.*,[46] the Court of Appeal held that there had been no waiver in circumstances where the landlord had proferred a deed of variation of the terms of the lease for execution by the tenant. The test adopted by the Court was whether the sending of the deed in the course of negotiations could be reasonably understood as unequivocally indicating the landlord's intention to treat the lease as subsisting. The decision illustrates the principle that the mere existence of negotiations will not be sufficient to show that the landlord participating in the negotiations is accepting that the tenancy does exist and that there has been no forfeiture. However, a waiver will arise when the landlord agrees to grant a new lease to commence from the regular determination of the existing lease.[47]

(6) *Inactivity*

In *Doe* d. *Shepherd* v. *Allen*[48] the tenant assigned the lease of shop premises to the defendant who partitioned the shop into two separate units. In breach of covenant in the lease, he then proceeded to carry on the business of a fishmonger in one part of the shop and a butcher in the other part. The landlord, who lived next door to the demised premises, passively lay by and witnessed the breach for a period of six years and subsequently brought an action for possession. The defendant had throughout this period paid his rent to the tenant. It was held that the landlord had not waived his right of forfeiture for the breach in the absence of some positive act of waiver. Heath J. said[49]:

"... there are a great many cases in the old books, where it is held, that a mere knowledge and acquiescence in an act constituting a forfeiture, does not amount to a waiver: there must be some act affirming the tenancy."

In this connection, Lord Mansfield C.J. in the same case suggested that, if the landlord had permitted the tenant to expend money or make improvements to the demised premises, this may be evidence of a

---

[46] [1986] Ch. 340.
[47] *Doe* d. *Weatherhead* v. *Curwood* (1835) 1 Har. & W. 140 and *Ward* v. *Day* (1864) 5 B. &. S. 359.
[48] (1810) 3 Taunt. 78; 128 E.R. 32, applied in *Perry* v. *Davis* (1858) 3 C.B. (N.S.) 769; 140 E.R. 945 (no waiver by mere standing by and seeing the tenant making alterations in breach of covenant).
[49] *Ibid.* p. 81; p. 33.

waiver.[50] There is also authority for the proposition that acquiescence in a particular breach over a very long period of time is capable of amounting to a permanent waiver in respect of that breach. In *Kelsey* v. *Dodd*[51] Jessel M.R. held that the plaintiffs, who were entitled to the benefit of a restrictive covenant against keeping a beershop on any part of the subject premises, had lost their right to seek an injunction to restrain a continued breach of the covenant on the ground of long and continued acquiescence. Similarly, in *Chelsea Estates Ltd.* v. *Kadri*,[52] a covenant in a lease to use the premises as a private dwelling-house only had been broken by the letting of several parts for about 50 years. The landlords sought possession of the premises from the tenants on the ground of breach of the covenant as to user. Goff J., in holding that the tenant's defence of acquiescence succeeded, said[53]:

> "... in the present case, there seemed a very long course of usage going back something like 50 years, which was inconsistent with the application of the covenant."

In these circumstances, despite the breach being a continuing one, the court may be drawn to infer that the landlord has licensed the acts in question or released the covenant.[54] In *Wolfe* v. *Hogan*,[55] Denning L.J. put the matter succinctly in this way[56]:

> "A breach of covenant not to use premises in a particular way is a continuing breach. Any acceptance of rent by the landlord, after knowledge, only waives the breaches up to the time of the acceptance of rent. It does not waive the continuance of the breach thereafter and, notwithstanding his previous acceptance of rent, the landlord can still proceed for forfeiture on this account. Indeed, in the case of a continuing breach, the acceptance of rent, after knowledge, is only a bar to a claim for forfeiture if it goes on for so long, or is accepted in such circumstances, that it can be inferred that the landlord has not merely waived the breach but has affirmatively consented to the tenant continuing to use the premises as he has done."

---

[50] See, *e.g. North Stafford Steel, Iron and Coal Co. (Burslem)* v. *Lord Camoys* (1865) 11 Jur. N.S. 555 and *Hume* v. *Kent* (1811) 1 Ball & B. 554.

[51] (1881) 52 L.J.Ch. 34.

[52] [1970] E.G.D. 425; 214 E.G. 1356.

[53] *Ibid.* p. 427.

[54] *Gibson* v. *Doeg* (1858) 2 H. & N. 623; 157 E.R. 253 (landlord had licensed the use of the premises); *Gibbon* v. *Payne* (1905) 22 T.L.R. 54 (release of covenant); *Hepworth* v. *Pickles* [1900] 1 Ch. 108 (waiver and release of covenant); *In Re Summerson* [1900] 1 Ch. 112–113 (licence or release of covenant); *Lloyds Bank* v. *Jones* [1955] 2 Q.B. 298 (facts did not raise inference of release of covenant) and *City and Westminster Properties (1934) Ltd.* v. *Mudd* [1959] 1 Ch. 129, 143–145, *per* Harman J. (no release of covenant on the facts).

[55] [1949] 2 K.B. 194.

[56] *Ibid.* p. 205.

The landlord may also be estopped from exercising his right of forfeiture in circumstances where he has led the tenant to believe that he will not rely upon his strict legal rights and the tenant has acted so as to change his position in reliance on the landlord's words or conduct.[57]

(7) No waiver of right to claim damages/injunction

It appears to be clearly established that a waiver which is implied from the acceptance of rent, whilst it constitutes a waiver of the right of re-entry, does not amount to a waiver of the right to sue for damages for breach of covenant[58] or claim an injunction to prevent its continuation.

Waiver of forfeiture for non-payment of rent

There is no distinction between a waiver of a breach consisting of non-payment of rent and a waiver of any other breach of covenant. This is so, notwithstanding that a right of re-entry operates as a security for the non-payment of the rent, since that security can be lost by waiver. Moreover, whilst the tenant can obtain relief from forfeiture for non-payment of rent simply by paying the rent due and the landlord's costs of the action, this does not justify any distinction between breach of covenant for non-payment of rent and other breaches of covenant. The rules as to waiver are the same for both categories of breach.[59] Thus, assuming two quarter's rent are in arrear, if the landlord accepts the second quarter's rent, he will waive the forfeiture for non-payment of rent because he thereby recognises that the lease continues to the second quarter. Whilst the landlord can still distrain or bring a rent action in respect of the other outstanding quarter, he cannot forfeit the lease for that quarter.[60]

Waiver and residential tenants

There is no doubt that the common law doctrine of waiver does not apply with the same force to a statutory tenancy under the Rent Act 1977 or to a secure periodic tenancy under the Housing Act 1988.

In *Trustees of Henry Smith's Charity* v. *Willson*,[61] the Court of Appeal held

---

[57] *City and Westminster Properties (1934) Ltd.* v. *Mudd* [1959] 1 Ch. 129; *Brikom Investments Ltd.* v. *Carr* [1979] Q.B. 467, *per* Lord Denning M.R.; *Millard* v. *Humphreys* (1918) 62 Sol. Jo. 505. See also, *Hughes* v. *Metropolitan Railway Co.* (1877) 2 App. Cas. 439.

[58] *Stephens* v. *Junior Army & Navy Stores Ltd.* [1914] 2 Ch. 516 and *Norman* v. *Simpson* [1946] K.B. 158, 165, *per* Du Parcq L.J.

[59] *London & County (A.D.)* v. *Wilfred Sportsman Ltd.* [1971] Ch. 764, (C.A.).

[60] *Ibid.* p. 785, *per* Russell L.J. Where the proviso specifies a period of grace (*e.g.* 21 days) before the right of forfeiture accrues, the landlord can demand rent during this period without waiving the right to forfeit for non-payment.

[61] [1983] 1 All E.R. 73. See also, *Marcroft Wagons Ltd.* v. *Smith* [1951] 2 K.B. 496; *Lewis* v. *MTC (Cars) Ltd.* [1975] 1 W.L.R. 457 and *Cardiothoracic Institute* v. *Shrewdcrest Ltd.* [1986] 2 E.G.L.R. 57.

that a single demand for future rent made with knowledge that a statutory tenant had granted an unlawful sub-tenancy did not amount to an election by the landlord to treat the sub-tenancy as lawful, since the landlord was entitled to demand rent from the statutory tenant until the statutory tenancy was properly terminated either by a notice to quit by the tenant or by court order. The question whether such a demand constitutes an unequivocal act of the affirmation of the statutory tenancy so as to operate as a waiver is a question of fact to be decided on the evidence. Thus, the Court of Appeal was able to distinguish the earlier case of *Carter* v. *Green*,[62] on the ground that there the landlord had accepted rent with full knowledge of the sub-letting on about six separate occasions before he attempted to claim that the sub-letting was unlawful, so that a waiver of the illegality was the obvious inference on the facts of that case. Slade L.J., who gave the leading judgment in the *Willson* case, also referred extensively to the judgment of Somervell L.J. in *Oak Property Co. Ltd.* v. *Chapman*,[63] in particular, to the following passage[64] as indicating that the question, in the context of a statutory tenancy, was ultimately one of fact in each individual case:

> "... as a question of fact, the acts of the landlords amounted, and were understood to amount, to such an unequivocal affirmance of the sub-tenancy that they must be taken to have waived their statutory rights and condoned the absence of consent."

In support of his view, Slade L.J. also cited the following passage from the judgment of Lord Denning M.R. in *Muspratt* v. *Johnstone*[65]:

> "We have been referred to the cases on waiver, particularly *Carter* v. *Green*, and I think the result of them is that in these Rent Act cases, there is not a waiver of an unlawful subletting from the mere acceptance of rent or the mere failure to write out a qualification at once. There has to be such a degree of acquiescence that a consent to a subletting can be inferred."

Since it is by no means clear on the present authorities just what kind of acts or degree of acquiescence by the landlord will be deemed to amount to an unequivocal waiver of the tenant's illegality, a safe rule for a landlord who has acquired full knowledge of a non-continuing breach of

---

[62] [1950] 2 K.B. 76, (C.A.).
[63] [1947] K.B. 886, (C.A.).
[64] *Ibid.* p. 900.
[65] [1963] 2 Q.B. 383, 393. In this case, the landlord received payment of rent without any qualification for a period of 18 months. Although the case was very near the line, the Court of Appeal felt there was sufficient evidence from which the trial judge could infer a waiver.

covenant by a statutory tenant is to demand and accept rent subject to an appropriate qualification firmly negativing the affirmance of the statutory or secure periodic tenancy.[66]

---

[66] *Oak Property Co. Ltd.* v. *Chapman* [1947] K.B. 886, 900, *per* Somervell L.J.

Part III: Relief against forfeiture

Chapter Seven

History of equity's jurisdiction to relieve against forfeiture of leases[1]

Introduction

From the earliest times, the Court of Chancery recognised an equitable jurisdiction to relieve against forfeitures where the injured party could be put back into the same position as if the covenant in question had not been broken. The underlying principle determining whether relief would be granted was whether the injured party could be adequately compensated for his loss occasioned by the other party's breach.[2] In the words of Farwell J. in *In Re Lord de Clifford's Estate, Lord de Clifford v. Quilter*[3]:

> "Now relief against the stringent rules of the common law in cases of forfeiture and the like was an old head of equity, which was applied on a thoroughly intelligible principle. The forfeiture being intended to secure the payment of money or the performance of a contract, equity gave no relief unless it could secure the payment of the money or the performance of the contract in favour of the person entitled to enforce the forfeiture, and it granted relief on the ground that it thereby gave effect to the real contract between the parties."

Thus, whilst there was no difficulty in "compensating" a landlord for a tenant's failure to pay rent in due time by simply permitting the tenant to

---

[1] See, generally, *White and Tudor's Leading Cases in Equity*, (9th ed., 1928), Vol. 2, pp. 222–227, 235–236 and 239–241; *Woodfall's Law of Landlord and Tenant*, (21st ed.), pp. 405–407 and *Platt on Leases*, Vol. 2, pp. 485 *et seq.*

[2] An early formulation of this principle is to be found in the judgment of Lord Nottingham L.C. in *Popham v. Bampfeild* (1682) 1 Vern. 79, 83; 23 E.R. 325, 326: "when the court can in any case compensate the party in damages for the non-precise performance of the condition, there it is just and equitable to relieve".

[3] [1900] 2 Ch. 707, 712.

tender late payment with interest and costs,[4] other breaches did not readily permit the placing of the landlord in the same position he would have been if no breach had occurred. For this reason, no relief could be given in respect of a tenant's breach of covenant not to assign or sub-let, to insure or to carry out repairs to the demised premises.[5] In each of these cases, the courts of equity declined to grant relief to the tenant upon terms that he should make compensation because it was not possible to quantify the extent of the landlord's loss or injury occasioned by the breach.

However, a number of early authorities did recognise an equitable jurisdiction to relieve against breaches of covenant other than those involving non-payment of a sum of money.

Cases prior to *Hill* v. *Barclay* (1811)

The earliest reported authority on the point appears to be *Cage* v. *Russell*,[6] where a testatrix devised certain lands to the executors of her will to pay the sum of £500 out of them to her son when he should attain the age of 21. The devise was made subject to the proviso that, if the father's son failed to give a release for the lands, then the sum of £500 was to be forfeited to the executors. The father refused to give a release whereupon the executors forfeited the £500. The father was subsequently willing to grant the release and the court decreed payment of the £500 to the son stating that:

> "It was the standing rule of the Court, that a forfeiture should not bind where a thing may be done afterwards, or any compensation made for it. As when the condition was to pay money or the like."

In *Webber* v. *Smith*,[7] the landlord forfeited the tenant's interest in a number of houses on the ground of the latter's failure to pay rent and repair the houses in accordance with the terms of the lease. The tenant had sub-let the premises and the sub-tenants were granted relief from forfeiture upon payment of the arrears and repair of all the houses. Similarly, in *Nash* v. *Earl of Derby*[8] the owner of two copyhold estates, who

---

[4] It was assumed that, if the money was paid with interest and costs, this was a sufficient indemnity to the landlord. Yet, in a number of cases, no doubt, considerable inconvenience was suffered by the landlord not having the money paid at the due time. Any such inconvenience, however, appears to have been disregarded by equity in granting relief. This was recognised by Lord Eldon in *Reynolds* v. *Pitt* (1812) 19 Ves. 134; 34 E.R. 468, where he said: "The failure of the payment at the time may be attended with mischievous consequences, that never can be cured in a rational sense by subsequent payment with the addition of interest."

[5] See Eden, *A Treatise on the Law of Injunctions*, (1821), p. 26 and Comyn, *Treatise on the Law of Landlord and Tenant*, (1821), pp. 494–495.

[6] (1681) 2 Vent. 352; 86 E.R. 481.

[7] (1689) 2 Vern. 103; 23 E.R. 676.

[8] (1705) 2 Vern. 537; 23 E.R. 948.

had wrongfully cut timber on the one in order to carry out repairs to the other, was relieved from forfeiture upon payment of the costs of the action.[9]

These cases, however, must be looked at in the light of subsequent developments and, in particular, the emergence of the principle that equity only had jurisdiction to relieve against a forfeiture where the object of the forfeiture clause was to secure payment of a definite sum of money. An early case in point is *Grimstone* v. *Bruce*,[10] where certain lands in Hertfordshire were devised upon condition that the devisee paid the testator's debts and legacies. One such legacy involved a payment of £30,000 to the testator's grand-daughter to be paid (initially) in instalments of £1,000 per year. The condition was broken but Lord Chancellor Cowper relieved against it upon payment of interest on each instalment from the time each fell due for payment together with the costs of the action. It was not, however, until 1721 that the principle was clearly formulated by Lord Macclesfield in one of the leading cases of the period. In *Peachy* v. *Duke of Somerset*,[11] the owner of a copyhold estate had entered into various leases contrary to the custom of the manor and without licence of the lord. He sought to be relieved from the forfeiture of his estate by offering to make recompense for the breach but Lord Macclesfield refused relief, stating[12]:

> "The true ground of relief against penalties is from the original intent of the case, where the penalty is designed only to secure money, and the court gives him all that he expected or deserved: but it is quite otherwise in the present case. These penalties or forfeitures were never intended by way of compensation, for there can be none.
>
> But even in the cases of copyholds there are some cases of forfeitures intended for a different purpose, as for non-payment of rents or fines, which are only by way of security of the rent or fine; and therefore where these are paid afterwards with interest, the money itself is paid according to the intent, only as to the circumstance of time; which is the true foundation of the relief which this Court gives in those cases."

This narrower view of the scope of equity's jurisdiction was also favoured in the subsequent case of *Descarlett* v. *Dennett*.[13] In that case, the defendant granted a lease to the plaintiff of certain lands in Essex for a

---

[9] There are other cases where relief has been granted against forfeiture of copyhold estates: See, *e.g. Thomas* v. *Porter* (1668) 1 Ch. Ca. 95, where the copyhold had been forfeited by cutting down timber and where the breach was held not to be wilful; *Cox* v. *Higford* 2 Vern. 664, where the court granted relief against forfeiture for want of repairs.
[10] (1707) 2 Vern 594; 23 E.R. 986.
[11] (1721) 1 Stra. 447; 93 E.R. 626.
[12] *Ibid.* p. 453; p. 630.
[13] (1722) 9 Mod. 22; 88 E.R. 290.

term of nine years. The lease contained a proviso for re-entry upon breach of various covenants including a covenant that the plaintiff should not suffer persons to make use of a way over part of the lands demised. In breach of this covenant, the plaintiff permitted people to pass over the lands whereupon the defendant forfeited the lease. The plaintiff then brought an action seeking relief from forfeiture offering to pay arrears of rent which had fallen due and to compensate the defendant by way of damages for breach of the covenant relating to the use of the way. Sir Joseph Jekyll M.R. refused to grant relief on the basis that:

"... the Court of Chancery cannot relieve the non-performance of a covenant or condition, the prejudice in breach of which cannot be estimated by damages."

Moreover, the learned Judge categorised the breach as a "wilful voluntary breach ... against which this Court cannot relieve." It is evident, therefore, that the learned Judge was only prepared to grant relief in a case where the breach could be estimated by an award of damages and where it was not wilful. Two years later, a similar conclusion was reached in the case of *Wafer* v. *Mocatto*,[14] where the plaintiff, the tenant of certain houses in London, assigned the same in breach of a covenant in the lease not to assign without the prior consent of the landlord. Lord Macclesfield took the opportunity to re-iterate the view he adopted in the *Peachy* case by saying[15]:

"Where a man makes a lease for life or for years, upon a condition of re-entry for a forfeiture, or that the lease shall be void if the lessee assign or alien it without licence, this is a forfeiture, and such a forfeiture against which this Court cannot relieve, because it is unknown what shall be the measure of damages; for this Court never relieves but in such cases where it can give some compensation in damages and where there is some rule to be the measure of damages, to avoid being arbitrary."

In this case, the court proceeded on the basis that the landlord could not be returned to his position prior to the tenant's breach because, where there was an assignee without licence, the court could not ascertain the pecuniary compensation which should be awarded to the landlord for having a new tenant forced upon him. In *Hack* v. *Leonard*,[16] however, (decided in then same year as the *Wafer* case) Lord Macclesfield appears to have adopted a more lenient approach to the granting of equitable relief in circumstances where the breach consisted of a failure to repair. In that case, a landlord had forfeited a lease of a barn on the ground of the

[14] (1724) 9 Mod. 12; 88 E.R. 348.
[15] *Ibid.* p. 349.
[16] (1724) 9 Mod. 90; 88 E.R. 335.

tenant's breach of covenant to keep it well-thatched. In his judgment, Lord Macclesfield intimated that he could not see what damage the landlord could sustain by the building being out of repair provided that the tenant kept the main timber free from going rotten and left all in good repair before the end of the term. Accordingly, he ordered an inquiry as to what damage had, in fact, been suffered by the landlord with a view to giving the tenant an opportunity to make compensation.

The principle that equity would only intervene in cases where it was possible for the court to grant compensation to the injured party was re-iterated by Lord Hardwicke in *Rose* v. *Rose*[17] where he said[18]:

"Equity will relieve against almost all penalties whatsoever ... against non-payment of money at a certain day; against forfeiture of copyholds: but they are all such cases where the Court can do it with safety to the other party; for if the Court cannot put him into as good condition as if the agreement had been performed, the Court will not relieve."

In *Northcote* v. *Duke*,[19] however, Lord Nottingham expressed a desire to extend equity's jurisdiction to relieve against forfeitures to cases where the breach was wilful and voluntary. He said[20]:

"It was said that Equity will not relieve where the act is voluntary. But the landlord may not have been injured at all, or in a manner for which I can compensate him. I take the rule to be, that in all cases where a person has broken a condition and forfeited a penalty Equity will relieve, if there can be a compensation. I think the court may relieve where a tenant cuts down timber."

The last sentence in this passage also suggests that the Lord Chancellor would grant relief in respect of breaches other than those involving non-payment of a sum of money provided only that the court could order appropriate compensation to the injured party. In *Eaton* v. *Lyon*,[21] on the otherhand, Lord Alvanley sought to restrict equitable relief to cases not involving wilful neglect or misconduct on the part of the defaulting tenant. In that case, the tenant had failed to serve a formal notice of exercise of an option to renew a lease within a specified time. In refusing the tenant relief, Lord Alvanley said[22]:

"At Law a covenant must be strictly and substantially performed according to the true intent and meaning of the parties, so far as

[17] (1756) Amb. 331; 27 E.R. 222.
[18] *Ibid*. p. 223.
[19] (1765) Amb. 511; 27 E.R. 330.
[20] *Ibid*. p. 330.
[21] (1798) 3 Ves. Jun. 691; 30 E.R. 1223.
[22] *Ibid*. pp. 692–693; p. 1224.

circumstances will admit; but if by unavoidable accident, if by fraud, by surprise, or ignorance not wilful default, parties may have been prevented from executing it literally, a Court of Equity will interfere; and upon compensation being made, the party having done every thing in his power and being prevented by the means I have alluded to, will give relief ... the party shall not avail himself of equitable circumstances, unless he shews, that there has been no wilful neglect or misconduct on his part."

In *Wadman* v. *Calcraft*,[23] the plaintiff was the tenant of lands under a lease for 21 years which contained a proviso for re-entry upon non-payment of rent or upon the plaintiff assigning or underletting the lands without the defendant's consent. The plaintiff fell into arrears with his rent and underlet the lands without prior consent from the defendant. Both Sir William Grant M.R. and Lord Eldon refused the plaintiff relief concluding that, whilst the court could relieve against forfeiture for non-payment of rent even where there was no fraud, accident surprise or mistake, it had no such jurisdiction in relation to the breach of other covenants whether wilful or otherwise.

However, a different conclusion was reached by Lord Erskine in the case of *Sanders* v. *Pope*,[24] who put forward a more expansive approach to equity's jurisdiction to grant relief. Here, a lease of a public house contained a covenant on the part of the tenants to expend the sum of £200 in improving and repairing the premises before the end of the first five years of the term. The tenants failed to carry out the repairs and the landlord forfeited the lease. The issue before the court was whether the tenants were entitled to relief in equity upon them laying out the sum of £200 in repairs or otherwise making compensation to the landlord for their breach. In granting relief,[25] Lord Erskine, in a classic judgment, said[26]:

"There is no branch of the jurisdiction of this Court more delicate than that which goes to restrain the exercise of a legal right. That jurisdiction rests only upon this principle; that one party is taking advantage of a forfeiture; and as a rigid exercise of the legal right would produce a hardship, a great loss and injury on the one hand arising from the going to the full extent of the right, while on the other the party may have the full benefit of the contract, as originally

[23] (1804) 10 Ves. Jun. 67; 32 E.R. 768.
[24] (1806) 12 Ves. Jun. 283; 33 E.R. 108.
[25] Lord Erskine intimated that the court's order would need to provide that, if the sum of £200 was not sufficient to put the premises in the state of repair in which they should have been placed by the time stipulated in the lease, an additional sum would have to be paid by the tenants. "If the price of materials and labour have increased, that must not be thrown upon the landlord": *ibid*. p. 294; p. 112. However, no order was actually made in the case, probably because the parties reached a settlement.
[26] (1806) 12 Ves. Jun. 283, 289; 33 E.R. 108, 110.

framed, the Court will interfere; where a clear mode of compensation can be discovered."

The central question, therefore, was whether the damage occasioned by the tenant's breach could be the subject of measurable compensation. In the instant case, the covenant provided for the expenditure of a specific sum of money (£200) on the property over a period of five years and, consequently, the difficulty of seeking to make an award of general damages to compensate for the breach did not arise. However, it is apparent that the court was not prepared to draw any distinction between expenditure of a specified sum on repairs within a prescribed period and payment of rent arrears. In this connection, Lord Erskine observed[27]:

"If it is a subject admitting of certain calculation, though not a specific sum of money or rent, relief may be given."

In the course of his judgment, Lord Erskine also had occasion to refer to the judgment of Lord Alvanley in *Eaton* v. *Lyon* (where, it will be recalled, his Lordship sought to confine equity's jurisdiction to cases where there was no wilful neglect or misconduct on the part of the party in breach) and said[28]:

"If the covenant is broken with the consciousness that it is broken, that is, if it is wilful, not by surprise, accident or ignorance, still if it is a case, where full compensation can be made, these authorities[29] say, not that it is imperative upon the Court to grant relief, but that there is a discretion."

A year later, Lord Erskine had occasion to re-iterate his view in the case of *Davis* v. *West*,[30] a case involving the forfeiture of a lease as a consequence of the tenant's failure to pay rent. The Lord Chancellor said[31]:

"In the late case of *Sanders* v. *Pope* . . . I was very unwilling to give the relief against breach of other covenants [i.e. other than to pay rent], but was compelled by a series of authorities[32] . . . establishing that, where the covenants are broken, and there is no fraud, and the party is capable of giving complete compensation, it is the province of a Court of Equity to interfere, and give the relief against the forfeiture for breach of other covenants, as well as those for payment of rent."

There is no doubt that the case of *Sanders* v. *Pope* marked a turning point

---

[27] *Ibid.* p. 290; p. 111.
[28] *Ibid.* p. 293; p. 112.
[29] See *Cage* v. *Russell* (1681) 2 Vent. 352; 86 E.R. 481; *Northcote* v. *Duke* (1765) Amb. 511; 27 E.R. 330; *Hack* v. *Leonard* (1724) 9 Mod. 90; 88 E.R. 335; *Wafer* v. *Mocatto* (1724) 9 Mod. 12; 88 E.R. 348 and *Eaton* v. *Lyon* (1798) 3 Ves. Jun. 691; 30 E.R. 1223.
[30] (1806) 12 Ves. 475; 33 E.R. 180.
[31] *Ibid.* p. 476; p. 180.
[32] See the cases referred to in n. 29 above.

in the evolution of equity's jurisdiction to grant relief against forfeitures. It paved the way for the acceptance by equity of a more robust attitude to do justice between the parties *irrespective* of the nature of the covenant broken and the wilfulness of the breach, provided only that the interests of the injured party could be adequately protected by an appropriate form of order. Where, therefore, strict reliance upon the forfeiture would produce an injustice to the party in breach, equity had a discretion to intervene so long as measurable compensation could be made to the injured party. This broad approach to equitable relief was, however, to be shortlived for in 1811 Lord Eldon, following his earlier judgment in *Wadman* v. *Calcraft*, declined to grant relief against the forfeiture of a lease for a wilful breach of covenant not involving the failure to pay rent even where the same was capable of adequate compensation.

Hill v. *Barclay* (1811) and subsequent cases

In *Hill* v. *Barclay*,[33] a covenant in the lease provided *inter alia* that if the tenants did not, within a specified time period, expend £150 on repairs to the demised premises or otherwise did not repair the premises within three months of being notified so to do by the landlord, the latter was entitled to re-enter upon the premises and forfeit the lease. The tenants failed to comply with the landlord's notice within the time period stipulated but, nevertheless, began the works following the landlord's action for ejectment. They then sought an injunction to restrain the landlord's action on the ground that the works would be completed and the premises put in a complete state of repair. Lord Eldon distinguished the earlier case of *Sanders* v. *Pope* on the basis that it involved the laying out of a specific sum of money by the tenant towards the repair of the demised premises and that the landlord had made no specific demand upon the tenant to repair the premises prior to commencing his action for ejectment. On the question of damages, he said[34]:

> "The Court has very long held in a great variety of classes of cases, that in the instance of a covenant to pay a sum of money the Court so clearly sees, or rather fancies, the amount of the damages, arising from non-payment at the time stipulated, that it takes upon itself to act, as if it was certain, that giving the money for years afterwards with interest it gives a complete satisfaction. That doctrine has been recognised without any doubt upon leases with reference to non-payment of rent . . . but, if a Court of Equity is to trust itself in all cases

---

[33] (1811) 18 Ves. Jun. 56; 34 E.R. 238. See also, 16 Ves. Jun. 402; 33 E.R. 1037, where Lord Eldon in an earlier motion in the case involving the tenant's claim for an injunction to restrain the landlord's ejectment said: ". . . a Court of Equity would not relieve against a breach of a general covenant to do repairs."

[34] *Ibid.* pp. 59–60 and 61; p. 240.

with the consideration of such a question as this, whether it is just, that a tenant should come here to prolong the duration of a lease, by his express contract determined, if the property has not been treated in a husband-like manner, the Court has not so sure a guide as the calculation of interest upon a sum of money; and, considering the depositions of surveyors in this Court, or the declarations of one of the Plaintiffs, as representing by the answer that the premises are in such circumstances that, whenever all the repairs are made it will be a bad business, the notion, that the Court upon such evidence can be sure, that it gives the party a compensation in damages, appears ridiculous."

In referring to the earlier cases, in particular *Hack* v. *Leonard*, Lord Eldon observed that a "very material consideration"[35] which had been over-looked was that equitable relief could not be given in circumstances where the breach of the covenant was wilful. Accordingly, on the basis that the breach in the case before him was both wilful and incapable of giving rise to an accurate estimate in damages, he dismissed the tenant's motion for an injunction to restrain the landlord's ejectment. His decision was, no doubt, influenced by a strong desire not to interfere with the contract made between the parties and, in particular, the landlord's unfettered legal right to re-enter for breach of covenant, in the absence of exceptional circumstances. He did, however, permit some degree of discretion for, when dealing with Lord Erskine's observations in *Sanders* v. *Pope* as to relieving against breaches of covenant to repair, he said[36]:

"A particular case might perhaps occur, such as was put by Lord Erskine ... in which it would be demonstrable that the landlord would sustain no injury by the relief; but still taking a prodigious liberty with a contract by which a tenant has undertaken forthwith to repair."

A similar approach was adopted in *Rolfe* v. *Harris*,[37] where the tenant had neglected to insure the premises in breach of covenant. In refusing relief, Sir T. Plumer V.C., following the earlier case of *Wadman* v. *Calcraft*, said:

"... where the Court will relieve, the omission and consequent failure, must be the effect of inevitable accident, and the injury or inconvenience arising from it must be capable of compensation; but where the transgression is wilful, or the compensation impracticable, the Court will refuse to interfere."

---

[35] *Ibid.* p. 62; p. 241
[36] *Ibid.* p. 62; p. 241.
[37] (1811) 2 Pri. 202; 146 E.R. 68.

The rationale for refusing relief is neatly summed up in the following extract from the judgment:

"Why in such cases as these, of relief against breach of contract, is a Court of Equity to be called on to make a new contract? The parties agree, that if the condition be broken, the lessor shall re-enter; and the Court is asked to give damages instead. What damages can the Court give? and what damages could reconcile a man to a tenant who breaks his contract, and brings his landlord before a Court of Equity by a bill, to be relieved against the effect of his own injurious neglect; and to defeat the landlord's remedy for the breach of the condition on which he holds, because he has done so? It seems to me to be a mischievous and arbitrary jurisdiction; and, if exercised at all, ought to be confined to cases of a pecuniary nature such as non-payment of rent, and money not paid by a day certain, and where such breach stands alone. In such cases, perhaps, compensation may be made; but when the principle of compensation is applied to other cases, such as waste, and not repairing, it becomes very difficult, if not impracticable to effect it. The only mode of measuring damages is by an issue, *quantum damnificatus*; and that may turn out to be wholly unsatisfactory and, in many instances, not capable of being carried into effect, by any means, as in breaches of covenant for assigning without leave. In this very sort of case too, how can we, when a risk has been run, estimate the quantum of that risk in damages? This is such a breach of covenant as is out of the measurement of damages; and the effect of giving the relief prayed would be, that any tenant may hereafter break this special covenant with impunity . . ."

Again in *Reynolds* v. *Pitt*,[38] the plaintiff was the tenant of a coffee house under a lease which contained a covenant on his part to insure the premises from fire during the term of the lease with a proviso for re-entry on breach of the covenant. The plaintiff neglected to renew the insurance during a period of two years, but effected the policy on the very same day that the landlord brought an action for ejectment. Lord Eldon, after an extensive review of the earlier authorities, concluded that equity had no jurisdiction to relieve against the wilful breach of a covenant to insure. The case proceeded on the basis that the risk which the landlord had incurred during the period when no insurance was in force was something which could not be the subject of compensation.

In *Lovat* v. *Lord Ranelagh*,[39] the landlord had brought an action for ejectment alleging that the tenant had cultivated a certain area of farm

[38] (1812) 19 Ves. 134; 34 E.R. 468.
[39] (1814) 3 Ves. & Bea. 24; 35 E.R. 388. See also *Macher* v. *The Foundling Hospital* 1 Ves. & Bea. 188; 35 E.R. 74 (relief refused where tenant had carried on a forbidden trade contrary to the terms of the lease).

land contrary to the terms of the lease which prescribed a particular mode of cultivation. The tenant claimed to be relieved from the forfeiture (on the basis *inter alia* that the landlord had never insisted on the tenant cropping the land according to the strict terms of the covenant) and offered to make compensation. Lord Eldon refused to grant the tenant an injunction to restrain the landlord's ejectment primarily on the ground that to do so would simply have activated the landlord into raising other breaches of covenant on the part of the tenant (such as his assignment of the lease without consent) which were not the subject of equitable relief.

A leading case of the time (and which merits detailed analysis) is *Bracebridge* v. *Buckley*,[40] where the Court of Exchequer refused to grant equitable relief to a tenant who was in breach of a covenant to lay out a sum of £1,000 on the demised premises within a stipulated time on the ground that it had no effective means of ascertaining precisely what compensation the landlord was entitled to in these circumstances. Moreover, relief was denied notwithstanding the fact that no damage had been sustained by the delay in carrying out the repair works and that the premises would be put into as good or even better condition than they would have been if the covenant had been punctually performed. Counsel for the tenant relied primarily on *Sanders* v. *Pope* in support of the contention that equity had jurisdiction to relieve in cases where the covenant provided for the expenditure of a specific sum of money. He also referred to a number of matters which he argued made it just and equitable that relief should be granted. First, the tenant was willing to submit to any terms the court thought fit to impose even if this meant placing the landlord in a better position than he would have been if the covenant had been strictly performed in accordance with the terms of the lease. Secondly, the tenant had been lulled into a false sense of security since the landlord had permitted him to continue in undisturbed possession of the premises for two years after the breach of covenant had occurred. Thirdly, it was contended that, despite the specific time limit for carrying out the repairs under the lease, the parties had, in fact, understood that the tenant was to take his own time to proceed with the repairs. It was submitted, therefore, that the tenant's breach could not be characterised as a wilful neglect to perform the covenant. Moreover, the landlord had given no prior notice of his intention to re-enter for the breach.[41] As to the court's difficulty in securing that precise compensation

---

[40] (1816) 2 Pri. 200; 146 E.R. 68.

[41] It was sought to distinguish *Hill* v. *Barclay* (1811) 18 Ves. Jun. 56; 34 E.R. 238 on this ground since, in that case, the landlord had demanded performance of the covenant prior to bringing his proceedings for ejectment. The earlier cases of *Rolfe* v. *Harris* 2 Pri. 202n; 146 E.R. 71n and *Reynolds* v. *Pitt* (1812) 19 Ves. 134; 34 E.R. 468, were also distinguished on the basis that the tenant's failure to insure the premises was wilful in that the landlord in each case had given notice requiring performance of the covenant but the tenant had ignored it.

was made to the landlord in cases of this kind, it was suggested on behalf of the tenant that the court could direct an inquiry as to what sum would be necessary to put the premises into the same state of repair as they would have been if the money had been applied according to the terms of the lease. In answer to this contention, Baron Richards said[42]:

"... as to the covenants such as the present, I know not how they are to be performed, unless according to the terms, or what compensation can be given for non-performance; or, if there could be any made, how it can be offered. Here, indeed, none is offered."

With reference to the case of *Hack* v. *Leonard*, he said[43]:

"But even this case had nothing to do with compensation; nor was any decreed. A reference was ordered to ascertain what damage had been done; but to whom, and how, is compensation to be given? Certainly not by decreeing a sum of money to the lessor, to enable him to repair, for he could not enter for that purpose; and are you to trust a jury to say what sum would be necessary to put the premises in repair? I do not, therefore, think this is a case which makes at all in favour of the plaintiff; nor does the ground of the determination appear, so as to offer a principle."

And referring to *Sanders* v. *Pope*, he said[44]:

"No doubt the contract of these parties required that £1,000 should be laid out within a year; and I wish to know how what they contracted for can now be done? If not done within the given time, the contract is not performed ... the lessor cannot enter to superintend the repair, and would the Master be directed to do so? ... The Chancellor has said, the Court will not superintend the repair. The Master cannot; it is impossible."

Baron Wood, on the other hand, gave a strong dissenting judgment and concluded that the tenant should be relieved on laying out the £1,000 towards the repairs to the premises and paying all the landlord's costs of the action. In his view, equity could grant relief wherever it was possible to award sufficient compensation in damages to the injured party: "Equity will relieve in almost all cases of forfeiture, if they can put the parties in as good a condition."[45] One exception to this broad principle was the breach of a covenant not to assign or underlet where no damage could be ascertained "because the tenant, though he might be perfectly solvent, may not be, in other respects, such a man as the landlord would

---

[42] (1816) 2 Pri. 200, 216; 146 E.R. 68, 75.
[43] *Ibid.* p. 216; p. 75.
[44] *Ibid.*
[45] *Ibid.* p. 221; p. 76.

chuse."[46] For the same reason, the breach of a covenant to insure could not be the subject of relief because the injury suffered by the landlord (*i.e.* the risk which the landlord would inevitably incur whilst the premises remained uninsured) was not susceptible of measurement by an award of damages. In the context of a tenant's neglect to repair, however, the learned Judge considered that the various objections to the practicability of granting relief were ill-founded: "The course of reference to the Master is an answer to all those difficulties."[47] Moreover, the principle that the court could not decree specific performance of a covenant to build or repair was subject to the qualification that such a remedy was available where the nature of the works and the subject premises were suitably defined.[48] This prompted the learned Judge to observe[49]: "There is no such objection here; the house is defined, and the sum to be laid out in repairs (expressly £1,000) is defined." A further apparent objection to the grant of relief was that the tenant might become bankrupt or insolvent whilst carrying out the works in compliance with the court's order. On this point, Baron Wood countered[50]: ". . . no doubt, in such a case, that fact would be a sufficient ground of refusal; but no such thing has happened, or was probable in this case." In the instant case, the tenant had not been guilty of any wilful neglect and the covenant was still capable of performance with equal (if not greater) advantage to the landlord than if carried out in accordance with the strict terms of the lease. In adopting, therefore, an expansive approach to equity's jurisdiction, he concluded[51]:

> "All the cases must depend on the tenant, and be governed by their own particular circumstances. Where, indeed, he has been guilty of wilful waste, or even presumptive waste, relief might properly be refused; but not for a mere want of repair, which, at the time of the application to be relieved, can be effectually supplied."

Baron Graham (the third member of the Court) agreed that equity could relieve where complete compensation could effectually be made by the tenant but felt unable to apply that principle to the facts of the case before him: "Equity never interferes, I think, except where the thing can be specifically done, as in the case of rent, or payment of a sum of money."[52] Chief Baron Thomson also concurred with the majority re-iterating that

[46] *Ibid.*
[47] *Ibid.* pp. 223–224; p. 77.
[48] See *City of London* v. *Nash* 3 Atk. 512, and *Moseley* v. *Virgin* (1796) 3 Ves. 184, *per* Lord Loughborough (Lord Chancellor).
[49] (1816) 2 Pri. 200, 224; 146 E.R. 68, 77.
[50] *Ibid.* p. 225; p. 77.
[51] *Ibid.*
[52] *Ibid.* p. 227; p. 78.

185

the court had no power to supervise the carrying out of works under a covenant to build or repair.

The principle established in the *Rolfe* and *Reynolds* cases was again applied by Lord Eldon in *White* v. *Warner*.[53] Here, the tenant had failed to keep the premises insured against fire but, unlike the earlier cases, had laid out £3,000 on repairs to the property. The tenant argued that, in view of the great hardship that would be caused to him if the landlord was permitted to sue at law, he should be relieved from the forfeiture on the principles enunciated by Lord Erskine in *Sanders* v. *Pope*. Lord Eldon, however, (in a short judgment) emphatically rejected the proposition which the tenant had sought to infer from the earlier authorities, namely, that equity would, in cases of forfeiture for breach of covenant, grant relief upon the court awarding appropriate compensation for any injury suffered by the landlord.

However, in *Hannan* v. *The South London Waterworks Company*,[54] (decided a year earlier) Lord Eldon, whilst reaffirming the principle that, in general, the court would not relieve against the breach of a covenant to repair, had occasion to grant equitable relief (in the form of an injunction restraining an action for ejectment) in favour of a tenant who was in breach of his covenant to repair the premises. The facts of this case were, however, considered by the Lord Chancellor to be exceptional in so far as the tenant had contracted to deliver up possession of the premises to a third party, who in turn intended to demolish the premises pursuant to the latter's statutory powers. It is interesting to refer to the form of the order made in this case since the injunction which was granted in favour of the tenant was specifically made conditional upon the payment by the tenant of the landlord's costs of the action and upon his undertaking to:

"obey such Orders as the Court should think proper to make upon any applications by the [landlords] requiring him to repair or rebuild any part of the premises, and also to obey such Orders as the Court should make upon any application by the [landlords] in case it should be made to appear that the [landlords], in any treaty which they might conclude with the [third party] for their interest in the premises as lessors, had been reasonably required to accept a less price for such interest, than they would have obtained if the premises had been by repairs or re-building, kept in or restored to the state and condition required by the lease."

It is evident, therefore, that in this case at least the court felt no

---

[53] (1817) 2 Mer. 459; 35 E.R. 1016. See also *Green* v. *Bridges* (1830) 4 Sim. 96; 58 E.R. 37 and *Shearman* v. *McGregor* (1853) 11 Hare 106; 68 E.R. 1206. In the latter case, relief was granted against an action on a bond in circumstances where the defaulting party had been misled as to the consequences of an omission to pay the insurance premium.

[54] (1816) 2 Mer. 65; 35 E.R. 863.

difficulty in granting equitable relief upon terms which would compel the tenant to perform his obligations under the repairing covenant and make appropriate compensation to the landlords in the event of a proven diminution in the value of their reversionary interest occasioned by the breach. Inevitably, any such compensation would fall to be measured by means of an inquiry as to the market value of the landlords' interest in the property in its unrepaired state and its condition on the assumption that the tenant had complied with his obligations under the lease. This, therefore, clearly marks a departure from the earlier authorities which denied relief for the very reason that the injury suffered by the landlord was not the subject of measurable compensation in cases involving disrepair.

Despite this apparent relaxation of the *Hill* v. *Barclay* principle, the courts, nevertheless, continued to adopt a restrictive approach to the scope of equity's jurisdiction to grant relief. A good example of this technical attitude is *Harries* v. *Bryant*,[55] where Sir John Leach M.R. extended the meaning of wilful breaches to include an omission occuring through negligence as a result of a failure to act with reasonable diligence or prudence. He said[56]:

> "Ignorance is considered to be wilful, where a person neglects the means of information, which ordinary prudence would suggest; and accident is not unavoidable, which reasonable diligence might have prevented."

In this case, a lease for lives contained a covenant entitling the tenant to renew it upon the dropping of a life provided an application was made for renewal within six months. The plaintiff (an assignee of the lease) omitted to apply for a renewal within the prescribed time limit and claimed relief on the ground that he was unaware of the death or that the deceased was named in the lease. Sir John Leach M.R. denied relief on the basis that the plaintiff tenant might have become aware of the relevant facts if he had used reasonable diligence to find out about them.

Again, in *Doe* d. *Mayhew* v. *Ashby*,[57] the Court of Queen's Bench held that it had no power to stay the landlord's action for ejectment (based on the tenant's breach of covenant to repair) in the absence of the landlord's

---

[55] (1827) 4 Russ. 89; 38 E.R. 738. See also *Gregory* v. *Wilson* (1852) 9 Hare 683; 68 E.R. 687, where Sir G.J. Turner V.-C. said: "Where a man, who knows that he is charged with a legal obligation, neglects to perform it, his neglect to do so must be deemed to be wilful and, if he persists in it, to be obstinate", and *Elliott* v. *Turner* (1843) 13 Sim. 477; 60 E.R. 185, where Sir Lancelot Shadwell V.-C. suggested that the word "wilful" meant "spontaneous" so that if the neglect or default arose from a voluntary act and not from the pressure of external circumstances over which the party in default had no control, the neglect or default fell to be classified as wilful. In his view, mere forgetfulness could amount to wilful neglect.

[56] *Ibid.* p. 91; p. 739.

[57] (1839) 10 Ad. & E. 71; 113 E.R. 28.

consent.[58] Similarly, in *Nokes* v. *Gibbon*,[59] Vice-Chancellor Kindersley held that, where there was a clear breach of covenant on the part of the tenant, equity had no jurisdiction to interfere with the landlord's legal rights and stay an action for ejectment.

In *Elliott* v. *Turner*,[60] the plaintiff gave a licence to the defendants to use his invention for the manufacture of covered buttons. The licence contained a covenant on the part of the defendants that they would render regular accounts of the quantities and value of buttons made by them under the licence with a proviso that, if the defendants "should be guilty of any wilful neglect or default" in the performance of the covenants, it would be lawful for the plaintiff to revoke the licence. The defendants defaulted in the production of accounts and the plaintiff revoked the licence. Sir Lancelot Shadwell V.C. refused relief from this forfeiture on the ground that equity could not intervene where compensation could not be made to the innocent party by the payment of a sum of money.

However, in *Bargent* v. *Thompson*,[61] Sir John Stuart V.C. granted the tenant relief from forfeiture (by restraining the landlord's action for ejectment) for non-repair of the premises on the ground that the remedial work was delayed because of poor weather conditions. He said[62]:

> "The bill in this case is filed upon an equity which has always been recognised in this Court – that of a tenant who has bound himself by covenants to repair, and who can shew to the Court equitable circumstances sufficient to entitle him either to a relief from a strict performance of the covenants, or to ensure him against a forfeiture of the lease by reason of neglect to perform them."[63]

In this case, the landlords had given the tenant three months' notice to carry out various works to the premises. Following the expiry of this period, the landlords (without further notice to the tenant) brought an

---

[58] The cases of *Hill* v. *Barclay*, *Bracebridge* v. *Buckley* and *White* v. *Warner* were cited as denying any jurisdiction to stay proceedings at law as well as in equity.

[59] (1856) 3 Drew. 681; 61 E.R. 1063.

[60] (1843) 13 Sim. 477; 60 E.R. 185.

[61] (1864) 4 Giff. 473; 66 E.R. 792. See also *Bamford* v. *Creasy* (1862) 3 Giff. 675; 66 E.R. 579, where Sir John Stuart V.-C. granted the tenant relief from forfeiture of her lease upon payment of the landlord's costs, arrears of rent and the amount due for repairing and insurance. The case, however, turned very much on its own special facts in so far as the landlord had obtained a default judgment for ejectment without the question whether the tenant had, in fact, breached any of the covenants being properly tried. In *ex p. Vaughan* (1823) 1 T. & R. 434, relief was granted against an ejectment for non-repair brought by the committee of a lunatic, on the principle that harsh proceedings would not be for the benefit of the lunatic's estate.

[62] *Ibid.* p. 477; p. 794.

[63] In *Hill* v. *Barclay*, Lord Eldon himself observed: "I do not mean to apply these observations to cases of accident and surprise; *the effect of the weather*, . . . or permissive want of repair, the landlord standing by and looking on" (emphasis supplied): (1811) Ves. Jun. 56, 62; 34 E.R. 238, 240.

action for ejectment. Out of the 22 items of disrepair, 20 had been commenced and 14 completed by the time of the expiry of the notice. On these facts, the Vice-Chancellor concluded that[64]:

"... the commencement of the action was a harsh and severe proceeding; and going on with it down to the notice of the trial, after an offer had been made [by the tenant], was still more so."

In the celebrated case of *Hughes* v. *Metropolitan Rly. Co.*,[65] the House of Lords, whilst re-affirming what had by then become the established view that "equity had no general power to relieve against forfeiture by way of mercy or by way merely of saving property from forfeiture",[66] held that equity could intervene to grant relief in the exceptional case where the party in default had been misled by the other party's conduct into believing that the latter's strict legal rights had been abandoned or suspended for a time. This well-known principle is neatly summarised in the following passage from the opinion of Lord Cairns[67]:

"... it is the first principle upon which all Courts of Equity proceed, that if parties who have entered into definite and distinct terms involving certain legal rights—certain penalties or legal forfeiture— afterwards by their own act or with their own consent—enter upon a course of negotiation which has the effect of leading one of the parties to suppose that the strict legal rights arising under the contract will not be enforced, or will be kept in suspense, or held in abeyance, the person who otherwise might have enforced those rights will not be allowed to enforce them when it would be inequitable having regard to the dealings which have thus taken place between the parties."

In *Hughes*, the landlords had served a notice on the tenant to repair various houses forming the subject-matter of the lease within a period of six months expiring on April 22, 1875. Upon service of this notice, the tenant made an offer to sell his interest in the premises to the landlords and various negotiations ensued culminating in a letter from the landlords (written on December 31, 1874) requiring a modification of the tenant's proposals. No further communication was made between the parties until April 1875 when the landlords wrote stating *inter alia* that the tenant had had ample time to complete the repairs since December 1874 when negotiations had broken off. Shortly after the expiry of the repair notice, the landlords brought an action for ejectment. The House of Lords held that the tenant was entitled to be relieved from the forfeiture on the

---

[64] *Ibid.* p. 478; 794.
[65] (1877) 2 App. Cas. 439. See also, *Bruner* v. *Moore* [1904] 1 Ch. 305.
[66] *Ibid.* p. 448, *per* Lord Cairns (L.C.).
[67] *Ibid.* p. 448.

basis that the negotiations had the effect of suspending the notice and that this suspension did not come to an end until December 31, 1874. Accordingly, till that time, the operation of the notice had been waived by the landlords so that no part of that time could be counted against the tenant in calculating the six months' notice to repair.

The reluctance of the court to expand the boundaries of equity's jurisdiction is also amply illustrated by the Court of Appeal decision in *Barrow v. Isaacs*.[68] In that case, the tenants underlet part of the demised premises without the prior consent of the landlord in breach of a covenant in the lease. The underletting had, in fact, been prepared by their solicitors who had omitted to look at the head lease and forgot that it contained the covenant not to underlet without consent. The undertenants were respectable and responsible persons and no injury had been suffered by the landlord by the grant of the underletting. Moreover, the landlord would have had no valid objection to the underletting had consent, in fact, been asked. Nevertheless, the Court of Appeal felt constrained to hold that the landlord was entitled to succeed in his action for possession on the ground that the omission to ask the landlord's consent was not a mistake falling within the recognised heads of equity's jurisdiction to grant relief. Lord Esher M.R. put the matter this way[69]:

> "The difficulty has been to find out under what head of equity the relief sought can be brought. Equity, it is said, will relieve against fraud, accident or mistake; and I think you must add that equity will only relieve when there can be complete compensation, or where there is no injury which requires any compensation. Under which head is this case brought? It is obvious that it is not fraud. This is not to be attributed to either of the parties. It is not accident, because it is the result of something which was done on behalf of one of the parties. Is it mistake? . . . if you treat mistake in its ordinary sense in the English language, is mere forgetfulness mistake? Can you, in English, say, 'I forgot', and is this the same thing as saying 'I was mistaken'? I think not."

It is noteworthy, however, that the learned Judge also concluded that, had the case been one of mistake, he would have granted equitable relief notwithstanding the fact that the tenants' agent had acted negligently in failing to observe the terms of the lease. Kay L.J.,[70] on the otherhand, in refusing equitable relief, felt no difficulty in holding the tenants responsible for the carelessness of their solicitors: " . . . equity will not relieve when the mistake arises from the negligence of the suitor who seeks its

---

[68] [1891] 1 Q.B. 417. See also, *Ellis* v. *Allen* [1914] 1 Ch. 904, 909; *Eastern Telegraph Co. Ltd.* v. *Dent* [1899] 1 Q.B. 835, (C.A.) and *Atkin* v. *Rose* [1923] 1 Ch. 522, 539.

[69] *Ibid.* p. 420.

[70] With whose judgment Lopes L.J. agreed.

help . . . If we were to grant [relief], hereafter lessees might avoid looking at their leases, lest they should be reminded by them of their obligations which it would be more convenient to ignore."[71] In a brief historical analysis of equity's jurisdiction to grant relief,[72] he had cause to conclude[73]:

"At first there seems to have been some hesitation whether this relief might not be extended to other cases of forfeiture for breach of covenants such as to repair, to insure, and the like, where compensation could be made; but it was soon recognised that there would be great difficulty in estimating the proper amount of compensation; and, since the decision of Lord Eldon in *Hill* v. *Barclay*, it has always been held that equity would not relieve, merely on the ground that it could give compensation, upon breach of any covenant in a lease except the covenant for payment of rent. But of course this left unaffected the undoubted jurisdiction to relieve in case of breach occasioned by fraud, accident, surprise or mistake."

Despite this obvious reluctance to interfere with well-established principles, there is a significant recognition in Kay L.J.'s judgment that the court's refusal to extend the limits of equity's jurisdiction to relieve against forfeitures had produced anomalous and harsh results. He observed[74]:

"[There] ensued a long period in which equity seems to have refused relief in cases of breach of any of the other covenants in a lease. Very hard cases occurred, in which unconscionable landlords insisted on their legal rights. Especially hard were these forfeitures for breach of the covenant to insure where no damage had ensued."

The decision in *Barrow* was applied in *Eastern Telegraph Company Ltd.* v. *Dent*[74a] where thoughtlessness on the part of the tenant or failure on his part to realise the gravity of a breach of covenant not to underlet without the landlord's consent were urged as grounds for relief against forfeiture. Romer L.J. concluded[74b]:

"The suggestion that it is a ground for relief in equity, against the enforcement by the landlord of his legal right, that the tenant has committed the breach of covenant either through thoughtlessness or

---

[71] *Ibid.* pp. 428–429.
[72] See also, *Howard* v. *Fanshawe* [1895] 2 Ch. 581, 586–589, *per* Stirling J. and *In Re Dixon, Heynes* v. *Dixon* [1900] 2 Ch. 561, *per* Rigby L.J.
[73] [1891] 1 Q.B. 417, 425.
[74] *Ibid.* p. 429.
[74a] [1989] 1 Q.B. 835, C.A.
[74b] *Ibid.*, 839.

because he thought the breach unimportant, has no foundation in principle or authority."

Where, however, the breach was occasioned by a *bona fide* belief, induced by the landlord's agents that the landlord had expressly consented to an underletting (as opposed to a mere mistake committed on the part of the tenant and his advisers) relief was granted.[74c]

The decision in *Barrow* was also referred to by Parker J. in *Matthew* v. *Smallwood*,[75] where the learned Judge said[76]:

> "Prior to the Conveyancing Acts the only breach of covenant against which equity relieved as a matter of course was the failure to observe the covenant for payment of rent. In no other case did equity relieve unless there was something additional in the nature of accident or mistake; and it was held that carelessness on the part of the person claiming relief could not be considered in a Court of Equity to be a mistake or accident of a nature which could afford a ground for relief."

It will be evident from the foregoing review[77] of the case-law that equity's jurisdiction to relieve from forfeitures of property was limited to essentially two specific heads of relief, namely, (a) where the right to forfeit was inserted by way of security for the payment of a specific sum of money and (b) where the breach had been occasioned by fraud, accident, mistake or surprise. The fact that the landlord stood to gain the premises in an improved state by insisting on the forfeiture was not taken into account as a basis for affording relief.

The emergence of this limited jurisdiction was, of course, largely attributable to the acceptance by the courts of the restrictive approach adopted by Lord Eldon in *Hill* v. *Barclay* as opposed to the more liberal and expansive view promulgated by Lord Erskine in *Sanders* v. *Pope*. At the heart of this dichotomy lay the court's inherent inability to compensate the injured party for any loss occasioned by the breach by means of an appropriate award of damages. It was, therefore, this inherent (procedural) disability of the Court of Chancery which precluded the development of a coherent set of equitable principles for the relief of forfeiture under English law. Because of this disability, the jurisdiction of equity was inevitably confined to very narrow limits where either the injured party could be "compensated" by payment of the specific money owed

---

[74c] *Upjohn* v. *Macfarlane* [1922] 2 Ch. 256.
[75] [1910] 1 Ch. 777. See also, *W.G. Clark (Properties) Ltd.* v. *Dupre Properties Ltd.* [1992] 1 All E.R. 596, 608.
[76] *Ibid.* p. 792.
[77] For a historical review: See also, *Shiloh Spinners Ltd.* v. *Harding* [1973] A.C. 691, 722, *per* Lord Wilberforce and *Billson* v. *Residential Apartments Ltd.* [1992] 1 All E.R., (H.L.), 141, 144, *per* Lord Templeman.

with interest and costs or where (because of his conduct) it would be manifestly unjust to permit a strict performance of his legal rights.

Coupled with this, however, was also the acceptance of Lord Eldon's view (in preference to that of Lord Erskine) that equity would not relieve against a wilful breach of covenant. In this connection, the "wilfulness" of the breach came to be regarded as a matter that went to the court's *jurisdiction* whether or not to grant relief and not merely as a factor that fell to be weighed (together with other factors) in exercising its *discretion* whether or not relieve in a particular case.

The foregoing remained the position[78] until 1973, when the House of Lords took the opportunity to review the whole question of the scope of equity's jurisdiction to relieve against forfeiture of property in the case of *Shiloh Spinners Ltd.* v. *Harding*.[79]

Shiloh Spinners Ltd. v. *Harding* (1973)

In *Shiloh*, the tenants of certain buildings assigned their interest in part thereof to a company who covenanted *inter alia* to fence the boundaries and to keep certain parts of the property in repair. The assignment contained a right on the part of the tenants to re-enter the assigned premises in the event of breach of the covenants. The company subsequently assigned their interest to the respondent, a demolition contractor, who had knowledge of the terms of the earlier assignment and who proceeded to demolish the buildings in breach of the covenants therein contained. The tenants claimed possession of the premises and the respondent disputed their right of re-entry and, alternatively, sought relief from forfeiture. The House of Lords held *inter alia* that the case fell within the class of cases in which a court of equity could intervene and grant relief against forfeiture but that relief should not be given in the instant case because the respondent had been guilty of clear and wilful breaches of the covenants and there was no evidence as to his ability to make good the consequences of his default. The leading speech was given by Lord Wilberforce who restated the basis for equitable relief in these terms[80]:

"... it remains true today that equity expects men to carry out their bargains and will not let them buy their way out by uncovenanted payment. But it is consistent with these principles that we should reaffirm the right of courts of equity in appropriate and limited cases to relieve against forfeiture for breach of covenant or condition *where the primary object of the bargain is to secure a stated result which can*

---

[78] Lord Simon of Glaisdale in the *Shiloh Spinners Ltd.* v. *Harding* [1973] 1 All E.R. 90, 104, refers to the "trail from *Hill* v. *Barclay*" as leading into a "juristic desert" and as demonstrating an "abnegation of equity."
[79] [1973] 1 All E.R. 90; [1973] A.C. 691.
[80] *Ibid.* p. 101.

effectively be attained when the matter comes before the court, and where the forfeiture provision is added by way of security for the production of that result. The word 'appropriate' involves consideration of the conduct of the applicant for relief, in particular whether his default was wilful, of the gravity of the breaches, and of the disparity between the value of the property of which forfeiture is claimed as compared with the damage caused by the breach." (emphasis supplied)

It is evident from this passage that Lord Wilberforce was not prepared to limit equity's jurisdiction to the two classical heads of relief referred to in the preceding section.[81] In his view, the policy of the law in granting the right to apply for relief from forfeiture for breaches of other covenants was the same as that in the case of rent, namely, to prevent a forfeiture where the landlord may be adequately compensated and receive proper undertakings as to future performance, so that the forfeiture clause is merely security to achieve these results.

As to the question whether Lord Eldon's view in *Hill* v. *Barclay* remained good law in relation to covenants to repair and similar covenants concerning the condition of the property (other than those now specifically dealt with by statute[82]) he said[83]:

> "Lord Eldon LC's decision was in fact based partly on the circumstance that he was concerned with a wilful default and partly on the impossibility of speculating whether the later doing of the repairs would compensate the landlord; such considerations remain relevant."

It seems apparent, therefore, that matters relating to the "wilfulness" of the breach and the adequacy or otherwise of compensation are now to be considered as mere factors influencing the court's discretion whether or not to grant relief in a particular case. Indeed, since the power of re-entry in the case before him was, clearly, inserted with the intention of securing enforcement of the various covenants contained in the assignment, his Lordship had no difficulty in holding that the court had the requisite equitable jurisdiction to grant relief. However, as a matter of

---

[81] Moreover, in his view, the fact that Parliament had intervened to provide specific machinery for the granting of relief against forfeiture of leases did not in any way negative an intention that equity's inherent jurisdiction should continue to operate outside the specific area of leases covered by the legislation. He referred to the view of Kay L.J. in *Barrow* v. *Isaacs* [1891] 1 Q.B. 417, 430, that covenants against assignment (which were excluded from the Conveyancing Act 1881) were left to be dealt with according to the general law. The question as to the extent to which equity's jurisdiction has been ousted by subsequent legislation is considered fully in Chap. 8.

[82] Relief under statute is considered in Chap. 10.

[83] *Ibid.* p. 102.

discretion, he concluded that the court ought not, in the circumstances, to grant relief to the respondent. He said[84]:

> "Failures to observe the covenants having occurred, it would be right to consider whether the assignor should be allowed to exercise his legal rights if the essentials of the bargain could be secured and if it was fair and just to prevent him from doing so. It would be necessary, as stated above, to consider the conduct of the assignee, the nature and gravity of the breach, and its relation to the value of the property which might be forfeited. Established and in my opinion sound principle requires that wilful breaches should not, or at least only in exceptional cases, be relieved against, if only for the reason that the assignor should not be compelled to remain in a relation of neighbourhood with a person in deliberate breach of his obligations."

Having examined all the evidence available to the trial judge, his Lordship concluded that the case was not one suitable for relief because of the respondent's clear and wilful breaches of the covenants and his inability to make good the consequences of his default.

The only other member of the House of Lords to give a substantive opinion was Lord Simon of Glaisdale, who, although expressing general agreement with the views expressed by Lord Wilberforce, went further and concluded that[85]:

> ". . . equity has an unlimited and unfettered jurisdiction to relieve against contractual forfeitures and penalties. What have sometimes been regarded as fetters to the jurisdiction are, in my view, more properly to be seen as considerations which the court will weigh in deciding how to exercise an unfettered jurisdiction."

---

[84] *Ibid.* p. 103. See also Viscount Dilhorne (*ibid.* p. 103), who said: ". . . the cases in which it is right to give relief against forfeiture where there has been a wilful breach of covenant are likely to be few in number and where the conduct of the person seeking to secure the forfeiture has been wholly unreasonable and of a rapacious and unconscionable character".

[85] *Ibid.* p. 104.

It is submitted that this view[86] has much to recommend it and it is regrettable that it has not found support in more recent judicial pronouncements.[87]

[86] Lord Simon had occasion to re-iterate his view in *Mardorf Peach & Co. Ltd.* v. *Attica Sea Carriers Corp. of Liberia, The Laconia* [1977] 1 All E.R. 545, a case involving a time charter-party which contained a clause permitting the owners to withdraw the vessel from the service of the charterers upon non-payment of the hire. See also, *Afovos Shipping Co. SA* v. *R. Pagnan and F. Lli, The Afovos* [1980] 2 Lloyd's Rep. 469, Lloyd J. and *Scandinavian Trading Tanker Co. AB* v. *Flota Petrolera Ecuatoriana, The Scaptrade* [1981] 2 Lloyd's Rep. 425, Lloyd J.

[87] *Scandinavian Trading Tanker Co. AB* v. *Flota Petrolera Ecuatoriana, The Scaptrade* [1983] 1 All E.R. 301, (C.A.) and [1983] 2 All E.R. 763, (H.L.), where the view put forward by Lord Simon in the *Shiloh* case was emphatically rejected as a "beguiling heresy": *ibid.* p. 766, *per* Lord Diplock. See also, *Sport Int. Bussum BV* v. *Inter-Footwear Ltd.* [1984] 1 All E.R. 376, (C.A.) and [1984] 2 All E.R. 321, (H.L.), (trade marks); *BICC plc* v. *Burndy Corp.* [1985] 1 All E.R. 417, (C.A.), (patent rights); *Jobson* v. *Johnson* [1989] 1 All E.R. 621, (C.A.), (shares in a football club); *Goker* v. *News Bank plc, The Times*, May 23, 1990 (C.A.), (car purchased under a hire-purchase agreement).

Chapter Eight

The inter-relationship of statutory and equitable jurisdictions to relieve against forfeiture of leases

A brief history of the statutory jurisdiction

It will be seen from the discussion that follows, that the court's statutory power to grant relief against forfeiture of leases has been gradually extended from the single case of non-payment of rent till it has reached its present dimensions of a broadly based jurisdiction, to relieve against virtually all forms of default occasioned by a tenant, sub-tenant or mortgagee.

(1) *Non-payment of rent*

From very early times, equity recognised a tenant's right to be relieved from breach of the covenant to pay rent upon payment of the arrears with costs.[1] Invariably, the tenant would seek relief in the Court of Chancery in the form of an injunction to restrain the landlord's action for ejectment. Moreover, even where the landlord had proceeded to judgment and final delivery up of possession, the tenant could still file a bill in the Court of Chancery seeking relief in terms of an order that the landlord should grant him a new lease of the premises.[2] Thus, the tenant could bring his claim for relief without limitation of time[3] and, in many cases, relief was sought (and obtained) long after the lease had been forfeited at law. In

---

[1] For a detailed historical account of equity's jurisdiction to relieve against forfeiture for non-payment of rent, see Chap. 7.

[2] *Bowser* v. *Colby* (1841) 1 Hare 109, 126; 66 E.R. 969, 976, *per* Wigram V.-C. and *Dendy* v. *Evans* [1910] 1 K.B. 263, 266–267, (C.A.), *per* Cozens-Hardy M.R.

[3] See, *Bowser* v. *Colby* (1841) 1 Hare 109, 125; 66 E.R. 969, 976, *per* Sir James Wigram V.-C.

order, therefore, to avoid hardship to a landlord caused by a late application for relief,[4] section 2 of the Landlord and Tenant Act 1730 provided that any bill for relief from forfeiture had to be filed within six months after judgment for execution was obtained in the common law courts, failing which the equitable jurisdiction to relieve was barred. Under section 4 of the Act, provided the tenant filed his bill within the prescribed time limit and tendered the full amount of the arrears of rent and costs, the landlord's proceedings for ejectment at common law were stayed and the original lease was revived as if no forfeiture had taken place.

The provisions of the 1730 Act were repealed and substantially re-enacted by sections 210 to 212 of the Common Law Procedure Act 1852, which continue to provide the main statutory framework for relief from forfeiture for non-payment of rent to the present day. Under section 210, the tenant's rights to relief at law and in equity (at or after the trial of the landlord's proceedings for possession) are barred unless all arrears of rent and costs are paid within six months of the execution of the order for possession. Section 211 gives statutory recognition to the tenant's right to apply for relief in equity but provides that the tenant's equitable right will be barred unless he pays into court the arrears of rent and costs claimed by the landlord. Section 212 of the 1852 Act provides for the granting of relief (in the form of a stay of the landlord's action for possession and a revival of the original lease) if at least six months rent is in arrears[5] and the tenant pays (or tenders) all the arrears and costs to the landlord or into court at any time before the trial of the landlord's action for possession.

The 1852 Act continues to govern proceedings for the granting of equitable relief in cases where the landlord is seeking to enforce his right of forfeiture of the lease by action through the courts. This statutory jurisdiction to grant equitable relief has, however, no application in circumstances where the landlord proceeds to forfeit the lease for non-payment of rent by actually physically re-entering[6] the demised premises without recourse to litigation. In this limited case, the tenant is entitled to rely upon equity's inherent jurisdiction to grant relief without any fixed

---

[4] See, *e.g. Doe* d. *Hitchins* v. *Lewis* (1751) 1 Burr. 614, 619; 97 E.R. 475, 478, *per* Lord Mansfield C.J.

[5] See s. 210 of the 1852 Act and *Standard Pattern Co. Ltd.* v. *Ivey* [1962] Ch. 432, where it was held that a tenant could not, by payment in of the sums necessary to meet the landlord's claim, compel a stay of proceedings under s. 212 where only one quarter's rent was unpaid. In such case, the tenant could seek relief under s. 46 of the Supreme Court of Judicature (Consolidation) Act 1925, currently s. 38(1) of the Supreme Court Act 1981.

[6] The landlord is not permitted to re-enter, otherwise than by court proceedings, where the premises are let as a dwelling and where any person is lawfully residing there: s. 2 of the Protection from Eviction Act 1977.

(statutory) time limit.[7] In *Thatcher* v. *C. H. Pearce & Sons (Contractors) Ltd.*,[8] the landlords peaceably re-entered the demised premises pursuant to a forfeiture clause in the lease for non-payment of a quarter's rent. The tenant sought relief from forfeiture but his writ was not issued within six months of the forfeiture as provided by the 1852 Act. Sir Jocelyn Simon P. held that since the landlord had re-entered peaceably without an order of the court, the court's power to grant relief from forfeiture was not statutory but arose from its equitable jurisdiction to which no statutory period of limitation applied.[9] However, relief could be refused on equitable grounds where, for example, the tenant had unduly delayed in bringing his claim for relief.[10] In the words of Sir Jocelyn Simon P.[11]:

> "I think that a court of equity—and it is such jurisdiction that I am exercising now—would look at the situation of the Plaintiff to see whether in all the circumstances he acted with reasonable promptitude. Naturally it would also have to look at the situation of the Defendants to see if anything has happened, particularly by way of delay on the part of the Plaintiff, which would cause a greater hardship to them by the extension of the relief sought than by its denial to the Plaintiff."

Although the courts of the common law were given power, under section 212 of the 1852 Act, to grant relief from forfeiture on payment of the arrears of rent and costs by the tenant before trial, relief after judgment for possession continued to be obtainable only from the Court of Chancery until the coming into effect of section 1 of the Common Law Procedure Act 1860. Section 1 of the 1860 Act was repealed and replaced by section 46 of the Supreme Court of Judicature (Consolidation) Act 1925, which empowered the High Court (in the case of any action for forfeiture brought for non-payment of rent) to give relief in a summary manner and subject to the same terms and conditions in all respects as to payment of rent, costs and otherwise as could formerly have been

---

[7] See, *Howard* v. *Fanshawe* [1895] 2 Ch. 581 *per* Stirling J. and *Lovelock* v. *Margo* [1963] 2 Q.B. 786, (C.A.). If the tenant's application is made in the county court, it will be governed by s. 139(2) of the County Courts Act 1984 whereby, subject to a time limit of six months from the date of the landlord's re-entry, the tenant may apply for such relief as the High Court could have granted.

[8] [1968] 1 W.L.R. 748. See also, *Bowser* v. *Colby* (1841) 1 Hare 109; 66 E.R. 969.

[9] Put at its highest, the time-limit of six months contained in the 1852 Act would probably be used as no more than a guide in the court's exercise of its equitable jurisdiction: *Howard* v. *Fanshawe* [1895] 2 Ch. 581, 589, *per* Stirling J. and *Thatcher* v. *C.H. Pearce & Sons (Contractors) Ltd.* [1968] 1 W.L.R. 748, 755–756, *per* Sir Jocelyn Simon P.

[10] See also, *Stanhope* v. *Haworth* (1866) 3 T.L.R. 34, where the landlord had relet the demised premises to a third party.

[11] [1968] 1 W.L.R. 748, 756.

enforced by the Court of Chancery. The provision is currently contained in section 38(1) of the Supreme Court Act 1981.[12]

By the County Courts Amendment Act 1856, the County Courts Acts 1934 and 1959 and, currently, sections 138 and 139 of the County Courts Act 1984, the county court was given statutory jurisdiction to relieve against forfeiture for non-payment of rent.[13] Under section 138(2) of the 1984 Act, if the tenant pays all the arrears of rent and costs of the action into court not less than five clear days before the date fixed for the hearing of the landlord's action, the landlord's action will automatically cease and the tenant will hold the demised premises under the original lease. Under section 138(3), where the tenant seeks relief at the trial, the court is obliged to make an order for possession unless the tenant pays into court all the arrears and costs within a time limit specified in the court order, which is fixed at the discretion of the court, but which must not be less than four weeks from the date of the order. If the tenant pays within the time limit fixed under the order, he will continue to hold under the lease but if he fails to pay within the time limit, he was formerly barred from all relief except that afforded by section 138(4),[14] which empowered the court at any time before the landlord recovered possession to extend the time limit. The current position, however, under section 55 of the Administration of Justice Act 1985, is that the tenant may still apply for relief where the landlord has recovered possession of the premises following a court order, provided that his application for relief is made within six months from the date when the landlord retook possession.

The foregoing county court provisions apply to cases where the landlord is proceeding *by action* to enforce a right of forfeiture for non-payment of rent. Where the landlord forfeits the lease by actually *physically re-entering*[15] the demised premises without recourse to the courts, section 139(2) (re-enacting section 191(3) of the County Courts Act 1959) expressly confers on the county court the same power to relieve against forfeiture for non-payment of rent as the High Court could have granted, provided that the application for relief is made within six months from the date of the landlord's peaceable re-entry.

---

[12] Under s. 38(2) of the 1981 Act, where the tenant (or a person deriving title under him) is granted relief under s. 38(1), he is deemed to hold the demised premises in accordance with the terms of the lease without the necessity for a new lease.

[13] For a historical survey of the relevant legislation, see *Di Palma* v. *Victoria Square Property Co. Ltd.* [1984] 1 Ch. 346, 365–367, *per* Scott J.

[14] s. 138(4) re-enacted s. 23 of the Administration of Justice Act 1965.

[15] The landlord is not permitted to re-enter, otherwise than by court proceedings, where the premises are let as a dwelling and whilst any person is lawfully residing therein: s. 2 of the Protection from Eviction Act 1977.

(2) Failure to insure

It was established in a series of cases[16] decided in the 19th century that equity had no power to relieve against forfeiture for wilful breach (*i.e.* not caused by fraud,[17] accident, surprise or mistake) of a covenant to insure. However, sections 4 to 9 of the Law of Property and Trustees Relief Amendment Act 1859 empowered a court of equity to grant relief in a case where no loss had occurred and the breach had been committed without fraud or gross negligence and there was insurance on foot at the time of the tenant's application to the court.[18] This provision was repealed and re-enacted by section 2 of the Common Law Procedure Act 1860 which extended equitable relief in cases of failure to insure (and non-payment of rent) to the courts of the common law. It was not until 1882, however, that relief against failure to insure was given a more broader base under section 14(1) and (2) of the Conveyancing and Law of Property Act 1881.[19]

(3) Other breaches of covenant[20]

Until the passing of the Conveyancing and Law of Property Act 1881, relief against forfeiture had been limited to cases involving non-payment of rent, failure to insure and other cases involving accident, surprise, mistake or fraud.[21]

Under section 14(1) of the 1881 Act (predecessor to the current provisions contained in section 146(1) of the Law of Property Act 1925), the landlord's right of forfeiture for breach of covenant (other than for rent) was made subject to the pre-condition of the service of a notice by him upon the tenant specifying the particular breach complained of and (if the breach was one capable of remedy) requesting the tenant to remedy the same within a reasonable period of time and (in any case) requesting the tenant to make compensation in money for the breach. Prior to the passing of the 1881 Act, a right of re-entry reserved in a lease conditional

---

[16] See *Rolfe* v. *Harris* (1811) 2 Pri. 202, 146 E.R. 68; *Reynolds* v. *Pitt* (1812) 19 Ves. 134, 34 E.R. 468; *Bracebridge* v. *Buckley* (1816) 2 Pri. 200, 146 E.R. 68 and *Green* v. *Bridges* (1830) 4 Sim. 96; 58 E.R. 37. For an historical survey of equity's jurisdiction in this area, see Chap. 7.

[17] *Meek* v. *Carter* (1858) 4 Jur. (N.S.) 992.

[18] The court had no power to relieve the same person more than once in respect of the same covenant or condition nor to grant any relief where a prior forfeiture had already been waived out of court in favour of the person seeking relief.

[19] The express provision for relief in cases of insurance covenants contained in s. 2 of the Common Law Procedure Act 1860 was expressly repealed by virtue of s. 14(7) of the 1881 Act.

[20] The provisions contained in s. 147 of the Law of Property Act 1925 (relief against landlord's notice to effect decorative repairs) and the Leasehold Property (Repairs) Act 1938 (restricting the landlord's right to forfeit and claim damages for disrepair) are considered in Chap. 10.

[21] For a detailed historical account of equity's jurisdiction to relieve against forfeiture of leases, see Chap. 7.

upon breach of a covenant to repair could be enforced by the landlord at common law without the tenant having any opportunity to meet the complaint and sometimes even without his knowing that a breach had, in fact, occurred.

A further purpose of the 1881 Act was to supplement equity and to enable a tenant to be relieved from the forfeiture of his lease. In the words of Lord Templeman in *Billson* v. *Residential Apartments Ltd.*[22]:

> "The need for such intervention was and is manifest because otherwise a tenant who had paid a large premium for a 999-year lease at a low rent could lose his asset by a breach of covenant which was remediable or which caused the landlord no damage. The forfeiture of any lease, however short, may unjustly enrich the landlord at the expense of the tenant."

Under section 14(2) of the 1881 Act,[23] the High Court was empowered to relieve the tenant against the forfeiture if it thought fit to do so "having regard to the proceedings and conduct of the parties . . . and to all other circumstances" and on such terms (if any) "as to costs, expenses, damages, compensation, penalty, or otherwise, including the grant of an injunction to restrain any like breach in the future." Although conferring a widely based statutory power to relieve against forfeiture, section 14(2) did not extend to covenants against assignment, underletting or parting with possession,[24] or to certain covenants in mining leases (*i.e.* covenants to permit the landlord to inspect books, accounts, records and weighing machines)[25] or to a condition for forfeiture on the bankruptcy of the tenant.[26] In this last case, relief was not made available until 1892 when section 2 of the Conveyancing and Law of Property Act 1892 provided a limited power on the court to relieve against forfeiture for bankruptcy or insolvency.[27] Moreover, by section 4 of that Act, jurisdiction was for the first time conferred on the court to relieve a sub-tenant of the whole or part of the demised premises from the forfeiture of his sub-lease.[28] In this connection, it was held in *Gray* v. *Bonsall*[29] that this section applied so as to

---

[22] [1992] 1 All E.R. 141, 145.
[23] See now s. 146(2) of the Law of Property Act 1925.
[24] See s. 14(6)(i) of the 1881 Act. Moreover, no relief could be obtained in such a case in equity: *Barrow* v. *Isaacs & Son* [1891] 1 Q.B. 417, (C.A.); *Ellis* v. *Allen* [1914] 1 Ch. 904, 909 and *Atkin* v. *Rose* [1923] 1 Ch. 522, 539. The statutory exclusion did not include a covenant against sharing possession (*Jackson* v. *Simons* [1923] 1 Ch. 373) or against assigning for the benefit of creditors (*Gentle* v. *Faulkner* [1900] 2 Q.B. 267) but did include a covenant against parting with possession of part of the premises (*Abrahams* v. *Mac Fisheries Ltd.* [1925] 2 K.B. 18 and *Carrington Manufacturing Co. Ltd.* v. *Saldin* (1925) 133 L.T. 432 but contrast *Russell* v. *Beecham* [1924] 1 K.B. 525, 536, *per* Scrutton L.J.).
[25] See s. 14(6)(ii) of the 1881 Act.
[26] See s. 14(6)(i) of the 1881 Act.
[27] See now, ss. 146(9) and (10) of the Law of Property Act 1925 discussed fully in Chap. 10.
[28] Effectively, overruling *Burt* v. *Gray* [1891] 2 Q.B. 98.
[29] [1904] 1 K.B. 601.

permit relief to be given to sub-tenants not only against breaches of covenant other than non-payment of rent but also against breaches of covenant to pay rent. The provision is now to be found in section 146(4) of the Law of Property Act 1925.[30] Under section 146(4), the court is empowered to make an order vesting for the whole term of the lease (or any less term) the property comprised in the lease (or any part thereof) in the sub-tenant, upon such conditions as to the execution of any deed or other document, payment of rent, costs, expenses, damages, compensation, giving security, or otherwise, as the court in the circumstances of each case, should think fit.

As to the exclusion in respect of covenants against assigning, subletting and parting with possession,[31] this was eventually repealed by section 78(1) of the Law of Property Act 1922[32] in respect of breaches occurring after January 1, 1926 where the premises concerned had not been assigned, underlet, etc., to a limited company.[33]

The current statutory provisions are to be found in section 146 of the Law of Property Act 1925 which repealed and re-enacted section 14 of the Conveyancing and Law of Property Act 1881 and sections 2 and 4 of the Conveyancing and Law of Property Act 1892. In addition, section 146 included[34] the power of the court to relieve against forfeiture for breach of covenant to assign, underlet and part with possession, which had already been given in modified form under section 78(1) of the Law of Property Act 1922.

The current scope of equity's jurisdiction

An interesting question which has vexed the courts during the past decade is the extent to which the inherent equitable jurisdiction to relieve against forfeiture of leases has been implicitly removed by legislation conferring statutory powers of relief in the landlord and tenant context. The question has arisen specifically in the context of the provisions of section 146 of the Law of Property Act 1925. In *Shiloh Spinners Ltd.* v. *Harding,*[35] in which the House of Lords recognised retrospectively the existence of an inherent equitable jurisdiction to relieve against forfeiture for wilful breaches of covenant (other than non-payment of rent) despite

---

[30] Relief available to sub-tenants is fully discussed in Chap. 10.
[31] See s. 14(6)(i) of the 1881 Act.
[32] See also, para. 30 of the Third Schedule to the Law of Property (Amendment) Act 1924, which enacted an absolute repeal of the exclusion without restrictions.
[33] Thus, curing the anomaly from 1892 to 1925 that the court had power only to grant relief against forfeiture for breach of a sub-tenant's but not a tenant's covenant against assignment, under-letting etc.: *Imray* v. *Oakshette* [1897] 2 Q.B. 218, (C.A.) and *Matthews* v. *Smallwood* [1910] 1 Ch. 777.
[34] See s. 146(8) of the 1925 Act. See also, *House Property & Investment Company Ltd.* v. *James Walker, Goldsmith and Silversmith Ltd.* [1948] 1 K.B. 257.
[35] [1973] A.C. 691.

the previously held view[36] that no such jurisdiction existed, Lord Wilberforce observed[37]:

"... a point of more difficulty arises from the intervention of Parliament in providing specific machinery for the granting of relief against forfeiture of leases ... This, it is said, negatives an intention that any corresponding jurisdiction should exist outside the case of leases. I do not accept this argument. In my opinion where the courts have established a general principle of law or equity, and the legislature steps in with particular legislation in a particular area, it must, unless showing a contrary intention, be taken to have left cases outside that area where they were under the influence of the general law. To suppose otherwise involves the conclusion that an existing jurisdiction has been cut down by implication by an enactment moreover which is positive in character (for it amplifies the jurisdiction in cases of leases) rather than negative."[38]

The upshot of this dictum appears to be that, if there is legislation in a particular area, it necessarily must exclude any inherent jurisdiction that also covers that area unless a contrary intention is shown from the wording of the statute. In this connection, there have been a number of cases decided since *Shiloh* which have raised the question whether the equitable jurisdiction to relieve from forfeiture of a lease has survived the relevant legislation giving the statutory right to such relief or whether such legislation has, in effect, impliedly extinguished the inherent jurisdiction in relation to leases.

In one group of cases, an inherent equitable jurisdiction to grant relief in relation to leases was upheld in circumstances where the condition for obtaining relief under the relevant statute did not apply.

In *Ladup Ltd.* v. *Williams & Glyn's Bank plc,*[39] the plaintiff recovered judgment for a sum of £43,000 in an action against the tenant of a residential flat and, in order to enforce the judgment, obtained a charging order in respect of the tenant's lease of the flat. Subsequently, the landlord brought proceedings against the tenant for the forfeiture of the lease for non-payment of rent and obtained possession of the flat. The plaintiff creditor then sought relief from the forfeiture as being a person interested in the lease by virtue of the charging order. Warner J. held that the court

---

[36] Emanating from the decision of Lord Eldon in *Hill* v. *Barclay* (1811) 18 Ves. Jun. 56; 34 E.R. 238.

[37] [1973] A.C. 691, 724–725.

[38] Lord Wilberforce referred to *Barrow* v. *Isaacs & Son* [1891] 1 Q.B. 417, 430, where Kay L.J. held that covenants against assigning (which were expressly excluded from the Conveyancing and Law of Property Act 1881 by virtue of s. 14(6)(i) thereof) were left to be dealt with according to the ordinary law.

[39] [1985] 2 All E.R. 577.

was entitled, in the exercise of its inherent equitable jurisdiction,[40] to grant relief to an equitable chargee who had no interest in the lease entitling him to possession of the demised premises. In his view, there was no fetter on the jurisdiction of a court of equity to relieve against forfeiture where the object of the right to forfeit was essentially to secure payment of a sum of money as in the case of a right to forfeit a lease for non-payment of rent.[41] The case can be explained on the basis that relief against forfeiture for non-payment of rent falls within a class of its own so that the relevant statutory provisions were not to be treated as being exhaustive.

In *Abbey National Building Society* v. *Maybeech*,[42] the plaintiff building society lent the tenant of a flat the sum of £17,609 on the security of a charge by way of legal mortgage over the lease of the demised premises. Subsequently, the landlord forfeited the lease for non-payment of rent and service charge contributions and obtained an order for possession of the premises. The plaintiff building society did not find out about the forfeiture until it was informed by the Land Registry that the landlord had applied to have the forfeited lease deleted from the register. The plaintiff then issued an originating summons seeking relief[43] from forfeiture of the lease in order to prevent the destruction of its security. This was opposed by the landlord on the ground that judgment had already been executed and that it was now too late to take advantage of section 146(4) of the Law of Property Act 1925 in view of the fact that the landlord was no longer "proceeding by action or otherwise" to enforce his right within the meaning of the sub-section. Nicholls J., however, held that, whilst no relief was available in respect of the failure to pay the service charge contributions under section 146(4) (which applied to other breaches of covenant as well as non-payment of rent) because there were no longer any landlord's proceedings during the pendency of which the plaintiff could apply for

---

[40] It was conceded that s. 146(2) of the Law of Property Act 1925 could not apply because, the landlord having recovered possession of the flat before the issue of the plaintiff's summons for relief, it could not be said that the landlord was "proceeding by action or otherwise to enforce a right of re-entry or forfeiture" within the meaning of that section. Similarly, s. 38 of the Supreme Court Act 1981 did not apply because the plaintiff's claim was not made "in any action in the High Court for the forfeiture of a lease for non-payment of rent" as required by that section.

[41] In so holding, Warner J. relied on the leading speech of Lord Wilberforce in *Shiloh Spinners Ltd.* v. *Harding* [1973] A.C. 691, 722–725.

[42] [1985] 1 Ch. 190. See also *Cardigan Properties Ltd.* v. *Consolidated Property Investment Ltd.* [1991] 07 E.G. 132, where Mr. P.J. Cox, Q.C., sitting as a deputy judge of the Queen's Bench Division, was prepared to grant relief under equity's inherent jurisdiction which, in his view, s. 146 of the 1925 Act had not, in the absence of express words, completely ousted.

[43] In this connection, whilst the plaintiff was entitled to claim relief in respect of the non-payment of rent under s. 210 of the Common Law Procedure Act 1852, relief was also needed in respect of the failure to pay service charges since they had not been made payable as "rent" in the lease.

relief under that section, nevertheless, this did not preclude the court from exercising its equitable jurisdiction to grant relief from a failure to pay a specific sum of money. In his view, neither section 4 of the Conveyancing and Law of Property Act 1892 nor its successor (section 146(4) of the Law of Property Act 1925) were intended as an exhaustive provision regarding the court's jurisdiction to grant relief to underlessees in either rent breach or other (non-rent) breach cases. In the course of his judgment, he referred to the Court of Appeal decision in *Lovelock* v. *Margo*,[44] which affirmed the continued existence of equity's inherent jurisdiction to grant relief to a tenant after a landlord had re-entered peaceably, notwithstanding sections 210 and 212 of the Common Law Procedure Act 1852 which did not expressly deal with such a case. Nicholls J. also gained considerable assistance from the Court of Appeal decision in *Gray* v. *Bonsall*,[45] where an underlessee was granted relief in respect of non-payment of rent due under the headlease. The question which arose in this case was whether the court's power to grant relief arose under section 1 of the Common Law Procedure Act 1860 or under section 4 of the Conveyancing and Law of Property Act 1892. The Court of Appeal held that relief could be granted to the underlessee under either provision since section 4 of the 1892 Act could not be construed as excluding the wider jurisdiction already in existence in the case of non-payment of rent under section 1 of the 1860 Act.[46]

In both the *Ladup* and *Maybeech* cases, very clear grounds existed for affording relief to the chargee and mortgagee, respectively, due to the gross disparity in both cases between the possible ultimate loss to the landlord in having to wait a little longer for his rent arrears and the value of the leasehold security which the applicants for relief stood to lose. In the *Ladup* case, Warner J., applying the principle that relief against forfeiture would be given in equity if it would be unconscionable for the landlord, who had received his rent in full with interest and costs, to insist on taking advantage of the right to forfeit the lease, granted relief so as to enable the chargee to effect a sale of the lease subject to the charge in order to recover his security. In the *Maybeech* case, Nicholls J. granted relief to the mortgagee upon terms that it should pay all arrears of rent and service contributions with interest and costs, observing[47]:

---

[44] [1963] 2 Q.B. 786. See also the decision of Stirling J. in *Howard* v. *Fanshawe* [1895] 2 Ch. 581.
[45] [1904] 1 K.B. 601.
[46] See also, *Nind* v. *Nineteenth Century Building Society* [1894] 1 Q.B. 472, relied on by Nicholls J., where once again the court was concerned with the question as to whether two statutory provisions could co-exist. In neither case was the court concerned with the question of the interaction between an express statutory provision and equity's inherent jurisdiction: See the observations of Sir Nicolas Browne-Wilkinson V.C. in *Billson* v. *Residential Apartments Ltd.* [1991] 3 All E.R. 265, 282.
[47] [1985] 1 Ch. 190, 205.

"... the value of the lease far exceeded the arrears of the unpaid sums, if relief is not granted the building society may well lose the whole of the amount outstanding and which was secured on the lease, and it is not suggested that the lessor has suffered any loss which will not be adequately recompensed ..."

It will now be convenient to turn to a second group of cases in which an inherent jurisdiction was denied in the face of the existence of a statutory jurisdiction covering the area in point. In *Official Custodian for Charities* v. *Parway Estates Development Ltd.*[48] (decided on the same day as the *Maybeech* case), the question in issue was whether the court had jurisdiction to grant equitable relief from the tenant's liquidation in circumstances where no such relief was available under section 146(10) of the Law of Property Act 1925 because the application for relief had not been made within one year of the tenant's liquidation as required by that section. The Court of Appeal, applying the dictum of Lord Wilberforce in the *Shiloh* case, held that where the legislature had enacted particular legislation in a particular area (as, for example, in section 146(10) of the 1925 Act), effect had to be given to it so that any wider equitable jurisdiction was thereby ousted. Dillon L.J. (who gave the leading judgment of the Court), considered that section 2 of the Conveyancing and Law of Property Act 1892 and, currently, section 146(9) and (10) of the 1925 Act, would not make any sense unless they fell to be regarded as comprehensive within their particular areas: "there is no sense in imposing a year's time limit for applications made by an insolvent lessee if the court has unlimited original jurisdiction to entertain applications made out of time."[49] In his view, therefore, since legislation had stepped into the area of law concerning relief against forfeiture in the event of bankruptcy or liquidation, any inherent equitable jurisdiction in this area had been effectively excluded.

The reasoning of Dillon L.J. in the *Parway* case was followed by Walton J. in *Smith* v. *Metropolitan City Properties Ltd.*,[50] a case involving the forfeiture of a lease for a tenant's breach of covenant to repair. Here, the tenant, against whom forfeiture proceedings had been completed (and the landlord had re-taken possession of the demised premises), sought to re-open the question of relief against forfeiture by invoking equity's inherent jurisdiction to grant relief. The landlords replied by issuing a motion to dismiss the tenant's summons for relief as being an abuse of the process of the court. The essence of the tenant's argument was that, although the statutory jurisdiction under section 146(2) of the Law of Property Act 1925 could not be relied on (as the landlords' forfeiture proceedings had been completed), the court still had an equitable jurisdiction to grant relief in

[48] [1985] 1 Ch. 151.
[49] *Ibid.* p. 165.
[50] (1986) 1 E.G.L.R. 52.

any circumstances in which the statutory jurisdiction was not available. Walton J., relying upon the dictum of Lord Wilberforce in the *Shiloh* case as explained by Dillon L.J. in *Parway*, held that such an argument was untenable on the authorities and "quite fantastic."[51] In his view, Lord Wilberforce's reference to equitable jurisdiction not been ousted only concerned cases outside the area of leases and underleases already covered by the provisions of section 146 of the 1925 Act. Accordingly, in his view, the equitable jurisdiction to relieve for breach of covenant as between landlord and tenant (other than for non-payment of rent) no longer existed. He, therefore, concluded that the reasoning applied by Dillon L.J. in the *Parway* case to section 146(9) and (10) of the 1925 Act applied equally to the rest of that section. With reference to Lord Wilberforce's dictum in *Shiloh*, he said[52]:

> "What Lord Wilberforce is saying in the plainest terms is: 'Look, the legislature has interfered with the old equitable jurisdiction to grant relief against forfeiture in the case of leases and underleases, but outside that area it has left the jurisdiction where it was.' If, I may add, the situation had been that even by stepping in with specific legislation, Parliament had not in fact interfered one bit with the equitable jurisdiction, then it is quite clear that Lord Wilberforce would have said: 'I do not know what you are talking about. However much legislation there has been, the equitable jurisdiction, even in the case of leases, as well as outside them, is left precisely where it is.' That, of course, is precisely what he did not say."

With reference to the decision of Nicholls J. in the *Maybeech* case, Walton J. observed[53]:

> "With great respect to the learned judge, first of all he did not have the very helpful and definite comments of Dillon L.J. [in the *Parway* case] and, second, in my judgment, he does not appear to have appreciated, perhaps lacking those particular comments of Dillon L.J., the precise effect of what Lord Wilberforce was getting at."

The Court of Appeal's hostility to acknowledging the existence of inherent equitable relief within the compass of statutory provision is also highlighted in the case of *Di Palma* v. *Victoria Square Property Ltd.*,[54] where the tenant sought equitable relief in the High Court, having failed to pay arrears of rent in due time in compliance with a court order made pursuant to the provisions of section 138 of the County Courts Act 1984. The Court of Appeal held[55] that a tenant sued in the county court for non-

---

[51] *Ibid.* p. 53.
[52] *Ibid.*
[53] *Ibid.*
[54] [1986] Ch. 150, (C.A.).
[55] Overruling *Jones* v. *Barnett* [1984] 3 All E.R. 129.

payment of rent could only seek relief from forfeiture under the provisions of section 138 of the 1984 Act and that the words "barred from all relief" contained in section 138(7)[56] meant that he was barred from obtaining all relief whatsoever, including relief that might be obtained other than under section 138, namely, in the High Court. Although the actual decision has been somewhat tempered since the amendment of section 138 by virtue of section 55 of the Administration of Justice Act 1985, the decision illustrates the modern trend of the caselaw to rule out the possibility of equitable relief in the face of statutory intervention.

This trend is now, perhaps, most vividly shown in the recent Court of Appeal decision in *Billson* v. *Residential Apartments Ltd.*[57] In this case, the landlords forfeited the tenants' lease of residential premises for breach of covenant not to make alterations without the landlord's previous consent in writing, by peaceably re-entering the premises and changing the locks. The re-entry was effected at 6am but four hours later on the same day, the tenants' workmen regained possession. The landlords then issued a writ claiming possession on the ground *inter alia* that their re-entry constituted a lawful and valid forfeiture of the tenants' lease. The court held that, although the landlords had been in possession (following their peaceable re-entry) for only a few hours, this precluded the court, under section 146(2) of the Law of Property Act 1925, from granting the tenants relief from forfeiture because a landlord who had already obtained possession of the premises was no longer "proceeding" to enforce his right within the meaning of the section.[58] In the absence of any statutory jurisdiction to grant relief, the tenants argued (in the alternative) that the court could, nevertheless, relieve them from the forfeiture under the inherent equitable jurisdiction. On this point, the majority of the Court of Appeal (Sir Nicolas Browne-Wilkinson V.C. and Parker L.J.) held that the inherent jurisdiction as between landlord and tenant to relieve against forfeiture from a wilful breach of covenant (other than non-payment of rent) had

---

[56] Formerly s. 191(1)(c) of the County Courts Act 1959.

[57] [1991] 3 All E.R. 265.

[58] The Court of Appeal's decision on this point was overruled on appeal by the House of Lords: See *Billson* v. *Residential Apartments Ltd.* [1992] 1 All E.R. 141. The cases of *Rogers* v. *Rice* [1892] 2 Ch. 170, *Quilter* v. *Mapleson* (1882) 9 Q.B.D. 672 and *Pakwood Transport Ltd.* v. *15 Beauchamp Place Ltd.* (1977) 245 E.G. 309, were relied on by the Court of Appeal. In the former two cases, it was established that once a landlord had obtained possession of the premises under order of the court, the statutory right to relieve the tenant against forfeiture was lost since it could not thereafter be said that the landlord "is" proceeding to enforce his rights. In the latter case, it was held that a tenant could apply for relief against forfeiture as soon as a s. 146 notice was served and before the landlord had started proceedings. The ground for so holding was that, in a case of peaceable re-entry, the right to relief would otherwise be illusory, since the tenant had no right to claim relief after peaceable re-entry.

been entirely extinguished by the provisions of section 146 of the Law of Property Act 1925.[59]

In the course of his judgment, Sir Nicholas Browne-Wilkinson V.C. took the opportunity to examine the effect of the legislation on the three recognised heads of equity jurisdiction[60] to relieve against forfeiture, namely, in case of (a) fraud, accident or mistake[61] (b) non-payment of rent or other specific sums of money and (c) wilful breach of covenant other than non-payment of rent where adequate compensation could be made for the breach.[62] Under (a), relief could still be granted in an appropriate case even where the fraud, accident or mistake arose in the context of a lease. On this point, the Vice-Chancellor observed[63]:

"In my judgment, the general equitable jurisdiction to relieve from the consequences of fraud, accident or mistake has never been affected by the statutory provisions and is not affected by section 146. Say a landlord was by fraud to procure the tenant to commit a breach of covenant and then forfeited the lease and obtained possession. Can it be doubted that the court would relieve against the forfeiture on the grounds of fraud even though the statutory jurisdiction to grant relief was no longer exercisable?"

Under (b), the Vice-Chancellor concluded that the equitable jurisdiction remained intact and that the relevant legislation (which was largely procedural) merely modified and limited equity's power to grant relief in certain respects, particularly in relation to time-limits. Moreover, the inherent jurisdiction to relieve without time-limit continued to apply in cases involving a forfeiture by peaceable re-entry.

Under (c), following a brief review of the earlier caselaw referred to above,[64] the Vice-Chancellor concluded that the equitable jurisdiction to relieve from wilful breaches of covenant (other than non-payment of rent), which had been resurrected retrospectively by the House of Lords in the *Shiloh* case, had been extinguished in the landlord and tenant context by reason of Parliament having legislated comprehensively in that field. He put the matter succinctly in this way[65]:

---

[59] In so doing, the majority applied the dictum of Lord Wilberforce in the *Shiloh* case and the observations of Dillon L.J. in *Parway*. The majority view was applied by Mummery J. in *British & West Building Society* v. *Turner* [1991] 37 E.G. 141, concerning the right of a mortgagee to seek relief following the landlord's peaceable re-entry of the premises.

[60] For a full historical survey of equity's jurisdiction to relieve against forfeiture, see Chap. 7.

[61] See, *Barrow* v. *Isaacs* [1891] 1 Q.B. 417.

[62] See, *Shiloh Spinners Ltd.* v. *Harding* [1973] A.C. 691.

[63] [1991] 3 All E.R. 265, 282.

[64] Notably, *Official Custodian for Charities* v. *Parway Estates Developments Ltd.* [1985] Ch. 151, *Abbey National Building Society* v. *Maybeech* [1985] Ch. 190 and *Smith* v. *Metropolitan City Properties Ltd.* (1986) 1 E.G.L.R. 52.

[65] [1991] 3 All E.R. 265, 281.

"Since, at the relevant times, no one thought that there was an inherent jurisdiction, the intention of Parliament in legislating must have been to lay down a comprehensive and exclusive code setting out the circumstances in which relief could be given."

Parker L.J. reached a similar conclusion relying predominantly on the dictum of Lord Wilberforce in the *Shiloh* case. He observed[66]:

"If it was believed that there was no relevant old law the parliamentary intent must, as it seems to me, have been the positive intent to create and thereafter maintain a comprehensive and exhaustive statutory provision."

Nicholls L.J., however, gave a strong dissenting judgment, pointing out the absurdity of denying relief in the circumstances of the case before him, since it meant that if a landlord chose to effect the forfeiture by physical re-entry he would be in a more favourable position than if he had effected his forfeiture by court proceedings for possession of the premises. In his view, sections 146(2) and (4) (conferring on the court power to grant relief to lessees and underlessees, respectively) were expressed in positive enabling terms and did not cut down any other jurisdiction of the court to grant relief. He rejected the "exhaustive code" interpretation of the sections stating[67]:

"When the statutes of 1881 and 1892 were enacted, the generally preferred view within the legal profession was the strict view of Lord Eldon LC in *Hill* v. *Barclay* . . . Thus, when enacting those statutes, and the same would be true of section 146 of the 1925 Act, Parliament is not to be taken as having intended that the relevant sections impliedly superseded and excluded the residual, ancient jurisdiction of the Court of Chancery . . . for this reason: *as generally perceived at that time* this residual jurisdiction seldom availed a tenant in non-rent cases. Thus there was nothing incongruous in the ancient jurisdiction and the new statutory jurisdiction existing side by side. For what it might avail him, a tenant could still seek to invoke the ancient jurisdiction even after 1881. For what it might be worth to him, the jurisdiction was still there and untouched by the new, enabling legislation, but it could not be expected to be of much help to him . . . However, in 1973 in the *Shiloh Spinners* case, the House of Lords reaffirmed, in more expansive terms, the right of courts of equity to grant relief against forfeiture."

In Nicholls L.J.'s view, therefore, the proper interpretation of section 146 of the 1925 Act, on the question whether that section constituted an

[66] *Ibid.* p. 286.
[67] *Ibid.* pp. 290–291.

exhaustive code or not, could not have been changed by the reawakening of the court of equity's relieving jurisdiction by the *Shiloh* case in 1973. The position, in his view, was that when the relevant statutes were passed, the various statutory provisions were seen as no more than enabling provisions which did not oust the existing jurisdiction of the court of equity and that this remained the position to this day. He approved his earlier decision in the *Maybeech* case[68] and concluded that the court should, on the facts, exercise its equitable jurisdiction to grant relief in circumstances where the landlords had re-entered by stealth and where the tenants had acted with promptitude in seeking relief.

---

[68] Nicholls L.J. felt able to dismiss the observations of Lord Wilberforce in the *Shiloh* case on the basis that the House of Lords was not concerned to examine in depth the position regarding covenants in leases.

Chapter Nine

Relief against forfeiture for non-payment of rent

Introduction

From very early times,[1] equity recognised that it had jurisdiction to relieve against a forfeiture where the object of the forfeiture clause was to secure payment of a definite sum of money.[2]

The underlying principle governing relief was whether the injured party could be put back into the same position as if the covenant had not been broken and this, in turn, depended upon whether the injured party could be adequately compensated for his loss occasioned by the other party's breach. Thus, in cases involving non-payment of rent, the Court of Chancery would invariably grant relief to the defaulting tenant upon payment of the arrears with interest and costs. In *Ladup Ltd.* v. *Williams and Glyn's Bank plc*[3] Warner J. accepted as unchallengeable the proposition that:

> "... a right to forfeit a lease for non-payment of rent is regarded by equity as simply a security for payment of the rent and that relief against forfeiture is granted by equity on the footing that in normal circumstances it would be unconscionable for a landlord who has received his rent in full, with any appropriate interest and costs, to insist (in the absence of any outstanding breach of any other covenant in the lease) on taking advantage of the right to forfeit ..."

This equitable jurisdiction to grant relief against forfeiture for non-

---

[1] The earliest reported case appears to be *Cage* v. *Russell* (1681) 2 Vent. 352; 86 E.R. 481. See further, Chap. 7.

[2] "If valuable property held as a security for a smaller sum than the value of the property was taken, when the smaller sum was once paid relief would be given from the forfeiture": *Wilson* v. *Bolton* (1893) 10 T.L.R. 17, *arguendo*.

[3] [1985] 1 W.L.R. 851, 860.

payment of rent remains intact to this day subject only to various statutory provisions[4] (discussed below) which have merely modified and limited equity's power to grant relief in certain procedural respects.[5] Thus, whilst these provisions differ as between the High Court and county court, the nature of relief in both jurisdictions continues to be rooted in equity's inherent power to relieve against forfeiture for non-payment of rent.

Moreover, the right to equitable relief is the same whether there is a proviso for re-entry for non-payment of rent, thereby determining the lease, or whether the lease is conditioned to be void on non-payment of rent.[6]

Relief in the High Court[7]

(1) Application for relief by tenant

In the High Court, equity's inherent jurisdiction to grant relief against forfeiture for non-payment of rent is placed on a statutory basis by sections 210 to 212 of the Common Law Procedure Act 1852.[8] In the words of Lord Denning M.R. in *Belgravia Insurance Co. Ltd.* v. *Meah*[9]:

> "In cases of non-payment of rent, relief is still based fundamentally on the jurisdiction of Courts of Equity to grant relief, subject to the limitations imposed by sections 210 and 212 of the Common Law Procedure Act 1852."

Under section 212 of the 1852 Act, the tenant[10] is entitled to be relieved

---

[4] For a history of the statutory provisions, see Chap. 8. A contract for the hire of a chattel is outside the scope of the statutory provisions: See *Barton Thompson & Co Ltd.* v. *Stapling Machines Co.* [1966] 2 All E.R. 222.

[5] *Billson* v. *Residential Apartments Ltd.* [1991] 3 W.L.R. 264, 277–278, (C.A.), *per* Sir Nicholas Browne-Wilkinson V.-C.

[6] *Bowser* v. *Colby* (1841) 1 Hare 109, 128; 66 E.R. 969, 977.

[7] For useful precedents, see Walter & Harris, *Claims to the Possession of Land: The Law and Practice*, (1987), App. 5.

[8] ss. 210 to 212 of the 1852 Act substantially re-enacted ss. 2 and 4 of the Landlord and Tenant Act 1730. For a form of statement of claim by the tenant seeking relief against forfeiture: See *Atkin's Court Forms*, (2nd ed., 1990) Vol. 24, p. 286, Form 50. For a statement of claim and form of summons seeking relief: See also Pt. VI of this work.

[9] [1964] 1 Q.B. 436, 443, (C.A.).

[10] Relief is not available under the section to a statutory tenant under the Rent Act 1977: *Brewer* v. *Jacobs* [1923] 1 K.B. 528 and *Dellenty* v. *Pellow* [1951] 2 K.B. 858, (C.A.). See also, *Smith* v. *Odder* (1949) 93 S.J. 433, (C.A.), (order for possession of controlled premises in default of appearance by tenant set aside on condition of payment of arrears. The setting aside of the original order held not to amount to relief against forfeiture under s. 212). *Quaere* whether ss. 210–212 apply to a tenant under an equitable lease. It has been held that the corresponding county court provisions do so apply: See, *Rickett* v. *Green* [1910] 1 K.B. 253, 259, *per* Darling J., (lease not under seal for a term exceeding three years void at law). Contrast *Sport International Bussum BV* v. *Inter-Footwear Ltd.* [1984] 1 All E.R. 376, 385, (C.A.), *per* Oliver L.J. From very early times, equity asserted a jurisdiction to relieve against forfeiture of a legal lease for non-payment of rent. It would be odd if equity viewed

in equity if at least six months' rent is in arrears[11] and, at any time before the trial of the landlord's action, he pays or tenders all the arrears and costs to the landlord or into court. The reference to "the trial of the action" in section 212 is a reference to an effective trial (and judgment) binding all necessary parties so that, if judgment for possession is entered against one only of two joint tenants, there will not be an effective trial and judgment within the meaning of the section so as to debar a tenant from tendering the rent due with costs.[12]

The landlord is not bound to accept tender of the arrears of rent from a third party which would not in law operate to discharge the debt or which would prejudice his position as against his tenant.[13] As to the question of discharge of the debt, it is well settled[14] that payment to a landlord by a stranger to the tenancy of a sum equivalent to the amount of rent owing by the tenant is not a good satisfaction of the rent, even if it is accepted by the landlord, unless it is made by the payer as agent for, and on behalf of,[15] or in the name and on account of, the tenant, or with his authority or subsequent ratification. As to the question of prejudice, the landlord may be entitled to refuse tender from a third party if his acceptance of the arrears would create a new tenancy in some person other than the tenant or would operate as a waiver of some default by the tenant which would otherwise have entitled the landlord to forfeit the lease.[16]

The relief under section 212 will take the form of a stay of the landlord's action and the tenant will continue to hold the demised premises under his original lease without any new lease. In *Standard Pattern Co. Ltd.* v. *Ivey*[17] it was held that relief under section 212 only applied where six months' rent was in arrear and, accordingly, a tenant could not, by payment of the sums necessary to meet the landlord's claim, compel a stay of proceedings under the section where only one quarter's rent was unpaid.[18]

Under section 210 of the 1852 Act, the tenant will also be entitled to

---

an equitable tenant less favourably. See, generally, P. Sparkes, *Forfeiture of Equitable Leases*, (1987) 16 Anglo-American L. Rev. 160, at pp. 167–169.

[11] See, s. 210 of the 1852 Act.

[12] *Gill* v. *Lewis* [1956] 2 Q.B. 1, (C.A.).

[13] *Richards* v. *De Freitas* (1974) 29 P. & C.R. 1. See also, *Matthews* v. *Dobbins* [1963] 1 W.L.R. 227, (C.A.).

[14] *Simpson* v. *Eggington* (1855) 10 Exch. 845, 847, *per* Parke B. followed by Humphreys J. in *Smith* v. *Cox* [1940] 2 K.B. 558. See also, *London and County (A. & D.) Ltd.* v. *Wilfred Sportsman Ltd.* [1971] 1 Ch. 764, (C.A.), (payment of arrears of rent by surety held to be payments in discharge of its personal contractual obligation and did not constitute payments of rent by or on behalf of the tenant).

[15] See, *Pellatt* v. *Boosey* (1862) 31 L.J.C.P. 281.

[16] *Richards* v. *De Freitas* (1974) 29 P. & C.R. 1, 8, *per* May J.

[17] [1962] Ch. 432. See, R.E.M. (1962) 78 L.Q.R. 168. Note, in this connection, the words "as often as it shall happen that one half year's rent shall be in arrear" in s. 210 of the 1852 Act.

[18] In such circumstances, the court's jurisdiction to grant relief under s. 38(1) of the Supreme Court Act 1981 should be invoked.

relief in equity at or after the trial of the landlord's action, if he pays all the arrears of rent and costs within six months of the execution of the order for possession. If, however, he fails so to do, his rights to all relief or remedy in law or equity will be barred and the landlord will then hold the premises discharged from the lease.[19] In this connection, section 211 of the 1852 Act gives statutory recognition to the tenant's right to apply for relief in equity but provides that the tenant's equitable right will be barred unless he pays into court the arrears of rent and costs claimed by the landlord.

It would appear that where there is less than six months' rent in arrears, the six months' limitation period has no application so as to confine the tenant to a period of six months after execution of the order for possession in which to bring his application for relief. In such circumstances, the court's inherent equitable jurisdiction would apply without strict statutory time-limit, although the six month period prescribed under section 210 of the 1852 Act would, no doubt, be taken as a guide in the exercise of the court's discretion whether to grant or refuse relief.[20]

Although the common law courts were given jurisdiction, under section 212, to grant relief from forfeiture on payment by the tenant of the arrears of rent and costs before trial, relief after judgment for possession was only obtainable from the courts of equity until the coming into effect of section 1 of the Common Law Procedure Act 1860. This section was repealed and replaced by section 46 of the Supreme Court of Judicature (Consolidation) Act 1925, which empowered the High Court (in the case of any action for forfeiture brought for non-payment of rent) to give relief in a summary manner and subject to the same terms and conditions in all respects as to the payment of rent, costs and otherwise as could formerly have been enforced by the Court of Chancery. This provision is currently contained in section 38(1) of the Supreme Court Act 1981.

Where relief is granted under section 38(1), the tenant (or a person deriving title under him) will continue to hold the demised premises in accordance with the terms of the original (forfeited) lease without the necessity for a new lease.[21]

Readiness to pay the arrears and costs[22] within the time specified by the

[19] s. 210 of the 1852 Act. See also, *In Re Brain* (1874) L.R. 18 Eq. 389; *Vesey* v. *Bodkin* (1830) 4 Bli. N.S. 64, (H.L.); 5 E.R. 23.
[20] *Di Palma* v. *Victoria Square Property Co. Ltd.* [1984] 1 Ch. 346, 366, *per* Scott J. upheld on appeal: [1986] Ch. 150, (C.A.).
[21] s. 38(2) of the 1981 Act.
[22] The tenant must bear the landlord's costs except so far as they have been increased by the landlord resisting his claim for relief: *Howard* v. *Fanshawe* [1895] 2 Ch. 581, 592, *per* Stirling J.; *Humphreys* v. *Morten* [1905] 1 Ch. 739, 741, *per* Swinfen Eady J. and *Belgravia Insurance Co. Ltd.* v. *Meah* [1964] 1 Q.B. 436, (C.A.). In *Newbolt* v. *Bingham* (1895) 72 L.T. 852, (C.A.), the costs were ordered to be paid on a solicitor and client basis. If the landlord obtains judgment for possession without costs, the tenant may obtain relief from forfeiture without being required to pay the landlord any costs other than those of the summons for

court is a necessary condition of a tenant's claim for relief.[23] In practice, therefore, the court will invariably grant relief[24] to the tenant upon payment of the rent due and the landlord's costs of the action. It would appear, however, that arrears of rent which are statute-barred under the Limitation Act 1980 need not be paid.[25]

In an appropriate case, the terms upon which relief is granted may also include a condition entitling the landlord to bring into operation a rent review provision contained in the lease[26] or to oblige the tenant to remedy other breaches of covenant.[27]

In *Nance* v. *Taylor*[28] a tenant's undertaking to pay the amount due and to give up possession of the premises in consideration of the landlord withholding the writ of possession for a period of three months was held not to afford sufficient reason for excluding the tenant from equitable relief under section 46 of the Supreme Court of Judicature (Consolidation) Act 1925. In this case, the agreement to allow the tenant further time was held not to be inconsistent with the right to relief being still subsisting. In the course of his judgment, Atkin L.J. observed[29]:

> "I can quite understand that an agreement might be entered into on the terms that if time were given the respondent would surrender his right to claim relief against forfeiture; or that an agreement might be made upon such terms that an agreement to surrender the right to relief must necessarily be implied; but it is a question of inference in each case whether such a term should be implied."

Thus, in *Howard* v. *Central Board of Finance of the Church of England*[30] a consent order in compromise of forfeiture proceedings was held to have been made on the footing that it was a final disposal of the litigation between the parties and that, by necessary implication, it amounted to an agreement to surrender the tenant's right to relief from forfeiture.

The court retains a discretion to refuse relief under the foregoing

---

relief: *Croft* v. *The London and County Banking Co.* (1885) 14 Q.B.D. 347, (C.A.). In *Woodtrek Ltd.* v. *Jezek* (1982) 261 E.G. 571 the tenant was awarded the substantial costs of the action on the ground that the landlord's claim for non-payment of service charge had been misconceived. In *Billson* v. *Residential Apartments Ltd.* [1992] 2 W.L.R. 15, (H.L.), it was held that in principle a tenant should not be ordered to pay costs on an indemnity basis.

[23] *Barton, Thompson & Co. Ltd.* v. *Stapling Machines Co.* [1966] Ch. 499, 509–510 *per* Pennycuick J., (a case involving a lease of chattels).

[24] It appears that advance relief (*i.e.* in advance of proceedings for possession or actual possession) has no place in the statutory provisions: *Barton, Thompson & Co. Ltd.* v. *Stapling Machines Co.* [1966] 2 All E.R. 222, 224, *per* Pennycuick J.

[25] See, *Re Howell's Application* [1972] Ch. 509.

[26] *Soteri* v. *Psylidies* [1991] 24 E.G. 161, (C.A.).

[27] *Piccadilly Estates Hotels Ltd.* v. *Total Property Investments Ltd.* (1974) 232 E.G. 590, (relief granted on terms that the tenant brought hotel premises into repair within four months).

[28] [1928] 1 K.B. 263, (C.A.).

[29] *Ibid.* p. 267.

[30] (1977) 244 E.G. 51.

statutory provisions in circumstances where the landlord (and any other interested parties) cannot be put back into their original position. Thus, in *Stanhope* v. *Haworth*[31] the tenant's application for relief (which was made towards the end of the period of six months allowed by section 210) was rejected on the ground that the landlord had so altered his position in the meantime that it would be inequitable to grant relief. In particular, the landlord had relet the demised premises (a colliery) to a third party who, in turn, had laid out substantial sums in purchasing plant to work it. In the words of Lord Esher M.R. in *Newbolt* v. *Bingham*[32]:

> "It seems to me that these Acts of Parliament give very large powers of relief to the court . . . If, at the time relief is asked for, the position has altered, so that relief could not be given without causing injury to third parties, I think that the case that was cited to us (*Stanhope* v. *Haworth*) applies. But if, at the time of the application, the position is not altered, so that no injustice will be done, I think, if the conditions mentioned in [section 210] are complied with, that, according to the settled practice in equity, there is no longer a discretion in the judge, but that he ought to make the order. It does not matter whether it is called discretionary or not, if the discretion ought always to be exercised in one way. If the conditions are complied with, and no interests of third parties have intervened, there is no longer any real discretion in the matter."

It has been suggested[33] that, in the exercise of the equitable jurisdiction to grant relief for non-payment of rent, it may be proper to consider the conduct of the parties and, in particular, breaches of other covenants in the lease and even conduct not amounting to a breach of covenant. This view, however, goes beyond the modern authorities and today it is not, generally speaking, legitimate to take into account other breaches of covenant committed by the tenant.[34] Save in very exceptional circumstances, therefore, the court is bound to exercise its discretion by granting relief to the tenant (upon payment of all the rent due and costs) without regard to any other matters of complaint that the landlord may have against the tenant. In *Gill* v. *Lewis*,[35] Jenkins L.J. said[36]:

> "The question is whether, provided all is paid up, the landlord will not have been fully compensated; and the view taken by the court is

---

[31] (1866) 3 T.L.R. 34, (C.A.).
[32] (1895) 72 L.T. 852, 853, (C.A.).
[33] *Bowser* v. *Colby* (1841) 1 Hare 109; 66 E.R. 969, *per* Sir James Wigram V.-C.
[34] *Gill* v. *Lewis* [1956] 2 Q.B. 1, 13, *per* Jenkins L.J. However, the decision in *Bowser* v. *Colby* remains "a useful authority as showing that the court is not to exercise this equitable jurisdiction, as it were, 'in blinkers' ": *ibid.*, 13. See also, *Howard* v. *Central Board of Finance of the Church of England* (1977) 244 E.G. 51, 53, *per* Goulding J.
[35] [1956] 2 Q.B. 1, (C.A.).
[36] *Ibid.* p. 13.

that if he gets the whole of his rent and costs, then he has got all he is entitled to so far as rent is concerned, and extraneous matters of breach of covenant, and so forth, are, generally speaking, irrelevant."

In the course of his judgment,[37] Jenkins L.J. alluded to an immoral user of the premises as constituting an exceptional circumstance disqualifying the tenant from seeking equitable relief. In *Gill* itself, evidence (a) that the landlords had experienced difficulties in extracting rent from the tenants in past (b) that they had experienced difficulties in finding the tenants for the purpose of bringing proceedings against them to recover the arrears of rent and (c) that one of the tenants had been convicted of two acts of indecent assault against two boys on the premises, was considered insufficient to warrant a denial of relief. In relation to (c), the acts of indecency involved one isolated incident and not a continuous course of conduct.

The fact that a tenant company has been a bad payer of rent in the past will not afford a sufficient reason for denying relief even where the tenant is in compulsory liquidation and has no assets with which to meet the rent in the future.[38] In this connection, once the arrears of rent are brought up to date, the landlord will be in no different position from any other lessor with an impecunious tenant. However, in *Public Trustee* v. *Westbrook*[39] relief was refused to a sub-tenant in circumstances where no rent had been paid for 22 years in respect of a sub-lease of a bombed site and where re-development of the site had been planned on the assumption that the sub-lease had gone altogether. Similarly, in *Tryfonos* v. *D. Landau & Son Ltd.*[40] Stevenson J. held that there were exceptional circumstances which entitled him to refuse relief in that one of the joint tenants was serving a prison sentence for arson, both tenants were insolvent, there were grave breaches of the covenant to repair and the landlords were well advised in negotiations to dispose of the premises elsewhere.

A further example of an "exceptional circumstance" justifying the refusal of relief is to be found in *Silverman* v. *AFCO (UK) Ltd.*[41] where the tenants had made a last minute application for relief against forfeiture following an assurance that they would not contest the landlords' proceedings for possession. The landlords had, on the basis of this assurance and an order for possession which had not been defended by the tenants, executed a new lease of the premises to a third party. The Court of Appeal

---

[37] *Ibid.* p. 14.

[38] *Re Brompton Securities Ltd. (No. 2)* [1988] 3 All E.R. 677. The application for relief on behalf of the insolvent company can be made by summons in the winding-up. See also, *Re Brompton Securities Ltd. (In Liquidation)* [1988] 2 E.G.L.R. 93.

[39] [1965] 1 W.L.R. 1160, (C.A.).

[40] (1961) 181 E.G. 405. See also, *Church Commissioners for England* v. *Nodjoumi* (1986) 51 P. & C.R. 155, 160–161, (tenant convicted of conspiring to defraud the Iranian Government).

[41] [1988] 1 E.G.L.R. 51, (C.A.).

held that relief should be refused on the ground that the position of the parties had altered and the right of a third party had intervened. Slade L.J. said[42]:

"... the court may, in the exercise of its discretion, properly refuse relief from forfeiture even to a tenant who belatedly tenders the full amount of outstanding rent and costs if, during the interim period, the landlord has, not unreasonably or precipitously, granted rights in the premises to third parties, on the footing that the original lease is at an end, and the court considers that, in all the circumstances, the grant of relief to the original tenants would cause injustice to the landlord or the third parties or both."

The provisions of the 1852 and 1981 Acts will govern proceedings for the granting of equitable relief in cases where the landlord is enforcing his right of forfeiture by action through the courts. However, these statutory provisions will have no application where the landlord proceeds to forfeit the lease for non-payment of rent by actually physically re-entering the demised premises without recourse to legal proceedings. In this limited case, therefore, the tenant is entitled to rely upon equitable relief[43] without any fixed (statutory) time limit although, by analogy with section 210 of the 1852 Act, a time-span of six months would probably be used by the court as a guide in the exercise of its equitable jurisdiction.[44] Moreover, in such a case, an order may be made under section 212 of the 1852 Act giving the tenant relief in equity and declaring that he may hold the demised premises according to the original lease without any new lease.[45] In *Thatcher* v. *C. H. Pearce & Sons (Contractors) Ltd.*[46] the landlords peaceably re-entered the demised premises for non-payment of rent. The tenant applied for relief from forfeiture but the landlords contended that his application was out of time, not having been issued within six months, as required by section 210 of the 1852 Act. Sir Jocelyn Simon P. held that, since the landlords had re-entered peaceably without court proceedings, the court's power to grant relief from forfeiture was not statutory but arose from its inherent equitable jurisdiction to which no statutory rules of limitation applied. However, in his view, equitable relief could be refused in appropriate circumstances where, for example, the tenant had unduly delayed in bringing his application for relief.[47]

---

[42] *Ibid.* p. 53.
[43] *Howard* v. *Fanshawe* [1895] 2 Ch. 581, approved in *Lovelock* v. *Margo* [1963] 2 Q.B. 787, (C.A.). See also, *Thatcher* v. *C. H. Pearce & Sons (Contractors) Ltd.* [1968] 1 W.L.R. 748 and *Bowser* v. *Colby* (1841) 1 Hare 109; 66 E.R. 969.
[44] *Howard* v. *Fanshawe* [1895] 2 Ch. 581, 589, *per* Stirling J. But see the observations of Sir Jocelyn Simon P. in *Thatcher* v. *C. H. Pearce & Sons (Contractors) Ltd.* [1968] 1 W.L.R. 748, 755.
[45] *Howard* v. *Fanshawe* [1895] 2 Ch. 581, 591–592, *per* Stirling J.
[46] [1968] 1 W.L.R. 748.
[47] *Ibid.* p. 756.

A mere squatter, who has acquired a title by adverse possession against the tenant, cannot apply for equitable relief unless there is evidence from which the court can infer a mutual intention to create a new relationship of landlord and tenant arising by operation of law from the payment or acceptance of rent.[48]

Where an order for relief against forfeiture is granted to the tenant on terms to be performed within a specified time, the court has jurisdiction to extend that time if circumstances are brought to its notice which would make it just and equitable that an extension should be granted.[49] In the words of Lord Greene M.R.[50]:

"The court, in exercising its jurisdiction to grant relief in cases of non-payment of rent is, of course, proceeding on the old principles of the court of equity which always regarded the condition of re-entry as being merely security for payment of the rent and gave relief if the landlord could get his rent. If an order of this kind, in which relief is granted on terms to be observed within a limited time, is to be treated as one which the court has no jurisdiction to modify in point of time even though circumstances justify modification, then the order becomes as vicious as the original forfeiture clause itself."

An extension of time will not be granted lightly and a tenant should not expect to get further indulgence from the court unless good grounds are shown for non-compliance with the time limit imposed under the original order.[51]

(2) *Application for relief by assignee of tenant*

The assignee of the tenant is entitled to claim relief under both sections 210 and 212 of the 1852 Act[52] but only upon payment (or tender) of all the arrears of rent due from him and all the arrears (if any) due from the original tenant under the lease.[53] Thus, in *Barratt v. Richardson and Cresswell*[54] it was held that an assignee seeking relief under section 212 was

---

[48] *Tickner* v. *Buzzacott* [1965] 1 Ch. 426. Moreover, the fact that the squatter was paying and the landlord accepting rent was held not sufficient to create an estoppel: *ibid.* p. 435, applying *Tichborne* v. *Weir* (1892) 8 T.L.R. 713, (C.A.).
[49] This is so although the order which prescribes the limitation of time does not give the tenant liberty to apply: *Chandless-Chandless* v. *Nicholson* [1942] 2 K.B. 321, 323, (C.A.) and *Cremin* v. *Barjack Properties Ltd.* (1985) 273 E.G. 299, 300, (C.A.), *per* Slade L.J. See also, *R.* v. *Bloomsbury and Marylebone County Court, ex p. Villerwest Ltd.* [1976] 1 W.L.R. 362, (C.A.) and *Starside Properties Ltd.* v. *Mustapha* [1974] 1 W.L.R. 816, (C.A.).
[50] *Chandless-Chandless* v. *Nicholson* [1942] 2 K.B. 321, 323.
[51] *Ibid.* pp. 324–325, *per* Lord Greene M.R.
[52] Both sections expressly make reference to the tenant "or his assignee". A person who agrees to take an assignment of the lease and who is in possession of the demised premises may apply for relief: *Re Brompton Securities Ltd. (No. 2)* [1988] 3 All E.R. 677.
[53] *Barratt* v. *Richardson and Cresswell* [1930] 1 K.B. 686, 698, *per* Wright J.
[54] [1930] 1 K.B. 686.

obliged to pay all the arrears of rent due (*i.e.* some 13 years' arrears) and not merely six years' arrears, since her liability fell to be measured by ascertaining what the landlord would have been entitled to recover in an action against the original tenant which was subject to a 20 year period of limitation on actions of debt for rent upon an indenture of demise and not a period of six years in actions for arrears of rent. The liability of the assignee to pay the full arrears of rent is supported by analogy with the decision in *Dingle* v. *Coppen*[55] where a mortgagor seeking to redeem his mortgage was held on general equitable principles to be under an obligation to pay all the arrears of interest and not merely such as might be recoverable in an action by the mortgagee. Thus, whilst section 19 of the Limitation Act 1980 limits the landlord's right to recover by action only six years' arrears of rent, nevertheless, on the basis of the *Barratt* and *Dingle* cases, an assignee may be liable to pay the full arrears of rent when claiming relief under the 1852 Act.

(3) *Application for relief by sub-tenant*[55a]

A sub-tenant is entitled to claim relief[56] from forfeiture of the tenant's headlease under sections 210 and 212 of the 1852 Act. Under section 210, the sub-tenant is a "person claiming or deriving under the [tenant's] lease" and, under section 212, although the relevant words are "the tenant or his assignee", he qualifies as a tenant under the section.[57] Thus, on an application under section 212, it is not necessary for the sub-tenant to prove his title as underlessee or assignee of the original tenant and the fact that the sub-tenant is "tenant" in possession of the premises is sufficient.[58]

If the sub-tenant applies for relief before judgment in the landlord's action for possession (*i.e.* before the lease is actually determined[59]), he is not obliged to make the original tenant (and his assignee) a party to the application.[60] This is because the form of relief in such a case does not involve the restoration of the headlease which remains intact in the absence of a judgment for possession. If, however, the sub-tenant applies for relief after judgment, he must (since the granting of relief will necess-

---

[55] [1899] 1 Ch. 726.
[55a] For a full discussion, see *Forfeiture of Leases: Relief for Underlessees and holders of other Derivative Interests*, S. Tromans, (1986) Conv. 187.
[56] For a form of summons: See *Atkin's Court Forms*, (2nd ed., 1990), Vol. 24, p. 300, Form 72 and Pt. VI of this work.
[57] *Doe* d.*Wyatt* v. *Byron* (1845) 1 C.B. 623; 135 E.R. 685; *Shine* v. *Gough* (1811) 1 Ball & B. 436.
[58] *Moore* v. *Smee and Cornish* [1907] 2 K.B. 8, (C.A.).
[59] *Dendy* v. *Evans* [1910] 1 K.B. 263, 266, *per* Cozens-Hardy M.R.
[60] See, *e.g. Doe* d. *Wyatt* v. *Byron* (1845) 1 C.B. 623; 135 E.R. 685, (where there was no judgment in ejectment so that the application for relief was to stay the landlord's proceedings and not to set up a lease which had determined). See also, *Hare* v. *Elms* [1893] 1 Q.B. 604, 609, *per* Day J. Contrast *Gray* v. *Bonsall* [1904] 1 K.B. 601, 606, *per* Romer L.J.

arily involve the setting up of the original lease) bring the original tenant (and, where the lease has been assigned, the last assignee) before the court or, alternatively, give some good reason for not doing so.[61] In this case, the revival of the forfeited lease would reimpose a liability on the tenant and, therefore, it ought not to be renewed in his absence and without giving him the opportunity of being heard. Thus, in *Hare* v. *Elms*[62] the landlord obtained judgment against the tenants in an action for forfeiture for non-payment of rent. Subsequently, mortgagees by way of sub-demise applied for relief against the forfeiture but did not make the original tenant a party to the application. It was held that relief ought not to be given in the absence of the original tenant. By way of contrast, in *Humphreys* v. *Morten*[63] mortgagees by sub-demise were excused from not making the original tenant and his assignee parties to the application for relief on the ground that the former had become a bankrupt and his trustee in bankruptcy had assigned the lease to the latter who had not been heard of for 26 years and could not be traced.

Relief will invariably be granted upon payment of the whole of the rent due under the headlease and the performance of the tenant's covenants.

Apart from sections 210 and 212 of the 1852 Act, a sub-tenant may also apply for relief from forfeiture of the headlease for non-payment of rent under section 146(4) of the Law of Property Act 1925[64] at any time before the landlord has actually obtained possession of the premises pursuant to an order of the court.[65] Indeed, the usual practice is to seek relief under section 146(4) where that can be done.

The effect of a vesting order under section 146(4) will be to create a new lease in favour of the sub-tenant in which the covenants and conditions as to rent and otherwise will be entirely at the discretion of the court unfettered by any limitation except that contained in the latter part of the sub-section, namely, that the sub-tenant shall not be entitled to require a lease for a term longer than he had under his original sub-lease. Invariably, the court will vest the premises comprised in the forfeited headlease in the sub-tenant for the residue of the term of the sub-lease and upon the same terms (as to rent and other covenants) as contained in the headlease.[66] Moreover, since the court has power, under section 146(4), to order the execution of a new lease directly in favour of the sub-tenant and since an order in this form will not affect the original tenant, it is not necessary for the latter (or his assignee) to be before the court before such

[61] *Hare* v. *Elms* [1893] 1 Q.B. 604, 607, *per* Day J.
[62] [1893] 1 Q.B. 604.
[63] [1905] 1 Ch. 739.
[64] s. 146(4) expressly applies to relief sought by an underlessee for non-payment of rent. See also, *Gray* v. *Bonsall* [1904] 1 K.B. 601, (C.A.).
[65] *Rogers* v. *Rice* [1892] 2 Ch. 170, (C.A.); *Quilter* v. *Mapleson* (1882) 9 Q.B.D. 672, (C.A.) and *Billson* v. *Residential Apartments Ltd.* [1992] 2 W.L.R. 15, 20–21, (H.L.).
[66] *Gray* v. *Bonsall* [1904] 1 K.B. 601, 608, (C.A.), *per* Romer L.J.

an order is made.[67] The principles governing relief under the equitable jurisdiction (which is preserved by section 38(1) of the Supreme Court Act 1981) are the same as those under section 146(4) of the Law of Property Act 1925.[68] Accordingly, in exercising its discretion, the court will invariably grant relief to a sub-tenant on the terms of paying the rent in arrear, performing the covenants and paying all the costs.[69] Relief, however, may be refused if the conduct of the sub-tenant is such as to make it inequitable that relief should be granted.[70]

Whilst, generally speaking, a landlord is entitled to be put back into the position that he would have been if the forfeiture had not occurred,[71] nevertheless, this may work injustice in a case where a sub-tenant of part only of the demised premises is seeking relief. Thus, in *Chatham Empire Theatre (1955) Ltd.* v. *Ultrans Ltd.*[72] Salmon J, in the exercise of his discretion, granted relief to sub-tenants upon payment of the proportion of arrears attributable to the property sublet to them under their sub-lease plus an element for the premium they had paid on the granting thereof. In the course of his judgment, he said[73]:

"One can envisage a case in which a block of property comprising a large number of shops and other premises is let to one corporation for £30,000 a year. The corporation then sublet the separate shops to various small shopkeepers at perhaps £300 a year each. After some time the corporation goes into liquidation owing perhaps half a year's rent. It is quite plain that the legislature gives the right to the small shopkeeper to come and ask for relief . . . I should have thought that if the shopkeeper paid his proportion of the arrears, namely, £150, and it was otherwise just and equitable that there should be relief, he should obtain relief on that basis."

The learned Judge was, however, mindful to point out that there might be cases in which it would be quite wrong to give a sub-tenant relief on this basis. For example, hardship could be caused to the landlord if granting relief to one or two of many sub-tenants would make it impossible for him to deal with the premises as a whole. Each case, therefore, falls to be decided on its own facts, bearing in mind that section 146(4)

---

[67] *Gray* v. *Bonsall* [1904] 1 K.B. 601, 608, (C.A.), *per* Romer L.J. and *Abbey National Building Society* v. *Maybeech Ltd.* [1985] 1 Ch. 190, 206, *per* Nicholls J.

[68] *Belgravia Insurance Co. Ltd.* v. *Meah* [1964] 1 Q.B. 436, (C.A.).

[69] *Gray* v. *Bonsall* [1904] 1 K.B. 601, (C.A.) and *Belgravia Insurance Co. Ltd.* v. *Meah* [1964] 1 Q.B. 436, (C.A.). As to contribution between sub-tenants: See, *Webber* v. *Smith* (1689) 2 Vern. 103.

[70] *Belgravia Insurance Co. Ltd.* v. *Meah* [1964] 1 Q.B. 436, 446, *per* Lord Denning M.R., citing *Bowser* v. *Colby* (1841) 1 Hare 109, 134; 66 E.R. 969, 979, *per* Wigram V.-C. and *Gill* v. *Lewis* [1956] 2 Q.B. 1, 17, *per* Hodson L.J.

[71] *Egerton* v. *Jones* [1939] 2 K.B. 702, 706, (C.A.), *per* Sir Wilfrid Greene M.R.

[72] [1961] 1 W.L.R. 817.

[73] *Ibid.* pp. 820–821.

confers upon the court the widest discretion as to the terms upon which relief should be granted.[74] Thus, in the earlier case of *London Bridge Buildings Co. v. Thomson*[75] Joyce J. gave the sub-tenant relief only upon terms that he should pay the whole of the rent in arrear in respect of the whole of the premises demised in the headlease.

(4) *Application for relief by mortgagee*[75a]

A mortgagee is entitled to claim equitable relief by virtue of section 38(1) of the Supreme Court Act 1981, section 210 of the Common Law Procedure Act 1852 and section 146(4) of the Law of Property Act 1925.

As stated earlier, section 38(1) merely confirms equity's inherent jurisdiction to grant relief in cases of non-payment of rent and this includes the power to grant relief to a mortgagee. It should be noted, however, that section 38(1) only confers power to grant relief "in an action in the High Court for forfeiture . . ." and, consequently, does not give the court jurisdiction once the landlord's proceedings are complete or in circumstances where the landlord forfeits by means of a physical re-entry without recourse to litigation. In these circumstances, a mortgagee will be obliged to rely upon the High Court's inherent (non-statutory) power to grant relief.[76] Thus, in *Ladup Ltd. v. Williams & Glyn's Bank plc*[77] the plaintiff recovered judgment for a sum of £43,000 in an action against the tenant of a residential flat and, in order to enforce the judgment, obtained a charging order in respect of the tenant's lease of the flat. Subsequently, the landlord brought proceedings against the tenant for forfeiture of the lease for non-payment of rent and obtained possession of the flat. The plaintiff, being a person interested in the lease by virtue of the charging order, then sought relief against the forfeiture under the court's inherent equitable jurisdiction. Warner J. held that the court was entitled, in the exercise of its inherent equitable jurisdiction, to grant relief to an equitable chargee who had no interest in the lease entitling him to possession of the demised premises. In his view, there was no fetter on equity's jurisdiction to relieve against forfeiture where the object of the right to forfeit was essentially to secure payment of a sum of money as in the case of a right to forfeit a lease for non-payment of rent.[78] In this case, it was conceded that

---

[74] *Ibid.* p. 820.

[75] (1903) 89 L.T. 50.

[75a] See above, n. 55a.

[76] *Howard v. Fanshawe* [1895] 2 Ch. 581, approved in *Lovelock v. Margo* [1963] 2 Q.B. 787, (C.A.). See also, *Thatcher v. C. H. Pearce & Sons (Contractors) Ltd.* [1968] 1 W.L.R. 748 and *Bowser v. Colby* (1841) 1 Hare 109; 66 E.R. 969.

[77] [1985] 1 W.L.R. 851.

[78] The equitable jurisdiction to grant relief from forfeiture for non-payment of rent remains intact notwithstanding its statutory modification in certain procedural respects: *Billson v. Residential Apartments Ltd.* [1991] 3 W.L.R. 264, 277–278, *per* Sir Nicolas Browne-Wilkinson V.-C.

225

section 38(1) of the Supreme Court Act 1981 had no application because the plaintiff's claim for relief was not made "in any action in the High Court for the forfeiture of a lease for non-payment of rent" as required by that section. Equally, section 146(2) of the Law of Property Act 1925 could not apply because, the landlord having recovered possession of the flat before the issue of the plaintiff's summons for relief, it could not be said that the landlord was "proceeding by action or otherwise to enforce a right of re-entry or forfeiture" within the meaning of that section.

By section 210 of the 1852 Act, the landlord's proceedings for possession for non-payment of rent under that section are subject to the following proviso:

> ". . . provided that nothing herein contained shall extend to bar the right of any mortgagee of such lease, or any part thereof, who shall not be in possession, so as such mortgagee shall and do, within six months after such judgment obtained and execution executed pay all rent in arrear, and all costs and damages sustained by such lessor . . . and perform all the covenants and agreements which, on the part and behalf of the first lessee, are and ought to be performed."

The effect of section 210 is that, if at least six months' rent is in arrears, a tenant's application for relief must be brought within a strict six month time period after execution of the order for possession.[79] It appears, however, that, in the context of a mortgagee's application for relief, the statutory time-limit imposed by section 210 will not bar relief. The point was recently considered by Mr David Neuberger Q.C. (sitting as a deputy judge of the Chancery Division) in *United Dominions Trust Ltd. v. Shellpoint Trustees Ltd.*[80] In that case, the tenant's mortgagee sought relief from forfeiture in the High Court of a leasehold flat which had been repossessed by the landlord pursuant to a county court judgment. The application for relief was opposed by the landlord on the grounds (*inter alia*) that the judgment was in respect of more than one-half year's rent and that, accordingly, after the expiry of six months following the execution of the judgment, the mortgagee became "barred and foreclosed from all Relief or Remedy in Law or Equity" within the meaning of section 210. The deputy judge[81] rejected this contention and held that the mortgagee's application for relief was not of a type barred by section 210 because he was not a party to the landlord's proceedings for possession. The relevant wording of section 210 is as follows:

---

[79] If less than six months' rent is in arrears, it would appear that the six months' limitation period has no application although, no doubt, it would be taken as a strong guide: *Di Palma v. Victoria Square Property Co. Ltd.* [1984] 1 Ch. 346, 366, *per* Scott J. upheld on appeal: [1986] Ch. 150, (C.A.).

[80] [1992] 39 E.G. 144. But see now the Court of Appeal decision, currently reported only in [1993] E.G.C.S. 57.

[81] Mr. David Neuberger Q.C.

" . . . and in case the Lessee or his Assignee, or other Person claiming or deriving under the said Lease, shall permit and suffer Judgment to be had and recovered on such Trial in Ejectment, and Execution to be executed thereon, without paying the Rent and Arrears, together with full Costs, and without proceeding for Relief in Equity within Six Months after such Execution executed, then and in such Case the said Lessee, his Assignee, and all other Persons claiming and deriving under the said Lease, shall be barred and foreclosed from all Relief or Remedy in Equity . . . "

At the time the section was enacted, it was not necessary to join the mortgagee as a party to a forfeiture action and this remains the position to this day. There was, therefore, a strong likelihood that the mortgagee would not know anything about the landlord's proceedings for possession,[82] the judgment for possession or the execution of the order for possession. In these circumstances, it was difficult to see how, as a matter of ordinary language, such a mortgagee could be said to have permitted or suffered judgment to be had and execution to be executed within the meaning of section 210. This was considered by the deputy judge to be a strong indication that the words "the Lessee or his Assignee, or other Person claiming or deriving under the said Lease" were not intended to apply to a mortgagee who had not been a party to the landlord's proceedings.[83]

A mortgagee of the lease will be entitled to relief against forfeiture for non-payment of rent upon the same terms as the tenant against whom possession is sought.[84] In *Newbolt* v. *Bingham*[85] relief under section 210 was granted to a mortgagee of a lease by sub-demise upon terms that all repairs required by the covenants were done to the satisfaction of a surveyor within one month of the order and that all rent in arrear and costs were paid. Relief, however, will be refused if third party rights have intervened making it inequitable to grant relief.[86] Moreover, if the landlord has obtained judgment against the tenant, a mortgagee by sub-demise will be refused relief if the tenant is not made a party to the application.[87]

Instead of invoking the court's equitable jurisdiction (under either section 38(1) of the Supreme Court Act 1981 or section 210 of the Common

[82] Today, if the landlord commences court proceedings to effect a re-entry, he is obliged to serve notice of those proceedings on any known underlessee (including a mortgagee): R.S.C. Ord. 6, r. 2 and C.C.R. Ord. 6, r. 3.

[83] The mortgagee's alternative argument, that the possession order executed by the landlord was not an order falling within s. 210 because it had not been established that there was insufficient distress on the premises, was not accepted by the deputy judge.

[84] *Doe* d. *Whitfield* v. *Roe* (1811) 3 Taunt. 402; 128 E.R. 160.

[85] (1895) 72 L.T. 852, (C.A.).

[86] *Ibid.* pp. 853–854, *per* Lord Esher M.R. and Rigby L.J., respectively.

[87] *Hare* v. *Elms* [1893] 1 Q.B. 604.

Law Procedure Act 1852), a mortgagee by sub-demise[88] or by way of legal charge[89] can claim relief as an "underlessee" under section 146(4) of the Law of Property Act 1925.[90] Accordingly, provided the landlord has not actually re-entered, the mortgagee will be entitled to relief against forfeiture of the tenant's lease in the same way as if he were an underlessee. Thus, in *Belgravia Insurance Co. Ltd.* v. *Meah*[91] the Court of Appeal made an order vesting the premises comprised in the lease in the mortgagee (by way of legal charge) for the residue of the term and upon the same conditions as the original lease upon payment of all the rent in arrear, performance of the tenant's covenant to repair and payment of all the costs of the application for relief except in so far as they had been incurred by the landlord's resistance to the claim for relief. Where relief is sought under section 146(4), it is not necessary to make the tenant a party to the application.[92]

Relief in the county court

In the county court, the equitable jurisdiction to relieve against forfeiture for non-payment of rent has been put on a statutory basis and the current provisions are contained in sections 138 and 139 of the County Courts Act 1984.

Section 140 of the 1984 Act contains interpretation provisions for the purposes of sections 138 and 139. The word "lease", for example, is expressed to include an original or derivative underlease and the word "lessee" includes an original or derivative underlessee and the persons deriving title under a lessee.[93]

(1) *Landlord proceeding by action*

Under section 138(2) of the 1984 Act, if the tenant pays into court (or to

---

[88] *Egerton* v. *Jones* [1939] 2 K.B. 702, (C.A.) and *Grangeside Properties Ltd.* v. *Collingwoods Securities Ltd.* [1964] 1 W.L.R. 139, (C.A.).

[89] *Grand Junction Co Ltd.* v. *Bates* [1954] 2 Q.B. 160; *Chelsea Estates Investment Trust Co. Ltd.* v. *Marche* [1955] 1 Ch. 328 and *Belgravia Insurance Co. Ltd.* v. *Meah* [1964] 1 Q.B. 436, (C.A.).

[90] An equitable mortgagee is also entitled to relief under s. 146(4): *Re Good's Lease, Good* v. *Wood* [1954] 1 W.L.R. 309.

[91] [1964] 1 Q.B. 436, (C.A.).

[92] *Belgravia Insurance Co. Ltd.* v. *Meah* [1964] 1 Q.B. 436, 446, (C.A.); *Gray* v. *Bonsall* [1904] 1 K.B. 601, 608, (C.A.) and *Abbey National Building Society* v. *Maybeech Ltd.* [1985] 1 Ch. 190, 206.

[93] The words "lessor", "under-lease" and "under-lessee" are also interpreted under s. 140. It has been held that the county court provisions apply to a tenant under an equitable lease: See, *Rickett* v. *Green* [1910] 1 K.B. 253, 259, *per* Darling J. Contrast *Sport International Bussum BV* v. *Inter-Footwear Ltd.* [1984] 1 All E.R. 376, 385, (C.A.), *per* Oliver L.J. See, generally, P. Sparkes, *Forfeiture of Equitable Leases*, (1987) 16 Anglo-American L. Rev. 160, at pp. 167–169.

the landlord[94]) not less than five clear days before the return day[95] all the rent in arrear and costs, the landlord's action will automatically cease and the tenant will hold the land according to the original lease without any new lease. However, the action will not cease under the sub-section if the payment into court (or to the landlord) is made by someone other than the tenant who is being sued by the landlord. In *Matthews* v. *Dobbins*[96] Ormerod L.J. said[97]:

> "It does not appear to me that the wording of the section is so wide as to put an end to the action whenever any person other than the person sued or someone on his behalf pays the arrears of rent and costs into court."

Moreover, section 138(2) will have no application if the landlord is proceeding in the same action to enforce a forfeiture on any other ground as well as for non-payment of rent or to enforce any other claim as well as the right of forfeiture and the claim for arrears of rent.[98]

Under section 138(3), where the tenant seeks relief at the trial of the landlord's action, the court is obliged to order[99] possession of the land to be given to the landlord at the expiration of such period, not being less than four weeks from the date of the order, as the court thinks fit, unless within that period the tenant pays into court all the rent in arrear and the costs[1] of the action. The court has power, under section 138(4), to extend the period for payment at any time before possession of the land is recovered by the landlord.[2] Moreover, under section 138(9), it may suspend any warrant which has been issued for the possession of the land during the period of extension and cancel it if, before the expiration of the

---

[94] See, s. 125(2) and para. 17 of Sched. 17 to the Courts and Legal Services Act 1990.
[95] The return day for the purposes of s.138 is the date referred to on the face of the form for a possession summons; *Swordheath Properties Ltd.* v. *Bolt* [1992] 38 E.G. 152.
[96] [1963] 1 W.L.R. 227, (C.A.).
[97] *Ibid.* p. 229.
[98] s. 138(6). The county court's power to grant relief against forfeiture in cases other than non-payment of rent is the same as that of the High Court: s. 146(13) of the Law of Property Act 1925.
[99] It is important that the correct form of order is used otherwise the order for possession will be discharged and the tenant let back into possession: *Spurgeons Homes* v. *Gentles* [1971] 1 W.L.R. 1514, (C.A.), where the landlord was not permitted to amend the form of order under the slip rule or the inherent powers of the court. For the correct form of order: see Forms N26–N28 of the County Court Forms.
[1] A legally aided tenant with a nil contribution may be ordered to pay the costs: *Three Stars Property Holdings* v. *Driscoll* (1988) C.L.Y. 2795, (C.A.). The "costs of the action" in s. 138(3) have been construed as meaning the costs of the action as awarded by the judge at the trial: *Sella House Ltd.* v. *Mears* (1989) 21 H.L.R. 147, 158–159, (C.A.), *per* Dillon L.J. In *Billson* v. *Residential Apartments Ltd.* [1992] 2 W.L.R. 15, (H.L.), it was held that in principle a tenant should not be ordered to pay costs on an indemnity basis. The landlord is entitled to recover not only his fixed court fee and fixed solicitors' costs specified in the possession summons but also any costs incurred in interlocutory proceedings prior to the date of the actual trial: *Swordheath Properties Ltd.* v. *Bolt* [1992] 38 E.G. 152.
[2] s. 138(4). See, *e.g. Varndean Estates Ltd.* v. *Buckland* (1967) 111 S.J. 684, (C.A.).

extended period, the tenant pays into court all the rent in arrear and all the costs of the action.

If the tenant pays the rent due and costs within the time limit fixed under the order (or any extension thereof), he will continue to hold under the original lease but, if he fails to pay within the time limit, the order for possession will be enforced[3] and the tenant will be barred from all relief[4] except that afforded by section 138(4) and (9A) of the 1984 Act.[5]

Under sub-section (9A), where the landlord recovers possession of the land at any time after the making of an order for possession (whether as a result of the enforcement of the order or otherwise), the tenant may, at any time within six months[6] from the date on which the landlord recovers possession, apply to the court for relief and, on such application, the court may, if it thinks fit, grant to the tenant such relief, subject to terms and conditions, as it thinks fit. Such an application may also be made by any person,[7] apart from the tenant, with an interest under the lease whether that interest was derived immediately from the tenant or otherwise.[8] Where relief is granted under sub-section (9A), the tenant will hold the land according to the original lease without any new lease.[9]

Section 138(7) of the 1984 Act provides that if the arrears of rent and costs are not paid into court within the specified time, then the tenant is to be "barred from all relief" except that afforded by subsections (8) and (9A). In this connection, subsection (9A) envisages the tenant as having six months following the landlord taking possession of the premises within which to seek relief from forfeiture. In the recent case of *United Dominions Trust Ltd.* v. *Shellpoint Trustees Ltd.*[10] the Court of Appeal held that a mortgagee of a leasehold flat was debarred from seeking relief from forfeiture in the High Court because its application for relief had been made outside the six month time-limit imposed by section 138(9A) of the

---

[3] Once it is established that the landlord has made out a case for forfeiture, the court is bound to order possession and there is no discretion in the matter: *R.* v. *A Circuit Judge (sitting at Norwich County Court), ex p. Wathen* (1977) 33 P. & C.R. 423.

[4] s. 138(7). See also, *Di Palma* v. *Victoria Square Property Ltd.* [1986] Ch. 150, (C.A.), where the tenant was denied equitable relief on the ground that the words "barred from all relief" in s. 138(7) of the 1984 Act meant barred from all relief whatsoever, including equitable relief in the High Court.

[5] Added to s. 138 by s. 55 of the Administration of Justice Act 1985. The amendment was prompted by the decision in *Di Palma* v. *Victoria Square Property Ltd.* [1986] Ch. 150, (C.A.).

[6] In *Haigside Ltd.* v. *Khan* [1989] 2 E.G.L.R. 239, (C.A.), the trial judge's attention was not drawn to s. 138(9A) and a rehearing was ordered.

[7] *e.g.* a mortgagee of the lease.

[8] subs. (9C) of the 1984 Act. On such an application, the court may make an order which vests the land (subject to such terms and conditions as the court thinks fit) in such person for the remainder of the term of the lease or for any less term. "Land" in this context includes part of the land: subs. (9C).

[9] subs. (9B) of the 1984 Act.

[10] [1993] E.G.C.S. 57, (C.A.).

1984 Act.[11] In this case, the landlord had re-taken possession of the flat pursuant to a court order and opposed the mortgagee's application for relief on the grounds that the High Court had no jurisdiction because section 138(7) excluded not only the jurisdiction of the county court to grant relief but also the High Court's jurisdiction.[12] At first instance,[13] Mr. David Neuberger Q.C. (sitting as a deputy judge of the Chancery Division) rejected this argument concluding that the consequences of construing section 138(7) in such a way as to debar the mortgagee (as opposed to a tenant) from any right whatever to seek relief would be draconian not least because a mortgagee was not normally a party to the possession proceedings.[14] Accordingly, despite the wide definition of "lessee" in section 140 of the 1984 Act, the reference to "the lessee" being barred from all relief in section 138(7) was held by the deputy judge not to extend to a mortgagee under the lease the subject of the forfeiture. In his view, the extension of the expressions "lease" and "lessee" in section 140 to include, for example, the original underlease and underlessee, was merely to emphasise that, if the lease that was the subject of the forfeiture proceedings was an underlease, then section 138 applied as much to the underlessee in whom the underlease was vested as it did to a headlease vested in a headlessee. The Court of Appeal has now reversed this decision emphasising that relief under section 138 can be achieved on payment by an underlessee of the rent arrears and costs even in cases where the action was brought against the headlessee and the underlessee was not a party to it.[15] According to the Court of Appeal, therefore, the applicant mortgagee was a "lessee" within the meaning of section 138 and since it had not made an application under subsection (9C) within the six month time period limited by subsection (9A) it was barred, by virtue of section 138(7), from all relief including relief in the High Court.

The right of a sub-tenant or mortgagee to apply for relief from forfeiture for non-payment of rent under section 146(4) of the Law of Property Act 1925 is expressly preserved by section 138(10)(b) of the 1984 Act.

It is important to observe that, in the case of a protected tenancy under the Rent Act 1977, section 138 of the 1984 Act only operates to terminate

---

[11] It is clear that it would have been open to the mortgagee to apply for relief from forfeiture in the county court under section 138(9C) within six months of the date on which the landlord recovered possession. However, by the time the mortgagee made its application for relief, the six months' time-limit had expired and it was, therefore, too late for the mortgagee to seek relief in the county court. For this reason, the mortgagee's application was made in the High Court.

[12] Relying on *Di Palma* v. *Victoria Square Property Ltd.* [1986] Ch. 150, (C.A.).

[13] [1992] 39 E.G. 144.

[14] In this case, the mortgage was, in fact, specifically identified, pursuant to Ord. 6, r. 3(1)(f) of the County Court Rules, in the particulars of claim as a person "who is entitled to claim relief against forfeiture" and was given notice of the proceedings. However, it was probably unaware of the fact that possession had been executed against the premises.

[15] A mortgagee is, of course, within the concept of an underlessee: See, for example, *Grand Junction Co. Ltd.* v. *Bates* [1954] 2 Q.B. 160.

the contractual tenancy held by the tenant and will not affect the further restrictions imposed by the 1977 Act on the actual attainment of possession once the contractual tenancy is determined.[15a] In this connection, the landlord must, in addition to showing that the contractual tenancy has determined by forfeiture, establish the relevant ground[16] for possession under the Rent Act 1977. Both these aspects, therefore, should be pleaded in the landlord's particulars of claim.[17] Moreover, the landlord's action for possession in such cases should be brought in the county court notwithstanding that the High Court also has jurisdiction.[18]

(2) *Landlord proceeding by re-entry without action*

The foregoing provisions apply to cases where the landlord is proceeding *by action* to enforce a right of forfeiture for non-payment of rent.[19] Where the landlord forfeits the lease by physically re-entering the demised premises without recourse to legal proceedings,[20] section 139(2) of the 1984 Act expressly confers on the county court[21] the same power to relieve against forfeiture for non-payment of rent as the High Court could have granted,[22] provided that the application for relief is made within six months from the date of the landlord's peaceable re-entry. Where the tenant is granted relief, he will hold the demised premises according to the original lease without any new lease.[23] An application under section 139(2) may be made by a person with an interest derived from the tenant (whether immediately or otherwise) and the court may make an order which (subject to such terms and conditions as it thinks fit) vests the land (or a part thereof) in such person for the remainder of the term of the lease or for any less term.[24]

Contract of hire of chattels

Hire is a form of bailment. It is a contract by which the hirer obtains the right to use the chattel hired in return for the payment to the owner of the

---

[15a] *Wolmer Securities Ltd. Corne* [1966] 2 Q.B. 243, (C.A.).

[16] See Case 1 of Sched. 15 to the Rent Act 1977, (rent lawfully due from the tenant has not been paid).

[17] The position is the same in respect of an assured or assured shorthold tenancy under the Housing Act 1988.

[18] *Peachey Property Corporation Ltd.* v. *Robinson* [1967] 2 Q.B. 543, (C.A.).

[19] See, s. 138(1).

[20] Physical re-entry is not available to a landlord where the premises are let as a dwelling and whilst any person is lawfully residing therein: s. 2 of the Protection from Eviction Act 1977. See also, s. 6 of the Criminal Law Act 1977.

[21] Provided, of course, that the demised premises are within the limits of the county court's jurisdiction.

[22] See, *e.g. Lovelock* v. *Margo* [1963] 2 Q.B. 786, (C.A.).

[23] s. 139(3) of the 1984 Act, inserted by s. 55(5) of the Administration of Justice Act 1985.

[24] *Ibid.*

price of hiring.[25] The general property in the chattel is not changed but remains in the owner although, upon delivery, the hirer becomes legally possessed of the chattel hired. Thus, for example, there is an implied warranty that the bailee/hirer will enjoy quiet possession of the goods for the period of the hire except so far as possession may be disturbed by the owner or other person entitled to the benefit of any charge or encumbrance disclosed or known to the hirer before the contract is made.[26] In *Palmer on Bailment* there appears the following passage[27]:

> "A bailment gives rise to a form of property because it creates a division of interests in rem within the compass of a single chattel. The division is chronological rather than geographical; as in the case of leaseholds, a bailment divides the ownership of the res "on a plane of time". The bailee obtains a legal interest in the form of possession, which is in many respects equivalent to an estate in land . . ."

It has recently been suggested that a hirer may have an equitable interest in the hired chattel where the contract of hire is specifically enforceable. In *Bristol Airport plc v.Powdrill*,[28] a case involving leasing agreements of aircraft, Browne-Wilkinson V.-C. opined[29]:

> "It is true that, to date, concepts of concurrent interests in personal property have not been developed in the same way as they have over the centuries in relation to real property. But modern commercial methods have introduced chattel-leasing . . . Although a chattel lease is a contract, it does not follow that no property interest is created in the chattel. The basic equitable principle is that if, under a contract, A has certain rights over property as against the legal owner, which rights are specifically enforceable in equity, A has an equitable interest in such property."

In *Barton Thompson & Co. Ltd.* v. *Stapling Machines Co.*[30] Pennycuick J. was called upon to consider whether relief could be granted against

---

[25] See, 2 *Halsbury's Law of England*, (4th ed., Re-Issue), para. 1850.
[26] s. 7(2) of the Supply of Goods and Services Act 1982.
[27] (1979), at p. 65. See also, Paton, *Bailment in the Common Law*, (1952), at pp. 29–36; *Story on Bailments*, (9th ed.), s. 370a; Winfield, *Province of the Law of Tort*, at pp. 100–103; Lawson, *Introduction to the Law of Property*, at pp. 109–110 and 118–119 and *Australian Guarantee Corporation Ltd.* v. *Ross* [1983] 2 V.R. 319, 329–330, (Supreme Court of Victoria), *per* Marks J. It has been suggested that the hirer has a proprietary interest in the hired goods: See, *e.g.*, *Bristol Airport plc* v. *Powdrill* [1990] Ch. 744, 759, (C.A.), *per* Browne-Wilkinson V.-C.; *A.L. Hamblin Equipment Property Ltd.* v. *Federal Commissioner of Taxation* [1974] Australian Tax Cases 4310, 4318, *per* Mason J. For a contrary view, see Barwick C.J. in *Hamblin*, at p. 4314, and *Australian Provincial Assurance Co. Ltd.* v. *Coroneo* (1938) 38 S.R. (N.S.W.), 700, 714–715, *per* Jordan C.J.
[28] [1990] Ch. 744, (C.A.).
[29] *Ibid.*, at p. 759.
[30] [1966] Ch. 499. *cf. Galbraith* v. *Mitchenhall Estates* [1965] 2 Q.B. 473, 482–484, *per* Sachs J., (forfeiture of instalments paid under a hire-purchase contract of a caravan).

forfeiture of an hiring agreement of chattels. In that case, the parties had entered into an agreement whereby the defendant leased to the plaintiff for a term of 25 years certain machines for making wirebound boxes. The agreement provided for rental and other payments. In the case of a breach by the plaintiff of any of the terms of the agreement, the defendant was entitled to serve 30 days' notice to remedy the breach and, in default, to terminate the agreement. The plaintiff defaulted in a number of payments and the defendant sent notice of intention to terminate the agreement and, after the expiry of the prescribed 30 day period, sent notice of immediate determination. The plaintiff then issued a summons claiming to be relieved from forfeiture of its interest in the machines. On a motion by the defendant to strike out the summons on the ground that it disclosed no reasonable cause of action, Pennycuick J. held[31] that it was arguable, as a matter of law, whether the court could (in the absence of unconscionable behaviour on the part of the defendant) grant relief from forfeiture in the case of a lease of chattels and, accordingly, permitted the plaintiff to argue the case if it was maintainable on other grounds.[32] However, in the instant case, the evidence did not show that the plaintiff was ready to discharge the arrears and the tenor of the plaintiff's affidavit was that it was not in a position to do so. In this connection, Pennycuick J. held that it was an invariable condition of relief from forfeiture for non-payment of rent that the arrears should be paid within a time specified by the court and that, therefore, readiness to pay the arrears within the time allocated was a necessary condition of a tenant's claim for relief. Whilst it was not strictly necessary for the tenant to aver such readiness specifically in his pleading or affidavit, nevertheless, where (as in the present case) the plaintiff's affidavit showed an absence of readiness the claim for relief was defective and fell to be struck out.

It is also useful to refer to the more recent case of *Lombard North Central plc* v. *Butterworth*[33] which also involved a lease of chattels. In that case, the plaintiffs, a finance company, leased a computer to the defendant for a period of five years on payment of an initial sum of £584.05 and 19 subsequent quarterly instalments of the same amount. The parties were referred to as "lessor" and "lessee" respectively and clause 2(*a*) provided as follows:

"THE LESSEE ... AGREES ...

2(*a*) to pay to the lessor: (i) punctually and without previous demand

---

[31] In so doing, he relied on the statements of principle enunciated by Rigby L.J. in *Re Dixon, Heynes* v. *Dixon* [1900] 2 Ch. 561, 576 and Lord Greene M.R. in *Chandless-Chandless* v. *Nicholson* [1942] 2 K.B. 321, 323 to the effect that a court of equity always regarded a forfeiture clause as being merely security for the payment of rent and provided the landlord could get his rent, relief was given.

[32] His view was approved by Edmund Davies L.J. in *Starside Properties Ltd.* v. *Mustapha* [1974] 1 W.L.R. 816, 822–823, (C.A.).

[33] [1987] 2 W.L.R. 7, (C.A.).

the rentals set out in Part 3 of the Schedule together with Value Added Tax thereon punctual payment of each which shall be of the essence of this Lease . . . "

Clause 5 of the agreement provided:

"IN THE EVENT THAT (a) the Lessee shall (i) make default in the due and punctual payment of any of the rentals . . . then upon the happening of such event . . . the Lessor's consent to the Lessee's possession of the Goods shall determine forthwith without any notice being given by the Lessor, and the Lessor may terminate this Lease either by notice in writing, or by taking possession of the Goods . . . "

The case revolved round the question whether the hirer's breach in failing to pay the rentals punctually amounted to a repudiation of the contract entitling the owner to recover all the arrears and future payments by way of damages. It is arguable, however, that the owner's exercise of its right to withdraw consent to the hirer's possession of the goods also constituted a forfeiture of the hirer's possessory/proprietary[34] rights in the goods and, as such, would have entitled the hirer to seek relief against the forfeiture. The point, however, did not strictly arise for consideration since, on the facts, the hirer had repudiated the contract and was no longer in a position to proceed with it.

A number of recent cases favour the court's power to grant relief from forfeiture in relation to contracts creating interests in property other than land. In *Scandinavian Trading Tanker Co. AB* v. *Flota Petrolera Ecuatoriana, The Scaptrade*[35] the House of Lords[36] suggested that equity's jurisdiction

---

[34] Assuming the hirer's *proprietary* interest in the goods is dependent on the availability of specific performance, his default in an essential condition of the contract may deprive him of this equitable remedy needed to support his proprietary right: See, *e.g.*, *Steedman* v. *Drinkle* [1916] 1 A.C. 275, (P.C.) and *Sport International Bussum BV* v. *Inter-Footwear Ltd.* [1984] 1 All E.R. 376, 385, (C.A.), *per* Oliver L.J. Hence, default in punctual payment (in cases where time is made of the essence of the contract) may involve the loss of the right to specific performance need to support the hirer's equitable interest in the goods rather than the forfeiture of the equitable interest. *cf.* P. Sparkes, *Forfeiture of Equitable Leases*, (1987) 16 Anglo-American L. Rev. 160. Moreover, it should be borne in mind that the discretion to order specific performance of a contract for the sale/hire of goods will be exercised only if an award of damages would not be an adequate remedy. Whilst the court will not refuse specific performance simply because the contract relates to chattels, the remedy will be denied if the chattel is "an ordinary article of commerce and of no special value or interest": See *Whiteley Ltd.* v. *Hilt* [1918] 2 K.B. 808, 819, (C.A.), *per* Swinfen Eady M.R., (a case involving the letting of a piano under a hire-purchase agreement). On the other hand, in *Bristol Airport plc* v. *Powdrill* [1990] Ch. 744, (C.A.), Browne-Wilkinson V.-C. suggested that a court would order specific performance of a contract to lease an aircraft on the ground that "each aircraft has unique features peculiar to itself": *ibid.*, at p. 759. See, generally, Jones and Goodhart, *Specific Performance*, (1986), at pp. 112–117.

[35] [1983] 1 All E.R. 301, (C.A.) and [1983] 2 All E.R. 763, (H.L.), (time charter).

[36] [1983] 2 All E.R. 763.

would extend to contracts "involving any transfer of proprietary or possessory rights."[37] However, in *Sport International Bussum BV* v. *Inter-Footwear Ltd.*,[38] the Court of Appeal[39] adopted a more restrictive approach and proceeded to hold that the availability of equitable relief was confined to cases where the subject-matter of the forfeiture was an interest in land. This narrow view was, however, not applied by the House of Lords[40] which adopted the wider statement of principle enunciated by Lord Diplock in the *Scaptrade* case without comment. The wider view was also accepted in *BICC plc* v. *Burndy Corporation*,[41] a case involving patent rights, in which the Court of Appeal held that, although relief was only available in respect of proprietary or possessory rights, it was *not* restricted to interests in real property but extended to interests in personal property as well. In that case, the relevant provision in the contract was construed as a forfeiture clause invoking the forfeiture by the defendant of its proprietary rights in personal property (namely, the patent rights) and accordingly, the Court had jurisdiction to grant the defendant relief by giving him an extension of time to comply with its obligations as to the payment of costs and fees under the contract. In the words of Dillon L.J.[42]:

> "There is no clear authority, but for my part I find it difficult to see why the jurisdiction of equity to grant relief against forfeitures should only be available where what is liable to forfeiture is an interest in land and not an interest in personal property. Relief is only available where what is in question is forfeiture of proprietary or possessory rights, but I see no reason in principle for drawing a distinction as to the type of property in which the rights subsist. The fact the right of forfeiture arises under a commercial agreement is highly relevant to the question whether relief against forfeiture should be granted, but I do not see that it can preclude the existence of the jurisdiction to grant relief, if forfeiture of proprietary or possessory rights, as opposed to merely contractual rights, is in question."

The question of the extent of equity's jurisdiction to relieve against forfeiture of personal property was further considered in *Jobson* v. *Johnson*,[43] which involved the purchase of a number of shares in a football club by instalments. The purchase agreement contained a clause that if the buyer defaulted in the payment of the instalments, he was required to transfer the shares back to the vendors for the sum of £40,000. When the

---

[37] *Ibid.* p. 767, *per* Lord Diplock.
[38] [1984] 1 All E.R. 376, (C.A.) and [1984] 1 W.L.R. 776, (H.L.), (trade marks).
[39] [1984] 1 All E.R. 376, 383, *per* Oliver L.J., giving the judgment of the Court of Appeal.
[40] [1984] 1 W.L.R. 776, 781, *per* Lord Templeman who gave the leading speech and with which the other Law Lords concurred.
[41] [1985] Ch. 232.
[42] [1985] Ch. 232, 252.
[43] [1989] 1 W.L.R. 1026, (C.A.).

buyer defaulted in the payment of the instalments, the vendors' successors sought specific performance of the agreement for the retransfer of the shares. The case proceeded on the basis that the re-transfer provision constituted a penalty clause and, as such, was subject to equitable relief in the sense that, if it was sued on by the vendors, it would not be enforced by the court beyond the amount of the vendors' actual loss. The Court of Appeal, however, also considered the question whether the re-transfer provision was unenforceable on the ground that it constituted a forfeiture clause which equity would relieve against on payment of the outstanding amounts with interest and costs. In this connection, Nicholls L.J. referred to the provision as "something of a hybrid"[44] possessing features which were common to both a penalty clause and a forfeiture clause. In substance, the provision gave the vendors the right to retake the property being sold in default of payment of the full price and, as such, fell squarely within equity's jurisdiction to relieve against the forfeiture of property. Since the provision was intended to provide the unpaid vendors with some security against non-payment by giving them an alternative remedy (namely, repossession of the shares) in the event of the buyer's default, it was a situation "which, par excellence, equity in its discretion, and having regard to all the circumstances, may grant relief."[45] Kerr L.J. was of the same view.[46] It is interesting to note that both Nicholls and Kerr L.JJ. were prepared to assume that equity would have jurisdiction to relieve against the forfeiture of the shares despite the fact that the subject-matter of the purchase agreement was personal property and not a proprietary or possessory interest in land. Indeed, no reference is made to this point in either of the judgments. Finally, reference may also be made to the recent case of *Goker* v. *News Bank plc*,[47] where Sir Gervase Sheldon concluded that, although the court had a general jurisdiction to provide relief from forfeiture of a chattel, it was unlikely to be utilised save in exceptional cases where the court was satisfied that no significant prejudice would result to the vendor from the grant of relief.

It will be apparent from the foregoing analysis that equity's jurisdiction to relieve against forfeitures extends to cases where the failure to comply with an instalment obligation under a contractual agreement results in the loss or termination of a proprietary or possessory right in some property other than land. In these cases, equity treats the forfeiture clause

---

[44] *Ibid.* p. 1043.

[45] *Ibid.* p. 1043. Nicholls L.J. relied on the extract from the speech of Lord Wilberforce in *Shiloh Spinners Ltd.* v. *Harding* [1973] A.C. 691, 722, (H.L.), where the latter said: "Where it is possible to state that the object of the transaction and of the insertion of the right to forfeit is essentially to secure the payment of money, equity has been willing to relieve on terms that the payment is made with interest, if appropriate, and also costs."

[46] *Ibid.* pp. 1046–1047. The third member of the Court, Dillon L.J., did not express any view on this aspect of the case.

[47] *The Times*, May 23, 1990.

as a mere security for the performance of the principal obligation to meet the instalment payments on time. Accordingly, relief will take the form of the grant of an extension of time within which to perform this principal obligation. However, such relief will only be granted on terms as to the payment of interest on the amounts outstanding and costs. It also seems apparent that relief will not be granted in every case where a forfeiture takes place and the party in default is willing and able to tender late performance. The exercise of the court's discretion whether or not to grant relief will depend on all the circumstances of the case,[48] including the conduct of the parties, the nature and gravity of the breach and its relation to the value of the property which might be forfeited.[49]

Contractual licence of land

In *Sport International Bussum BV* v. *Inter-Footwear Ltd.*[50] Lord Templeman had occasion to remark[51]:

> "The recognised boundaries [of the equitable doctrine of relief against forfeiture] do not include mere contractual licences . . . "

This statement of principle was made in the specific context of a licence to use certain names and trade marks and it is unclear to what extent it was also intended to apply to contractual licences for the occupation of land. In this connection, the weight of academic opinion[52] favours the view that contractual licences of land do not give rise to proprietary rights and are not capable of binding third parties as interests in land. There are several authorities which clearly confirm this proposition. For example, in *King* v. *David Allen and Sons, Billposting Ltd.*[53] the parties entered into an agreement whereby the defendant gave the plaintiff permission to affix posters and advertisements to the flank walls of a cinema for a period of four years at a rent of £12 per year. The House of Lords held that the agreement did not create an interest in land but created merely a personal obligation on the part of the licensor to allow the licensee the use of the wall for advertisements. The Court of Appeal decision in *Clore* v. *Theatrical Properties Ltd.*[54] is to the same effect. In that case, Lord Wright M.R., referring to the document in that case, concluded:[55]

[48] See, *e.g. BICC plc* v. *Brundy Corporation* [1985] Ch. 232, 253, *per* Dillon L.J. and *Jobson* v. *Johnson* [1989] 1 W.L.R. 1026, 1043, *per* Nicholls L.J.
[49] See, *Shiloh Spinners Ltd.* v. *Harding* [1973] A.C. 691, 725, (H.L.), *per* Lord Wilberforce.
[50] [1984] 1 W.L.R. 776, (H.L.).
[51] *Ibid.*, at p. 794.
[52] Numerous academic writers have ventured into this great debate. See, *e.g.*, Wade, (1952) 68 L.Q.R. 337; Cheshire, (1953) 16 M.L.R. 1; Sheridan, (1953) 17 Conv. 440; Briggs, [1981] Conv. 212 and [1983] Conv. 285; Moriarty, (1984) 100 L.Q.R. 376; Dawson & Pearce, *Licences Relating to the Occupation and Use of Land*, (1979), Ch. 11.
[53] [1916] 2 A.C. 54, (H.L.).
[54] [1936] 3 All E.R. 483. See also, *Re Solomon* [1967] Ch. 573.
[55] *Ibid.*, at p. 490.

"I think... that this is not a document which creates an estate in land, but merely one which is a personal contract between the parties named therein and is only enforceable among parties between whom there is privity of contract."

In *National Provincial Bank Ltd.* v. *Hasting Car Mart Ltd.*[56] Russell L.J. remarked[57]:

"In the case of contractual licences, their elevation for purposes of title to a status equivalent to an estate or interest in land might be thought desirable, at least in the case of licences to occupy; but, if so, it is a matter for legislation..."

It is equally clear, however, that a contractual licensee may be able to enforce a right against a third party if the facts give rise to some other legal relationship outside the sphere of contract (*i.e.* under the doctrine of proprietary estoppel or of the constructive trust). In these cases, the licensee will acquire an equitable interest either as an estoppel licensee or as a beneficiary under a trust.[58]

It has already been mentioned earlier[59] that the term "forfeiture" involves the loss or termination of an estate in property or a proprietary or possessory right in property.[60] Unfortunately, there are few reported cases in which relief against forfeiture has been raised as an equitable defence to the termination of a licence to occupy land. In *Starside Properties Ltd.* v. *Mustapha*[61] the plaintiffs agreed to sell the freehold of a house to the defendant for £5,950. Under the agreement, the defendant was to pay a deposit of £350 and be allowed into occupation as a licensee pending completion of the sale. She agreed to pay 10 per cent interest per annum in monthly instalments and additional monthly payments off the purchase price. After payment of a total of £1,250 off the purchase price, she was to be entitled to completion on payment of the balance due. Paragraph 7 of the agreement provided that, if she was in arrears with her payments for more than 14 days, the plaintiffs were to have the right to rescind the contract and forfeit all the sums paid by her by way of deposit and she would vacate the property. The defendant defaulted under the agreement and the plaintiffs sued for possession. The Court of Appeal held that the power to grant equitable relief in the form of an extension of

[56] [1964] Ch. 665, (C.A.).
[57] *Ibid.*, at p. 699.
[58] See, *e.g.*, *Errington* v. *Errington and Woods* [1952] 1 K.B. 290; *Binions* v. *Evans* [1972] Ch. 359; *Ashburn Anstalt* v. *Arnold* [1989] Ch. 1; *D.H.N. Food Distributors Ltd.* v. *Tower Hamlets London Borough Council* [1976] 1 W.L.R. 852 and *Re Sharpe* [1980] 1 W.L.R. 219.
[59] See under the heading "Contract of hire of chattels", *ante*.
[60] See, *Scandinavian Trading Tanker Co. AB* v. *Flota Petrolera Ecuatoriana, The Scaptrade* [1983] 2 All E.R. 763, 767, *per* Lord Diplock and *BICC plc* v. *Burndy Corporation* [1985] Ch. 232, (C.A.), 252, *per* Dillon L.J.
[61] [1978] 1 W.L.R. 816, (C.A.).

time to make payment was not confined to cases of forfeiture for non-payment of rent and remitted the defendant's application to the trial judge for consideration on its merits. The Court found it unnecessary to refer to the fact that all the cases[62] cited by them were cases where it was sought to forfeit an interest in land, whereas the instant case was one where the plaintiff was a mere licensee, albeit under a license "coupled with an interest".

In *Underground (Civil Engineering) Ltd.* v. *Croydon London Borough Council*[63] a company agreed at its own expense to construct a workshop building and ancillary offices on land belonging to the defendant Council. The company covenanted to complete the works by the beginning of October 1988 and the Council agreed that, within one month of the date of practical completion, it would grant the company a 125 year lease of the land. By clause 6(*a*) of the agreement, it was agreed that if the company's works were not completed within the period specified, at the option of the Council, the agreement "shall cease and determine and the [Council] may re-enter upon and take possession of the . . . land together with the buildings and erections thereon . . . " By March 1988, the company had spent some £8,000 on carrying out the works and the only work that required completion was the erection of a steel-framed building and landscaping which was estimated to cost £20,000 and could have been completed within two or three weeks. In the same month, the company was informed that Sutton London Borough Council had resolved to compulsorily purchase the land for a new road and, following the advice of that Council (and later its own professional advisers), the company ceased to carry out further work. By a letter, dated October 31, 1988, the Council purported to determine the agreement and take possession of the land whereupon the company claimed that the power of termination in clause 6(*a*) was penal and amounted to a forfeiture provision and sought relief from forfeiture. Mr. T. A. Morison Q.C. (sitting as a deputy judge of the High Court) held that clause 6(*a*) was not penal in its effect since the sensible purpose of the clause was no more than an ordinary power of re-entry to be found in a lease. However, he concluded that the clause amounted to a forfeiture provision and that, as a matter of principle, the court had jurisdiction to grant relief. The learned deputy judge distinguished the contract from an ordinary building agreement on the ground that the company went into occupation of the land with a view to becoming a long leaseholder of it. It, therefore, had an insurable interest and a right to specific performance of the Council's obligation to grant the lease. On this basis, therefore, it had a "proprietary or possessory inter-

---

[62] See, *e.g. In Re Dagenham (Thames) Dock Co.* (1873) 8 Ch. App. 1022; *Kilmer* v. *British Columbia Orchard Land Ltd.* [1913] A.C. 319, (P.C.) and *Steedman* v. *Drinkle* [1916] A.C. 275, (P.C.), (purchaser let into possession of the land as a tenant).
[63] [1990] E.G.C.S. 48.

est" and relief from forfeiture was granted on terms that the building be completed within ten weeks.

In the absence of clear authority on the point, it remains uncertain to what extent equitable relief against forfeiture is applicable to a mere contractual right to possession of land. It is, at least, arguable[64] that a mere possessory right which is capable of enforcement by means of an order for specific performance falls within equity's jurisdiction to grant relief. In *Verrall* v. *Great Yarmouth Borough Council*[65] the Court of Appeal granted specific performance of a contractual licence to allow the National Front to hold its annual conference at one of the defendant Council's halls on two days in October 1979. The Court took the view that it had a duty to protect by injunction[66] or specific performance any right in or over land regardless whether it was a legal estate or a mere license, when appropriate to do so. The *Verrall* case is, therefore, significant in the present context because it emphatically rejects the argument[67] that specific performance will be granted only if a contract creates a proprietary interest in land. Moreover, it appears that any interest in land, including a licence to occupy land, is unique and has "a peculiar and special value"[68] so that specific performance will not be denied on the ground that damages would provide an adequate remedy. An inherent difficulty, however, is that the courts are reluctant to decree specific performance when the party seeking it has to do so on the basis that he himself is in default in performing one of the essential terms of the contract.[69]

---

[64] But see the *obiter* remarks of Oliver L.J. (giving the judgment of the Court of Appeal) in *Sport International Bussum BV* v. *Inter-Footwear Ltd.* [1984] 1 All E.R. 376, 385: " . . . we have considerable doubt whether, outside the sphere of landlord and tenant, the equitable jurisdiction could in any event be exercised in a case where the forfeited interest depends on contract only and where relief, in effect, involves specifically performing that contract."

[65] [1981] Q.B. 202, (C.A.).

[66] See, *e.g.*, *Winter Garden Theatre (London) Ltd.* v. *Millennium Productions Ltd.* [1948] A.C. 173, (H.L.) and *Hounslow London Borough Council* v. *Twickenham Garden Developments Ltd.* [1971] Ch. 233.

[67] See, *e.g.*, *Booker* v. *Palmer* [1942] 2 All E.R. 674, 677, *per* Lord Greene M.R.

[68] Story, *Equity Jurisprudence*, (1st ed., 1836), at p. 24.

[69] See, *e.g.*, *Steedman* v. *Drinkle* [1916] 1 A.C. 275, (P.C.) and *Sport International Bussum BV* v. *Inter-Footwear Ltd.* [1984] 1 All E.R. 376, 385, (C.A.), *per* Oliver L.J. The point was not taken in *Starside Properties Ltd.* v. *Mustapha* [1974] 1 W.L.R. 816, (C.A.).

Chapter Ten

Relief against forfeiture for breaches of covenant (other than non-payment of rent)

Application for relief by tenant[1]

(1) Introduction

In cases other than non-payment of rent, the court's inherent equitable jurisdiction[2] to grant relief against forfeiture from a wilful[3] breach of covenant has been entirely replaced by the statutory jurisdiction contained in section 146(2) of the Law of Property Act 1925[4] in respect of leases and underleases covered by the sub-section.[5] Thus, if the tenant cannot obtain relief under section 146(2), he has no recourse to any underlying equitable jurisdiction to be relieved against a wilful breach of covenant in order to preserve his lease.[6] Section 146(2) provides as follows:

> "Where a lessor is proceeding, by action or otherwise, to enforce such a right of re-entry or forfeiture, the lessee may, in the lessor's

---

[1] For useful precedents, see *Atkin's Court Forms*, (2nd. ed., 1990) Vol. 24, pp. 374–376 Forms 173–175 and Part VI of this work.

[2] See, *Shiloh Spinners Ltd.* v. *Harding* [1973] A.C. 691, (H.L.).

[3] *i.e.* not involving fraud, accident or mistake. The equitable jurisdiction to relieve against the consequences of fraud, accident or mistake is unaffected by s. 146: *Billson* v. *Residential Apartments Ltd.* [1991] 3 W.L.R. 264, 284, (C.A.).

[4] *Billson* v. *Residential Apartments Ltd.* [1991] 3 W.L.R. 264, (C.A.).

[5] A contract for hire of chattels is outside the subsection because it does not constitute a lease of land. In this case, the hirer would be entitled to relief under the court's inherent equitable jurisdiction: *Shiloh Spinners Ltd.* v. *Harding* [1973] A.C. 691, (H.L.), (assignment of lease). See also, *Barton Thompson & Co Ltd.* v. *Stapling Machines Co.* [1966], Ch. 499 (non-payment of instalments under a contract of hire of machines).

[6] See cases discussed in Chap. 8, at pp. 203–212.

action, if any, or in any action brought by himself, apply to the court[7] for relief; and the court may grant or refuse relief, as the court, having regard to the proceedings and conduct of the parties under the foregoing provisions of this section, and to all the other circumstances, thinks fit, and in case of relief it may grant it on such terms, if any, as to costs, expenses, damages, compensation, penalty, or otherwise, including the granting of an injunction to restrain any like breach in the future, as the court, in the circumstances of each case, thinks fit."

The combined effect of section 146(1) and (2) is to give the tenant the benefit of double protection against the forfeiture of his lease, namely, (a) the landlord cannot exercise his right to forfeit unless he has first served a notice on the tenant requiring the tenant to remedy the breach complained of and the tenant fails to remedy the same within a reasonable time[8] and (b) the tenant can apply to the court for relief against forfeiture at any time before the landlord has actually obtained possession of the demised premises pursuant to an order of the court. In *Billson* v. *Residential Apartments Ltd.*,[9] Lord Templeman explained the purpose behind Parliament's intervention to enable a tenant to be relieved from the forfeiture of his lease[10]:

"In 1881[11] Parliament interfered to supplement equity and to enable any tenant to be relieved from forfeiture. The need for such intervention was and is manifest because otherwise a tenant who had paid a large premium for a 999-year lease at a low rent could lose his asset by a breach of covenant which was remediable or which caused the landlord no damage. The forfeiture of any lease, however short, may unjustly enrich the landlord at the expense of the tenant."

The nature of a legal lease is such as to confer on the tenant a legal term of years (an estate in land) and it is this proprietary interest which the tenant stands to lose upon the exercise of the landlord's remedy of forfeiture. Where, however, the parties have merely entered into an agreement for a lease (as opposed to a valid lease at law), the agreement is only recognised in equity under the rule in *Walsh* v. *Lonsdale*.[11a] This

---

[7] The application will usually be assigned to the Chancery Division of the High Court (s. 203(4) of the 1925 Act), although the Queen's Bench Division also has jurisdiction to relieve in an action before it. The county court's jurisdiction under ss. 146 and 147 of the Law of Property Act 1925 has now been extended without limit: See, the High Court and County Courts Jurisdiction Order 1991 made on March 19, 1991 under s. 1 of the Courts and Legal Services Act 1990. The Order came into force on July 1, 1991: See, S.I. 1991 No. 724.

[8] The pre-requisite of a s. 146 notice is discussed in Chap. 5.

[9] [1992] 2 W.L.R. 15, (H.L.).

[10] *Ibid*. p. 18–19.

[11] Lord Templeman's reference is to s. 14(2) of the Conveyancing and Law of Property Act 1881, predecessor to s. 146(2) of the 1925 Act.

[11a] (1882) 21 Ch. D. 9.

decision dictates that an agreement for a lease is to be treated as a lease in equity if specific performance of the agreement is available. Subsequent cases[12] have confirmed that specific performance is not available if the tenant must admit his own breach of covenant under the agreement. It follows that breach of an agreement for a lease does not involve any forfeiture of the equitable term but simply the loss of the right to specific performance needed to create the equitable term. The consequence is that a legal tenant, who is in breach of covenant and who loses his lease by forfeiture, may claim relief but an equitable tenant appears to be unprotected because his inequitable conduct will deny him the equitable remedy of specific performance on which his equitable rights depend. Equity, however, may grant specific performance despite breaches of covenant if they were caused by accident, surprise or other excuse.[12a] These exceptional circumstances, which would enable the court to grant specific performance, would presumably also enable the court to grant relief from forfeiture. Moreover, for the purposes of section 146 of the Law of Property Act 1925, the term "lease" is defined to include an "agreement for a lease where the lessee has become entitled to have his lease granted".[13] The traditional view is that this wording does not affect the common law position and that section 146 is not applicable to equitable leases.[13a] An alternative view[14] is that the words "but for the forfeiture sued upon" ought to be inserted after the word "entitled" in section 146(5) of the 1925 Act. Even if there may be no lease in equity, it may still be possible to infer a common law periodic tenancy where the tenant under the agreement has entered into possession and paid rent by reference to a period.[14a]

If the landlord is proceeding by action to enforce his right of forfeiture, the tenant's application for relief may be made in the landlord's action by way of counterclaim.[15] If, however, the landlord is effecting a forfeiture by physically re-entering the demised premises, the tenant may himself

---

[12] See, *e.g. Coatesworth* v. *Johnson* (1886) 55 L.J.Q.B. 220, (C.A.); *Swain* v. *Ayres* (1888) 21 Q.B.D. 289, (C.A.).

[12a] *Swain* v. *Ayres* (1888) 21 Q.B.D. 289, 294, *per* Lord Esher M.R.

[13] See, s. 146(5)(*a*) of the 1925 Act.

[13a] *Greville* v. *Parker* [1910] A.C. 335, (P.C.); *Charrington & Co. Ltd.* v. *Camp* [1902] 1 Ch. 386 and *Strong* v. *Stringer* (1889) 61 L.T. 470.

[14] See, Woodfall, *Law of Landlord and Tenant*, at para. 1–1934. See also, *Sport International Bussum BV* v. *Inter-Footwear Ltd.* [1984] 1 All E.R. 376, 385, *per* Oliver L.J.; *Shodroske* v. *Hadley* (1908) 27 N.Z.L.R. 377 and *Greenwood Village Property* v. *Tom the Cheap (W.A.) Property* [1975] W.A.R. 49; P. Sparkes, *Forfeiture of Equitable Leases*, 16 Anglo-American L. Rev. 160 and Keeton & Sheridan's *Equity*, (3rd ed., 1987), at p. 70.

[14a] See further, P.H. Pettit, *The Tenant under an Agreement and Section 146 of the Law of Property Act 1925*, (1960) 24 Conv. (N.S.) 125, at pp. 128–129.

[15] *Warden and Governors of Cholmeley's School, Highgate* v. *Sewell* [1893] 2 Q.B. 254, a case concerning s. 146(4) of the 1925 Act. For a form of counterclaim: See *Atkin's Court Forms* (2nd ed., 1990) Vol. 24, p. 374, Form 173 and Pt. VI of this work.

bring an action[15a] and apply for relief from forfeiture. In the former case, it is not essential that the tenant's pleadings contain an application for relief and it is sufficient if the application is made in the landlord's action by way of summons[16] or even informally in the course of an appeal against an order for possession founded on the forfeiture of the lease.[16a] However, the tenant's failure to make an application for relief at the hearing of the landlord's action is not a ground for setting aside a judgment for possession and ordering a new trial.[17] Where the landlord is proceeding to enforce his right of forfeiture otherwise than by action, section 146(2) requires the tenant to make his application in "any action brought by himself" and it has been held[17a] that an application brought by originating summons will be bad since it is not a summons taken out in "an action" as required by the subsection.

The court only has power, under section 146(2), to grant relief from the consequences of a past act of forfeiture and cannot condone a continuing or proposed breach of covenant in the future.[18] A mere squatter, who has acquired a title by adverse possession against the tenant, cannot apply for relief unless there is evidence from which the court can infer a mutual intention to create a new relationship of landlord and tenant arising by operation of law from the payment or acceptance of rent.[19]

In *Warner* v. *Sampson*[20] Ashworth J. held *inter alia* that relief cannot be granted where the forfeiture arises out of a denial of the landlord's title. In his view, such a forfeiture arises by operation of law and not under "any proviso or stipulation in a lease" within the meaning of section 146(1) of the 1925 Act.[21] However, in *W. G. Clark (Properties) Ltd.* v. *Dupre Properties Ltd.*,[22] Mr. T. R. A. Morison Q.C. (sitting as a deputy judge of the High Court) opined[23] that relief against forfeiture may be granted under section

---

[15a] Either by Writ or by Originating Summons: R.S.C. Ord. 5, r.4. negativing *Lock* v. *Pearce* [1893] 2 Ch. 271, (C.A.).

[16] *Mitchison* v. *Thomson* (1883) Cab. & El. 72 and *Jacques* v. *Harrison* (1884) 12 Q.B.D. 165, (C.A.). See also, *Golding* v. *Cavendish Holdings* (1959) 174 E.G. 577, (application in High Court where landlord's action in county court). For a form of summons and affidavit in support: See *Atkin's Court Forms* (2nd ed., 1990) Vol. 24, pp. 375–376, Forms 174 and 175 and Pt. VI of this work.

[16a] *Lam Kee Ying* v. *Lam Shes Tong* [1975] A.C. 247, 257 (P.C.), *per* Sir Harry Gibbs. See also, *Quilter* v. *Mapleson* (1882) 9 Q.B.D. 672, (C.A.), in relation to the powers of the Court of Appeal.

[17] *Ezekiel* v. *Orakpo* [1977] Q.B. 260, 266, *per* Shaw L.J., (C.A.).

[17a] *Lock* v. *Pearce* [1893] 2 Ch. 271, 275, *per* Lord Esher M.R., (C.A.). But see now, R.S.C. Ord. 5, r.4.

[18] *Batson* v. *The School Board for London* (1904) 69 J.P. 9, *per* Channel J. But see, *Duke of Westminster* v. *Swinton* [1948] 1 K.B. 524, where a continuing breach was sanctioned for two years pending remedial works.

[19] *Tickner* v. *Buzzacott* [1965] 1 Ch. 426.

[20] [1958] 1 Q.B. 404. The decision of Ashworth J. (but not on this point) was reversed by the Court of Appeal: [1959] 1 Q.B. 297.

[21] *Warner* v. *Sampson* [1958] 1 Q.B. 404, 424–425.

[22] [1991] 3 W.L.R. 579.

[23] *Ibid.* pp. 589–591.

146(2) where the forfeiture arises out of a disclaimer of the landlord's title on the ground that section 146(1) was not confined to breaches of express conditions but extended to breaches of implied conditions, such as the implied condition that the tenant would not do anything that might prejudice the title of the landlord.

In *Brewer* v. *Jacobs*[24] it was held that relief under section 146(2) was not available to a statutory tenant under the Rent Act 1977. The court has also no jurisdiction under section 146(2) to grant relief to joint lessees unless all of them apply for relief under the subsection. Thus, in *T. M. Fairclough and Sons Ltd.* v. *Berliner*[25] the landlord served section 146 notices on two joint tenants alleging breaches of repairing covenants. The tenants originally appeared by the same solicitors and put in a defence signed by counsel on their behalf. At the date of the hearing, however, one tenant asked for relief against forfeiture but the other preferred to give up possession. Maugham J. held that relief against forfeiture, where there were joint tenants, could not be granted on the application of only one of them and ordered possession of the premises. He said[26]:

> "... there seems to me to be a very great objection to a provision which would enable him to apply to the Court, unless the provision also in some way enabled the Court in granting relief to absolve the other joint lessee from future liability ... if I were to accede to the application on behalf of the second defendant, the result would be that the first defendant would continue to be liable under the onerous covenants contained in these leases, including the onerous obligation to pay rent up to the termination of the leases without, it may be, any prospect of being able to recoup himself by the use of the premises."

It has been held[27] that a right to relief against forfeiture is a true equitable defence to the landlord's claim for possession and that a tenant's counterclaim for such relief ought to result in an order for unconditional leave to defend in proceedings for summary judgment brought under R.S.C. Ord. 14. In the words of Parker L.J.[28]:

> "Although the right to relief against forfeiture is now statutory, it is in origin an equitable defence. It was a means by which equity stepped in to prevent the enforcement of a legal right. It is inextricably mixed with the claim for forfeiture, and it is, in my judgment, a true equitable defence to the legal claim for forfeiture."

---

[24] [1923] 1 K.B. 528.
[25] [1931] 1 Ch. 60.
[26] *Ibid.* p. 66.
[27] *Liverpool Properties Ltd.* v. *Oldbridge Investments Ltd.* (1985) 276 E.G. 1352, (C.A.).
[28] *Ibid.* p. 112. See also, *G.M.S. Syndicate Ltd.* v. *Gary Elliott Ltd.* [1982] 1 Ch. 1, 11, *per* Nourse J.: "Relief against forfeiture was a process by which equity restricted a landlord from enforcing his rights at law."

It appears that unconditional leave to defend will only be refused if the tenant's claim for relief from forfeiture is either not genuine or has no prospect of success. Indeed, since the court's discretion to grant relief under section 146(2) of the Law of Property Act 1925 is very wide, it is likely to be a fairly rare case where the court would be able to say that a genuine claim for relief from forfeiture was bound to fail.[29]

The right of a tenant to be relieved from the forfeiture of his lease is a chose in action which will vest in his trustee in bankruptcy and the trustee is entitled to sell such right and to assign it to a purchaser.[30]

It will be observed that the opening words of section 146(2) limit the tenant's right to claim relief in circumstances where "a lessor is proceeding, by action or otherwise, to enforce" his right of forfeiture. In *Rogers* v. *Rice*[31] the Court of Appeal held that, once a landlord had obtained a judgment of the court entitling him to re-enter on a forfeiture and had re-entered the premises in reliance on that judgment, the statutory right to relieve the tenant against forfeiture was lost since it could not thereafter be said that the landlord "is" proceeding to enforce his rights. In the words of Lindley L.J. in the earlier case of *Quilter* v. *Mapleson*[32]:

> "So long as the tenant has not been turned out of possession he is within the terms of the enactment, for the lessor is 'proceeding to enforce' his right of re-entry."

In *Pakwood Transport Ltd.* v. *15 Beauchamp Place Ltd.*[33] the Court of Appeal held that a landlord who serves a section 146 notice is at that stage "proceeding to enforce a right of re-entry or forfeiture" and that, consequently, a tenant could apply for relief as soon as a section 146 notice was served and before the landlord had started proceedings for forfeiture. The ground for so holding was that, in a case of peaceable re-entry, the right to relief would otherwise be illusory, since the tenant had no right to claim relief after a peaceable (physical) re-entry[34] onto the premises by the landlord.

The actual decision (but not the reasoning) in *Pakwood* was recently approved by the House of Lords in *Billson* v. *Residential Apartments Ltd.*,[35] where the landlords, having previously served a section 146 notice, forfeited the tenants' lease of residential premises for breach of covenant

---

[29] *Sambrin Investments Ltd.* v. *Taborn* [1990] 01 E.G. 69.

[30] *Howard* v. *Fanshawe* [1895] 2 Ch. 581, 589, *per* Stirling J.

[31] [1892] 2 Ch. 170. See also, *Lock* v. *Pearce* [1893] 2 Ch. 271, 274, *per* Lord Esher M.R., (C.A.).

[32] (1882) 9 Q.B.D. 672, 676, (C.A.). In this case, unlike *Rogers* v. *Rice* [1892] 2 Ch. 170, the tenant had been granted a stay of execution of the landlord's judgment for possession.

[33] (1977) 245 E.G. 309.

[34] As opposed to court proceedings for possession.

[35] [1992] 2 W.L.R. 15. See, generally, P. F. Smith, *The Clipping of a Dubious and Dangerous Method*, [1992] Conv. 273.

not to make alterations by peaceably re-entering the premises and changing the locks. The re-entry was effected at 6am (when the premises were
vacant) but four hours later on the same day, the tenants' workmen
regained possession. The landlords then issued a writ claiming possession on the ground that their re-entry constituted a lawful and valid
forfeiture of the tenants' lease. In the Court of Appeal,[36] it was held that,
although the landlords had been in possession (following their peaceable
re-entry) for only a few hours, this precluded the court, under section
146(2), from granting the tenants relief because a landlord who had
already obtained possession of the premises was no longer "proceeding"
to enforce his rights within the meaning of the subsection. On the contrary, he *had* succeeded in enforcing them and the act of forfeiture was
complete. Following the Court of Appeal decision, the advice given to
tenants was to instruct solicitors to issue proceedings for relief from
forfeiture as soon as a section 146 notice was received from the landlord
or, alternatively, to obtain an undertaking from the landlord that he
would not peaceably re-enter pending the issue of the tenant's application for relief. This, however, did not necessarily avail a tenant who had
committed an irremediable[37] breach of covenant (for example, a covenant
against assignment) since, in that case, the landlord could technically
serve his notice and thereafter physically re-enter with little delay,[38]
giving the tenant only a minimal opportunity to consider his legal position. The position was even more acute if the tenant of vacant premises
was unaware of the service of the notice because it was left at the premises
or because he was away on holiday when it was served. Equally, a
mortgagee[39] (and even a sub-tenant) was vulnerable because he might not
receive prompt (or any) notice of intended action by the landlord.

It is, perhaps, not surprising, therefore, that the House of Lords in
Billson reached an opposite conclusion to the Court of Appeal and upheld
the tenant's right to apply for relief against forfeiture under section 146(2)
even after the landlord had forfeited the lease by physically re-entry on
the premises. In Lord Templeman's view,[40] with whom the other Law

---

[36] [1991] 3 W.L.R. 264. See, "*Peaceable Re-entry and Relief against Forfeiture*", P. F. Smith [1992]
Conv. 32. See also, S. Goulding [1991] Conv. 380.

[37] For a discussion of remediable/irremediable breaches of covenant, see Chap. 5, pp. 000.

[38] In *Scala House & District Property Co. Ltd.* v. *Forbes* [1974] Q.B. 575, (C.A.), 14 days was held
to be sufficient time between the service of the notice and the date of the writ of summons
claiming forfeiture of the lease for breach of covenant against assigning, subletting and
parting with possession.

[39] Whilst the landlord is obliged to notify a mortgagee (and anyone else in possession of
whom he is aware) of his proceedings for forfeiture (see R.S.C. Ord. 6, r. 2 and C.C.R.
Ord. 6, r. 3), there is no such corresponding obligation where the landlord seeks to forfeit
by peaceable re-entry. Indeed, the landlord is not even obliged to inform the mortgagee or
sub-tenant that he has served a s. 146 notice.

[40] Lord Templeman referred to the judgment of Larkin J.A. in *Rexdale Investments Ltd. and
Gibson* [1967] 1 O.R. 251, 259, dealing with provisions in the Ontario legislation identical to
s. 146(2), in support of his view.

Lords[41] agreed, a tenant could apply for relief under section 146(2) where the landlord was "proceeding" by action and also where the landlord was proceeding "otherwise" than by action, namely, where the landlord was proceeding to forfeit by physical re-entry after the expiry of a section 146 notice. In the former case, the tenant could apply for relief after the writ/summons had been served and, in the latter case, after the landlord had physically re-entered.[42] Accordingly, section 146(2) enabled the tenant to apply for relief whenever and however the landlord claimed that the lease had been determined for breach of covenant. However, the settled[43] principle that a tenant cannot apply for statutory relief[44] after the landlord has recovered judgment for possession and has re-entered in reliance on that judgment remains unaffected unless, of course, such judgment is set aside or successfully appealed. Further, where a tenant applies for relief after a landlord has forfeited by physical re-entry without court action, his claim for relief may fail on equitable grounds where, for example, he has not brought his application with reasonable promptitude.[45] It is apparent, however, that a landlord may remain vulnerable to the tenant's application for relief for some time after his election to forfeit by physically re-entering on the premises. In order, therefore, to debar the tenant from making any such application in the future, the landlord would be well advised to obtain a final judgment for possession of the premises from the court.[46]

(2) Court's discretion to grant relief

Section 146(2) provides that the court[47] may grant or refuse relief, having regard to the proceedings and conduct of the parties and to all other circumstances, as it thinks fit. Moreover, in case of relief, the court may

[41] The only other Law Lord who delivered a speech (as opposed to simply concurring with Lord Templeman) was Lord Oliver, *ibid.*, 150–152.

[42] The tenant can, of course, still apply for relief as soon as a s. 146 notice is served and before the landlord has started his proceedings or physically re-entered on the premises: *ibid.*, 148, *per* Lord Templeman, referring to the decision in *Pakwood Transport Ltd.* v. *15 Beauchamp Place Ltd.* (1977) 245 E.G. 309.

[43] *Rogers* v. *Rice* [1892] 2 Ch. 170 and *Quilter* v. *Mapleson* (1882) 9 Q.B.D. 672.

[44] Moreover, the tenant has no recourse to any inherent equitable jurisdiction (except in cases involving fraud, accident or mistake) since this has been effectively ousted by s. 146: *Smith* v. *Metropolitan City Properties Ltd.* (1986) 1 E.G.L.R. 52 and *Billson* v. *Residential Apartments Ltd.* [1991] 3 W.L.R. 264, (C.A.), not following *Abbey National Building Society* v. *Maybeech* [1985] 1 Ch. 190.

[45] *Billson* v. *Residential Apartments Ltd.* [1992] 2 W.L.R. 15, 23, 26–27, *per* Lords Templeman and Oliver, respectively.

[46] *Ibid.* pp. 26–27, *per* Lord Oliver.

[47] On appeal from a master, the judge must treat the question of relief as if it had come before him for the first time. Thus, although he must give due weight to the master's decision, he is in no way bound by it and he must exercise his discretion on the basis of the evidence at the date when the matter comes before him: *Cremin* v. *Barjack Properties Ltd.* (1985) 273 E.G. 299, (C.A.).

grant it on "such terms, if any, as to costs, expenses, damages, compensation, penalty, or otherwise, including the granting of an injunction to restrain any like breach in the future" as, in the circumstances of each case, it thinks fit. Whilst there is no doubt that the court's discretion is unfettered and very wide,[48] it is equally clear that it must be exercised judicially,[49] having regard to the circumstances of each individual case[50] and to the specific matters referred to in section 146(2), and with the object of ensuring that the landlord is not substantially prejudiced or damaged by the revival of the tenant's lease.[51]

In *Rose* v. *Hyman*[52] the Court of Appeal sought to lay down some general guidelines regarding the exercise of the court's discretion in granting relief under the subsection. Cozens-Hardy M.R. said[53]:

"In the first place the applicant must, so far as possible, remedy the breaches alleged in the notice and pay reasonable compensation for the breaches which cannot be remedied. In the second place, if the breach is of a negative covenant, such as not to carry on a particular business on the demised premises, the applicant must undertake to observe the covenant in the future, or at least must not avow his intention to repeat the breach complained of. In the third place, if the act complained of, though not a breach of a negative covenant, is of such a nature that the Court would have restrained it during the currency of the lease on the ground of waste, the applicant must undertake to make good the waste if it be possible to do so. In the fourth place, if the act complained of does not fall under either the second or the third head, but is one in respect of which damages, other than nominal, might be recovered in an action on the covenant, the applicant must undertake not to repeat the wrongful act or to be guilty of a continuing breach. In short, subject only to the maxim de minimis, the applicant must come into Court with clean hands, and ought not to be relieved if he avows an intention to continue or to repeat a breach of covenant."

Whilst the House of Lords in *Hyman*[54] discouraged the laying down of any rigid rules for guiding the court's discretion, the above-cited passage from the judgment of Cozens-Hardy M.R. continues to provide a useful

---

[48] *Hyman* v. *Rose* [1912] A.C. 623, 631, *per* Earl Loreburn L.C. In *Sood* v. *Baker* [1991] 23 E.G. 112, the fact that (1) nothing that the tenant had said in evidence could be accepted (2) there had been falsehood in the proceedings and (3) the tenant's points could not be regarded as put forward in good faith, were all considered relevant to the exercise of the court's discretion in refusing relief.

[49] *Egerton* v. *Esplanade Hotels, London Ltd.* [1947] 2 All E.R. 88, 92, *per* Morris J.

[50] *Duke of Westminster* v. *Swinton* [1948] 1 K.B. 524.

[51] *Billson* v. *Residential Apartments Ltd.* [1992] 2 W.L.R. 15, 19, (H.L.), *per* Lord Templeman.

[52] [1911] 2 K.B. 234, (chapel premises converted into a theatre).

[53] *Ibid.* p. 241.

[54] [1912] A.C. 623, reversing the Court of Appeal decision.

summary of the underlying principles which may influence the court in granting/refusing relief under section 146(2). The House of Lords, however, did recognise that there may be cases in which all or any of them may be disregarded.[55]

A combination of one or more of the following considerations[56] will usually determine whether or not relief will be granted in a given case:

(1) Whether the tenant is able and willing to remedy and/or recompense the landlord for the breach;
(2) Whether the breach was wilful;
(3) Whether the breach involves an immoral/illegal user;
(4) The gravity of the breach;
(5) The extent of the diminution in the value of the landlord's reversionary interest as compared to the value of the leasehold interest threatened with forfeiture;
(6) The conduct of the landlord;
(7) The personal qualifications of the tenant;
(8) The financial position of the tenant.

It will now be convenient to examine each of the above considerations in more detail.

(a) *Ability and willingness to remedy and/or recompense landlord for the breach*

The court will usually require the breach to be remedied as a condition precedent to granting relief.[57] In the words of Lord Denning M.R. in *Bathurst* v. *Fine*:[58]

> "In the ordinary way relief is almost always granted to a person who makes good the breach of covenant and is able and willing to fulfil his obligations in the future."

There is, however, no rule that relief against forfeiture should only be given on the condition that the breach of covenant complained of should be immediately rectified. Thus, in *Duke of Westminster* v. *Swinton*[59] an underlease contained covenants to use the premises as a private dwell-

---

[55] *Ibid.* p. 631, Earl Loreburn L.C.
[56] In *Shiloh Spinners Ltd.* v. *Harding* [1973] A.C. 691, 723, Lord Wilberforce, in the context of the court's equitable jurisdiction to grant relief, referred to the conduct of the tenant, the nature and gravity of the breach, and its relation to the value of the property to be forfeited.
[57] *Hyman* v. *Rose* [1912] A.C. 623, 631, *per* Earl Loreburn L.C.
[58] [1974] 1 W.L.R. 905, 908, (C.A.).
[59] [1948] 1 K.B. 524. Compare *Eyre* v. *Rea* (1947) 63 T.L.R. 171.

ing-house only and not to alter the structure or appearance of the house. The sub-underlessee, in breach of the covenants, converted the house into six separate flats which he then let to six separate individuals. Denning J. granted relief to the underlessee on condition that the house be restored to its original state within two years or within such additional period allowed by the court. In this case, the conversion could not be rectified at once for a variety of reasons, including the fact that the remedial work could not be done without the prior licence of the local authority and because of the difficulty of evicting the six occupants without the provision of alternative accommodation.

In *St. Marylebone Property Co. Ltd.* v. *Tesco Stores Ltd.*[60] the tenants granted an underlease on terms which totally disregarded the undertakings contained in the landlords' licence to underlet. Hoffman J. refused the tenants relief primarily on the ground that, by granting the underlease on terms which disregarded the undertakings in the licence, they had put it out of their power to ensure that the undertakings would be observed.

Where the tenant remedies the breach(es) specified in the landlord's section 146 notice, he will only be required to make compensation when the landlord has, in fact, suffered some loss as a result of the breach(es). In the words of Fry L.J. in *Skinners' Company* v. *Knight*[61]:

"... it is evident that many cases may occur in which, where the breach has been perfectly made good and no expense or loss incurred, there may be nothing for which to make compensation, and we are therefore of opinion that, notwithstanding the general terms of the notice required by the statute, the lessee is bound to make compensation, not absolutely in every case, but only where there is something to compensate."

Although the word "damages" is not used in section 146(1) of the 1925 Act, it is clear[62] that compensation under the subsection falls to be measured by the same rules as damages for breach of covenant. Thus, where the breach comprises a breach of a covenant to repair, the appropriate measure of damages will be that applicable to breaches of repairing covenants.[63] As to other breaches of covenant, the proper measure of damages is such sum as reasonably represents the damage which the covenantee has sustained.[64] In an appropriate case, this may represent

---

[60] [1988] 27 E.G. 72.
[61] [1891] 2 Q.B. 542, 544–545, (C.A.).
[62] *Ibid.* p. 545, *per* Fry L.J.
[63] As to damages for breach of covenant to repair see, M. Pawlowski, "Construction and Enforcement of Repairing Obligations in Leases" (1990) 6, Const. L. J. 113.
[64] *Duke of Westminster* v. *Swinton* [1948] 1 K.B. 524, 533–534, *per* Denning J., (conversion of house into separate flats in breach of covenants to use the house as a private dwelling-house only and not to alter the structure and appearance of the house).

the cost of restoring the premises to their original state plus any loss of rent during the work of restoration.[65]

Where a long standing breach of a covenant to build results in the forfeiture of the lease and the tenant wishes to appeal for relief on the basis of change of circumstances, the burden of proof is on the tenant to show precisely where the finance is to come from to rectify the breach and explain why it was not available when the matter was before the trial judge.[65a]

(b) *Wilful breaches*

If a breach of covenant arises from the tenant's voluntary and conscious act, his neglect or default will fall to be classified as wilful.[66] In other words, the breach must be deliberate in the sense that the tenant purposely does not comply with an obligation of which he is aware.[67] In *Shiloh Spinners Ltd.* v. *Harding*,[68] Lord Wilberforce, referring to the court's equitable jurisdiction to grant relief, said[69]:

> "Established and, in my opinion, sound principle requires that wilful breaches should not, or at least should only in exceptional cases, be relieved against, if only for the reason that the [lessor] should not be compelled to remain in a relation of neighbourhood with a person in deliberate breach of his obligations."

In *Southern Depot Co. Ltd.* v. *British Railways Board*,[70] Morritt J. did not accept the proposition that relief under section 146(2) could only be granted in an exceptional case in relation to a wilful breach of covenant. In his view, Lord Wilberforce's remarks in the *Shiloh* case were confined to the exercise of the court's inherent jurisdiction to grant relief and not to cases falling under section 146(2). Accordingly, although giving considerable weight to the fact that two out of the three breaches before him were wilful, he concluded that he was not required to find an exceptional case before granting relief from forfeiture. It is, perhaps, noteworthy that Morritt J. also took the opportunity to re-emphasise that the wilfulness of

---

[65] *Eyre* v. *Rea* [1947] 1 K.B. 567, Atkinson J., (conversion of premises into five flats in breach of covenant *inter alia* not to permit the premises to be used otherwise than as a private dwelling-house in one occupation).

[65a] *Darlington Borough Council* v. *Denmark Chemists Ltd.* [1993] 02 E.G. 117, (C.A.). Any enrichment by the landlord Council in recovering possession of the premises with the benefit of the building erected by the tenant was held not to be unjust; *Ibid.* 122, *per* Neill L.J.

[66] See, *e.g. Elliott* v. *Turner* (1843) 13 Sim. 477; 60 E.R. 185 and *Gregory* v. *Wilson* (1852) 9 Hare 683; 68 E.R. 687.

[67] *Southern Depot Co. Ltd.* v. *British Railways Board* [1990] 2 E.G.L.R. 39, 43, *per* Morritt J.

[68] [1973] A.C. 691, (H.L.).

[69] *Ibid.* p. 725.

[70] [1990] 2 E.G.L.R. 39.

a breach of covenant would continue to remain a relevant consideration in granting or refusing relief. He said, in this context[71]:

"... the court should not in exercising its discretion encourage a belief that parties to a lease can ignore their obligations and buy their way out of any consequential forfeiture."

Thus, for example, in *Eyre* v. *Rea*[72] Atkinson J. refused relief on the ground that the tenant had deliberately broken the covenant to keep the dwelling-house in one occupation and, moreover, had obtained the lease with the intention of breaking it. In *Tulapan Properties Ltd.* v. *De Almeida*[73] relief was refused where the tenants had committed breaches of user covenant and the covenant against sharing possession of the premises. The tenants were fully aware that they were in breach of the covenants and took no steps to remedy them despite having had many opportunities to do so. In *Cremin* v. *Barjack Properties Ltd.*,[74] the tenants' conduct just fell short of being classified as wilful and deliberate.[75] In *Duke of Westminster* v. *Swinton*,[76] relief was granted to the lessee and an underlessee who were wholly unaware of the breaches of user covenant but refused to an underlessee who had deliberately caused the same. Similarly, in *Scala House & District Property Co. Ltd.* v. *Forbes*,[77] relief was granted to a tenant who, through the fault of his solicitors, granted a sublease in breach of covenant whilst, in fact, intending only to create a form of licence.

In the case of a building lease, the landlord is usually empowered to forfeit the lease on the tenant's failure to comply with his obligation to build. There is no relief in equity against forfeiture for non-completion of the works if not occasioned by the landlord's default[77a] but the tenant may be entitled to relief from forfeiture under section 146 of the 1925 Act.

(c) *Immoral/illegal user*

Relief from forfeiture will normally be refused where the tenant has permitted immoral or illegal user[78] of the demised premises in breach of

---

[71] *Ibid.* p. 43.
[72] (1947) 63 T.L.R. 171.
[73] (1981) 260 E.G. 919.
[74] (1985) 273 E.G. 299, (C.A.).
[75] *Ibid.* p. 303, *per* Eveleigh L.J.
[76] [1948] 1 K.B. 524.
[77] [1974] Q.B. 575, (C.A.). See also, *Cardigan Properties Ltd.* v. *Consolidated Property Investments Ltd.* [1991] 07 E.G. 132, (tenant's failure to insure not deliberate but brought about by a combination of circumstances beyond its control).
[77a] *Croft* v. *Goldsmith* (1857) 24 Beav. 312; 53 E.R. 378.
[78] In the absence of immorality/illegality, a tenant in appropriate circumstances will obtain relief from forfeiture following a breach of a negative covenant just as readily as for non-compliance with a positive covenant: *Bass Holdings Ltd.* v. *Morton Music Ltd.* [1988] Ch. 493, 526–527, *per* Kerr L.J.

covenant in the lease. Thus, in *Egerton* v. *Esplanade Hotels, London Ltd.*[79] the tenants allowed rooms in an hotel to be used as a brothel in breach of covenant in the lease. The evidence pointed to the fact that the tenants knew and had tolerated what was happening and, in these circumstances, relief was refused. Similarly, in *Borthwick-Norton* v. *Romney Warwick Estates Ltd.*[80] the sub-tenant of a flat was convicted of keeping the premises as a brothel. Complaints regarding the sub-tenant's conduct and the manner in which she was using the flat were made to the tenants by their sub-tenants in other flats in the building, but the tenants took no steps to discover whether or not the allegations were true. Indeed, the evidence showed that the tenants had deliberately shut their eyes to the true state of affairs. The Court of Appeal held that the discretion under section 146(2) was not to be exercised in favour of tenants who either knew or could have known (if they had not deliberately refrained from taking notice) what was going on on their premises.[81] Again, in *British Petroleum Pension Trust Ltd.* v. *Behrendt*,[82] relief was refused on the ground that the tenant had deliberately shut his eyes to what he knew or ought to have known was taking place on the demised premises[83] and made no attempt to heed the warnings from the landlords except when they were backed up by the service of section 146 notices.

In an appropriate case, however, where the tenant is genuinely ignorant of the facts, relief may be granted. In *Glass* v. *Kencakes Ltd.*,[84] the sub-tenant of residential flats permitted the premises to be used for the purposes of prostitution in breach of covenant but this was unknown to the head-tenants until they were served with a section 146 notice by their landlord. They then served notice of forfeiture on the sub-tenant and the immoral user ceased. Paull J. expressed the view *obiter* that, since the user for prostitution had taken place through no fault of the tenants, the case was a suitable one for the the grant of relief. Similarly, in *Central Estates (Belgravia) Ltd.* v. *Woolgar (No. 2)*[85] the majority[86] of the Court of Appeal concluded that "in a proper case"[87] the court could grant relief from

---

[79] [1947] 2 All E.R. 88. See also, *Hoffman* v. *Fineberg* [1949] 1 Ch. 258, (relief refused where illegality consisted of unlawful gambling on club premises) and *Church Commissioners for England* v. *Maxwell* (1962) 106 S.J. 329, (premises used for illegal abortions).

[80] [1950] 1 All E.R. 798, (C.A.). See also, [1950] 1 All E.R. 362, (Hilberry J.) and *Borthwick-Norton* v. *Dougherty* [1950] W.N. 481, (Pritchard J.).

[81] The suggestion that relief was not to be exercised in favour of persons who suffered premises to be used as a brothel has been criticised as being too restrictive: See *Central Estates (Belgravia) Ltd.* v. *Woolgar (No. 2)* [1972] 1 W.L.R. 1048, 1053, (C.A.), *per* Lord Denning M.R. But see, *ibid.* pp. 1055–1056, *per* Buckley L.J.

[82] [1985] 2 E.G.L.R. 97, (C.A.). See also, *Dunraven Securities Ltd.* v. *Holloway* (1982) 264 E.G. 709, (C.A.), (premises used as a sex shop for sale of pornographic material).

[83] The flat in question was being used for the purposes of prostitution.

[84] [1966] 1 Q.B. 611

[85] [1972] 1 W.L.R. 1048, (C.A.).

[86] Lord Denning M.R. and Cairns L.J., Buckley L.J. *dubitante*.

[87] *Ibid.* p. 1053, *per* Lord Denning M.R.

forfeiture even for a breach of covenant against immoral user. In that case, the tenant was convicted of unlawfully keeping a brothel at the demised premises. The combination of circumstances was somewhat exceptional, including the tenant's age and health, the fact that there was no evidence that the landlords' good name or the value of their estate had suffered from the breach, and that they stood to gain and the tenant to lose about £9,000 from a forfeiture of the lease. Moreover, there was no evidence suggesting that the immoral user continued over a long period or that the tenant persisted in such user after initial warning from the landlord.[88] In view, therefore, of the many mitigating factors in favour of the tenant, the Court was not prepared to interfere with the trial judge's discretion in granting relief. In *G.M.S. Syndicate Ltd.* v. *Gary Elliott Ltd.*[89] Nourse J., referring to the *Woolgar* decision, observed[90]:

"It is the established practice of the court not to grant relief in cases where the breach involves immoral user, save in very exceptional circumstances . . ."

This view has been recently re-affirmed by Millett J. in *Ropemaker Properties Ltd.* v. *Noonhaven Ltd.*[91] where he said[92]:

"The mere fact that the breach in question involves immoral user does not itself preclude the court from granting relief . . . It will, however, be in only the rarest and most exceptional circumstances that the court will grant relief in such a case, particularly where the breach of covenant has been both wilful and serious."

In the *Ropemaker* case, two night clubs had been used for the purposes of prostitution in breach of user covenants in the lease. The tenants of the premises were a private company owned and controlled by a sole director. He had distanced himself from the actual running of the clubs but was presumed, on the evidence, to have known that the hostesses at the clubs were engaged in prostitution. Despite the admittedly grave nature of the breaches, Millett J. regarded the case as exceptional and granted relief against forfeiture, listing the following considerations as having influenced the exercise of his discretion:

(a)   the substantial value of the lease (being worth over 250,000);

---

[88] Contrast *Borthwick-Norton* v. *Romney Warwick Estates Ltd.* [1950] 1 All E.R. 362, (Hilberry J.) and [1950] 1 All E.R. 798, (C.A.).
[89] [1982] Ch. 1.
[90] *Ibid.* p. 10. See also, *Central Estates (Belgravia) Ltd.* v. *Woolgar (No. 2)* [1972] 1 W.L.R. 1048, 1055, *per* Buckley L.J.
[91] [1989] 2 E.G.L.R. 50. See P. F. Smith, "Immoral User Covenants – Relief against Forfeiture", (1990) R.R.L.R. 23.
[92] *Ibid.* p. 56.

(b)   a financial loss to the tenants out of proportion to their offence or to any conceivable damage to the landlords[93];

(c)   the immoral user had been ended and was unlikely to be renewed (the tenants were willing to enter into a deed of variation of the lease prohibiting the presence of hostesses at the premises[94]);

(d)   any "stigma" attaching to the premises would be shortlived and might already have disappeared;

(e)   evicting the tenants would not help to remove any remaining stigma since those who ran the clubs had already gone;

(f)   the grant of relief would not saddle the landlords with unacceptable tenants as in all respects, save the one complained of in the present action, the tenants had been excellent lessees;

(g)   the director of the tenant company was in seriously poor health and had been thinking of retiring and disposing of the lease. He had offered to use his best endeavours to find a purchaser within some appropriate time-scale if relief was granted.

In the recent case of *Van Haarlam* v. *Kasner*[94a] Harman J. was prepared to grant relief to a tenant who had been convicted of various offences under the Official Secrets Acts on the ground that the advantage to the landlords of obtaining vacant possession of the flat (where there was over eighty years to run at a very low ground rent), was wholly disproportionate to the damage done to it by the tenant's acts of illegality. In that case, the tenant had used the flat for various spying activities in breach of covenant not to use the premises for any illegal or immoral purposes. None of these activities were *per se* offensive and refusal of relief would, in effect, have resulted in punishing the tenant twice over for his offences. In the words of Harman J.[95]:

"It seems to me that it would be to punish him twice to take away from him the flat for which he paid £36,000 only four or five years ago as well as having been sent to prison. It is quite true that he has no need of the flat as a residence because he is in prison and then he will be deported, but it is an asset which he may well be desirous of exploiting by assignment."

It has been held[95a] that the statutory protection given to residential

---

[93] See, *Van Haarlam* v. *Kasner Charitable Trust* [1992] 36 E.G. 135, (damage caused to landlord far less than that caused to tenant who had been convicted of an offence under the Official Secrets Act 1920 and whose behaviour had been in no way offensive).

[94] As to the wording of this deed of variation: See, *Ropemaker Properties Ltd.* v. *Noonhaven Ltd.* (*No. 2*) [1991] 09 E.G. 125.

[94a] [1992] 36 E.G. 135.

[95] *Ibid.*, 146.

[95a] *Yates* v. *Morris* [1950] 2 All E.R. 577, (C.A.). See also, *Frederick Platts Co. Ltd.* v. *Grigor* [1950] W.N. 194, (a Rent Act case in which the tenant was a prostitute using the premises for her trade).

tenants under the Rent Act 1977 was not intended to apply where the premises were being used for immoral purposes and, therefore, the principle which applied in cases under section 146(2), that the discretion of the court would not generally be exercised in favour of a tenant who suffered the premises to be used for immoral purposes, was one that would equally be applied in cases under the Rent Act 1977. In such cases, therefore, the court would *prima facie* make an immediate order for possession.[96]

The court has jurisdiction to grant relief against forfeiture in respect of part only of the property comprised in the lease. In *G.M.S. Syndicate Ltd.* v. *Gary Elliott Ltd.*[97] the property consisted of the ground floor and basement of a building let to the first defendant for the purpose of a retail clothing business. The first defendant sub-let the basement to two sub-lessees for use as a sauna bath, gymnasium and health club. The sub-lessees, in turn, assigned the benefit of the sub-tenancy to a husband and wife who used the basement premises for immoral purposes. The land-lord claimed forfeiture in respect of both the ground floor and basement but he was willing for the first defendant to continue to use the ground floor for the purpose of its business. Nourse J. held[98] that it was possible for a landlord to forfeit in respect of part only of demised premises (the basement) and for the court to grant relief against forfeiture in respect of the other part (the ground floor) where, as in the present case, the demised premises were physically separated into two parts and not only could both parts be separately let and enjoyed but the immoral user had been confined to one part.

(d) *The gravity of the breach*

The court will invariably refuse relief where there has been a serious breach of covenant. In *Mitchison* v. *Thomson*,[99] however, relief was granted where the premises were substantially out of repair.

In *Angell* v. *Burn*[1] the breach consisted of using the premises for busi-ness purposes in breach of a covenant by which the user of the premises was restricted to a private dwelling-house only. The evidence showed that, whilst the district in which the premises were situate had originally been residential, it had now become a centre of business and only one out of ten houses was still entirely occupied as a private dwelling-house. Mackinnon J., not surprisingly, granted relief but on terms that within

---

[96] *Ibid.* p. 580. The Court of Appeal was, however, in the instant case, not prepared to depart from the trial judge's suspended order for possession, in view of the tenant's innocence of the use made of the premises.

[97] [1982] Ch. 1.

[98] Relying on *Dumpor's Case* (1603) 4 Co. Rep. 119b.

[99] (1883) Cab. & El. 72.

[1] (1933) 77 S.J. 337.

one month application was made under section 84 of the Law of Property Act 1925 to vary the covenant.

(e) *Diminution in the value of the reversion as compared to the value of the tenant's interest*

In *Southern Depot Co. Ltd.* v. *British Railways Board,*[2] Morritt J. paraphrased section 146(2) of the 1925 Act by posing the questions whether the damage sustained by the landlords was proportionate to the advantage they would obtain if no relief was granted and, if not, whether in all the circumstances it was just that the landlords should retain that advantage. In the case before him, on the assumption that no relief was granted, the landlords stood to obtain an advantage worth not less than £1.4m from breaches which had caused them no lasting damage. On this basis, therefore, relief was granted.

In *Cremin* v. *Barjack Properties Ltd.,*[3] the value of the lease to be forfeited was about £45,000, representing a substantial loss to the tenants as compared to the minimal extent of the outstanding breaches of repair which still required to be remedied. In view of the fact, therefore, that the amount of work outstanding was relatively very small in relation to the total work required to be done and the total value of the property, relief was granted. This balancing process was recently applied by Harman J. in *Van Haarlam* v. *Kasner*[3a] where the advantage to the landlords of obtaining vacant possession of a flat (where there was still over eighty years left to run and for which the tenant had paid £36,000 only four or five years ago) was considered wholly disproportionate to the damage done to it by the tenant's illegal spying activities.

Similarly, in *Fuller* v. *Judy Properties Ltd.,*[4] it was held that the tenant's assignee should not lose a lease for which it had paid a premium of £30,000 on assignment and relief from forfeiture was granted.

In *Cardigan Properties Ltd.* v. *Consolidated Property Investments Ltd.,*[5] a case concerning a breach of covenant to insure, there was no evidence that the value of the landlord's reversion had been materially affected by the non-insurance.

(f) *Conduct of the landlord*

In *Segal Securities Ltd.* v. *Thoseby,*[6] the landlord's conduct, which was

---

[2] [1990] 2 E.G.L.R. 39.
[3] (1985) 273 E.G. 299, (C.A.).
[3a] [1992] 36 E.G. 135. See also, *Iperion Investments Corporation* v. *Broadwalk House Residents Ltd.,* [1992] 2 E.G.L.R. 235, (lease valued at between £1.4m and £2m and no evidence of diminution in value of reversion—relief granted).
[4] [1992] 14 E.G. 106, (C.A.).
[5] [1991] 07 E.G. 132.
[6] [1963] 1 Q.B. 887.

calculated to harass the tenant, was taken into account in granting the tenant unconditional[7] relief from forfeiture for breach of a covenant to use the demised premises for the purpose of a private residence in the occupation of one household only.

(g) *Personal qualifications of the tenant*

In *Bathurst* v. *Fine,*[8] the landlord let a large country house of historic interest to the tenant, an American citizen, for a term of 20 years. There were stipulations in the lease that the tenant should put the place into good order, do considerable repairs and maintain it to the high standard befitting such a property. There was a proviso for re-entry if the tenant *inter alia* suffered any distress or execution to be levied on his goods. The tenant went to France and was banned from re-entering Britain. He failed to pay a quarter's rent and execution was levied on his goods at the premises in respect of a judgment debt obtained by a London store for some £89. The landlord forfeited the lease whereupon the tenant, although still abroad, paid the arrears of rent, discharged the judgment debt and applied for relief from forfeiture. The Court of Appeal held[9] that the personal qualifications of the tenant were of importance for the preservation of the value and character of the property and, since the tenant was shown to be unsuitable personally,[10] relief was refused. The case may be viewed as somewhat exceptional in so far as the personal qualifications and suitability of the tenant "were very much at the heart of this lease."[11]

(h) *The financial position of the tenant*

In *Mascherpa* v. *Direct Ltd.*[12] the landlord brought an action against the tenant company for forfeiture of its lease for failure to comply with the repairing covenants therein. The tenant counter-claimed for relief from forfeiture and the landlord in reply alleged that the tenant was not financially sound and was, therefore, unable to comply with its obligations under the lease. The Court of Appeal held that the landlord was entitled, on a claim for relief against forfeiture of a lease, to discovery of documents limited to the issue of the financial soundness of the tenant

---

[7] In particular, no condition was imposed for the payment of costs.
[8] [1974] 1 W.L.R. 905, (C.A.).
[9] Despite the fact that the tenant had spent at least about £5,000 on improving the premises.
[10] *i.e.* he was not a British subject and had been banned from entering Britain.
[11] *Ibid.* p. 907, *per* Lord Denning M.R.
[12] [1960] 1 W.L.R. 447, (C.A.). See also, *Harry Lay Ltd.* v. *Fox* (1963) 186 E.G. 15.

and this did not infringe the rule[13] that discovery would not be ordered for the purpose of establishing a forfeiture.

In *Geland Manufacturing Co.* v. *The Levy Estates Co.*[14] Wilberforce J. held that relief from forfeiture of a lease held by a company in liquidation could not be obtained by a proposed assignment of the tenancy to a subsidiary of the company which, though itself solvent, was insubstantial, even though the tenant company could provide an acceptable guarantor for future rent. It would not be proper to impose such an assignment on the landlord which was quite different from an assignment to a satisfactory and responsible assignee.[14a]

(3) *Terms of relief*

If the court is mindful to grant relief to the tenant, it may grant it on "such terms, if any, as to costs, expenses, damages, compensation, penalty, or otherwise, including the granting of an injunction to restrain any like breach in the future"[15] as, in the circumstances of each case, it thinks fit. Thus, in *Quilter* v. *Mapleson*,[16] relief was granted in respect of a breach of covenant to insure on terms *inter alia* that the tenant repaid to the landlord, with interest, the premiums of insurance that the landlord had paid on his behalf together with the costs of the action. In *North London Freehold Land and House Co.* v. *Jacques*,[17] equitable mortgagees were held entitled to be relieved from the forfeiture of a lease on terms *inter alia* of their undertaking to comply with a covenant in the lease to complete certain buildings on the property by a certain time. In *Southern Depot Co. Ltd.* v. *British Railways Board*,[18] Morritt J. granted relief to tenants, who had permitted another company to enter into possession of the premises and to make use of the same in breach of covenant, upon terms which included payment of all rent and outgoings due and payments for the unauthorised use of the premises, both with interest, and payment of the costs of the action on an indemnity basis.

Although the tenant will invariably be ordered to pay the costs of the

---

[13] *Earl of Mexborough* v. *Whitwood Urban District Council* [1897] 2 Q.B. 111; *Seddon* v. *Commercial Salt Co. Ltd.* [1925] Ch. 187 and *Colne Valley Water Co.* v. *Watford & St. Albans Gas Co.* [1948] 1 K.B. 500.

[14] (1962) 181 E.G. 209.

[14a] See *Pakwood Transport Ltd.* v. *15 Beauchamp Place Ltd.* (1978) 36 P. & C.R. 112 (C.A.).

[15] See, s. 146(2).

[16] (1882) 9 Q.B.D. 672, (C.A.).

[17] (1883) 49 L.T. 659. See also, *Bond* v. *Freke* [1884] W.N. 47.

[18] [1990] 2 E.G.L.R. 39. See also, *Associated Omnibus Co. Ltd.* v. *Idris & Co.* (1919) 148 L.T. Jo. 157 for terms imposed where landlord had suffered no real damage as a result of the breach. If the breach is a continuing one, the court will grant relief upon terms that there should be no future breach: *Wrotham Park Settled Estates* v. *Naylor* (1990) 62 P. & C.R. 233, 241, *per Hoffman J.*

action[18a] as a condition of the grant of relief, the court retains a discretion in the matter and there may be circumstances which will justify the tenant being awarded the costs of the action. For example, in *Woodtrek Ltd.* v. *Jezek*[19] the landlord's action for forfeiture of a lease of a flat in respect of non-payment of service charge was held to be misconceived although technically justified in respect of arrears of rent. The court granted the tenant relief against forfeiture and, in the circumstances, held that he was entitled to the costs of the action subject to a deduction from taxed costs because of the arrears of rent. It has been usual in the past for a landlord to obtain the payment of costs on an indemnity basis from the tenant on any application for relief under section 146(2). This has been the case even against a legally-aided tenant.[20] However, it has recently been held[21] that in principle a tenant should not be ordered to pay costs on an indemnity basis on the ground that they "encourage lawyers and surveyors and other advisers to charge large fees."[22]

If the tenant declines to perform the conditions upon which relief is granted, the court has no power to compel him to do so and, in these circumstances, the order for relief must be treated as abandoned.[23] Where, however, an order for relief is granted on terms to be performed within a specified time, the court has jurisdiction to extend that time if circumstances are brought to its notice which would make it just and equitable that an extension should be granted.[24] This is so although the

---

[18a] Costs have been awarded on a variety of different bases: See, *e.g. Scala House Ltd.* v. *Forbes* [1974] Q.B. 575, (C.A.), (standard basis); *Southern Depot Co. Ltd.* v. *British Railways Board* [1990] 2 E.G.L.R. 39, (indemnity basis); *Newbolt* v. *Bingham* (1895) 72 L.T. 852 (C.A.), (solicitor and client basis). The landlord will invariably be entitled to the costs of the tenant's application for relief as well as the costs of the forfeiture action. However, the tenant will not bear the landlord's costs in so far as they have been increased by the landlord unreasonably resisting his claim for relief: See, *e.g. Belgravia Insurance Co. Ltd.* v. *Meah* [1964] 1 Q.B. 436, (C.A.).

[19] (1982) 261 E.G. 571.

[20] *Three Stars Property Holdings* v. *Driscoll* (1988) C.L.Y. 2795, (C.A.).

[21] *Billson* v. *Residential Apartments Ltd.* [1992] 2 W.L.R. 15, (H.L.). But see, *Iperion Investments Corporation* v. *Broadwalk House Residents Ltd.*, [1992] 2 E.G.L.R. 235, where despite the remarks of Lord Templeman in *Billson*, the judge would have ordered the tenant to pay costs on an indemnity basis in view of the fact that he had positively invited litigation.

[22] *Ibid.* p. 24, *per* Lord Templeman. The landlord's costs of a forfeiture action cannot be charged to the tenant under service charge provisions in the lease as a "proper cost of management": See, *Sella House Ltd.* v. *Mears* [1989] 1 E.G.L.R. 65, (C.A.), applied in *Iperion Investments Corporation* v. *Broadwalk House Residents Ltd.*, [1992] 2 E.G.L.R. 235.

[23] *Talbot* v. *Blindell* [1908] 2 K.B. 114, where the order merely imposed conditions and did not contain an undertaking by the tenants to perform them and, therefore, the landlord could not hold the tenants to performance.

[24] *Chandless-Chandless* v. *Nicholson* [1942] 2 K.B. 321, (C.A.), a case involving non-payment of rent. See also, *R.* v. *Bloomsbury and Marylebone County Court, ex p. Villerwest Ltd.* [1976] 1 W.L.R. 362, (C.A.), (extension of time for payment of arrears of rent into court). But the court's power to extend time is not limited to non-payment of rent cases: *Starside Properties Ltd.* v. *Mustapha* [1974] 1 W.L.R. 816, (C.A.); *Ridley* v. *Brookpyle Investments Ltd.* (1961) 179 E.G. 387, (C.A.).

order which prescribes the limitation of time does not give the tenant liberty to apply. Where relief is granted subject to conditions, the tenant (pending performance of those conditions) will not hold the premises under the lease but as tenant at will or on sufferance.[25]

Where the tenant obtains a court order granting him relief from forfeiture under section 146(2), the effect of the order will be to restore the lease as if it had never become forfeited.[26] Thus, the original (forfeited) lease will continue in existence without the necessity for the execution of a new lease in favour of the tenant. This is to be contrasted with the position under section 146(4) of the 1925 Act, in respect of relief granted to a sub-tenant[27] or mortgagee,[28] where relief takes the form of the grant of a new lease in favour of the applicant.

A tenant's right to apply for relief, under section 147 of the Law of Property Act 1925, in respect of a landlord's notice relating to internal decorative repairs, is considered under a separate heading.[29]

Application for relief by sub-tenant

The jurisdiction to relieve a sub-tenant from the forfeiture of his sub-lease is to be found in section 146(4) of the Law of Property Act 1925,[30] which provides as follows:

"Where a lessor is proceeding by action or otherwise to enforce a right of re-entry or forfeiture under any covenant, proviso, or stipulation in a lease, or for non-payment of rent, the court may, on application[31] by any person claiming as underlessee[32] any estate or

---

[25] *City of Westminster Assurance Co. Ltd.* v. *Ainis* (1975) 29 P. & C.R. 469.

[26] *Dendy* v. *Evans* [1910] 1 K.B. 263, (C.A.). As to the status of a lease during the twilight period between its forfeiture and the determination of the tenant's application for relief, see Chap. 3, pp. 81–89. If before the court order is granted, the landlord re-lets to a third party who acquires the premises with notice of the tenant's application, the effect of relief is to bind the third party with the tenant's equity so that the latter may re-possess. If, on the other hand, the third party acquires with no notice of the application, he will obtain a good title and the relief will operate to make the tenant the immediate landlord of the third party: See, *Fuller* v. *Judy Properties Ltd.* (1992) 14 E.G. 106, (C.A.).

[27] See, *e.g. Cadogan* v. *Dimovic* [1984] 1 W.L.R. 609, (C.A.).

[28] See, *e.g. Chelsea Estates Investment Trust Co. Ltd.* v. *Marche* [1955] Ch. 328.

[29] See, *post* pp. 279–280.

[30] Formerly s. 4 of the Conveyancing and Law of Property Act 1892.

[31] In the High Court, an application will usually be made by a counterclaim in the landlord's action where the sub-tenant has been joined as a party, otherwise by summons issued by the sub-tenant in the landlord's action asking to be joined as a party and seeking relief. For a form of summons: see Part VI of this work.

[32] "Underlease" includes an agreement for an underlease where the underlessee has become entitled to have his underlease granted to him and "underlessee" includes any person deriving title under an underlessee: s. 146(5) (*d*) and (*e*) of the 1925 Act. An underlessee may claim the benefit of s. 146(4) notwithstanding that the lease or covenant falls within s. 146(8), (9) or (10): s. 1 of the Law of Property Amendment Act 1929. See also, *Jarrott* v. *Ackerley* (1916) 85 L.J. Ch. 135, (unregistered society not an underlessee).

interest in the property comprised in the lease or any part thereof,[33] either in the lessor's action (if any) or in any action brought by such person for that purpose, make an order vesting, for the whole term of the lease or any less term, the property comprised in the lease or any part thereof in any person entitled as under-lessee to any estate or interest in such property upon such conditions as to execution of any deed or other document, payment of rent, costs, expenses, damages, compensation, giving security, or otherwise, as the court in the circumstances of each case may think fit, but in no case shall any such under-lessee be entitled to require a lease to be granted to him for any longer term than he had under his original sub-lease."

Under this subsection, the court has power to grant relief to a sub-tenant against conditions of forfeiture on bankruptcy,[34] forfeiture for non-payment of rent[35] and for breach of other covenants contained in the headlease and the sub-tenant[36] is entitled to be served with a copy of the landlord's action for forfeiture.[37]

It has already been stated elsewhere[38] that the effect of a forfeiture is to determine not only the lease but all sub-leases created under it.[39] Indeed, the forfeiture operates to vest in the landlord the whole of the rights in the demised premises[40] free from the lease and any mortgage subject to it entered into by the tenant.[41] The effect, therefore, of a vesting order under section 146(4) is to create a new lease in favour of the sub-tenant in which the covenants and conditions as to rent and otherwise are entirely at the discretion of the court unfettered by any limitation except that contained in the latter part of the subsection, namely, that the sub-tenant shall not

---

[33] The earlier provision contained in s. 14(2) of the Conveyancing and Law of Property Act 1881 did not permit a sub-tenant of part of the demised premises to obtain relief: *Burt* v. *Gray* [1891] 2 Q.B. 98.

[34] *The Wardens and Governors of Cholmeley School, Highgate* v. *Sewell* [1894] 2 Q.B. 906.

[35] s. 146(4) expressly extends to relief for non-payment of rent. Relief against forfeiture for non-payment of rent is discussed in Chap. 9. See also *Gray* v. *Bonsall* [1904] 1 K.B. 601, (C.A.).

[36] or the tenant's mortgagee.

[37] R.S.C. Ord. 6, r. 2(1)(*c*)(iii) and (2) and C.C.R. Ord. 6, r. 3(1)(*f*) and (2).

[38] See, Chap. 3, p. 84.

[39] But note that the security of tenure of certain sub-tenants of residential premises will be preserved by statute: See, s. 137 of the Rent Act 1977.

[40] *Ewart* v. *Fryer* [1901] 1 Ch. 499, (C.A.).

[41] *Official Custodian for Charities* v. *Mackey* [1985] 1 Ch. 168, where it was held that the mortgagees' receivers had no right to collect the rents or manage the demised premises once the landlord had effectively forfeited the lease. The fact that the receivers' acts might be retrospectively validated on the tenant's appeal against the refusal of relief against forfeiture was not a sufficient defence.

be entitled to require a lease for a term longer than he had under his original sub-lease.[42] In the words of Romer L.J. in *Ewart* v. *Fryer*[43]:

> "The Legislature has taken care not to hamper the Court. It has taken care to give to the Court the fullest powers of adjusting matters, and doing what is right when the whole circumstances of the case are regarded. Those circumstances would involve the terms of the original lease, the terms of the underlease, the circumstances of the forfeiture, what has been caused by the forfeiture, and the position of the parties generally."

The new lease is not, therefore, a restoration of the original sub-lease but a new grant where the premises demised,[44] term, rent[45] and other provisions may differ from those of the forfeited sub-lease.[46] In *Hammersmith and Fulham London Borough Council* v. *Top Shop Centres Ltd.*,[47] Warner J. had occasion to observe[48]:

> "Thus, the court may, under section 146(4), order that the new lease should be at a rent different from that reserved by the original underlease, as it did in *Ewart* v. *Fryer*. It may order that the new lease should be for a term ending sooner than the term granted by the original underlease. It may order that the new lease should contain different covenants and it may, on my reading of the subsection, order that the new lease should comprise a lesser part of the property demised by the forfeited lease than was comprised in the original underlease."

In this respect, the position of a sub-tenant is quite different from that of a tenant under section 146(2) of the 1925 Act.[49] The court's jurisdiction in respect of sub-tenancies is not to grant relief against forfeiture as such but to grant a new lease where the tenant will be a person who was not a party to the original headlease and where the demised premises, term of the lease and conditions on which it is held may also be different. Thus, any interest (for example, an underlease) derived from the original lease will

---

[42] *Ewart* v. *Fryer* [1901] 1 Ch. 499, (C.A.); *Sejeant* v. *Nash, Field & Co.* [1903] 2 K.B. 304, 313, (C.A.), *per* Stirling L.J.; *Cadogan* v. *Dimovic* [1984] 1 W.L.R. 609, (C.A.) and *Factors (Sundries) Ltd.* v. *Miller* [1952] 2 All E.R. 630, (C.A.).

[43] [1901] 1 Ch. 499, 516, (C.A.).

[44] The court has power, *e.g.* to grant relief in respect of part only of the premises originally demised: *London Bridge Buildings Company* v. *Thomson* (1903) 89 L.T. 50, 52, *per* Joyce J.

[45] *Ewart* v. *Fryer* [1901] 1 Ch. 499, 516, *per* Romer L.J. See also, *The Wardens and Governors of Cholmeley School, Highgate* v. *Sewell* [1894] 2 Q.B. 906, 913, *per* Charles J.

[46] *Cadogan* v. *Dimovic* [1984] 1 W.L.R. 609, 613–614, 615 *per* Fox and Robert Goff L.JJ.

[47] [1990] Ch. 237.

[48] *Ibid.* pp. 251–252.

[49] The two provisions are independent of each other and, accordingly, s. 146(4) enables the court to grant relief to a sub-tenant in cases where it would have no power, under s. 146(2), to grant relief to the tenant: *The Wardens and Governors of Cholmeley School, Highgate* v. *Sewell* [1894] 2 Q.B. 906; *Imray* v. *Oakshette* [1897] 2 Q.B. 218, (C.A.).

not automatically be reinstated upon the court vesting a new lease under section 146(4), since any such interest may not fit into the provisions of the new lease ordered by the court.[50]

Whilst the court has a wide discretion in the matter, generally speaking, the same terms and conditions as those contained in the original headlease will be implied into the new lease.[51] In appropriate cases, the court may make an order for the vesting of the unexpired term of the headlease in the sub-tenant, but where the term of the headlease has come to an end by virtue of the forfeiture prior to the hearing of the application for relief, the court is precluded, under section 146(4), from making a vesting order in respect of any such term in the sub-tenant which no longer exists. Instead, the court, in the exercise of its discretion, may grant a new lease in favour of the sub-tenant. In *Cadogan* v. *Dimovic*,[52] it was held that section 24(2) of the Landlord and Tenant Act 1954 does not preclude the court from giving the sub-tenant under a business tenancy relief by way of the grant of a new lease for an appropriate term. In this connection, the restriction in section 146(4) which prevents the grant of a new lease to an underlessee "for any longer term than he had under his original sub-lease" refers to the term which the under-lessee would have had but for the forfeiture and, in the case of a business tenancy, this term is, by virtue of section 24(1) of the 1954 Act, the period which would elapse before the tenancy could be terminated in accordance with Part II of the 1954 Act following the expiry of the term granted by the underlease. In *Hill* v. *Griffin*,[53] this meant that the court had jurisdiction, under section 146(4), to order the grant of no more than a monthly tenancy to the sub-tenant.

The court is not precluded from making a vesting order in respect of a periodic tenancy. Thus, in *Factors (Sundries) Ltd.* v. *Miller*,[54] the court made a vesting order under section 146(4) in the case of a monthly tenancy, although the tenancy would (but for the forfeiture) have continued indefinitely until determined by notice of the appropriate length. In this case, the tenant was precluded from relying on (what is now) section 137 of the Rent Act 1977 because his sub-tenancy was unlawful but this did not prevent him from seeking relief under section 146(4) of the 1925 Act. However, the fact that, at the expiration of the monthly tenancy granted to him under that subsection, he could claim the protection of the Rent Act was a relevant circumstance for the court to consider in deciding

---

[50] *Hammersmith and Fulham London Borough Council* v. *Top Shop Centres Ltd.* [1990] Ch. 237, 252, *per* Warner J.
[51] *Ewart* v. *Fryer* [1901] 1 Ch. 499, 515, *per* Romer L.J. and *Chelsea Estates Investment Trust Co. Ltd.* v. *Marche* [1955] 1 Ch. 328.
[52] [1984] 1 W.L.R. 609, (C.A.).
[53] [1987] 1 E.G.L.R. 81, (C.A.).
[54] [1952] 2 All E.R. 630, (C.A.).

whether to grant relief. Thus, in *Clifford* v. *Personal Representatives of Johnson Deceased*[55] relief was refused to the sub-tenant on the ground that, if relief was granted, the landlord would be saddled with a protected tenancy of the premises.

It has been held[56] that the jurisdiction to grant relief under section 146(4) should be exercised sparingly because it may force upon the landlord a person whom he has never accepted as tenant and create *in invitum* privity of contract between them.[57] The court will, in these circumstances, only be prepared to vest the residue of the term of the headlease in the sub-tenant if the same (or not less stringent) covenants are included in the new lease as those contained in the original headlease.[58] Thus, in *Hill* v. *Griffin*[59] relief was refused to a sub-tenant as he was not prepared to enter into repairing obligations as extensive as those under the forfeited headlease. In *St. Marylebone Property Co. Ltd.* v. *Tesco Stores Ltd.*,[60] the tenant granted an underlease of various lock-up shops on terms which totally disregarded the undertakings in the landlords' licence to underlet. In refusing relief to the sub-tenant, Hoffman J. was influenced by the fact that (a) the sub-tenant had been guilty of continuing to trade in breach of the restrictions contained in the licence after promising not to do so (b) he was likely to be in financial difficulties if he operated in accordance with the restrictions and (c) the landlords should not have to accept the sub-tenant as their tenant by way of relief against forfeiture when they never accepted him as a tenant in the first place. In *Imray* v. *Oakshette*,[61] the Court of Appeal emphasised that, where the breach consists of an unlawful sub-letting without consent, the jurisdiction to grant relief under section 146(4) should be exercised with caution and sparingly and the sub-tenant asking for its exercise must show that he is blameless and has taken all precautions which a reasonably cautious and careful person would use. In that case, the sub-tenant had been negligent in entering into a contract for the purchase of an underlease which precluded him from investigating the leasehold title containing the restriction on subletting. The Court of Appeal held that relief against forfeiture by the tenant for breach of the covenant ought not to be granted to the sub-

---

[55] (1979) 251 E.G. 571, (C.A.).

[56] *Creery* v. *Summersell and Flowerdew & Co. Ltd.* [1949] 1 Ch. 751, 767, *per* Harman J., (court not prepared to compel landlord to concede a wider use of the demised premises than the user prescribed in the headlease).

[57] The position may be different if the circumstances show that it would have been unreasonable for the landlord to withhold his consent to a sub-letting had it been sought: *Lam Kee Ying* v. *Lam Shes Tong* [1975] A. C. 247, 258, (P.C.), *per* Sir Harry Gibbs.

[58] *Creery* v. *Summersell and Flowerdew & Co. Ltd.* [1949] 1 Ch. 751, 767.

[59] [1987] 1 E.G.L.R. 81, (C.A.). See also, *Gray* v. *Bonsall* [1904] 1 K.B. 601, 608, *per* Romer L.J., (breaches of repairing covenants ought to be remedied as a condition of making vesting order in favour of sub-tenant).

[60] [1988] 27 E.G. 72.

[61] [1897] 2 Q.B. 218, (C.A.), applied in *Matthews* v. *Smallwood* [1910] 1 Ch. 777, 792.

tenant because of his negligence. Where, however, a lease is forfeited for breaches by the tenant of a covenant to repair, the fact that a sub-tenant has been guilty of breaches of a similar covenant in the sub-lease will not disentitle the latter to relief under section 146(4).[62] But the court will be reluctant to grant relief to a sub-tenant who is guilty of a deliberate breach of a covenant against under-letting in the absence of extenuating circumstances mitigating the breach.[63]

The court has a wide discretion to order the sub-tenant to pay the costs of the landlord's proceedings as a condition of granting relief under section 146(4).[64] An award of costs, as a condition of relief, may even be made against a sub-tenant who is an assisted person with a nil contribution under the Legal Aid Scheme.[65] In *London Bridge Buildings Company* v. *Thomson*,[66] relief was granted to a sub-tenant upon terms as to the payment of all the arrears of rent due under the headlease together with the costs of the landlord's action to recover possession. Such costs may include the costs of an inquiry necessary to determine the rent payable under the new lease[67] but not the landlord's costs of employing a solicitor and surveyor/valuer in respect of the preparation of a section 146 notice in reference to the breach which gives rise to the right of forfeiture.[68] In the absence of a covenant of indemnity contained in the sub-lease, the costs of proceedings for relief incurred by a tenant as a result of his own breaches of covenant in the headlease are irrecoverable against his sub-tenant.[69]

Since the court has power, under section 146(4), to order the execution of a new lease directly in favour of the sub-tenant and since an order in this form will not affect the original tenant, it is not necessary for the latter to be before the court before such an order is made.[70]

A vesting order made by the court under section 146(4) does not have retrospective effect so as to divest a landlord of his proprietary rights during the period prior to the making of such an order. Thus, the court has no power, under the subsection, to impose as a condition precedent

---

[62] *Hurd* v. *Whaley* [1918] 1 K.B. 448, where McCardie J. confined the decision in *Imray* v. *Oakshette* [1897] 2 Q.B. 218 to the case of a forfeiture for breaches of covenant not to assign, underlet or part with possession which were expressly excepted from the operation of s. 14 of the Conveyancing and Law of Property Act 1881 by subs. (6) of that section.

[63] *Atkin* v. *Rose* [1923] 1 Ch. 522, 539–540.

[64] *Factors (Sundries) Ltd.* v. *Miller* [1952] 2 All E.R. 630, (C.A.), (order that sub-tenant pay costs on a solicitor and client basis upheld).

[65] *Factors (Sundries) Ltd.* v. *Miller* [1952] 2 All E.R. 630, (C.A.).

[66] (1903) 89 L.T. 50.

[67] *Ewart* v. *Fryer* (1902) 86 L.T. 676.

[68] *Nind* v. *Nineteenth Century Building Society* [1894] 2 Q.B. 226, (C.A.).

[69] *Clare* v. *Dobson* [1911] 1 K.B. 35.

[70] *Abbey National Building Society* v. *Maybeech Ltd.* [1985] 1 Ch. 190, 206, *per* Nicholls J. Contrast the position where relief was sought in equity for non-payment of rent, where the original tenant was required to be before the court: *Hare* v. *Elms* [1893] 1 Q.B. 604 and *Humphreys* v. *Morten* [1905] 1 Ch. 739.

to a vesting order the requirement that a landlord pay over rents received from occupiers of the premises between the date of forfeiture and the date of the vesting order to the tenant's mortgagees applying for relief.[71] Conversely, a landlord will have no right to recover rents from the mortgagees' receivers paid to them by the occupiers of the premises during the period between the forfeiture of the lease and the date of the vesting order made in favour of the mortgagees either as money had and received by the receivers to their use or in equity or as mesne profits for the receivers' own trespass.[72]

It is now apparent that section 146(4) provides an exhaustive code for the granting of relief to underlessees and that there is no residual equitable jurisdiction to grant relief[73] outside the provisions of the subsection.[74] In appropriate circumstances, however, a sub-tenant may be entitled to remain in occupation of the premises on the basis of an equitable estoppel. In *Hammersmith and Fulham London Borough Council* v. *Top Shop Centres Ltd.*,[75] the trustees of an estate leased it to a development company (Parway) under a lease which contained a provision entitling the trustees to re-enter the property and forfeit the lease if Parway went into liquidation. Parway mortgaged its lease and developed the estate and then granted underleases to various tenants including the plaintiff Council. Parway later went into liquidation and the trustees obtained an order of forfeiture under which all interests derived from Parway's lease (including the mortgage and the Council's underleases) ceased to exist. Notwithstanding the forfeiture, the mortgagee's receivers continued to collect rent from the Council as though the underleases still subsisted. Subsequently, a vesting order was made, under section 146(4) of the 1925 Act, granting the mortgagee a new lease of the estate. The mortgagee then purchased the freehold of the property from the trustees and sold it to a third party together with the lease, which was sold subject to the underleases granted by Parway in so far as they still subsisted or had been affirmed. Warner J. held that, whilst the Council had not lost its right to apply for relief under section 146(4), it was entitled to succeed on the alternative basis of an equitable estoppel since the mortgagee in whom the new lease was vested had, with the co-operation of the trustees, encouraged the Council to assume to its detriment that its underleases

---

[71] *Official Custodian for Charities* v. *Mackey* [1985] 1 Ch. 168.

[72] *Official Custodian for Charities* v. *Mackey (No. 2)* [1985] 1 W.L.R. 1308. The judgment of Nourse J. also contains an interesting discussion as to the terms on which a new lease to the tenant's mortgagees should be granted.

[73] Except in cases involving fraud, accident or mistake: *Barrow* v. *Isaacs* [1891] 1 Q.B. 417 and *Billson* v. *Residential Apartments Ltd.* [1991] 3 W.L.R. 264, 285.

[74] See *Billson* v. *Residential Apartments Ltd.* [1991] 3 W.L.R. 264, (C.A.) and *Smith* v. *Metropolitan City Properties Ltd.* [1986] 1 E.G.L.R. 52, not following *Abbey National Building Society* v. *Maybeech* [1985] 1 Ch. 190. The current scope of equity's jurisdiction is discussed in Chap. 8.

[75] [1990] Ch. 237.

still existed and it would be unconscionable for the third party to be permitted to deny that state of affairs.

Application for relief by mortgagee

A mortagee by sub-demise is an "underlessee" within the meaning of section 146(4) of the Law of Property Act 1925 and, as such, entitled to relief against forfeiture under that subsection.[76] Thus, in *Grangeside Properties Ltd.* v. *Collingwoods Securities Ltd.*,[77] relief was granted to a mortgagee by sub-demise who was in a sound financial position to stand in the place of the tenant and where consent to the mortgage could not have reasonably been refused by the landlord if it had been asked for by the tenant.

A mortagee by way of legal charge has, by section 87(1) of the Law of Property Act 1925, "the same protection, powers and remedies" as a mortgagee by way of sub-demise and, accordingly, where a lease is forfeited for breach of covenant by the tenant, a mortgagee of the lease by way of legal charge is also entitled to relief against forfeiture under section 146(4) in the same way as if he were an underlessee.[78] Thus, in *Chelsea Estates Investment Trust Co. Ltd.* v. *Marche*[79] a mortgagee by way of legal charge was granted, by way of relief, a new lease of the demised premises upon the same terms and conditions as those contained in the original (forfeited) lease. Moreover, such new lease (being for the protection of the mortgagee) fell to be regarded as a substituted security and, accordingly, subject to the mortgage with the consequence that the mortgagor had a right to redeem it notwithstanding that the original lease had been forfeited. In *Purley Automobile Co. Ltd.* v. *Aldon Motors Ltd.*[80] relief was granted on terms that the remainder of the leasehold term be vested in the mortgagees at the same rent on condition that they remedy the breach of covenant to repair and bear all the costs[81] incurred.

---

[76] *Egerton* v. *Jones* [1939] 2 K.B. 702, (C.A.), (premises used as a brothel), where the mortgagees were granted relief upon terms that they pay all the landlord's costs (which were irrecoverable from the tenant) on a solicitor and own client basis. The landlord was, however, ordered to transfer the benefit of the judgment for such costs if the mortgagees so desired.

[77] [1964] 1 W.L.R. 139, (C.A.).

[78] *Grand Junction Co. Ltd.* v. *Bates* [1954] 2 Q.B. 160, (premises used for immoral purposes), applied in *Belgravia Insurance Co. Ltd.* v. *Meah* [1964] 1 Q.B. 436, (C.A.) and *Regent Oil Co. Ltd.* v. *J. A. Gregory (Hatch End) Ltd.* [1966] 1 Ch. 402, (C.A.).

[79] [1955] 1 Ch. 328, (arrears of rent). Relief was made conditional upon the payment of the arrears and the costs of the action in the usual way. See also, *Abbey National Building Society* v. *Maybeech Ltd.* [1985] 1 Ch. 190, 206.

[80] (1968) 112 S.J. 482, (C.A.), (tenants went into compulsory liquidation and were in breach of repairing covenants).

[81] The ordinary rule is for the mortgagee to pay the landlord's costs of the action not only on a party and party basis but on a common fund basis: *Grangeside Properties Ltd.* v. *Collingwoods Securities Ltd.* [1964] 1 W.L.R. 139, 144, *per* Harman L.J.

271

A guarantor, having the right to call for a legal charge or mortgage of the demised premises, is also entitled to claim relief under section 146(4) since he is a person having an "agreement for an underlease" within the meaning of section 146(5)(d) of the 1925 Act.[82]

The court's discretion to grant relief under section 146(4) to a mortagee is unfettered and must be exercised according to the circumstances of each particular case.[83] However, a mortagee will lose his right to apply for relief once the landlord has re-entered the demised premises pursuant to a judgment for possession.[84] This is because the opening words of section 146(4) limit the applicant's right to claim relief in circumstances where "a lessor is proceeding, by action or otherwise, to enforce" his right of forfeiture. Thus, once a landlord has obtained possession of the premises in reliance on a judgment entitling him to re-enter on a forfeiture, the statutory right to relief will be lost since it cannot thereafter be said that the landlord "is" proceeding to enforce his rights.

It is now also apparent that, if a mortgagee cannot obtain relief under section 146(4) of the 1925 Act, he has no recourse to any inherent jurisdiction to grant relief in equity.[85] In this connection, the Court of Appeal in *Billson* v. *Residential Apartments Ltd.*,[86] has held that equity's jurisdiction to relieve against forfeiture from a wilful breach of covenant (other than non-payment of rent) had been entirely extinguished by the provisions of section 146(2) and (4), which provide an exhaustive and comprehensive code setting out the circumstances in which relief can be given in cases falling within these provisions. It seems apparent, however, that if the landlord peaceably re-enters without recourse to court action, a mortgagee will be entitled to invoke the court's inherent equitable jurisdiction to grant relief from forfeiture.[86a]

A writ in a forfeiture action must be indorsed with the name and address of, and be sent to, any person whom the landlord knows to be entitled to claim relief against forfeiture under section 146(4) (or in accordance with section 38 of the Supreme Court Act 1981), as underlessee or

---

[82] *Re Good's Lease, Good* v. *Wood* [1954] 1 W.L.R. 309, (non-payment of rent).

[83] *Egerton* v. *Jones* [1939] 2 K.B. 702, 705, *per* Sir Wilfrid Greene M.R.

[84] *Rogers* v. *Rice* [1892] 2 Ch. 170, (C.A.); *Egerton* v. *Jones* [1939] 2 K.B. 702, 707 and *Abbey National Building Society* v. *Maybeech* [1985] 1 Ch. 190. See also, *Billson* v. *Residential Apartments Ltd.* [1992] 2 W.L.R. 15, (H.L.) dealing with s. 146(2) of the 1925 Act.

[85] Except in cases involving fraud, accident or mistake: *Barrow* v. *Isaacs* [1891] 1 Q.B. 417 and *Billson* v. *Residential Apartments Ltd.* [1991] 3 W.L.R. 264, 285.

[86] [1991] 3 W.L.R. 264, not following *Abbey National Building Society* v. *Maybeech* [1985] 1 Ch. 190.

[86a] See, *Billson* v. *Residential Apartments Ltd.* [1992] 2 W.L.R. 15, (H.L.). The earlier cases of *Egerton* v. *Jones* [1939] 2 K.B. 702 (C.A.) and *Bristol & West Building Society* v. *Turner* [1991] 37 E.G. 141 no longer represent the law on this point.

mortgagee.[87] A mortgagee may apply to set aside a judgment for possession by default provided he acts promptly and shows good cause.[88]

Recovery of solicitors' and surveyors' costs

Section 146(3)[89] of the Law of Property Act 1925 provides as follows:

"A lessor shall be entitled to recover as a debt due to him from a lessee, and in addition to damages (if any), all reasonable costs and expenses properly incurred by the lessor in the employment of a solicitor and surveyor or valuer, or otherwise, in reference to any breach giving rise to a right of re-entry or forfeiture which, at the request of the lessee, is waived by the lessor, or from which the lessee is relieved, under the provisions of this Act."

In *Skinners' Company* v. *Knight*,[90] the Court of Appeal held that a landlord was not entitled to recover, by way of compensation under section 146(1) of the 1925 Act, the costs incurred by the landlord in consulting and employing a solicitor and surveyor in respect of the preparation of a notice required by that subsection. Such costs were held to arise, not from a breach of covenant, but solely from the requirement (as to service of a notice) imposed by section 146(1) on the enforcement of the cause of action arising from such a breach. However, in *Bridge* v. *Quick*,[91] it was held that the court may, in the exercise of its discretion in granting relief from forfeiture under section 146(2) of the 1925 Act, order the payment by the tenant of the landlord's costs and expenses of employing a surveyor and solicitor to prepare and serve a section 146 notice including a schedule of dilapidations.

Under section 146(3)[92] of the 1925 Act, such reasonable expenses are also recoverable where either (a) the landlord waives the breach at the request of the tenant or (b) when the tenant is relieved from the forfeiture by the court under the provisions of the 1925 Act. These are the only two cases in which the landlord can recover such expenses under the subsection.[93] If, therefore, the tenant complies with the landlord's section 146 notice by remedying the breach within a reasonable time (and makes reasonable compensation) and so avoids the forfeiture, section 146(3) has no application.[94] In these circumstances, the tenant is not "relieved" from

---

[87] R.S.C. Ord. 6, r. 2(1)(*c*)(iii) and (2) and C.C.R. Ord. 6, r. 3(1)(*f*) and (2).
[88] *Jacques* v. *Harrison* (1884) 12 Q.B.D. 165, (C.A.). See also, R.S.C. Ord. 13, r.9 and Ord. 19, r.9 and C.C.R. Ord. 37, r.4.
[89] Re-enacting s. 2(1) of the Conveyancing and Law of Property Act 1892.
[90] [1891] 2 Q.B. 542, (C.A.).
[91] (1892) 61 L.J.Q.B. 375. See also, *Bond* v. *Freke* [1884] W.N. 47.
[92] It seems that s. 146(3) was passed to repeal the effect of the decision in *Skinners' Company* v. *Knight* [1891] 2 Q.B. 542, (C.A.).
[93] *Middlegate Properties Ltd.* v. *Gidlow-Jackson* (1977) 34 P. & C.R. 4, 7, *per* Megaw L.J.
[94] *Nind* v. *Nineteenth Century Building Society* [1894] 2 Q.B. 226, (C.A.).

a forfeiture so as to bring the subsection into operation. In order to avoid this difficulty, it is common practice to insert in the lease an express covenant which obliges the tenant to pay all expenses (including solicitors' costs and surveyors' fees) incurred by the landlord incidental to the preparation and service of a notice under section 146(1) of the 1925 Act.

Where the Leasehold Property (Repairs) Act 1938 applies, the landlord will not be entitled to the benefit of section 146(3) of the 1925 Act unless he makes an application for leave to the court and, on such an application, the court has power to direct whether and to what extent the landlord is to be entitled to the benefit thereof.[95] In *Bader Properties Ltd.* v. *Linley Property Investments Ltd.*,[96] Roskill J. held that there was nothing in the various statutory provisions[97] to prevent effect being given to an express covenant in the lease obliging the tenant to pay the landlord's expenses incidental to the preparation and service of a section 146 notice. The decision in *Bader* was approved by the Court of Appeal in *Middlegate Properties Ltd.* v. *Gidlow-Jackson*[98] where the lease contained covenants by the tenant to repair and to pay the landlords' legal costs and surveyors' fees of and incidental to the preparation of *inter alia* any statutory notice relating to a breach of covenant. The specific issue before the court was whether sections 1(3) and 2 of the Leasehold Property (Repairs) Act 1938 applied to prevent the landlords recovering these costs, it being admitted that they had not obtained leave of the court in accordance with those provisions. The Court of Appeal held that section 2 of the 1938 Act was inapplicable since it applied only where the landlord was claiming to be entitled to the benefit of section 146(3) of the 1925 Act and, in the present case, the landlords were not relying on that subsection but claiming only under an express covenant in the lease. Moreover, section 1(3) of the 1938 Act had no application since the landlords' claim was not for damages for a breach of contract but for a debt due under the lease.

It has been held[99] that a sub-tenant is not, as between himself and the head landlord, a "lessee" within the meaning of section 146(3) and, consequently, such landlord cannot recover from him the costs and expenses mentioned in the subsection.

Relief against forfeiture for assignment, underletting and parting with possession without consent

Although section 14(2) of the Conveyancing and Law of Property Act

---

[95] s. 2 of the Leasehold Property (Repairs) Act 1938. See also, *Re Metropolitan Film Studios Ltd.* v. *Twickenham Film Studios Ltd.* [1962] 1 W.L.R. 1315, where an order under s. 2 was made.
[96] (1968) 19 P. & C.R. 620.
[97] In particular, s. 2 of the Leasehold Property (Repairs) Act 1938.
[98] (1977) 34 P. & C.R. 4.
[99] *Nind* v. *Nineteenth Century Building Society* [1894] 2 Q.B. 226, (C.A.).

1881[1] conferred a widely based statutory power to relieve a tenant against forfeiture, it did not extend to covenants against assignment, underletting or parting with possession.[2] This exclusion was eventually repealed by section 78(1) of the Law of Property Act 1922 in respect of breaches occurring after January 1, 1926 where the premises concerned had not been assigned, underlet, etc., to a limited company. An absolute repeal of the exclusion without restrictions was enacted under the Law of Property (Amendment) Act 1924[3] and the current statutory provisions are to be found in section 146(2) of the Law of Property Act 1925.

The upshot of the foregoing was that statutory relief[4] against forfeiture could not be granted to a tenant in respect of breaches of covenants or conditions against assigning, underletting or parting with possession committed prior to January 1 1926.[5] With respect to such breaches committed after this date, the provisions of section 146 of the 1925 Act apply in relation to the service of a landlord's notice[6] and the tenant's right to apply for relief.

Whether relief will be granted in the case of such irremediable breaches will depend very much on the facts of each individual case. Thus, for example, in *House Property & Investment Company Ltd.* v. *James Walker, Goldsmith and Silversmith, Ltd.*,[7] relief, under section 146(2), was granted to a tenant who had, in breach of covenant, underlet the premises to a Government department under threat of requisition if it refused to do so. In *Scala House & District Property Co. Ltd.* v. *Forbes*,[8] the Court of Appeal granted relief where the tenant, who had never intended to sublet or part with possession, instructed his solicitor to prepare a form of licence agreement and the latter (in error) produced a document which constituted an unlawful sub-letting. The sub-letting could not have done any damage to the landlord and was one from which the landlord could not reasonably have withheld his consent had it been asked for by the

---

[1] Predecessor to the current provisions contained in s. 146(1) of the Law of Property Act 1925.

[2] See s. 14(6)(i) of the 1881 Act. The reason for this exclusion was the subject of some speculation by Romer J. in *Jackson* v. *Simons* [1923] 1 Ch. 373, 381.

[3] See para. 30 of the Third Schedule to the 1924 Act.

[4] Whilst equity could still grant relief in cases of fraud, accident or mistake, where the omission to ask for consent arose from mere neglect or forgetfulness, relief could not be granted: *Barrow* v. *Isaacs & Son* [1891] 1 Q.B. 417, (C.A.); *Eastern Telegraph Co. Ltd.* v. *Dent* [1899] 1 Q.B. 835, (C.A.) and *Ellis* v. *Allen* [1914] 1 Ch. 904, 909.

[5] See s. 146(8) of the Law of Property Act 1925.

[6] The breach of such a covenant is classified as irremediable and the landlord's notice need not require the tenant to remedy it: *Scala House & District Property Co. Ltd.* v. *Forbes* [1974] Q.B. 575, (C.A.).

[7] [1948] 1 K.B. 257.

[8] [1974] 1 Q.B. 575, (C.A.).

tenant.[8a] In *Lam Kee Ying* v. *Lam Shes Tong*[9] an important factor in granting relief was the fact that it would have been unreasonable for the landlord to have withheld its consent to the assignment of the lease had such consent been sought by the tenant. Thus, where it is clear that consent could not have been refused, it appears that relief against forfeiture will generally be granted.

It should, perhaps, be pointed out that relief against forfeiture for breach of covenant against assignment, underletting, etc., was first made available to a sub-tenant under section 4 of the Conveyancing and Law of Property Act 1892. The effect of the early legislation was, therefore, somewhat anomalous since from 1892 to 1925 the court had power only to grant relief against forfeiture for breach of a sub-tenant's but not a tenant's covenant against assignment, underletting, etc.[10] In the case of a sub-tenant, it has been held that the jurisdiction to grant relief should be exercised sparingly and with caution.[11] In particular, the sub-tenant must show that he is blameless and has taken all precautions which a reasonably cautious and careful person would use. Thus, in *Imray* v. *Oakshette*,[12] relief was refused to a sub-tenant who had been negligent in entering into a contract for the purchase of an underlease which precluded him from investigating the leasehold title containing a restriction on sub-letting.

Relief against forfeiture on bankruptcy or taking of lease in execution[13]

The relief given to a tenant under section 14(2) of the Conveyancing and Law of Property Act 1881 did not extend to a condition for forfeiture on the bankruptcy of the tenant.[14] Indeed, relief was not made available until 1892 when section 2 of the Conveyancing and Law of Property Act 1892 gave the court a limited power to relieve against forfeiture for the bankruptcy[15] of the tenant. The current provisions are contained in sections 146(9) and (10) of the Law of Property Act 1925.

Under section 146(9), on the occurrence of the forfeiture of the lease on the tenant's bankruptcy or the taking in execution of the tenant's interest

---

[8a] In this case also the sub-tenancy was surrendered and the parting with possession ended: *ibid.*, 589, *per* Russell L.J.

[9] [1975] A.C. 247, (P.C.).

[10] See, *e.g. Matthews* v. *Smallwood* [1910] 1 Ch. 777, 794, *per* Parker J. and the earlier case of *Imray* v. *Oakshette* [1897] 2 Q.B. 218, (C.A.).

[11] *Imray* v. *Oakshette* [1897] 2 Q.B. 218, (C.A.).

[12] [1897] 2 Q.B. 218, (C.A.), applied in *Matthews* v. *Smallwood* [1910] 1 Ch. 777.

[13] See also, Chap. 5, pp. 103–104.

[14] See s. 14(6)(i) of the 1881 Act.

[15] "Bankruptcy" includes the liquidation of a company: s. 205(1)(i) of the Law of Property Act 1925. See also, *Horsey Estate Ltd.* v. *Steiger* [1899] 2 Q.B. 79, (C.A.) and *Fryer* v. *Ewart* [1902] A.C. 187, (H.L.), where it was held that a voluntary liquidation for the purpose of reconstruction or amalgamation came within s. 2(2) of the 1892 Act. See also, *Re Walker, ex p. Gould* (1884) 13 Q.B.D. 454.

in the lease, the landlord's right to forfeit is unaffected by the provisions of section 146 if the lease is of (a) agricultural or pastoral land (b) mines or minerals (c) a house used or intended to be used as a public-house or beershop (d) a house let as a dwelling-house, with the use of any furniture, books, works of art, or other chattels not being in the nature of fixtures or (e) any property with respect to which the personal qualifications[16] of the tenant are of importance for the preservation of the value or character of the property, or on the ground of neighbourhood to the landlord or to any person holding under him.[16a] Thus, in the case of leases falling within section 146(9), the tenant has no statutory right to relief against the forfeiture of his lease on the occasion of his bankruptcy or the taking in execution of his interest in the lease. Moreover, it is apparent from the Court of Appeal decision in *Official Custodian for Charities* v. *Parway Estates Development Ltd.*[17] that the court has no residual equitable jurisdiction to grant relief from forfeiture on the tenant's bankruptcy or liquidation in circumstances where no such relief is available under the statutory provisions.

In the case of leases falling outside section 146(9), the landlord's right to forfeit on bankruptcy or taking in execution is subject to the provisions of section 146 (including the tenant's right to apply for relief from forfeiture) if the tenant's interest is sold within one year from the date of the bankruptcy or taking in execution.[18] If, however, the tenant's interest is not sold before the expiration of that year, section 146 only applies to the forfeiture condition in the lease during the first year from the date of the bankruptcy or taking in execution.[19] The upshot of the foregoing is, therefore, that, in the case of leases outside section 146(9), the provisions of section 146 as to notice and relief apply during the first year after bankruptcy or taking in execution and, if the lease is sold within that first year, they continue to apply indefinitely. In the words of Russell J. in *Civil Service Co-operative Society Ltd.* v. *McGrigor's Trustee*[20]:

"The right of entry or forfeiture on bankruptcy of the lessee, or on taking in execution of the lessee's interest is fettered; if the lessee's interest be not sold within the one year the fetter is removed at the end of the year; if the lessee's interest be sold within the one year the fetter is not removed, but continues."

[16] See, *e.g. Bathurst* v. *Fine* [1974] 1 W.L.R. 905, (C.A.) in a different context.
[16a] *Hockley Engineering Co. Ltd.* v. *V. & P. Midlands Ltd.* [1993] 18 E.G. 129.
[17] [1985] 1 Ch. 151, followed in *Smith* v. *Metropolitan City Properties Ltd.* (1986) 1 E.G.L.R. 52, a case involving a tenant's breach of repairing covenant. See also, *Billson* v. *Residential Apartments Ltd.* [1991] 3 W.L.R. 264, (C.A.), where the forfeiture was effected by a peaceable re-entry onto the demised premises. The current scope of equity's jurisdiction to relieve against forfeiture is discussed fully in Chap. 8.
[18] s. 146(10)(*a*) of the 1925 Act.
[19] s. 146(10)(*b*) of the 1925 Act.
[20] [1923] 2 Ch. 347, 355. See also, *Gee* v. *Harwood* [1933] 1 Ch. 712, 737, (C.A.), *per* Lord Hanworth M.R.

Thus, in the *McGrigor* case itself, where the tenant's interest had not been sold, the landlord was held entitled to enforce his right of re-entry on the bankruptcy of the tenant during the first year but subject to the service of a valid section 146 notice.

Again, in *Horsey Estate Ltd.* v. *Steiger*,[21] the lease contained a proviso for re-entry if the tenant company should enter into liquidation, whether compulsory or voluntary. The tenant passed a resolution for a voluntary winding-up, not by reason of insolvency, but for the purpose of reconstruction with additional capital. The Court of Appeal held that a sufficient notice under (what is now) section 146(1) of the 1925 Act was a condition precedent to enforcing the forfeiture on the tenant's liquidation where landlord's action was brought within a year from the resolution for winding-up.

In *Gee* v. *Harwood*,[22] the landlord demised certain lands comprising a spa to the tenant company for a term of 50 years less one month. The company was compulsorily wound-up and, four months later, the liquidator brought proceedings seeking, *inter alia*, relief from forfeiture. It was held that the Court had a discretion, under section 146 of the 1925 Act, to grant relief from forfeiture as the case fell within section 146(10)(*b*), which entitled the liquidator to apply for relief within a year of the winding-up, when the demised land had not been sold, and which neither limited the grant of relief to that period nor made it necessary that the application should be heard within that period.

The reason why the right to relief does not cease after a year when the lease is sold was referred to by Lord Hanworth M.R. in *Gee* v. *Harwood*[23]:

"It may often happen in the case of a liquidation that the company may be in possession of a lease which is of saleable value. It may not be easy to disentangle the affairs of the company or to ascertain the rights within a short time, and still less may it be possible to effect a sale of the lease within a short time; and, as I read [section 146(10)], its purpose is to give a twelve months' period during which the liquidator can apply for relief and, further, in the case where there is a sale effected (it may be towards the end of the twelve months' period), to insure that the liquidator should not find himself brought up against a time limit which would imperil the success of his realization of the assets."

In order for a sale to come within section 146(10), it must be a sale

[21] [1899] 2 Q.B. 79, (C.A.).

[22] [1933] Ch. 712, (C.A.), affirmed by the House of Lords: *Pearson* v. *Gee and Braceborough Spa Ltd.* [1934] A.C. 272.

[23] *Ibid.* pp. 736–737.

completed by conveyance or, alternatively, the contract for sale must be absolute and not merely conditional.[24]

A lease may contain a proviso for forfeiture not only on the tenant's bankruptcy but also if he makes a voluntary arrangement with his creditors. In *Re Mohammed Naeem (A Bankrupt) (No. 18 of 1988)*[24a] Hoffman J. held that a voluntary arrangement made by the bankrupt tenant with his creditors, under section 260 of the Insolvency Act 1986, under which *inter alia* the tenant's leasehold interest was to be marketed and sold, did not affect the landlord's proprietary right to forfeit the lease on the grounds of arrears of rent and the tenant's bankruptcy. In this case, the arrangement permitted the demised premises to be marketed and sold in so far as the tenant bankrupt was able to obtain relief from forfeiture under section 146(2) of the 1925 Act.

In the event of relief being granted, the effect of the arrangement will be to modify the landlord's claim for arrears of rent in the same way as the claims of other creditors of the bankrupt tenant. Thus, since the landlord's right to the arrears of rent will be extinguished and replaced by his right in the arrangement, it is unlikely that the tenant will be obliged to make full repayment of the arrears as a condition of relief.

Finally, it should be noted that, where a leasehold interest is disclaimed by the tenant's trustee in bankruptcy, the disclaimed lease will remain operative (in the absence of a vesting order) in the sense that a failure to perform any of the covenants will continue to justify a forfeitue. Thus, if the tenant bankrupt has sub-let any part of the demised premises, the headlease will not be entirely extinguished by disclaimer by his trustee in bankruptcy and the sub-tenant will (in the absence of a vesting order) be liable to forfeiture for failure to perform any covenant in it.[25]

Relief against notice to carry out decorative repairs

A special form of relief is available to a lessee in respect of a landlord's notice served on him relating to the internal decorative repairs to a house or other building under section 147 of the Law of Property Act 1925. Upon the lessee's application[25a] for relief, the court may[26] relieve the tenant from liability for such repairs if "having regard to all the circumstances of the

---

[24] *Re Henry Castle and Sons Ltd., Mitchell* v. *Henry Castle and Sons Ltd.* (1906) 94 L.T. 396; *Ferguson & Co. Ltd.* v. *Ferguson* [1924] I.R. 22, (C.A.) and *Gee* v. *Harwood* [1933] 1 Ch. 712, 725, *per* Luxmoore J.

[24a] [1990] 1 W.L.R. 48.

[25] See, *Re Thompson & Cottrell's Contract* [1943] Ch. 97, 100, *per* Uthwatt J. and *Re A. E. Realisations (1985) Ltd.* [1988] 1 W.L.R. 200, 211–213, *per* Vinelott J.

[25a] The application need not be in an action and may be made by originating summons: s. 203(2) of the Law of Property Act 1925. For a form of summons: See *Atkin's Court Forms*, (2nd ed., 1990), Vol. 24, p. 376, Form 176.

[26] The power of the court is purely discretionary and is exercised with regard to the circumstances of each particular case.

case (including in particular the length of the lessee's term or interest remaining unexpired), the court is satisfied that the [landlord's] notice is unreasonable."[27] The subsection does not apply (a) where the liability arises under an express covenant or agreement to put the property in a decorative state of repair and the covenant or agreement has never been performed[28] (b) to any matter necessary or proper for putting or keeping the property in a sanitary condition or for the maintenance or preservation of the structure[29] (c) to any statutory liability to keep a house in all respects reasonably fit for human habitation[30] and (d) to any covenant or stipulation to yield up the property in a specified state of repair at the end of the term.[31]

The word "lease" includes an underlease and an agreement for a lease, and "lessee" has a corresponding meaning and includes any person[32] liable to effect the repairs.[33] The section will have effect notwithstanding any stipulation to the contrary.[34]

The county court has jurisdiction under the section where the net annual value for rating of the house or other building does not exceed the county court limit.[35]

Relief from obligation to repair in case of war damage

The Landlord and Tenant (War Damage) Act 1939[36] provides statutory relief where property subject to a lease suffers war damage.[37]

Where, under section 1 of the 1939 Act, an obligation to repair (whether express or implied) is modified or suspended or an obligation to make good war damage as such is extinguished, all rights and remedies by way of damages, forfeiture, re-entry, sale, foreclosure or otherwise arising out of the non-fulfilment of the obligation, including all rights against any person who has guaranteed the fulfilment of the obligation, are by section 1(4) of the Act modified or suspended or extinguished accordingly. The section only affords relief against an obligation to repair as between landlord and tenant and it gives no defence to proceedings for failure to abate a statutory nuisance.[38]

---

[27] s. 147(1).
[28] s. 147(2)(i).
[29] s. 147(2)(ii) (a) and (b).
[30] s. 147(2)(iii).
[31] s. 147(2)(iv).
[32] e.g. a tenant's surety or mortgagee in possession.
[33] s. 147(3).
[34] s. 147(4).
[35] s. 147(5), added by the Sched. 2, para. 6 to the County Courts Act 1984.
[36] See also, the Landlord and Tenant (War Damage) (Amendment) Act 1941.
[37] The obligation to repair may also be extinguished under the common law doctrine of frustration which has now been held to apply in principle to leases: *National Carriers Ltd.* v. *Panalpina (Northern) Ltd.* [1981] A.C. 675.
[38] *Turley* v. *King* [1944] 2 All E.R. 489.

Relief in respect of long residential tenancies

Part I of the Landlord and Tenant Act 1954 gives security of tenure to a tenant who occupies a dwelling-house on a long tenancy at a low rent to which the Rent Act 1977 would apply but for the low rent. Such a tenancy will not come to an end by effluxion of time but will continue until such time as certain procedures which can be initiated by the landlord under Part I have been successfully completed. These can take the form of either (a) a landlord's notice proposing a statutory tenancy or (b) a landlord's notice to resume possession. If successful, the former will result in the tenant becoming a statutory tenant under the Rent Act 1977 and the latter in the landlord obtaining possession of the dwelling-house.

Part I of the 1954 Act now only applies to long tenancies at a low rent granted before January 15, 1989. For such tenancies granted on or after this date which (but for the low rent) would be assured tenancies under the Housing Act 1988, the relevant provisions are contained in section 186 (and Schedule 10) of the Local Government and Housing Act 1989. Under the 1989 Act, the long tenancy will continue until such time as certain statutory procedures (contained in Schedule 10 to the 1989 Act) have been completed. Here again, the landlord may take the initiative by serving on the tenant either (a) a landlord's notice proposing an assured tenancy or (b) a landlord's notice to resume possession.

A tenant under a long tenancy enjoys as of right the benefit of two special provisions for relief against forfeiture and damages other than for failure to pay rent or rates, failure to insure or breach of covenant against illegal or immoral user of the premises.[39] These provisions apply to both 1954 Act and 1989 Act long residential tenancies.[39a] First, where the tenant has applied in the landlord's proceedings for relief under section 16(1)(b) of the Act, no order for possession or damages may be made during the last seven months of the tenancy[40] (but an order for damages in respect of a failure, as respects any premises, to comply with the terms of a tenancy may be made if, when the order is made, the tenancy has come to an end[41]). Secondly, if there is more than seven months of the tenancy to run from the date of the order for possession (or damages) and the tenant has applied[42] in the landlord's proceedings for relief under section 16(1)(b) of

---

[39] s. 16(4) of the 1954 Act.
[39a] See, para. 20(1) of Sched. 10 to the Local Government and Housing Act 1989.
[40] s. 16(3) of the 1954 Act.
[41] s. 16(3) proviso, *ibid*.
[42] In the High Court, the application may be made in the applicant's pleading (R.S.C. Ord. 97, r. 12(*a*)) or by summons at any time before the trial (R.S.C. Ord. 97, r. 12(*b*)) or at the trial (R.S.C. Ord. 97, r. 12(*c*)). For a form of counterclaim for relief: See, *Atkin's Court Forms*, (2nd ed., 1990), Vol. 24, p. 543, Form 397. The tenant can only apply if, at the time, the qualifying condition (defined in s. 2(1)) of the 1954 Act is fulfilled: See s. 16(7) of the 1954 Act which excludes s. 2(3).

the 1954 Act and the tenant notifies (under section 16(2)) both the landlord and the court[43] in writing within 14 days[44] of the making of the order that he claims the benefit of the section, the order merely operates so far as it provides for the payment of costs[45] and to bring the tenancy to an end seven months later.[46] In other words, the landlord does not obtain possession but his opportunity to terminate the tenancy by notice under section 4 of the 1954 Act is accelerated. Thus, the landlord may serve a notice proposing a statutory (assured) tenancy or a notice to resume possession specifying a date of termination seven months after the making of the order of possession.

A tenant who applies for relief under section 16(1)(b) of the 1954 Act is not thereby precluded from making a claim to acquire the freehold or an extended lease under the Leasehold Reform Act 1967.[47] However, if he gives notice under section 16(2) of the 1954 Act, any claim made by him to acquire the freehold or an extended lease under the 1967 Act will be of no effect, or, if already made, will cease to have effect.[48]

The parties cannot contract out of Part I, but the tenant is at liberty to surrender his tenancy if so minded.[49]

---

[43] The tenant must lodge a copy of his notice in court: s. 16(2), *ibid*.
[44] The order for possession is suspended for a period of 14 days from the making thereof: s. 16(2), *ibid*.
[45] s. 16(2)(*a*), *ibid*.
[46] s. 16(2)(*b*), *ibid*.
[47] See para. 4(4) of Sched. 3 to the Leasehold Reform Act 1967.
[48] *Ibid*.
[49] s. 17 of the 1954 Act. See also, *Re Hennessey's Agreement, Hillman* v. *Davison* [1975] 2 W.L.R. 159.

Chapter Eleven

Relief against forfeiture of options to renew leases

Introduction

In this Chapter, a number of English and Commonwealth authorities are examined with reference to the question whether equity has any jurisdiction to relieve a tenant from the consequences of his failure to comply with the pre-conditions for the exercise of an option to renew his lease. Invariably, the consequences of such failure will involve the tenant in the loss of his interest in the demised premises arising under the option to renew.

Although there is considerable judicial (and academic) controversy as to whether an option to purchase land constitutes an irrevocable offer[1]; or a conditional contract,[2] it appears that the true nature of an option falls to be determined by reference to its specific terms so that an option can be expressed either in the form of an irrevocable offer or in the form of a conditional contract.[3] Provided, however, that the option does not constitute a mere (revocable) offer, it will confer on the grantee an equitable interest in the land[4] which may be protected by registration and, as such, will fall to be classified as a proprietary interest in that land.[5] Moreover, the loss of such an option (following the grantee's failure to exercise it in

---

[1] *United Dominions Trust (Commercial) Ltd.* v. *Eagle Aircraft Services Ltd.* [1968] 1 W.L.R. 74, 82, *per* Lord Denning M.R.; *Mountford* v. *Scott* [1975] Ch. 258; *United Scientific Holdings Ltd.* v. *Burnley Borough Council* [1978] A.C. 904, 928–929 *per* Lord Diplock, 945 *per* Lord Simon of Glaisdale, and 951 *per* Lord Salmon. See, W.J. Mowbray, *Who can Exercise an Option* (1958) 74 L.Q.R. 242, 250 and *Halsbury's Laws of England*, (4th ed.), Vol. 42, at p. 20.
[2] *Griffith* v. *Pelton* [1958] 1 Ch. 205, 225. See, C.J. Rossiter, *Options to Acquire Interests in Land—Freehold and Leasehold* (1982) 56 A.L.J. 576, 576–577.
[3] See, A. G. Lang, *Forfeiture of Interests in Land* (1984) 100 L.Q.R. 427, 449–450 referring to a number of Australian authorities.
[4] *London and South Western Railway Co.* v. *Gomm* (1882) 20 Ch. D. 562, 580–581; *Stromdale & Ball Ltd.* v. *Burden* [1952] Ch. 223; *Mountford* v. *Scott* [1975] Ch. 258 and *Griffith* v. *Pelton* [1958] 1 Ch. 205. See, Barnsley, *Land Options* (1st. ed), p. 26.
[5] *Re Button's Lease* [1964] 1 Ch. 263, 271, *per* Plowman J.

compliance with its requirements) is properly characterised (it is submitted) as a forfeiture of that proprietary interest by the grantor. In this connection, it has been held by the Court of Appeal in *Richard Clarke & Co. Ltd.* v. *Widnall*[6] that an option contained in a lease giving the landlord the right to terminate the tenancy upon the tenant's breach of covenant constituted a forfeiture clause although the tenant, strictly speaking, had been deprived of his interest by the exercise of the option. This is, of course, analogous to the grantor of an option depriving the grantee of the benefit of the option because of the grantee's failure to observe the pre-conditions of the option itself.

In Australia and New Zealand, statutes[7] have given the courts power to grant relief to a tenant against the forfeiture of an option contained in a lease resulting from a breach of covenant. In *Evanel Property Limited* v. *Stellar Mining N.L.,*[8] the Supreme Court of New South Wales[9] held that the principles on which relief should be exercised in respect of options should be similar to those on which relief is granted against the forfeiture of a lease. In that case, the lease gave the tenant an option of renewal for three years subject to the giving of due notice and the punctual payment of rent, and the due performance and observance of the covenants contained in the lease. There was a history of late payment of rent. The tenant gave notice of the exercise of the option and the landlord responded with a notice, made pursuant to section 133F of the Conveyancing Act 1919, that it proposed to treat *inter alia* the tenant's arrears of rent as having precluded the tenant from exercising his right of renewal. In this connection, the relevant provisions of the 1919 Act,[10] which apply to options contained in a lease, give the tenant a right to require the landlord (a) to sell or offer to sell to the tenant the reversion expectant on the lease or (b) to grant or to offer to grant to the tenant a renewal or extension of the lease or a further lease of the demised premises or a part thereof.[11] If the landlord wishes to rely on a breach of the lease by the tenant as precluding the tenant from exercising an option, he is obliged, within 14 days after the purported exercise of the option, to serve on the tenant a notice specifying the acts or omissions and stating that, subject to an order of the court under section 133F, he proposes to treat the breach as having precluded the tenant from exercising the option. The tenant then has a period of one month in which to seek relief from the court against the effect of the breach.[12] The court is given jurisdiction to make such orders

---

[6] [1976] 1 W.L.R. 845.
[7] See, *e.g.* s. 133 C-G of the Conveyancing Act 1919 (N.S.W.); s. 128 of the Property Law Act 1974 (Queensland); s. 83A–83E of the Property Law Act 1969 (Western Australia) and ss. 120–121 of the Property Law Act 1952 (New Zealand).
[8] (1982) 1 N.S.W.L.R. 380.
[9] Wootten J.
[10] See ss. 133C, 133D, 133E, 133F, and 133G.
[11] See s. 133C.
[12] See s. 133E.

as it thinks fit for the purpose of granting the relief sought, or to refuse relief. It is also empowered to make an order on such terms as to costs, damages, compensation or penalty, or on such other terms as it thinks fit.[13] In considering whether or not to grant relief, the court is entitled to take into consideration (a) the nature of the breach complained of (b) the extent to which, at the date of the institution of proceedings, the landlord was prejudiced by the breach (c) the conduct of the landlord and tenant, including conduct after the giving of the prescribed notice (d) the rights of persons other than the landlord and tenant (e) the operation of section 133G[14] and (f) any other circumstances considered by the court to be relevant. In the *Evanel* case, Wootten J., following a review of several New Zealand authorities[15] on a similarly worded provision, concluded that it was appropriate to regard the primary object of the conditions attached to the right to exercise the option as the securing of a result which could effectively be attained when the matter came before the court and to regard the forfeiture provision (the loss of the right to exercise the option) as added by way of security for the production of that result.[16] It was suggested in argument that there was an essential difference between the concept of a forfeiture of a lease and the forfeiture of an option to renew but in the Court of Appeal, Hope J.A. (with whom Glass and Samuels JJ.A. agreed) dismissed this on the basis that: "the two obligations and the power to grant relief are essentially analogous in kind, and that it is appropriate that similar principles should be applied in each case."[17] On the facts, relief was granted to the tenant[18] on the basis that the arrears of rent had been tendered to the landlord prior to the proceedings and that, therefore, the landlord was no longer prejudiced by the breach in regard to rent. Moreover, no injury had been done to the leased property but, on the contrary, considerable improvements had been effected by the tenant which he would stand to lose if relief was refused.

Conditions must be strictly observed

Where an option (or right of pre-emption) is conditional upon the performance by the grantee of some act in a stated manner or at a stated

---

[13] See s. 133F(2) and (4).

[14] s. 133G provides for the continuation of the lease until the issue of relief is decided by the court.

[15] See, *Re A Lease Kennedy to Kennedy* [1935] N.Z.L.R. 564; *Re Lease McNaught to McNaught* [1958] N.Z.L.R. 72; *Vince Bevan Ltd.* v. *Findgard Nominees Ltd.* [1973] 2 N.Z.L.R. 290 and *Henderson* v. *Ross* [1981] 1 N.Z.L.R. 417. All these cases emphasise the court's wide and unfettered jursidiction under the relevant legislation: See ss. 120 and 121 of the Property Law Act 1952.

[16] See *Shiloh Spinners Ltd.* v. *Harding* [1973] A.C. 691, 723–724, *per* Lord Wilberforce.

[17] *Stellar Mining N.L.* v. *Evanel Property Ltd.* (1983) N.S.W. Conv. R., para. 55–118.

[18] On terms that the tenant should provide a satisfactory guarantor of its obligation to pay the rent under the renewed lease.

time, the act must be performed strictly in order to entitle the grantee to exercise the right.

The principle that conditions must be strictly observed is rooted in old authorities. For example, in *Barrell* v. *Sabine*,[18a] a case involving the sale of land with a right of re-purchase, it was held that the time limited to re-purchase ought to be precisely observed. In *Davis* v. *Thomas*[19] Sir John Leach M. R. said[20]:

> "In all cases of the payment of money, where penalty or forfeiture is introduced for the purpose of security, there a Court of Equity will relieve against the penalty or forfeiture, upon the ground of full compensation by giving interest. But where there is no stipulation for penalty or forfeiture, but a privilege is conferred, provided money be paid within a stated time, there the party claiming that privilege must show that the money was paid accordingly."

The principle has been applied in a variety of legal contexts including options to renew[21] and determine[22] leases. In *Burch* v. *Farrows Bank Ltd.*[23] a lease contained the usual tenant's covenant to repair the demised premises and a proviso entitling him to determine the lease upon giving written notice to the landlord and performing all the tenant's covenants under the lease. The tenant duly gave notice under the proviso and subsequently commenced repairs to the premises which were completed a few days after the date of the determination of the lease. Neville J. held that the performance of the covenant to repair was a condition precedent to the determination of the lease and that, accordingly, the condition not having been fulfilled, the notice was bad and the lease had not been validly terminated. The case may be contrasted with *Simons* v. *Associated Furnishers Ltd.*[24] where Clauson J. held that as the breaches of repairing covenant (although unremedied at the date of the notice) had been remedied by the time the tenant's notice expired, the condition precedent was fulfilled with the result that the lease had been effectively determined. In *Hare* v. *Nicoll*,[25] a case involving an option to re-purchase shares in a private company, Willmer L.J. had occasion to remark[26]:

[18a] (1684) 1 Vern. 268; 23 E.R. 462. See also, *Joy* v. *Birch* (1836) 4 Cl. & Fin. 57, (H.L.); 7 E.R. 22.

[19] (1831) 1 Russ. & M. 506; 39 E.R. 195. See also, *Ensworth* v. *Griffiths* (1706) 5 Bro. Parl. Cas. 184; 2 E.R. 615. Both these cases concerned the release of the equity of redemption to the mortgagee coupled with the grant of a right of re-purchase to the mortgagor within a year upon payment of a stipulated sum.

[20] *Ibid.*, 507–508; 195–196.

[21] *Greville* v. *Parker* [1910] A.C. 335, (P.C.); *West Country Cleaners (Falmouth) Ltd.* v. *Saly* [1966] 1 W.L.R. 1485, (C.A.).

[22] *Burch* v. *Farrows Bank Ltd.* [1917] 1 Ch. 606 and *Simons* v. *Associated-Furnishers Ltd.* [1931] 1 Ch. 379.

[23] [1917] 1 Ch. 606.

[24] [1931] 1 Ch. 379.

[25] [1966] 2 Q.B. 130, (C.A.).

[26] *Ibid.*, 141.

"It is well established that an option for the purchase or repurchase of property must in all cases be exercised strictly within the time limited for the purpose. The reason for this, as I understand it, is that an option is a species of privilege for the benefit of the party on whom it is conferred. That being so, it is for that party to comply strictly with the conditions stipulated for the exercise of the option."

The decision in *Hare* was applied by the Court of Appeal in *West Country Cleaners (Falmouth) Ltd.* v. *Saly,*[27] where tenants were held to be disqualified by reason of their breaches of a painting covenant (albeit that the breaches were only trivial) from exercising their option to renew the lease for an extended term. Moreover, in the recent case of *Bairstow Eves (Securities) Ltd.* v. *Ripley,*[28] the Court of Appeal confirmed the proposition that a tenant seeking to enforce an option to renew in a lease, where compliance with repairing obligations was a condition precedent to the exercise of the option, could not excuse himself by saying that the want of repair was trivial or merely a technical breach.

Equitable relief against late compliance with conditions

In England, there are a number of early decisions (from the 18th and 19th centuries) concerned with leases for lives containing covenants for renewal upon the dropping of a life and requiring an application for renewal to be made within a stated period after the death.[29] In these cases, the courts were concerned with the question whether equity could relieve the tenant against the forfeiture of his right of renewal notwithstanding his failure to comply strictly with the terms of the option covenant.

The earliest reported case appears to be *Ross* v. *Worsop,*[30] where a lease for lives contained a landlord's covenant to renew the lease in the event of the dropping of any of the lives upon the tenant nominating a new life in place thereof and paying a fine of £100 within a specified time. The lease contained a proviso that, if the tenant defaulted in these pre-conditions, it would be lawful for the landlord to refuse a renewal. The tenant neglected to name a new life and pay the fine within the time specified, whereupon the landlord refused to grant a renewal. The tenant then sought specific performance of the landlord's covenant contending that the landlord had waived his right to rely upon the tenant's default by promising to accept late tender. The tenant's claim for specific performance was upheld in the

---

[27] [1966] 1 W.L.R. 1485, (C.A.).
[28] [1992] E.G.C.S. 83, (C.A.).
[29] See, generally, Comyn, *Treatise in the Law of Landlord and Tenant*, (1821), pp. 483–485 and Woodfall's *Law of Landlord and Tenant*, (21st ed.). pp. 470–472.
[30] (1740) 1 Bro. Parl. Cas. 281; 1 E.R. 568.

House of Lords on appeal from the Irish Court of Chancery,[31] the House accepting that equity had jurisdiction to relieve a tenant against the forfeiture of his right of renewal under the lease in circumstances where he had failed to comply strictly with the terms of the renewal covenant. A more restrictive approach, however, was applied in *Bateman* v. *Murray*,[32] where a lease of lands in Ireland for three lives contained a covenant for perpetual renewal upon the tenant tendering a sum of money by way of fine to the landlord within three months after the death of each life. The tenant allowed all three lives to drop without applying for a renewal or making any tender of the fines. He subsequently claimed specific performance in the Court of Chancery in Ireland against the landlord to compel a renewal of the lease for three lives which he had now nominated. The Irish Court granted the decree but, on appeal, the House of Lords refused the tenant equitable relief. Lord Thurlow L.C. set out the relevant principles in the following terms[33]:

> "Courts of equity will relieve the lessee, if he has lost his right by fraud of the lessor, or accident on his own part; but will never assist him where he has lost his right by his own gross laches or neglect . . . Where the lessee has lost his legal right, he must prove some fraud on the part of the lessor by which he was debarred the exercise of his right, or some accident or misfortune on his part, which he could not prevent, by means whereof he was disabled from applying for a renewal at the stated times, according to the terms of his lease."

In *Bayley* v. *The Corporation of Leominster*,[34] a lease for three lives contained a landlord's covenant to renew the lease upon the dropping of a life. The tenants allowed two lives to drop without applying for a renewal and, in these circumstances, their claim for a renewal was dismissed. Lord Thurlow (L.C.) said:

> "If [the lessees] wish to make a new bargain upon the old footing,

---

[31] There are several Irish decisions in point but all appear to have depended on the fact of there being a fine payable under the covenant as a pre-condition of renewal. The Irish courts, therefore, proceeded on the basis that, if the tenant paid the fine together with interest from the time it had become due, the court would indulge him with a renewal of the lease. See, *e.g. Butler* v. *Mulvihill* (1819) 1 Bli. 137, (H.L.); 4 E.R. 49; *Trant* v. *Dwyer* (1828) 2 Bli. N.S. 11; 4 E.R. 1034. For Irish cases involving non-payment of rent: See *Mulloy* v. *Goff* (1850) 1 I. Ch. R. 27; *M'Donnell* v. *Burnett, Burnett* v. *Going* (1841) 4 I. Ch. R. 216; *Fitzgerald* v. *O'Connell* (1844) 6 I. Eq. R. 455.

[32] (1779) 5 Bro. P.C. 20; 2 E.R. 506. See also, *Vijon* v. *Rowley* Dom. Proc. (1774) and *Kane* v. *Hamilton* (1776) 1 Ridgway 180, where the House of Lords also differed from the judgments of the Court of Ireland which were held to be based upon a local equity.

[33] (1779) 5 Bro. P.C. 20; 2 E.R. 506.

[34] (1792) 3 Bro. C.C. 529; 30 E.R. 446.

they do not treat the [lessor] fairly . . . this case has been determined over and over in the House of Lords upon Irish cases."[35]

The reasoning of this case was that if the tenant had desired to avail himself of the benefit of the landlord's covenant to renew, he should have strictly performed the conditions upon which the renewal was to be granted.

In *Rawstone* v. *Bentley*,[36] Sir Richard Arden M.R., whilst expressing agreement[37] with the statement of principle enunciated by Lord Thurlow in the *Bateman* case, nevertheless, granted the tenant a renewal of the lease largely on the basis that the intention of the original parties was that the tenant should consider himself as already having an interest of 99 years and that a local law was the only obstacle to this full term being granted at the outset. In fact, the lease was expressed to be for an initial period of 21 years with a landlord's covenant to renew it for successive periods in order to eventually make up the full 99 year term originally envisaged by the parties. On the basis of the parties' original understanding, the tenant had constructed a house on the premises at a cost of £1,000. At the expiration of the first term, the tenant made no application for renewal and, since there were arrears of rent, the landlord brought an action for ejectment and obtained possession of the premises. The tenant then claimed a renewal of the lease on payment of the rent arrears with interest. In view of the exceptional circumstances, the Court felt compelled to grant relief but without discrediting in any way previous House of Lords' authority.

In *Eaton* v. *Lyon*,[38] another case involving a lease for lives with renewal for further lives, the tenants covenanted that they would (a) within six months after the death of any of the three named lives in the lease, give notice thereof to the landlord and (b) within the next six months, surrender the lease and accept a new lease adding one or two lives to the life or lives then in being, and paying a fine for the addition of the life or lives. The landlord, in turn, covenanted to grant a new lease in return for the stipulated fines. Within six months of the death of one of the lives, the tenant's agent went to the landlord's house in order to seek a renewal of the lease. The agent did not see the landlord and was told he was too ill to speak. The agent did not ask the person to whom he spoke to inform the landlord of his business. Sir Richard Arden M.R. held that the tenant had lost her right of renewal since she had not done everything in her power

---

[35] For a review of the Irish cases which gave rise to the Irish Tenantry Acts, see Lord Lifford's judgment in *Boyle* v. *Lysaght*, Vernon & Scrivener's Reports, 135, 142 *et seq.* See also, *Magrath* v. *Lord Muskerry*, Vernon & Scrivener's Reports, 166.
[36] (1793) 4 Bro. C.C. 415; 29 E.R. 966.
[37] See also, *Baynham* v. *Guy's Hospital* (1796) 3 Ves. 295; 30 E.R. 1019.
[38] (1798) 3 Ves. Jun. 689; 30 E.R. 1223.

to give notice of renewal. Applying Lord Thurlow's views in the *Bayley* case, he said[39]:

> "At Law a covenant must be strictly and literally performed: in Equity it must be really and substantially performed according to the true intent and meaning of the parties, as far as circumstances will admit: but if by unavoidable accident, if by fraud, by surprise, or ignorance not wilful, parties may have been prevented from executing it literally, a Court of Equity will interfere; and upon compensation being made, the party having done everything in his power, and being prevented by the means, I have alluded to, will give relief . . . the party shall not avail himself of equitable circumstances, unless he shows, that there has been no wilful neglect or misconduct on his part."

The learned Judge then considered the facts and refused the tenant's claim for relief stating[40]:

> ". . . Equity will interpose, and go beyond the stipulations of the covenant at law, only where a literal performance has been prevented by means, I have mentioned, and no injury is done to the lessor."

The decision in *Eaton* was subsequently applied and followed in *Maxwell* v. *Ward*,[41] where equitable relief was denied on the ground that[42]:

> ". . . ignorance of a party's own rights, or of instruments in his possession or power—an ignorance to which the adverse party is in no way auxiliary, cannot excuse a non-performance of any thing encumbent on that party to perform."

In *Harries* v. *Bryant*,[43] a lease for lives contained a covenant for renewal on the dropping of any life upon payment of a small fine and provided application was made within six months by the tenant. A life dropped in January 1822 and the tenant failed to make the requisite application until November 1822. He subsequently applied for relief on the ground that he did not, within the six month period, know that the person had died or

---

[39] *Ibid.* pp. 692–693; p. 1224.

[40] *Ibid.* p. 695; 1226.

[41] (1824) 13 Price 674; 148 E.R. 192.

[42] *Ibid.* p. 676; p. 194, *per* Lord Alexander C.B. In this case, the notice of renewal was not given because the tenant's successor in title was unaware of the existence of the covenant.

[43] (1827) 4 Russ. 89; 38 E.R. 738. See also, *Reid* v. *Blagrave* (1831) 9 L.J.(O.S.) Ch. 245, 248, concerning a lease for lives renewable on notice and payment of a fine, in which Sir John Leach M.R. said: ". . . the rule is now established, that no accident will entitle a party to renew unless it be unavoidable. I am of opinion that nothing but accident, which could not have been avoided by reasonable diligence, will entitle the plaintiff to a renewal in this court"; In *Jackson* v. *Saunders* (1814) 2 Dow. P.C. 388; 3 E.R. 923, the House of Lords held that the tenant had forfeited his rights to renewal on the ground of unreasonable delay.

that the deceased was one of the lives named in the lease. It was argued that the only injury suffered by the landlord had been the non-payment of the fine and that the tenant's conduct in omitting to renew had not been wilful but a matter of misfortune since the deceased had been an obscure individual whose death would not have been immediately known beyond the circle of his immediate friends. Sir John Leach M.R., however, refused a new lease on the ground that the tenant could have known the facts if he had used reasonable diligence and acted with ordinary prudence. He said:

> "A Court of Equity will relieve against the effect of an express covenant, where strict performance of the condition is prevented by ignorance not wilful, or by unavoidable accident. Ignorance is considered to be wilful, where a person neglects the means of information, which ordinary prudence would suggest; and accident is not unavoidable, which reasonable diligence might have prevented. When the Plaintiff became the assignee of a lease containing such a conditional covenant for renewal, ordinary prudence would have suggested, and reasonable diligence would have required, that he should have ascertained who the lives were, and have taken measures to secure early information of their deaths. All this he appears to have neglected, his ignorance, therefore, was wilful and the accident not unavoidable ..."

In *London Corporation* v. *Mitford*,[44] the covenant for renewal was one whereby the landlord would, a month previously to the expiration of the lease, upon request grant another lease. The tenant did not apply for a renewal within the time allowed. Lord Eldon, dismissing the tenant's claim for specific performance, said:

> "... where there has been default of this kind in making a request, unless it has been excused by circumstances, there is no authority for decreeing a specific performance ..."

Exceptional circumstances may, therefore, exist which will justify the tenant's failure to give proper notice of his desire for a renewal. Such circumstances were found to exist in the case of *Hunter* v. *Earl of Hopetoun*,[45] where the tenant under a lease for 19 years, perpetually renewable on 12 months' previous notice before the expiry of each term, brought an action to compel the landlord to renew the lease for the period from 1842 to 1861. In his defence, the landlord pleaded that the lease had been

---

[44] (1807) 14 Ves. 41; 33 E.R. 437.

[45] (1865) 13 L.T. 130. See also, *Statham* v. *Liverpool Dock Co.* (1830) 3 Y. & J. 565; 148 E.R. 1304, where, in unusual circumstances, the tenant was relieved from the strict performance of his obligations under the renewal covenant since, otherwise, the landlord would have been enabled to take advantage of his own wrong.

forfeited for breaches of various covenants on the part of the tenant. The tenant's action remained dormant whilst the parties negotiated over a draft renewal of the lease. These negotiations continued for some time (the delay being caused primarily by the landlord) and, in due course, the time arrived for the tenant to give notice of renewal of another term from 1861 to 1880. The tenant failed to give such notice and the landlord commenced an action seeking a declaration that, because the tenant had failed in 1860 to demand a renewal, the lease had become forfeited and he was no longer bound to give a renewal. The House of Lords rejected this argument and held that, whilst the *lis pendens* as to the existence of the lease existed, the tenant was excused from making a demand for a further renewal. The basis for the decision appears to be that it would have been inequitable for the landlord to insist on compliance with the terms of the covenant for renewal of which he himself was denying the existence in the tenant's action.

In *Brooke* v. *Garrod*,[46] a case involving a right of pre-emption contained in a will, it was opined by Lord Cranworth[47] that equitable relief would be available in circumstances where, although the grantee was ready and willing to comply with a condition precedent, he was prevented from doing so by reason of the delay or contrivance of the other contracting party. Similarly, relief will be available where the condition is in the nature of a penalty.[48]

Although it is difficult to extract from the cases any underlying theory governing relief from the forfeiture of options, nevertheless, it is submitted that a tenant, whose diligent efforts to comply with his obligations are unavailing *through no fault of his own*,[49] will be placed in the same position as he would have acquired had he strictly complied with the requirements of his lease.

Specific performance of the renewal covenant

Analogous to the issue whether the tenant is entitled to seek relief against the forfeiture of his right of renewal upon the non-fulfilment of the pre-conditions contained in the renewal covenant, is the question whether he may successfully claim specific performance of the renewal covenant in circumstances where he has committed breaches of *other* covenants in the lease in respect of which the landlord has sued for possession of the premises.[50]

[46] (1857) 2 De G. & J. 62; 44 E.R. 911.
[47] *Ibid.*, 67; 913.
[48] *Wallis* v. *Crimes* (1667) 1 Cas. in Ch. 89; 22 E.R. 708 and *Priestley* v. *Holgate* (1857) 3 K. & J. 286, 288; 69 E.R. 1116, 1117, *per* Sir Page Wood V.-C.
[49] See, *Clarke* v. *Parker* (1812) 19 Ves. 1, 17–18; 34 E.R. 419–425, *per* Lord Eldon L.C.
[50] See, generally, White & Tudor's *Leading Cases in Equity*, (9th ed., 1928), Vol. 2, pp. 233–235; Woodfall's *Law of Landlord and Tenant*, (21st ed.) p. 145.

The question arose in *Thompson* v. *Guyon*.[51] In this case, a lease for 21 years contained a proviso for re-entry on non-performance of any of the tenant's covenants. It also contained a covenant that at the end of the term, if it should not be sooner determined by the tenant's acts or defaults, the landlord would grant the tenant a lease for a further term of 14 years. Following the expiry of the term, the landlord brought an action for ejectment alleging a breach of the tenant's covenant to insure during the term. It was significant that the landlord was not aware of the tenant's breach until only after the expiry of the term. The tenant filed a bill for specific performance of the covenant to renew and for an injunction to restrain the landlord's action. The issue before the court was not whether the tenant should be relieved from any forfeiture but whether the breach of covenant to insure deprived him of his right to specific performance. It was argued that the landlord's covenant to renew was not dependent on the tenant paying the rent and performing the other covenants in the lease. However, Sir Lancelot Shadwell V.-C., refusing the tenant's motion, stated[52]:

> "If, during the existence of a lease, such a breach of covenant is committed by a tenant, as that a Court of Equity would not have interfered to prevent the landlord from taking advantage of the forfeiture of the lease, had he known of the breach and proceeded to determine the lease, he ought not to be placed in a worse situation after the expiration of the term than he would have been in had he known of the breach and availed himself of it before the term expired."

The case confirmed the view that a landlord could not be called on to fulfil his covenant to renew unless the tenant had properly performed his covenants in the lease. The same conclusion was reached in *Walker* v. *Jeffreys*,[53] where various mines were conveyed to a trustee on trust to grant a lease of the same for 42 years and, at the request of the tenants at any time after the expiry of the lease, to grant a further lease of the mines for 21 years to commence at the expiration of the first term. Shortly before the first term expired, the tenants applied for a renewal which was refused. There was evidence that the tenants had, in breach of covenant, discontinued working the mines. On this point, Sir James Wigram V.-C. observed[54]:

> "The general rule in equity I take to be that a party who asks the Court to enforce an agreement in his favour must aver and prove that he

---

[51] (1831) 5 Sim. 65; 58 E.R. 262.
[52] *Ibid.* p. 72; p. 264.
[53] (1842) 1 Hare 342; 66 E.R. 1064. See also, *Gregory* v. *Wilson* (1852) 9 Hare 683; 68 E.R. 687.
[54] *Ibid.* p. 352; p. 1069.

has performed, or been ready and willing to perform, the agreement on his part. Where, however, the strict application of this general rule would work injustice the Court will relax it . . . But if it has been by the default of the [tenants] that the beneficial interest of the [landlords] in the mines has been wholly destroyed or suspended, and if . . . the [tenants] work the mines only to support and protect their buildings on the surface, and did not intend to work the mines, whether able or unable to work them, I am satisfied that I ought to refuse the decree which the [tenants] ask."

Again, in *Job* v. *Banister*,[55] specific performance of a covenant to renew was refused on the basis that the tenant was in breach of his covenant to insure and repair the premises.[56] The refusal of relief in this case was particularly harsh since the tenant had expended thousands of pounds in building ten houses on the premises during the term of the lease which considerably increased their value. In the words of Sir William Page Wood V.-C.[57]:

"I believe the only case in which this Court will now interfere is where the omission is to perform a covenant to make a simple money payment. The expenditure upon the property which the Plaintiff has made affords no ground for relief. He was then the owner of it, and was at liberty to build on it as he pleased. The landlord was not bound to interfere and prevent him doing so, because his interest might be determined."

Similarly, in *Greville* v. *Parker*[58] the Privy Council held that a tenant, who had persistently neglected to perform various repairing covenants in the lease, could not enforce an option for an extended term which was expressed in the lease to be conditional upon performance of the covenants. Accordingly, the tenant's claim for specific performance of the renewal covenant was rejected.

Modern authorities

There is virtually no modern English authority on the extent and scope of equity's jurisdiction to relieve against the forfeiture of a tenant's inter-

---

[55] (1856) 2 K. & J. 374; 69 E.R. 827. See also, *Finch* v. *Underwood* (1876) 2 Ch. D. 310; *Bastin* v. *Bidwell* (1881) 18 Ch. D. 238; *West Country Cleaners (Falmouth) Ltd.* v. *Saly* [1966] 1 W.L.R. 1485, (C.A.).

[56] The landlord covenanted "provided the rents should have been paid and the covenants kept" at the request in writing of the tenant, to provide a licence from the lord of the manor to demise the premises for a further term of 21 years and, on obtaining such licence, to grant a new lease with the same covenants including the covenant for renewal.

[57] *Ibid.* p. 379; p. 829.

[58] [1910] A.C. 335, (P.C.).

est under an option to renew a lease.[59] The only case directly in point is *Peeling* v. *Guidice*,[60] where a clause in the lease gave the tenant a right to extend the term for a further period of two years provided that he gave notice to the landlord asking for the extension not less than three months before the end of the original term. The tenant was serving a sentence of imprisonment at the relevant time and was not able to serve his notice of extension until after his release. Although the Court of Appeal accepted that, as a matter of principle, equity could relieve against the strictness of time in an option to renew in respect of accident or misfortune on the tenant's part which he could not prevent by reasonable diligence, the fact that the tenant was in prison at the material time was not considered a valid reason for affording relief.

The decision of Goff J. in *Boobyer* v. *Thornville Properties Ltd.*,[61] concerning the failure of a purchaser to give proper notice of the exercise of a conditional contract of sale, is also illuminating. Here, the purchaser, less than the required three months before the expiration of three years from the date of the contract, gave written notice to extend the contract. The vendor contended that the contract had become unenforceable because the provision as to notice had not been complied with. The purchaser, whilst conceding that the notice was defective, argued that there was jurisdiction in equity to relieve against ignorance or mistake, relying on the case of *Harries* v. *Bryant*. Goff J., whilst accepting that he had jurisdiction where the mistake was not the result of lack of diligence or failure to take reasonable precautions, refused equitable relief on the ground that the purchaser had failed to explain how or why the mistake as to notice had arisen. He said[62]:

> "... that there is nothing to take the case out of the ordinary well established rule that an option must be exercised strictly within the prescribed time."

A similar point arose in *Samuel Properties (Development) Ltd.* v. *Hayek*,[63] a case concerning a landlords' failure to serve due notice of a rent review on the tenant. The landlords' review notice was held invalid on the ground that it had been served out of time contrary to the mandatory time-limits set out in the lease.[64] The Court of Appeal also held that there was no

---

[59] If an option to purchase is not made conditional on the performance of the tenant's obligations, the landlord cannot destroy the option, after its exercise but before completion is due, by himself exercising a power of re-entry: *Rafferty* v. *Schofield* [1897] Ch. 937. See also, *Penman* v. *Mackay* [1922] S.C. 385.

[60] (1963) 186 E.G. 113.

[61] (1968) 19 P. & C.R. 768.

[62] *Ibid.* p. 771.

[63] [1972] 1 W.L.R. 1296, (C.A.). See also, *Hynes Ltd.* v. *Independent Newspapers* [1980] I.R. 204.

[64] This part of the decision is no longer good law following the House of Lords decision in *United Scientific Holdings Ltd.* v. *Burnley Borough Council* [1978] A.C. 904.

jurisdiction in equity to relieve the landlords from the consequences of their failure to serve notice in time. A number of authorities were cited on behalf of the landlords in support of the contention that the Court had jurisdiction to relieve, including *Eaton* v. *Lyon, Harries* v. *Bryant* and *Reid* v. *Blagrave* but all these cases were considered to be against the landlords on the ground that they limited relief to cases of either fraud, mistake or unavoidable accident. In the instant case, the landlords' failure to give proper notice was characterised as being due to gross negligence. Edmund Davies L.J. said[65]:

> "... the power of a lessor on due notice to increase rent involves, in effect, the making of a new contract between the parties, subject in the present case to compliance by the lessor with a condition precedent. It resembles options and these are undoubtedly required to be exercised in strict conformity with the terms by which they were created ... if that is not done, relief will in general be granted only where, by unconscionable conduct by the proposed recipient of the notice to exercise the option, the other party has been led to believe that strict adherence to its terms will not be insisted upon."[66]

Although the Court of Appeal's ruling that it had no jurisdiction to grant relief rendered academic any question as to whether, as a matter of discretion, relief should be given on the particular facts, nevertheless, Edmund Davies L.J. ventured to suggest that it would not be proper to grant relief in any event, having regard to the conduct of the tenant against whom relief was sought (in no way had the tenant misled the landlords) and the prejudice that he would suffer which could not be overcome by monetary compensation if relief was granted. In this connection, because of the landlords' default, the tenant had been assured of seven more years of occupation at the old rent and the only compensation offered by the landlords to counter-balance the loss of this valuable accrued right was that the new rent would only become payable from the date of its determination and not retrospectively from an earlier date.

Some conclusions

It will be apparent from the foregoing review of the English caselaw, that equitable relief will not normally be available to a tenant who fails to comply strictly with the terms of a renewal covenant. It will, in general, be granted only in respect of accident or misfortune which the tenant could not prevent by reasonable diligence or where, as a result of unconscionable conduct on the part of the landlord, the tenant has been misled to

---

[65] *Ibid.* p. 1307.
[66] In *Hinds* v. *Randall* (1961) 177 E.G. 733, due to the tenant's mistake, the renewal notice did not refer to all of the subject premises. The notice was construed strictly and held invalid.

believe that strict compliance with the terms of the renewal/option covenant will not be insisted upon. There is no modern case where such relief
has been granted to a tenant seeking a renewal.

As to whether relief is available against the loss of a right of renewal in
circumstances where the tenant is in breach of other covenants in the
lease, English authority has consistently denied relief regardless of the
hardship caused to the defaulting tenant.[67] In the words of Wootten J. in
Evanel Property Ltd. v. *Stellar Mining N.L.*[68]:

> "Neither equity's traditional jurisdiction to relieve against forfeiture,
> nor the long standing statutory provisions relating to forfeiture of
> leases, extended to relief against the loss of a right to exercise an
> option."[69]

Although in England, as in most Commonwealth jurisdictions, statute[70] provides for relief against forfeiture of *a lease* based on a tenant's
failure to perform a covenant, it is evident that this statutory jurisdiction
has no application where a landlord is resisting specific performance of a
covenant to renew which is conditional on the performance of the
tenant's covenants. This was established in *Greville* v. *Parker*,[71] where the
Privy Council held that there was nothing in section 94(1) of the New
Zealand Property Law Act 1908[72] which gave the court jurisdiction to
grant relief against the performance of a condition precedent. It was this
lack of jurisdiction which prompted several states in Australia and New
Zealand to enact legislation giving the courts power to grant relief against
the loss of a right to exercise an option. There is much to be said for this
legislation and it is regrettable that in England the matter is still governed
by old authorities which (in the absence of fraud, accident or surprise)
deny any form of relief to the defaulting tenant regardless of the merits of
the case.

---

[67] See, *e.g. Job* v. *Banister* (1856) 2 K. & J. 279; 69 E.R. 827.

[68] [1982] 1 N.S.W.L.R. 380, 386.

[69] The provision for an option subject to performance of the conditions of the lease has been
regarded simply as a conditional offer, and unless the conditions were fulfilled, the offer
could not be accepted: See, *Gilbert J. McCaul (Aust.) Property Limited* v. *Pitt Club Ltd.* (1959)
S.R. (N.S.W.) 122.

[70] See, s. 146 of the Law of Property Act 1925. For an historical review of the statutory
provisions providing for relief against forfeiture, see Chap. 7.

[71] [1910] A.C. 335.

[72] This is virtually identical to the English provision contained now in s. 146 of the Law of
Property Act 1925.

Part IV: Proposals for reform

Chapter Twelve

Reform of the law of forfeiture of leases

Introduction

In 1985, the Law Commission, as part of its programme for the cod-ification of the law of landlord and tenant, published a report entitled, *Forfeiture of Tenancies*[1] which examined various defects in the current law and recommended the replacement of the present structure with an entirely new system. Over seven years have now passed since the publi-cation of this Report, but there is still little expectation that the Law Commission's recommendations will become law in the foreseeable future.[2]

The justification for a radical change is that the present law "besides being unnecessarily complicated, is no longer coherent and may give rise to injustice."[3] The proposed new scheme would simplify the law by providing for a system of termination orders under which either the landlord or the tenant would be entitled to terminate the tenancy upon the fault of the other. At present, where the landlord is in breach of his obligations under the lease, the tenant may have no means of bringing the relationship of landlord and tenant to an end because his lease is unlikely to contain a right to terminate on the part of the tenant.[4] The inclusion of a tenant's right to terminate in the new scheme would, therefore, introduce a novel right not previously enjoyed by tenants.

---

[1] (1985) Law Com. No. 142. See also, P. F. Smith, "Reform of the Law of Forfeiture", (1986) Conv. 165.
[2] Work continues on a draft bill to give effect to the Law Commission's scheme: See 26th Annual Report (1991) of the Law Commission, para. 2.44., Law Com. No. 206.
[3] See para. 1.3, *ibid*.
[4] But see, *Hussein* v. *Mehlman* [1992] 32 E.G. 59, where it was held that a lease could come to an end by the tenant's acceptance of his landlord's repudiatory conduct.

Defects in the present law

The Law Commission noted three major sources of difficulty under the present law, namely (1) the doctrine of re-entry (2) the doctrine of waiver and (3) the separate regimes for forfeiture for non-payment of rent and all other breaches of covenant. Essentially, its report recommends abolition of the first two defects and assimilation of the rules of forfeiture for non-payment of rent and other breaches of covenant into a single comprehensive code. It will be convenient to consider each of the three defects separately.

(1) *The doctrine of re-entry*[5]

Under the doctrine of re-entry, a landlord forfeits a lease by re-entry upon the demised premises and the lease terminates on the date on which the re-entry takes place. In the case of an actual re-entry, this means that the lease will become forfeited from the moment the landlord physically re-enters upon the premises. However, the practice of actual physical re-entry has now largely given way to what the Law Commission terms "constructive re-entry", namely, re-entry which is not actual but which involves the initiation by the landlord of court proceedings for possession of the premises. In this case, a notional re-entry is deemed to take place from the date when the writ or summons is served on the tenant.[6] This gives rise to the anomaly that, although the lease is notionally forfeited from that date, nevertheless, the tenant remains in possession of the premises for an indefinite period until the final outcome of the landlord's proceedings. Accordingly, the date of the service of the writ or summons has no real legal significance and there is no reason why it should mark the ending of the lease. Moreover, because the lease is deemed to end when the landlord's proceedings are served on the tenant, the proceedings themselves have taken an artificial form. Instead of taking the form of proceedings to end the tenancy, they are framed as proceedings for possession.

Because the lease is deemed to end at the time of re-entry, there is the further difficulty that all the obligations which it imposes upon the tenant terminate also at that time.[7] As noted earlier, the tenant will remain in possession for an indefinite period after forfeiture and, during this period, he will be under no obligation to pay rent or to perform any of his other covenants in the lease unless he is subsequently granted relief from forfeiture. During this twilight period, the status of the lease is somewhat

[5] See paras. 3.3–3.10, *ibid*.
[6] *Canas Property Co. Ltd.* v. *K.L. Television Services Ltd.* [1970] 2 Q.B. 433, (C.A.).
[7] See further, Chap. 3, pp. 86–87.

obscure, the landlord is deprived of his right to claim rent or to seek any equitable remedy (*e.g.* an injunction) to enforce the tenant's covenant's and any damages payable for breaches by a tenant of his covenant to repair are assessable only down to the service of the writ or summons.

In view of these difficulties, the Commission recommended[8] the abolition of the doctrine of re-entry and its replacement by a scheme under which (apart from termination by agreement) court proceedings and a termination order would always be necessary to end a lease and until that time it would simply continue in full force. The recommendation is eminently sensible and would do away with all the present difficulties associated with the doctrine of re-entry.

(2) *The doctrine of waiver*[9]

The Law Commission viewed the doctrine of waiver of forfeiture as artificial and grounded in the doctrine of re-entry. At present, the landlord may lose his right of forfeiture for a particular breach by the mere act of a demand or acceptance of rent irrespective of his intention. With the introduction of the scheme for termination orders, the lease would remain in existence until the court decided whether or not, in its discretion, to terminate it and rent would continue to be payable until that time. Accordingly, there would no longer be any justification for inferring a waiver from the mere demand or acceptance of rent or, moreover, from any conduct by the landlord amounting merely to a recognition of the continued existence of the lease. The Commission would, therefore, replace the current doctrine of waiver with a new rule to the effect that the landlord would lose his right to a termination order only if his conduct, after he had actual knowledge of the event, was such that it would lead a reasonable tenant to believe, and did in fact lead the actual tenant to believe, that he would not seek a termination order on the ground of that event.[10] This would be a question of fact to be decided in the light of the circumstances of each individual case and, if the event was a continuing breach of covenant, it would equally be a question of fact whether and how far the landlord's conduct indicated a waiver for the future as well as for the past. Such a formulation, however, has the disadvantage of uncertainty and may be more difficult to apply in some cases than the present doctrine of waiver. The Commission, however, counter such disadvantage by noting that any uncertainty would be shortlived because it would soon be overtaken by the passing of the six months' time period for the bringing of termination proceedings.[11]

[8] See para. 3.7, *ibid.*
[9] See para. 3.35 and Pt VI, *ibid.*
[10] See para. 6.8, *ibid.*
[11] See para. 6.11, *ibid.*

(3) *Separate regimes for forfeiture for non-payment of rent and all other breaches of covenant*[12]

The Law Commission noted that the present distinction, in relation to relief against forfeiture, between cases involving non-payment of rent and other breaches of covenant, gave rise to unnecessary complexity in the law. The distinction has an historical basis in so far as from early times equity granted relief against non-payment of rent upon payment of the arrears and costs of the action, viewing the landlord's right to forfeit on this ground as no more than security for the payment of a specific sum of money. On the other hand, so far as other breaches of covenant were concerned, the old Court of Chancery considered that the forfeiture clause should be fully enforced (even if the default could be put right) unless there was some element of fraud, accident, mistake or surprise which rendered it equitable to grant relief.[13] Coupled with this attitude lay equity's inherent inability to compensate the landlord for any loss occasioned by a breach other than non-payment of rent by means of an appropriate award of damages.

Whilst the jurisdiction to grant relief in non-rent cases was considerably extended by legislation during the nineteenth century, equity's inherent power to relieve in cases of non-payment of rent was also embodied in separate legislative provisions during this period, with the result that there now exists two parallel systems of relief each operating to produce very similar results. The Law Commission, accordingly, proposed the removal of these two regimes and their replacement by a much simplified, unified structure. There is no doubt that such a reform is long overdue, particularly because, as has been shown, the reason for having two separate systems for relief is largely historical.

(4) *Other defects*

In addition to the major defects outlined above, the Commission also noted[14] other defects which its new scheme of termination orders would remove. These defects may conveniently be summarised as follows:

   (a)   The rule that a landlord cannot forfeit for breach of covenant unless the tenancy contains a forfeiture clause adds unnecessary verbiage to leases;

   (b)   The implied condition against denial of the landlord's title is anomalous and outdated;

   (c)   The law concerning relief against forfeiture contains many

---

[12] See paras. 3.11–3.13, *ibid*.
[13] See further, Chap. 7.
[14] See paras. 3.14–3.23, *ibid*.

shortcomings quite apart from the dichotomy between cases of non-payment of rent and other breaches of covenant already mentioned earlier. Thus, to take one example, unnecessary differences exist in the parties' rights depending on whether proceedings are commenced in the High Court or in a county court;

(d) The law concerning formal demand for rent is obsolete;

(e) The exceptional cases in which the tenant is prevented by section 146 of the Law of Property Act 1925 from claiming relief are a source of potential unfairness and should not be reproduced in a new scheme;

(f) The requirement of the service of a section 146 notice on the tenant in all cases (other than non-payment of rent) causes difficulties and uncertainties. In this connection, the Law Commission considered that, whilst there was no justification for maintaining the two separate regimes which exist under the present law, there was a strong case for retaining a special notice requirement for cases involving breaches of covenant to repair;

(g) The fact that a breach of covenant, once remedied, cannot be the subject of forfeiture proceedings may be unfair to the landlord, particularly because it prevents a lease being ended for persistent breaches (*e.g.* of the covenant to pay rent);

(h) Conversely, the doctrine of "stigma", which leads to relief being invariably refused in cases of illegal or immoral user of the premises, may be unfair to the tenant;

(i) The rules concerning relief for sub-tenants and other holders of derivative interests are inadequate in many respects and require complete revision;

(j) The court's present inability to grant relief to fewer than all of a number of joint tenants is a source of potential unfairness.

An outline of the new scheme

The new scheme contains essentially two main elements, namely, (1) a termination order procedure under which a landlord[15] is given the right to terminate a lease[15a] for fault on the part of the tenant by means of either an "absolute" termination order or a termination order made absolute on failure by the tenant to comply with a "remedial" termination order and (2) a termination order procedure under which the tenant is given the

---

[15] It is intended that the scheme would bind the Crown: see paras. 3.68 and 14.4, *ibid.*
[15a] The Law Commission's proposals would apply to a lease, underlease and any other tenancy whether formal or informal and whether legal or equitable. Thus, an equitable lease arising by virtue of an agreement for a lease under the rule in *Walsh* v. *Lonsdale* (1882) 21 Ch. D. 9 would be included but not a statutory tenancy under the Rent Act 1977: See, para. 1.6.

right to terminate the lease for non-compliance by the landlord of his obligations under the lease.

(1) *The landlord's termination order procedure*[16]

As already mentioned, the general intention of the new scheme is to abolish the present law of forfeiture[17] (in particular, the doctrine of re-entry) and to replace it with a structure which makes no distinction between termination for non-payment of rent and termination for other breaches of covenant and under which the lease continues in full force until the date on which the court orders that it should terminate. The scheme is, therefore, intended to apply to existing tenancies as well as to those granted in the future.[18]

A landlord is permitted to apply for a termination order only upon the happening of a "termination order event" which may include any of the following:

(a) *Breaches of covenant*[19]

Under this heading, all breaches of covenant by the tenant (including express and implied obligations) are to be classified as termination order events. It would not be necessary to make any of the tenant's obligations subject to a right of forfeiture in the lease but, in the case of leases granted before the new legislation came into force, a breach of covenant would be the subject of the termination scheme only if it was covered by a proviso for re-entry in the lease.

(b) *Disguised breaches of covenant*[20]

These would, broadly, be breaches by the tenant of obligations imposed on him otherwise than by covenant. Thus, a termination order event would include all events (involving fault on the part of the tenant[21]) on the happening of which the lease (whether through the inclusion of a

---

[16] See paras. 3.26–3.71 and 4.1–16.18, *ibid*.

[17] The scheme would apply to the exclusion of the present law of forfeiture, except where the landlord had a ground for forfeiture and had taken action on it before the "operative date" for the scheme. Termination order events occurring before the operative date would be capable of founding termination proceedings provided the landlord had not, before that date, become disqualified (*e.g.* through waiver or remedial action) from forfeiting the lease because of them: See paras. 3.69–3.71 and 15.1–15.16, *ibid*.

[18] Transitional provisions are dealt with in paras. 3.69–3.71, *ibid*.

[19] See paras. 5.2–5.9, *ibid*.

[20] See paras. 5.10–5.18, *ibid*.

[21] Neutral events (*e.g.* grant of planning permission), the happening of which do not connote fault on the part of the tenant, would fall outside the scheme: See paras. 5.11–5.14, *ibid*.

condition or limitation or for any other reason) was expressed to cease (whether immediately or after a period) or the landlord was to have the right (whether or not on notice) to apply for a termination order.[22]

(c) *Insolvency events*[23]

These are events which are concerned with the tenant's insolvency and on which the lease has been made terminable by the landlord.

In relation to breaches of covenant generally, it is proposed that non-payment of rent should become a termination order event, without a formal demand for rent, whenever rent is overdue for 21 days or for such other period as may be prescribed in the lease. There would no longer be any implied condition about denial of the landlord's title so that such a denial by the tenant would not qualify as a termination order event unless prohibited by express wording in the lease.

As mentioned earlier, the new scheme would abolish the present doctrine of waiver and replace it with the rule that "the landlord loses his right [to seek a termination order] . . . only if his conduct is such that a reasonable tenant would believe, and the actual tenant does in fact believe, that he will not seek a termination order."[24] A further innovation is that a termination order event would, generally speaking, remain available as a ground for a termination order despite the fact that its consequences may have been remedied.[25] The rule is aimed, for example, at a tenant who, although eventually pays his rent, is persistently late in doing so. The rule would not, however, be confined to such cases and would apply equally to other persistent breaches of covenant and to single/isolated breaches (whether remediable or not).

Under the new scheme, a landlord's right to take termination proceedings founded on a particular termination order event would continue for only six months after he first had knowledge of that event.[26] The position would differ if the event was a continuing breach of covenant in so far as the six month limitation period would run from the date on which the breach was last continuing.

There would be no general requirement (such as now exists under section 146(1) of the Law of Property Act 1925) for the landlord to serve notice on the tenant before commencing termination proceedings.[27] In the case of disrepair, however, the giving of notice would still be compulsory and, if the tenant served a counter-notice, the landlord would not

[22] See para. 5.18, *ibid*.
[23] See paras. 5.19–5.20, *ibid*.
[24] para. 3.35, *ibid*.
[25] See para. 3.36 and Pt VII, *ibid*.
[26] para. 3.37 and Pt VIII, *ibid*.
[27] para. 3.38 and Pt VIII, *ibid*.

be able to start termination proceedings without leave of the court.[28] In other cases, there would be an optional notice procedure which would involve the landlord serving notice on the tenant giving details of the breach and specifying the remedial action required.[29] This would then extend the six month limitation period (mentioned earlier) so that it ended six months after the service of the landlord's notice.

At the hearing of the proceedings, the court would essentially have three basic options, namely, (a) to make an absolute order which would terminate the lease unconditionally on a date specified in the order; (b) to make a remedial order which would operate to terminate the lease only if the tenant failed to take prescribed remedial action[30] by a date specified or (c) to decline to make an order of either kind.[31] The court would also have powers to make consequential orders in relation to the payment of costs and rent/mesne profits and the imposition of terms (for example, by injunction or the payment of damages).[32] Needless to say, the ending of the lease by means of a termination order (whether absolute or remedial) would not prejudice any statutory security of tenure (for example, under the Rent Act 1977 or Housing Act 1988) which the tenant might enjoy.[33]

The Law Commission set out guidelines as to the circumstances in which an absolute order should be made by the court.[34] In paragraph 3.46 of their Report, they state that an absolute order should be made only:

"Where the court is satisfied, by reason of the serious character of any termination order events occurring during the tenure of the present tenant, or by reason of their frequency, or by a combination of both factors, that he is so unsatisfactory a tenant that he ought not in all the circumstances to remain tenant of the property."

This formulation is intended to achieve a number of objectives. First, it is intended to ensure that the court considers the tenant's breaches in the wider context of providing an indication that the tenant is so unsatisfactory that he should not be allowed to remain as tenant. Thus, it is designed to change the tendency of the present law to look backwards rather than forwards in relation to the tenant's conduct. Secondly, it is intended to militate against the current doctrine of "stigma" under which breaches involving illegality or immorality are assumed to cast a stigma on the premises thereby precluding the tenant from successfully claiming relief from forfeiture. The broad effect of the new provisions would be to

[28] See currently, the Leasehold Property (Repairs) Act 1938 (considered in detail in Chap. 5, pp. 124–132).
[29] See para. 3.40 and Pt VIII, *ibid.*
[30] As to the form of remedial action envisaged, see para. 3.44, *ibid.*
[31] See para. 3.41 and Pt IX, *ibid.*
[32] See para. 3.42, *ibid.*
[33] See para. 3.45, *ibid.*
[34] See para. 3.46 and Pt IX, *ibid.*

replace the present law on relief from forfeiture by a primary discretion which would be exercisable by the court when the landlord applied for a termination order.

The Law Commission envisaged three other cases in which an absolute order would be appropriate. The first is intended to prevent the possibility of an absolute order being avoided by a last minute assignment of the lease by the tenant to an associated person or company. The second makes special provision for cases where the termination order event is itself an assignment of the lease in breach of covenant or is an insolvency event.[35] In these cases, the test would be whether any remedial action which the court could order would be adequate and satisfactory to the landlord.[36] The third arises if the court, though it would otherwise wish to make a remedial order rather than an absolute one, is not satisfied that the tenant is willing, and is likely to be able, to carry out the remedial action which would be required of him.[37]

Because of the stringent requirements associated with the making of an absolute order, the Commission envisaged that, in most cases, the remedial order would be the normal type of order made by the courts. (The third option, namely, to make no order at all, would only be exercised if remedial action had already been taken or if it was impossible or unnecessary).[38] So far as costs are concerned, this would be entirely at the discretion of the court subject to a specific power to make the landlord pay the tenant's costs if satisfied that the tenant would have taken appropriate remedial action before the hearing if the landlord had given him a sufficient opportunity of doing so.[39]

The subject of derivative interests is dealt with at some length in the Commission's Report.[40] Essentially, the Commission would preserve the current rule under which the ending of the lease necessarily involves the automatic termination of any sub-tenancies, mortgages or other interests derived from it.[41] At the same time, it would introduce entirely new powers for a landlord to voluntarily preserve derivative interests if he wished so to do. Relief would also be available to holders of derivative interests along the lines of the present law, except that (a) there would be a new definition of those eligible for relief ("the derivative class"); (b) the court would have new powers to preserve the existing interests of members of the derivative class as opposed to ordering the grant of new interests to them and (c) the court's existing powers to order the grant of

---

[35] See para. 3.50, *ibid.*
[36] See para. 3.51, *ibid.*
[37] See para. 3.52, *ibid.*
[38] See para. 3.53, *ibid.*
[39] See para. 3.54, *ibid.*
[40] See paras. 3.55–3.59 and Pt X, *ibid.*
[41] The existing exception in s. 137 of the Rent Act 1977 would also be maintained.

new leases would be extended and several difficulties under the present law, (for example, the anomalous position which arises when a new lease is granted to a former mortgagee) would also be resolved. So as to ensure that the derivative class would have an opportunity to seek relief, the landlord would have new powers to obtain their identity and to serve warning notices upon them.

Several important changes to the present law were also recommended in relation to abandoned premises.[42] Under the new scheme, if the landlord reasonably believed the demised premises to have been abandoned, he would have the right to secure and preserve them, absolved from any liability in trespass which he might otherwise incur under the general law. Moreover, if the landlord reasonably believed the premises to have been abandoned and there was at least one termination order event in respect of which he would be entitled to seek a termination order, he would have the right to serve notices which would operate, if no response was made within six months, to terminate the lease without the need for court proceedings. These notices would be served (by substituted service if necessary) on the tenant and any members of the derivative class of whom the landlord had knowledge. If any response was forthcoming, the landlord would be obliged to initiate termination order proceedings in the normal way.

On the subject of joint tenants,[43] the Commission felt that the court should have power, on application, to preserve a lease in favour of one or more joint tenants provided that this would not cause unjustifiable prejudice to the landlord. A similar power would be available in favour of joint holders of derivative interests.

With the abolition of the doctrine of re-entry under the proposed scheme, it was necessary for the Commission to deal specifically with the case where, under the present law, the landlord has the power to end a tenancy by re-entry on the happening of a specified event which does not connote fault on the part of the tenant. Under the new structure, the landlord would have the power to end the lease in these cases by one month's written notice to the tenant.[44]

(2) *The tenant's termination order procedure*[45]

Under the present law, it is very unusual to find terms in a lease entitling the tenant to terminate it for fault on the part of the landlord.[46]

---

[42] See paras. 3.60–3.62 and Pt XI, *ibid.*
[43] See paras. 3.63–3.65 and Pt XII, *ibid.*
[44] See paras. 3.66 and Pt XIII, *ibid.* Waiver and the six months' limitation period would apply to these cases.
[45] See paras. 3.72–3.93 and Pt XVII, *ibid.*
[46] There is, of course, nothing in theory to prevent the parties from incorporating such a provision in their lease should they so desire.

This part of the scheme, therefore, would create entirely new law. It would enable the tenant to bring termination proceedings (despite any stipulation to the contrary) upon the occurrence of one particular termination order event, namely, breaches of covenant by the landlord.[47] The new provisions regarding waiver and remediable breaches (applicable to landlords) would apply equally to tenants so that, for example, a tenant could seek a termination order, even though the breach had been remedied, so as to allow him to take action on the basis of persistent breaches by the landlord (*e.g.* of the covenant to repair).[48] The scheme would also incorporate a six months' time limit for initiating proceedings and a provision for optional notice (thereby allowing the six months' period to be extended). There would, however, be no compulsory preliminary notice, even in cases where the landlord was in breach of his repairing obligations.[49]

At the hearing, the court would have the same three basic options, namely, (a) to make an absolute termination order (b) to make a remedial order or (c) to refuse to make a termination order altogether.[50] It would also have the power to make ancillary orders in relation to costs and the imposition of terms.[51]

A further innovation under the scheme would be to give the tenant the right to claim damages from the landlord for breach of covenant and for any loss suffered through the loss of his lease as a result of the operation of the termination order. In this connection, the Commission recognised that for most tenants with a term of years, the termination order scheme would serve little purpose without the right to claim damages because the tenant would lose the value of his lease which would not be covered by any current award of damages for breach of covenant.[52]

As regards derivative interests, the provisions of this part of the scheme would differ significantly from those applicable to landlords' termination orders. Most importantly, the lease could not be ended at the tenant's instance unless the court was satisfied:

> "(i) that all derivative interest holders who are sub-tenants will be adequately compensated for any losses arising through termination, and that any objections they may have are not sufficient to outweigh the desirability of termination taking place, or
> (ii) that they have consented to termination."[53]

With regard to derivative interest holders who were mortgagees,

---

[47] See para. 3.76 and Pt XVIII, *ibid*.
[48] See para. 3.77, *ibid*.
[49] See para. 3.78, *ibid*.
[50] See para. 3.79 and Pt XIX, *ibid*.
[51] See para. 3.80, *ibid*.
[52] See para. 3.81, *ibid*.
[53] See para. 3.90. See also, Pt XX, *ibid*.

requirement (i) above would be modified so as to require merely that they should receive the amount of the debt or the value of the security (whichever is the less). It is envisaged that compensation for all holders of derivative interests should come initially from the tenant himself and the extent to which he could recover it from the landlord would be largely determined by applying existing rules about remoteness of damage for breach of contract.

As to joint landlords, the Commission recognised that it would be impossible to have a situation in which some only of those who held the reversion would be bound by the lease. A lease would, therefore, have to be terminated or else continued against all joint landlords.[54]

---

[54] See para. 3.91 and XXI, *ibid*.

Part V: Main statutory provisions

Statutory provisions

Below are set out the main statutory provisions relating to the forfeiture of leases.

CONTENTS

The Common Law Procedure Act 1852[1]

Proceedings in ejectment by landlord for nonpayment of rent

210. In all cases between landlord and tenant, as often as it shall happen that one half year's rent shall be in arrear, and the landlord or lessor, to whom the same is due, hath right by law to re-enter for the nonpayment thereof, such landlord or lessor shall and may, without any formal demand or re-entry, serve a writ in ejectment for the recovery of the demised premises, . . . which service . . . shall stand in the place and stead of a demand and re-entry; and in case of judgment against the defendant for nonappearance, if it shall be made appear to the court where the said action is depending, by affidavit, or be proved upon the trial in case the defendant appears, that half a year's rent was due before the said writ was served, and that no sufficient distress was to be found on the demised premises, countervailing the arrears then due, and that the lessor had power to re-enter, then and in every such case the lessor shall recover judgment and execution, in the same manner as if the rent in arrear had been legally demanded, and a re-entry made; and in case the lessee or his assignee, or other person claiming or deriving under the said lease, shall permit and suffer judgment to be had and recovered on such trial in ejectment, and execution to be executed thereon, without paying the rent and arrears, together with full costs, and without proceeding for relief in equity within six months after such execution executed, then and in such case the said lessee, his assignee, and all other persons claiming and deriving under the said lease, shall be barred and foreclosed from all relief or remedy in law or equity, other than by bringing error for reversal of such judgment, in case the same shall be erroneous, and the said landlord or lessor shall from thenceforth hold the said demised premises discharged from such lease; . . . provided that nothing herein contained shall extend to bar the right of any mortgagee of such lease, or any part thereof, who shall not be in possession, so as such mortgagee shall and do, within six months after such judgment obtained and execution executed pay all rent in arrear, and all costs and damages sustained by such lessor or person entitled to the remainder or reversion as aforesaid, and perform all the covenants and agreements which, on the part and behalf of the first lessee, are and ought to be performed.

Lessee proceeding in equity not to have injunction or relief without payment of rent and costs

211. In case the lessee, his assignee, or other person claiming any right,

---

[1] Printed as amended by the Statute Law Revision Act 1892.

title, or interest, in law or equity, of, in, or to the said lease, shall, within the time aforesaid, proceed for relief in any court of equity, such person shall not have or continue any injunction against the proceedings at law on such ejectment, unless he does or shall, within 40 days next after a full and perfect answer shall be made by the claimant in such ejectment, bring into court, and lodge with the proper officer such sum and sums of money as the lessor or landlord shall in his answer swear to be due and in arrear over and above all just allowances, and also the costs taxed in the said suit, there to remain till the hearing of the cause, or to be paid out to the lessor or landlord on good security, subject to the decree of the court; and in case such proceedings for the relief in equity shall be taken within the time aforesaid, and after execution is executed, the lessor or landlord shall be accountable only for so much and no more as he shall really and bona fide, without fraud, deceit, or wilful neglect, make of the demised premises from the time of his entering into the actual possession thereof; and if what shall be so made by the lessor or landlord happen to be less than the rent reserved on the said lease, then the said lessee or his assignee, before he shall be restored to his possession, shall pay such lessor or landlord what the money so by him made fell short of the reserved rent for the time such lessor or landlord held the said lands.

Tenant paying all rent, with costs, proceedings to cease

212. If the tenant or his assignee do or shall, at any time before the trial in such ejectment, pay or tender to the lessor or landlord, his executors or administrators, or his or their attorney in that cause, or pay into the court where the same cause is depending, all the rent and arrears, together with the costs, then and in such case all further proceedings on the said ejectment shall cease and be discontinued; and if such lessee, his executors, administrators, or assigns, shall, upon such proceedings as aforesaid, be relieved in equity, he and they shall have, hold, and enjoy the demised lands, according to the lease thereof made, without any new lease.

The Law of Property Act 1925

Creation and disposition of equitable interests

4.—(3) All rights of entry affecting a legal estate which are exercisable on condition broken or for any other reason may after the commencement of this Act, be made exercisable by any person and the persons deriving title under him, but, in regard to an estate in fee simple (not being a rentcharge held for a legal estate) only within the period authorised by the rule relating to perpetuities.

Actions for possession by mortgagors

98.—(1) A mortgagor for the time being entitled to the possession or receipt of the rents and profits of any land, as to which the mortgagee has not given notice of his intention to take possession or to enter into the receipt of the rents and profits thereof, may sue for such possession, or for the recovery of such rents or profits, or to prevent or recover damages in respect of any trespass or other wrong relative thereto, in his own name only, unless the cause of action arises upon a lease or other contract made by him jointly with any other person.

(2) This section does not prejudice the power of a mortgagor independently of this section to take proceedings in his own name only, either in right of any legal estate vested in him or otherwise.

(3) This section applies whether the mortgage was made before or after the commencement of this Act.

Rent and benefit of lessee's covenants to run with the reversion

141.—(1) Rent reserved by a lease, and the benefit of every covenant or provision therein contained, having reference to the subject-matter thereof, and on the lessee's part to be observed or performed, and every condition of re-entry and other condition therein contained, shall be annexed and incident to and shall go with the reversionary estate in the land, or in any part thereof, immediately expectant on the term granted by the lease, notwithstanding severance of that reversionary estate, and without prejudice to any liability affecting a covenantor or his estate.

(2) Any such rent, covenant or provision shall be capable of being recovered, received, enforced, and taken advantage of, by the person from time to time entitled, subject to the term, to the income of the whole or any part, as the case may require, of the land leased.

(3) Where that person becomes entitled by conveyance or otherwise, such rent, covenant or provision may be recovered, received, enforced or taken advantage of by him notwithstanding that he becomes so entitled

after the condition of re-entry or forfeiture has become enforceable, but this subsection does not render enforceable any condition of re-entry or other condition waived or released before such person becomes entitled as aforesaid.

(4) This section applies to leases made before or after the commencement of this Act, but does not affect the operation of—

(a) any severance of the reversionary estate; or

(b) any acquisition by conveyance or otherwise of the right to receive or enforce any rent covenant or provision;

effected before the commencement of this Act.

Restrictions on and relief against forfeiture of leases and underleases

146.—(1) A right of re-entry or forfeiture under any proviso or stipulation in a lease for a breach of any covenant or condition in the lease shall not be enforceable, by action or otherwise, unless and until the lessor serves on the lessee a notice—

(a) specifying the particular breach complained of; and

(b) if the breach is capable of remedy, requiring the lessee to remedy the breach; and

(c) in any case, requiring the lessee to make compensation in money for the breach;

and the lessee fails, within a reasonable time thereafter, to remedy the breach, if it is capable of remedy, and to make reasonable compensation in money, to the satisfaction of the lessor, for the breach.

(2) Where a lessor is proceeding, by action or otherwise, to enforce such a right of re-entry or forfeiture, the lessee may, in the lessor's action, if any, or in any action brought by himself, apply to the court for relief; and the court may grant or refuse relief, as the court, having regard to the proceedings and conduct of the parties under the foregoing provisions of this section, and to all the other circumstances, thinks fit; and in case of relief may grant it on such terms, if any, as to costs, expenses, damages, compensation, penalty, or otherwise, including the granting of an injunction to restrain any like breach in the future, as the court, in the circumstances of each case, thinks fit.

(3) A lessor shall be entitled to recover as a debt due to him from a lessee, and in addition to damages (if any), all reasonable costs and expenses properly incurred by the lessor in the employment of a solicitor and surveyor or valuer, or otherwise, in reference to any breach giving rise to a right of re-entry or forfeiture which, at the request of the lessee, is waived by the lessor, or from which the lessee is relieved, under the provisions of this Act.

(4) Where a lessor is proceeding by action or otherwise to enforce a right of re-entry or forfeiture under any covenant, proviso, or stipulation in a lease, or for non-payment of rent, the court may, on application by any person claiming as under-lessee any estate or interest in the property comprised in the lease or any part thereof, either in the lessor's action (if any) or in any action brought by such person for that purpose, make an order vesting, for the whole term of the lease or any less term, the property comprised in the lease or any part thereof in any person entitled as under-lessee to any estate or interest in such property upon such conditions as to execution of any deed or other document, payment of rent, costs, expenses, damages, compensation, giving security, or otherwise, as the court in the circumstances of each case may think fit, but in no case shall any such under-lessee be entitled to require a lease to be granted to him for any longer term than he had under his original sub-lease.

(5) For the purposes of this section—

(a) "Lease" includes an original or derivative under-lease; also an agreement for a lease where the lessee has become entitled to have his lease granted; also a grant at a fee farm rent, or securing a rent by condition;

(b) "Lessee" includes an original or derivative under-lessee, and the persons deriving title under a lessee; also a grantee under any such grant as aforesaid and the persons deriving title under him;

(c) "Lessor" includes an original or derivative under-lessor, and the persons deriving title under a lessor; also a person making such grant as aforesaid and the persons deriving title under him;

(d) "Under-lease" includes an agreement for an underlease where the underlessee has become entitled to have his underlease granted;

(e) "Underlessee" includes any person deriving title under an underlessee.

(6) This section applies although the proviso or stipulation under which the right of re-entry or forfeiture accrues is inserted in the lease in pursuance of the directions of any Act of Parliament.

(7) For the purposes of this section a lease limited to continue as long only as the lessee abstains from committing a breach of covenant shall be and take effect as a lease to continue for any longer term for which it could subsist, but determinable by a proviso for re-entry on such a breach.

(8) This section does not extend—

(i) To a covenant or condition against assigning, underletting,

321

parting with the possession, or disposing of the land leased where the breach occurred before the commencement of this Act; or

(ii) In the case of a mining lease, to a covenant or condition for allowing the lessor to have access to or inspect books, accounts, records, weighing machines or other things, or to enter or inspect the mine or the workings thereof.

(9) This section does not apply to a condition for forfeiture on the bankruptcy of the lessee or on taking in execution of the lessee's interest if contained in a lease of—

(a) Agricultural or pastoral land;

(b) Mines or minerals;

(c) A house used or intended to be used as a public-house or beershop;

(d) A house let as a dwelling-house, with the use of any furniture, books, works of art, or other chattels not being in the nature of fixtures;

(e) Any property with respect to which the personal qualifications of the tenant are of importance for the preservation of the value or character of the property or on the ground of neighbourhood to the lessor, or to any person holding under him.

(10) Where a condition of forfeiture on the bankruptcy of the lessee or on taking in execution of the lessee's interest is contained in any lease, other than a lease of any of the classes mentioned in the last subsection, then—

(a) if the lessee's interest is sold within one year from the bankruptcy or taking in execution, this section applies to the forfeiture condition aforesaid;

(b) if the lessee's interest is not sold before the expiration of that year, this section only applies to the forfeiture condition aforesaid during the first year from the date of the bankruptcy or taking in execution.

(11) This section does not, save as otherwise mentioned, affect the law relating to re-entry or forfeiture or relief in case of non-payment of rent.

(12) This section has effect notwithstanding any stipulation to the contrary.

(13) The county court has jurisdiction under this section—

(a) in any case where the lessor is proceeding by action in court to enforce the right of entry or forfeiture; and

(b) where the lessor is proceeding to enforce the said right otherwise than by action, in a case where the net annual value for rating of the property comprised in the lease does not exceed the county court limit.[2]

Relief against notice to effect decorative repairs

147.—(1) After a notice is served on a lessee relating to the internal decorative repairs to a house or other building, he may apply to the court for relief, and if, having regard to all the circumstances of the case (including in particular the length of the lessee's term or interest remaining unexpired), the court is satisfied that the notice is unreasonable, it may, by order, wholly or partially relieve the lessee from liability for such repairs.

(2) This section does not apply:—

  (i)   where the liability arises under an express covenant or agreement to put the property in a decorative state of repair and the covenant or agreement has never been performed;
  (ii)   to any matter necessary or proper—

    (a)   for putting or keeping the property in a sanitary condition, or
    (b)   for the maintenance or preservation of the structure;

  (iii)   to any statutory liability to keep a house in all respects reasonably fit for human habitation;
  (iv)   to any covenant or stipulation to yield up the house or other building in a specified state of repair at the end of the term.

(3) In this section "lease" includes an underlease and an agreement for a lease, and "lessee" has a corresponding meaning and includes any person liable to effect the repairs.

(4) This section applies whether the notice is served before or after the commencement of this Act, and has effect notwithstanding any stipulation to the contrary.

(5) The county court has jurisdiction under this section where the net annual value for rating of the house or other building does not exceed the county court limit.[3]

Waiver of a covenant in a lease

148.—(1) Where any actual waiver by a lessor or the persons deriving title under him of the benefit of any covenant or condition in any lease is

---

[2] subs. 13 was added by The County Courts Act 1984, s. 148 (1), sched. 2, Pt II, para. 5.
[3] subs. 5 was added by The County Courts Act 1984, s. 148 (1), sched. 2, Pt II, para. 6.

proved to have taken place in any particular instance, such waiver shall not be deemed to extend to any instance, or to any breach of covenant or condition save that to which such waiver specially relates, nor operate as a general waiver of the benefit of any such covenant or condition.

(2) This section applies unless a contrary intention appears and extends to waivers effected after the twenty-third day of July, eighteen hundred and sixty.

Regulations respecting notices

196.—(1) Any notice required or authorised to be served or given by this Act shall be in writing.

(2) Any notice required or authorised by this Act to be served on a lessee or mortgagor shall be sufficient, although only addressed to the lessee or mortgagor by that designation, without his name, or generally to the persons interested, without any name, and notwithstanding that any person to be affected by the notice is absent, under disability, unborn, or unascertained.

(3) Any notice required or authorised by this Act to be served shall be sufficiently served if it is left at the last-known place of abode or business in the United Kingdom of the lessee, lessor, mortgagee, mortgagor, or other person to be served, or, in case of a notice required or authorised to be served on a lessee or mortgagor is affixed or left for him on the land or any house or building comprised in the lease or mortgage, or, in case of a mining lease, is left for the lessee at the office or counting-house of the mine.

(4) Any notice required or authorised by this Act to be served shall also be sufficiently served, if it is sent by post in a registered letter addressed to the lessee, lessor, mortgagee, mortgagor, or other person to be served, by name, at the aforesaid place of abode or business, office, or counting-house, and if that letter is not returned through the post-office undelivered; and that service shall be deemed to be made at the time at which the registered letter would in the ordinary course be delivered.

(5) The provisions of this section shall extend to notices required to be served by any instrument affecting property executed or coming into operation after the commencement of this Act unless a contrary intention appears.

(6) This section does not apply to notices served in proceedings in the court.

THE LANDLORD AND TENANT ACT 1927

Provisions as to covenants to repair

18.—(1) Damages for a breach of a covenant or agreement to keep or put premises in repair during the currency of a lease, or to leave or put premises in repair at the termination of a lease, whether such covenant or agreement is expressed or implied, and whether general or specific, shall in no case exceed the amount (if any) by which the value of the reversion (whether immediate or not) in the premises is diminished owing to the breach of such covenant or agreement as aforesaid; and in particular no damage shall be recovered for a breach of any such covenant or agreement to leave or put premises in repair at the termination of a lease, if it is shown that the premises, in whatever state of repair they might be, would at or shortly after the termination of the tenancy have been or be pulled down, or such structural alterations made therein as would render valueless the repairs covered by the covenant or agreement.

(2) A right of re-entry or forfeiture for a breach of any such covenant or agreement as aforesaid shall not be enforceable, by action or otherwise, unless the lessor proves that the fact that such a notice as is required by section 146 of the Law of Property Act 1925, had been served on the lessee was known either—

(a) to the lessee; or
(b) to an under-lessee holding under an under-lease which reserved a nominal reversion only to the lessee; or
(c) to the person who last paid the rent due under the lease either on his own behalf or as agent for the lessee or under-lessee;

and that a time reasonably sufficient to enable the repairs to be executed had elapsed since the time when the fact of the service of the notice came to the knowledge of any such person.

Where a notice has been sent by registered post addressed to a person at his last known place of abode in the United Kingdom, then, for the purposes of this subsection, that person shall be deemed, unless the contrary is proved, to have had knowledge of the fact that the notice had been served as from the time at which the letter would have been delivered in the ordinary course of post.

This subsection shall be construed as one with section 146 of the Law of Property Act 1925.

(3) This section applies whether the lease was created before or after the commencement of this Act.

The Leasehold Property (Repairs) Act 1938[4]

Restriction on enforcement of repairing covenants in long leases of small houses

1.—(1) Where a lessor serves on a lessee under sub-section (1) of section 146 of the Law of Property Act, 1925, a notice that relates to a breach of a covenant or agreement to keep or put in repair during the currency of the lease all or any of the property comprised in the lease, and at the date of the service of the notice three years or more of the term of the lease remain unexpired, the lessee may within 28 days from that date serve on the lessor a counter-notice to the effect that he claims the benefit of this Act.

(2) A right to damages for a breach of such a covenant as aforesaid shall not be enforceable by action commenced at any time at which [three] years or more of the term of the lease remain unexpired unless the lessor has served on the lessee not less than one month before the commencement of the action such a notice as is specified in subsection (1) of section 146 of the Law of Property Act, 1925, and where a notice is served under this subsection, the lessee may, within 28 days from the date of the service thereof, serve on the lessor a counter-notice to the effect that he claims the benefit of this Act.

(3) Where a counter-notice is served by a lessee under this section, then, notwithstanding anything in any enactment or rule of law, no proceedings, by action or otherwise, shall be taken by the lessor for the enforcement of any right of re-entry or forfeiture under any proviso or stipulation in the lease for breach of the covenant or agreement in question, or for damages for breach thereof, otherwise than with the leave of the court.

(4) A notice served under subsection (1) of section 146 of the Law of Property Act, 1925, in the circumstances specified in subsection (1) of this section, and a notice served under subsection (2) of this section shall not be valid unless it contains a statement, in characters not less conspicuous than those used in any other part of the notice, to the effect that the lessee is entitled under this Act to serve on the lessor a counter-notice claiming the benefit of this Act, and a statement in the like characters specifying the time within which, and the manner in which, under this Act a counter-notice may be served and specifying the name and address for service of the lessor.

(5) Leave for the purposes of this section shall not be given unless the lessor proves—

(a) that the immediate remedying of the breach in question is

---

[4] Printed as amended by the Landlord and Tenant Act 1954 s. 51, and The County Courts Act 1959, s. 204 and Sched. 3.

requisite for preventing substantial diminution in the value of his reversion, or that the value thereof has been substantially diminished by the breach;

(*b*)   that the immediate remedying of the breach is required for giving effect in relation to the premises to the purposes of any enactment, or of any byelaw or other provision having effect under an enactment, or for giving effect to any order of a court or requirement of any authority under any enactment or any such byelaw or other provision as aforesaid;

(*c*)   in a case in which the lessee is not in occupation of the whole of the premises as respects which the covenant or agreement is proposed to be enforced, that the immediate remedying of the breach is required in the interests of the occupier of those premises or of part thereof;

(*d*)   that the breach can be immediately remedied at an expense that is relatively small in comparison with the much greater expense that would probably be occasioned by postponement of the necessary work; or

(*e*)   special circumstances which in the opinion of the court, render it just and equitable that leave should be given.

(6) The court may, in granting or in refusing leave for the purposes of this section, impose such terms and conditions on the lessor or on the lessee as it may think fit.

Restriction on right to recover expenses of survey, etc.

2. A lessor on whom a counter-notice is served under the preceding section shall not be entitled to the benefit of subsection (3) of section 146 of the Law of Property Act, 1925, (which relates to costs and expenses incurred by a lessor in reference to breaches of covenant), so far as regards any costs or expenses incurred in reference to the breach in question, unless he makes an application for leave for the purposes of the preceding section, and on such an application the court shall have power to direct whether and to what extent the lessor is to be entitled to the benefit thereof.

Saving for obligation to repair on taking possession

3. This Act shall not apply to a breach of a covenant or agreement in so far as it imposes on the lessee an obligation to put premises in repair that is to be performed upon the lessee taking possession of the premises or within a reasonable time thereafter.

4. [Repealed]

Application to past breaches

5. This Act applies to leases created, and to breaches occurring, before or after the commencement of this Act.

Court having jurisdiction under this Act

6.—(1) In this Act the expression "the court" means the county court, except in a case in which any proceedings by action for which leave may be given would have to be taken in a court other than the county court, and means in the said excepted case that other court.

(2) [Repealed]

Application of certain provisions of 15 & 16 Geo. 5 c. 20

7.—(1) In this Act the expressions "lessor", "lessee" and "lease" have the meanings assigned to them respectively by sections 146 and 154 of the Law of Property Act, 1925, except that they do not include any reference to such a grant as is mentioned in the said section 146, or to the person making, or to the grantee under such a grant, or to persons deriving title under such a person, and "lease" means a lease for a term of seven years or more, not being a lease of an agricultural holding within the meaning of the Agricultural Holdings Act, 1948.

(2) The provisions of section 196 of the said Act (which relate to the service of notices) shall extend to notices and counter-notices required or authorised by this Act.

Short title and extent

8.—(1) This Act may be cited as the Leasehold Property (Repairs) Act, 1938.

(2) This Act shall not extend to Scotland or to Northern Ireland.

THE LANDLORD AND TENANT (WAR DAMAGE) ACT 1939

Relief from obligation to repair in cases of war damage

1.—(1) Where, by virtue of the provisions (whether express or implied) of a disposition or of any contract collateral thereto, an obligation (in this Part of this Act referred to as an "obligation to repair") is imposed on any person to do any repairs in relation to the land comprised in the disposition, those provisions shall be construed as not extending to the imposition of any liability on that person to make good any war damage occurring to the land so comprised.

(2) Where war damage occurs to land comprised in a disposition, then, in so far as compliance with an obligation to repair, as modified by the provisions of the preceding subsection, is, having regard to the extent of the war damage—

> (*a*) impracticable, or only practicable at a cost which is unreasonable in view of all the circumstances; or
>
> (*b*) of no substantial advantage to the person who, but for the provisions of this subsection, would be entitled to the benefit of the obligation;

the obligation shall be suspended until the war damage is made good to such an extent that compliance with the obligation is practicable at a reasonable cost and is of substantial advantage to the person entitled to the benefit thereof.

(3) Any disposition or contract collateral thereto containing a provision whereunder an obligation to make good war damage as such is imposed on any person, shall have effect as if that provision were not contained therein.

(4) Where, under the foregoing provisions of this section, an obligation to repair is modified or suspended or an obligation to make good war damage as such is extinguished, all rights and remedies (whether by way of damages, forfeiture, re-entry, sale, foreclosure or otherwise) arising out of the non-fulfilment of the obligation, including all rights against any person who has guaranteed the fulfilment of the obligation, shall be modified or suspended or extinguished accordingly.

(5) In this section the expression "disposition" means any instrument (including an enactment) or oral transaction, whether made before or after the commencement of this Act, creating or transferring any interest in land.

(6) Where a disposition is made under or in pursuance of an enactment which imposes an obligation to repair in relation to the land the subject of the disposition, the obligation shall be deemed for the purposes of this

329

section to have been imposed by virtue of the provisions of the disposition.

(7) The provisions of this section shall have effect subject to the provisions of Part II of this Act relating to notices of retention and notices to avoid disclaimer.

The Landlord and Tenant Act 1954

Relief for tenant where landlord proceeding to enforce covenants

16.—(1) The provisions of the next following subsection shall have effect where, in the case of a tenancy to which section one of this Act applies,—

    (a) the immediate landlord has brought proceedings to enforce a right of re-entry or forfeiture or a right to damages in respect of a failure to comply with any terms of the tenancy,

    (b) the tenant has made application in the proceedings for relief under this section, and

    (c) the court makes an order for the recovery from the tenant of possession of the property comprised in the tenancy or for the payment by the tenant of such damages as aforesaid, and the order is made at a time earlier than seven months before the term date of the tenancy.

(2) The operation of the order shall be suspended for a period of 14 days from the making thereof, and if before the end of that period the tenant gives notice in writing to the immediate landlord that he desires that the provisions of the two following paragraphs shall have effect, and lodges a copy of the notice in the court,—

    (a) the order shall not have effect except if and in so far as it provides for the payment of costs, and

    (b) the tenancy shall thereafter have effect, and this Part of this Act shall have effect in relation thereto, as if it had been granted for a term expiring at the expiration of seven months from the making of the order.

(3) In any case falling within paragraphs (a) and (b) of subsection (1) of this section, the court shall not make any such order as is mentioned in paragraph (c) thereof unless the time of the making of the order falls earlier than seven months before the term date of the tenancy:

Provided that (without prejudice to section 10 of this Act) this subsection shall not prevent the making of an order for the payment of damages in respect of a failure, as respects any premises, to comply with the terms of a tenancy if, at the time when the order is made, the tenancy has come to an end as respects those premises.

(4) The foregoing provisions of this section shall not have effect in relation to a failure to comply with—

    (a) any term of a tenancy as to payment of rent or rates or as to insuring or keeping insured any premises, or

331

(*b*) any term restricting the use of any premises for immoral or illegal purposes.

(5) References in this section to proceedings to enforce a right to damages in respect of a failure to comply with any terms of a tenancy shall be construed as including references to proceedings for recovery from the tenant of expenditure incurred by or recovered from the immediate landlord in consequence of such a failure on the part of the tenant.

(6) Nothing in the foregoing provisions of this section shall prejudice any right to apply for relief under any other enactment.

(7) Subsection (3) of section two of this Act shall not have effect in relation to this section.

THE SEXUAL OFFENCES ACT 1956

Tenant permitting premises to be used as a brothel

35.—(1) It is an offence for the tenant or occupier, or person in charge, of any premises knowingly to permit the whole or part of the premises to be used as a brothel.

(2) Where the tenant or occupier of any premises is convicted (whether under this section or, for an offence committed before the commencement of this Act, under section 13 of the Criminal Law Amendment Act 1885) of knowingly permitting the whole or part of the premises to be used as a brothel, the First Schedule to this Act shall apply to enlarge the rights of the lessor or landlord with respect to the assignment or determination of the lease or other contract under which the premises are held by the person convicted.

(3) Where the tenant or occupier of any premises is so convicted, or was so convicted under the said section 13 before the commencement of this Act, and either—

(*a*) the lessor or landlord, after having the conviction brought to his notice, fails or failed to exercise his statutory rights in relation to the lease or contract under which the premises are or were held by the person convicted; or

(*b*) the lessor or landlord, after exercising his statutory rights so as to determine that lease or contract, grants or granted a new lease or enters or entered into a new contract of tenancy of the premises to, with or for the benefit of the same person, without having all reasonable provisions to prevent the recurrence of the offence inserted in the new lease or contract;

then, if subsequently an offence under this section is committed in respect of the premises during the subsistence of the lease or contract referred to in paragraph (*a*) of this sub-section or (where paragraph (*b*) applies) during the subsistence of the new lease or contract, the lessor or landlord shall be deemed to be a party to that offence unless he shows that he took all reasonable steps to prevent the recurrence of the offence.

References in this subsection to the statutory rights of a lessor or landlord refer to his rights under the First Schedule to this Act or under subsection (1) of section five of the Criminal Law Amendment Act 1912 (the provision replaced for England and Wales by that Schedule).

The Leasehold Reform Act 1967

Schedule 3, Part I (Restrictions on claims by tenant, and effect of claims on other notices, forfeitures, etc.).

4—(1) Where a tenant makes a claim to acquire the freehold or an extended lease of any property, then during the currency of the claim no proceedings to enforce any right of re-entry or forfeiture terminating the tenancy shall be brought in any court without the leave of that court, and leave shall not be granted unless the court is satisfied that the claim was not made in good faith; but where leave is granted, the claim shall cease to have effect.

(2) Where a claim is made to acquire the freehold or an extended lease of property comprised in a tenancy, the tenancy shall be deemed for purposes of the claim to be a subsisting tenancy notwithstanding that the claim is made when proceedings are pending to enforce a right of re-entry or forfeiture terminating the tenancy and notwithstanding any order made afterwards in those proceedings, and if the claim is effective, the court in which the proceedings were brought may set aside or vary any such order to such extent and on such terms as appear to that court to be appropriate:

Provided that if it appears to that court that the claim is not made in good faith, or there has been unreasonable delay in making it, and that apart from the claim effect should be given to the right of re-entry of forfeiture, the court shall order that the tenancy shall not be treated as subsisting nor the claim as valid by virtue of this sub-paragraph.

(3) Where a court other than the county court—

    (a)   grants leave under sub-paragraph (1) above; or

    (b)   makes an order under the proviso to sub-paragraph (2) above on the ground that a claim was not made in good faith;

the court may make any such order as the county court is authorised to make by section 20(5) or (6) of this Act.

(4) A tenant who, in proceedings to enforce a right of re-entry or forfeiture or a right to damages in respect of a failure to comply with any terms of the tenancy, applies for relief under section 16 of the Landlord and Tenant Act 1954 is not thereby precluded from making a claim to acquire the freehold or an extended lease; but if he gives notice under section 16(2) (under which the tenant is relieved from any order for recovery of possession or for payment of damages, but the tenancy is cut short), any claim made by him to acquire the freehold or an extended lease of property comprised in the tenancy, with or without other property, shall be of no effect, or, if already made, shall cease to have effect.

(5) Sub-paragraph (4) above shall apply in relation to proceedings relating to a superior tenancy with the substitution for the references to section 16 and to section 16(2) of the Landlord and Tenant Act 1954 of references to paragraph 9 and to paragraph 9(2) of Schedule 5 to that Act.

THE CRIMINAL LAW ACT 1977

Violence for securing entry

6.—(1) Subject to the following provisions of this section, any person who, without lawful authority, uses or threatens violence for the purpose of securing entry into any premises for himself or for any other person is guilty of an offence, provided that—

(a) there is someone present on those premises at the time who is opposed to the entry which the violence is intended to secure; and

(b) the person using or threatening the violence knows that that is the case.

(2) The fact that a person has any interest in or right to possession or occupation of any premises shall not for the purposes of sub-section (1) above constitute lawful authority for the use or threat of violence by him or anyone else for the purpose of securing his entry into those premises.

(3) In any proceedings for an offence under this section it shall be a defence for the accused to prove—

(a) that at the time of the alleged offence he or any other person on whose behalf he was acting was a displaced residential occupier of the premises in question; or

(b) that part of the premises in question constitutes premises of which he or any other person on whose behalf he was acting was a displaced residential occupier and that the part of the premises to which he was seeking to secure entry constitutes an access of which he or, as the case may be, that other person is also a displaced residential occupier.

(4) It is immaterial for the purposes of this section—

(a) whether the violence in question is directed against the person or against property; and

(b) whether the entry which the violence is intended to secure is for the purpose of acquiring possession of the premises in question or for any other purpose.

(5) A person guilty of an offence under this section shall be liable on summary conviction to imprisonment for a term not exceeding six months or to a fine not exceeding [level 5 on the standard scale] or to both.

(6) A constable in uniform may arrest without warrant anyone who is, or whom he, with reasonable cause, suspects to be, guilty of an offence under this section.

(7) Section 12 below contains provisions which apply for determining

when any person is to be regarded for the purposes of this Part of this Act as a displaced residential occupier of any premises or of any access to any premises.

THE PROTECTION FROM EVICTION ACT 1977

Restriction on re-entry without due process of law

2.—Where any premises are let as a dwelling on a lease which is subject to a right of re-entry or forfeiture it shall not be lawful to enforce that right otherwise than by proceedings in the court while any person is lawfully residing in the premises or part of them.

THE SUPREME COURT ACT 1981

Relief against forfeiture for non-payment of rent

38.—(1) In any action in the High Court for the forfeiture of a lease for non-payment of rent, the court shall have power to grant relief against forfeiture in a summary manner, and may do so subject to the same terms and conditions as to the payment of rent, costs or otherwise as could have been imposed by it in such an action immediately before the commencement of this Act.

(2) Where the lessee or a person deriving title under him is granted relief under this section, he shall hold the demised premises in accordance with the terms of the lease without the necessity for a new lease.

THE COUNTY COURTS ACT 1984[5]

Provisions as to forfeiture for non-payment of rent

138.—(1) This section has effect where a lessor is proceeding by action in a county court (being an action in which the county court has jurisdiction) to enforce against a lessee a right of re-entry or forfeiture in respect of any land for non-payment of rent.

(2) If the lessee pays into court or to the lessor not less than 5 clear days before the return day all the rent in arrear and the costs of the action, the action shall cease, and the lessee shall hold the land according to the lease without any new lease.

(3) If—

    (*a*)   the action does not cease under subsection (2); and

    (*b*)   the court at the trial is satisfied that the lessor is entitled to enforce the right of re-entry or forfeiture,

the court shall order possession of the land to be given to the lessor at the expiration of such period, not being less than four weeks from the date of the order, as the court thinks fit, unless within that period the lessee pays into court or to the lessor all the rent in arrear and the costs of the action.

(4) The court may extend the period specified under subsection (3) at any time before possession of the land is recovered in pursuance of the order under that subsection.

(5) . . . if—

    (*a*)   within the period specified in the order; or

    (*b*)   within that period as extended under subsection (4),

the lessee pays into court or to the lessor—

    (i)   all the rent in arrear; and

    (ii)   the costs of the action,

he shall hold the land according to the lease without any new lease.

(6) Subsection (2) shall not apply where the lessor is proceeding in the same action to enforce a right of re-entry or forfeiture on any other ground as well as for non-payment of rent, or to enforce any other claim as well as the right of re-entry or forfeiture and the claim for arrears of rent.

(7) If the lessee does not—

    (*a*)   within the period specified in the order; or

    (*b*)   within that period as extended under subsection (4), pay into court or to the lessor—

---

[5] Printed as amended by the Administration of Justice Act 1955, ss. 55 and 67(2), and Sched. 8, Pt III and by the Courts and Legal Services Act 1990, s. 125(2), and Sched. 17 para. 17.

(i)   all the rent in arrear; and

(ii) the costs of the action,

the order shall be enforceable in the prescribed manner and so long as the order remains unreversed the lessee shall, subject to subsections (8) and (9A), be barred from all relief.

(8) The extension under subsection (4) of a period fixed by a court shall not be treated as relief from which the lessee is barred by subsection (7) if he fails to pay into court or to the lessor all the rent in arrear and the costs of the action within that period.

(9) Where the court extends a period under subsection (4) at a time when—

(a)   that period has expired; and

(b)   a warrant has been issued for the possession of the land, the court shall suspend the warrant for the extended period; and, if, before the expiration period, the lessee pays into court or to the lessor all the rent in arrear and all the costs of the action, the court shall cancel the warrant.

(9A) Where the lessor recovers possession of the land at any time after the making of the order under subsection (3) (whether as a result of the enforcement of the order or otherwise) the lessee may, at any time within six months from the date on which the lessor recovers possession, apply to the court for relief; and on any such application the court may, if it thinks fit, grant to the lessee such relief, subject to such terms and conditions, as it thinks fit.

(9B) Where the lessee is granted relief on an application under subsection (9A) he shall hold the land according to the lease without any new lease.

(9C) An application under subsection (9A) may be made by a person with an interest under a lease of the land derived (whether immediately or otherwise) from the lessee's interest therein in like manner as if he were the lessee; and on any such application the court may make an order which (subject to such terms and conditions as the court thinks fit) vests the land in such a person, as lessee of the lessor, for the remainder of the term of the lease under which he has any such interest as aforesaid, or for any lesser term.

In this subsection any reference to the land includes a reference to a part of the land.

(10) Nothing in this section or section 139 shall be taken to affect—

(a)   the power of the court to make any order which it would otherwise have power to make as respects a right of re-entry or forfeiture on any ground other than non-payment of rent; or

(b)   section 146(4) of the Law of Property Act 1925 (relief against forfeiture).

Service of summons and re-entry

139.—(1) In a case where section 138 has effect, if—

(a)   one-half-year's rent is in arrear at the time of the commencement of the action; and

(b)   the lessor has a right to re-enter for non-payment of that rent; and

(c)   no sufficient distress is to be found on the premises countervailing the arrears then due,

the service of the summons in the action in the prescribed manner shall stand in lieu of a demand and re-entry.

(2) Where a lessor has enforced against a lessee, by re-entry without action, a right of re-entry or forfeiture as respects any land for non-payment of rent, the lessee may . . . at any time within six months from the date on which the lessor re-entered apply to the county court for relief, and on any such application the court may, if it thinks fit, grant to the lessee such relief as the High Court could have granted.[6]

(3) Subsections (9B) and (9C) of section 138 shall have effect in relation to an application under subsection (2) of this section as they have effect in relation to an application under subsection (9A) of that section.

Interpretation of sections 138 and 139

140.—For the purposes of sections 138 and 139—
"lease" includes—

(a)   an original or derivative under-lease;

(b)   an agreement for a lease where the lessee has become entitled to have his lease granted; and

(c)   a grant at a fee farm rent, or under a grant securing a rent by condition;

"lessee" includes—

(a)   an original or derivative under-lessee;

(b)   the persons deriving title under a lessee;

(c)   a grantee under a grant at a fee farm rent, or under a grant securing a rent by condition; and

(d)   the persons deriving title under such a grantee;

---

[6] The words omitted from subs. 2 were repealed by the High Court and County Courts Jurisdiction Order 1991 (S.I. 1991 No. 724, art. 2(8), Sched.)

"lessor" includes—

(a)   an original or derivative under-lessor;

(b)   the persons deriving title under a lessor;

(c)   a person making a grant at a fee farm rent, or a grant securing a rent by condition; and

(d)   the persons deriving title under such a grantor;

"under-lease" includes an agreement for an under-lease where the under-lessee has become entitled to have his underlease granted; and

"under-lessee" includes any person deriving title under an under-lessee.

Part VI: Selection of forms

Selection of forms

The aim of this part of the book is to provide the reader with a selection of forms to assist him/her in the drafting of pleadings and other documents associated with the forfeiture of leases. The forms included here (which are by no means intended to be exhaustive) should be treated merely as examples and not as standard precedents. The reader is referred to *Atkin's Court Forms*, (2nd. ed., 1990), Vol. 24 and also to Walter & Harris's book on *Claims to the Possession of Land: Law and Practice* (1987) Appendix 5, pp. 456–477 for a further selection of useful forms in this area.

CONTENTS

Form 1: Landlord's notice under section 146 of the Law of Property Act 1925 alleging breach of covenant to repair

NOTICE UNDER SECTION 146 OF THE LAW OF PROPERTY ACT 1925

TO   , the Lessee of the premises situate at
and known as   , comprised in and
demised by a Lease, dated   day of   199 , and made
between   of the one part and yourselves of the other
part (hereinafter referred to as "the said Lease")

AND to all others whom it may concern

WE, Messrs.   of   , as Solicitors and Agents of
your Landlords the said   , whose registered office is situate at   , who are
entitled to the reversion of the above mentioned premises expectant on
the said Lease

HEREBY pursuant to the provisions of section 146 of the Law of Property Act 1925 give you notice that you have committed breaches of the
covenant contained in sub-clause   of clause   of the said Lease
whereby you covenanted as follows:
[set out covenant in full]

PARTICULARS of the said breaches of the said covenant are set forth in
the Schedule of Dilapidations annexed hereto and consist of the failure to
carry out the works therein mentioned

WE HEREBY require you to remedy the said breaches of covenant
within a reasonable time from the date of service of this notice upon you

WE HEREBY further give you notice that unless you remedy the said
breaches within a reasonable time from the date of service hereof your
said Landlords will proceed to enforce their right of re-entry under the
said Lease and will take such further or other steps or proceedings as they
may be advised

AND further take notice that your said Landlords HEREBY require you
to make reasonable compensation in money in respect of the aforesaid
breaches of covenant and to pay, pursuant to clause   of the said
Lease, all expenses including solicitors' costs and surveyors' fees incurred

by your said Landlords in relation or incidental to the preparation and service of this notice

YOU ARE HEREBY notified that you are entitled within 28 days of the service of this notice upon you to serve on your said Landlords a counter-notice claiming the benefit of the Leasehold Property (Repairs) Act 1938 (as amended). Such counter-notice may be served by leaving the same or sending the same by registered or recorded delivery post to us, your Landlords' said Solicitors, or otherwise as provided by section 196 of the Law of Property Act 1925 (as amended) and section 23(2) of the Landlord and Tenant Act 1927.

DATED this   day of   199 .

(*Signed*)

Solicitors and Agents
for the Landlords

Form 2: Landlord's notice under section 146 of the Law of Property Act 1925 alleging breach of covenant against assigning, sub-letting and parting with possession

NOTICE UNDER SECTION 146 OF THE LAW OF PROPERTY ACT 1925

TO   , the Tenant of the premises
situate at and known as   , comprised in and
demised by a Lease, dated the   day of   199 , and made
between   of the one part and
                    of the other part (hereinafter referred to as "the
said Lease")

AND to all others whom it may concern

WE, Messrs.   of   , as Solicitors and Agents of your said Landlords   whose
registered office is situated at   , who are entitled
to the reversion of the above-mentioned premises expectant on the said
Lease

HEREBY pursuant to the provisions of section 146 of the Law of Property Act 1925 give you notice that you have broken the covenant contained in sub-clause   of clause   of the said Lease which provides as follows:

"Not to assign, under-let or part with possession of the demised premises or any part thereof without the consent of the Landlords such consent not to be unreasonably withheld in the event of a respectable and responsible assignee or under-tenant being proposed."

Particulars of the said breach of the said covenant are as follows, namely, that you have parted with possession of the said demised premises by permitting or suffering the same to be occupied by one   , without obtaining the consent of your said Landlords and further or in the alternative that you have assigned or under-let the said demised premises to the said   without obtaining such consent as aforesaid

WE HEREBY require you to remedy the said breach of covenant and HEREBY further give you notice that unless you remedy the said breach within 14 days from the date of service of this notice upon you, your said

351

Landlords will proceed to enforce their right of re-entry under the said Lease and will take such further or other steps or proceedings as they may be advised

DATED this   day of   199 .

(*Signed*)

Solicitors and Agents
for the Landlords

Form 3: Landlord's notice under section 146 of the Law of Property Act 1925 alleging tenant's liquidation

NOTICE UNDER SECTION 146 OF THE LAW OF PROPERTY ACT 1925

TO A.B. Co. Ltd. (in liquidation) whose registered office is situate at , the Tenant of the premises situate at and known as , comprised in and demised by a Lease, dated the day of 199 , and made between of the one part and A.B. Co. Ltd. of the other part (hereinafter referred to as "the said Lease")

AND TO [*insert name and address of liquidator*]

AND TO all others whom it may concern

WE, Messrs. of , as Solicitors and Agents for your said Landlord of , who is entitled to the reversion of the above mentioned premises expectant on the said Lease

HEREBY pursuant to the provisions of section 146 of the Law of Property Act 1925 give you notice that:

1. By and in a proviso contained in clause of the said Lease it was provided and agreed that it should be lawful for your said Landlord to re-enter upon the said premises if the Tenant should *inter alia* become bankrupt or enter into liquidation whether compulsory or voluntary (except where the liquidation is for the purpose of amalgamation or reconstruction of a solvent company);

2. On the day of 199 , you were placed in creditors' Voluntary Liquidation, pursuant to section 98 of the Insolvency Act 1986, and as a consequence the said Lease is liable to forfeiture;

3. By reason of your liquidation, your said Landlord intends to enforce his right of re-entry under the said Lease by action or otherwise and take such further or other steps or proceedings as he may be advised.

DATED this day of 199 .

(*Signed*)

Solicitors and Agents
for the Landlords

353

Form 4: Tenant's counter-notice claiming the benefit of the Leasehold (Property) Repairs Act 1938

TO: [*landlord*]   of

COUNTER-NOTICE

I hereby give you notice that with reference to the Notice, dated , served on me by you on the   day of , I claim the benefit of the Leasehold Property (Repairs) Act 1938.

This is not an acceptance that your Notice is a valid notice and I reserve the right to contest its validity at any later stage.

Yours faithfully,

[*signature of tenant*]

Form 5: Landlord's Originating summons seeking leave to bring proceedings under the Leasehold Property (Repairs) Act 1938

IN THE HIGH COURT OF JUSTICE   199... A. No...

QUEEN'S BENCH DIVISION

In the Matter of the Leasehold Property (Repairs) Act 1938

And in the Matter of the Lease, dated   , between A.B. and
C.D. of premises known as   .

And in the Matter of an Intended Action.

BETWEEN:

A.B.   *Plaintiff*

and

C.D.   *Defendant*

LET C.D., whose registered office is situate at   , attend before the Master in Chambers Room No.   , Central Office, Royal Courts of Justice, Strand, London, WC2A 2LL on   day the   day of   199 at   o'clock on the hearing of an application by the Plaintiff for:

1. An Order giving the Plaintiff leave to take proceedings for the enforcement of his right of re-entry by reason of breaches of the covenants to repair contained in a Lease made on the   19   between the Plaintiff of the one part and the Defendant of the other part, whereby the premises known as   were demised by the Plaintiff to the Defendant for the term of   years from the   19 ;

2. An Order giving the Plaintiff leave to take proceedings for damages for breaches of the covenants;

3. A Direction under section 2 of the above-mentioned Act that the Plaintiff has the benefit of section 146(3) of the Law of Property Act 1925 in relation to the costs and expenses incurred in reference to the said breaches;

4. An Order that the costs of this application be taxed by the Taxing Master and paid by the Defendant to the Plaintiff.

AND LET the Defendant within 14 days after service of this summons on it counting the day of service return the accompanying Acknowledgment of Service to the appropriate Court Office.

DATED this   day of   199 .

Note: This summons may not be served later than four calendar months beginning with the above date unless renewed by order of the Court.

This summons was taken out by Messrs.   , Solicitors to the Plaintiff whose address is   .

Note: If a Defendant does not attend personally or by his Counsel or Solicitor at the time and place where mentioned such order will be made as the Court may think just and expedient.

Important

Directions for Acknowledgment of Service are given with the accompanying form.

Form 6: Landlord's Affidavit in support of Originating Summons seeking leave to bring proceedings under the Leasehold Property (Repairs) Act 1938

IN THE HIGH COURT OF JUSTICE   199... A. No...

QUEEN'S BENCH DIVISION

In the Matter of the Leasehold Property (Repairs) Act 1938

And in the Matter of the Lease, dated   , between A.B. and
C.D. of premises known as   .

And in the Matter of an Intended Action.

BETWEEN:

A.B.	*Plaintiff*
and	
C.D.	*Defendant*

I,   of   , MAKE OATH and say as follows:

1. I am [*state professional qualifications*] and [*state position held within firm of surveyors*]. I have had   years experience as a full-time (building) surveyor in private practice and have on numerous occasions acted in disputes between landlords and their tenants concerning liability under repairing covenants in leases. Save where it otherwise appears, the facts and matters deposed to by me herein are within my own personal knowledge. I am duly authorised to make this Affidavit on behalf of the Plaintiff.

2. I am informed by Messrs.   , Solicitors acting for the Plaintiff and verily believe that the document now produced and shown to me marked " 1" is a true copy of the Lease made on the   between the Plaintiff of the one part and the Defendant of the other part whereby the Plaintiff demised to the Defendant the premises known as   for the term of   years from the   19 .

3. The said Lease contains (*inter alia*) the following covenants on the part of the Defendant as lessee, namely:
[*set out relevant repairing covenants in full*]

4. In   19 , my firm was engaged by the Plaintiff to inspect the

357

said premises and to prepare a schedule of dilapidations accrued at the said premises under the said covenants contained in clauses   of the said Lease. On   19 , I inspected the said premises and prepared the Schedule of Dilapidations annexed to a Notice, dated   , under section 146 of the Law of Property Act 1925, which I am informed by the Plaintiff's said Solicitors and verily believe was served upon the Defendant by [recorded delivery] post on or about   19 . I am further informed and verily believe that by letter, dated   19 , the Defendant served upon the Plaintiff a counter-notice, dated   19 , claiming the benefit of the Leasehold Property (Repairs) Act 1938. A true copy of the said Notice and Schedule of Dilapidations and the said Counter-notice are now produced and shown to me in a bundle marked "   2".

5. In the said Schedule, a number of breaches are specified the immediate remedying whereof is, in my opinion, necessary for preventing substantial diminution in the value of the Plaintiff's reversionary interest or which have already caused substantial diminution in the value of the Plaintiff's reversion, and I have marked on the said Schedule each such breach with the letter "A" in the left-hand margin. [*Continue by giving full particulars.*]

6. Furthermore, certain of the said breaches can, in my opinion, be immediately remedied at an expense that is relatively small in comparison with the much greater expense that would probably be occasioned by postponement of the necessary work and I have marked each such item with the letter "B" in the said margin on the said Schedule. [*Continue by giving full particulars.*]

7. In addition, there are the following special circumstances which I respectfully submit render it just and equitable that the leave sought in the Originating Summons herein should be given, namely, that I have been informed by the Plaintiff and verily believe that the said premises have never been used or occupied by the Defendant since the said Lease was granted to it in 19   and the same are deteriorating substantially through non-use. In particular, the said premises have not received any heating, cleaning and general maintenance during the period from   19 to   19 . In fact, my inspection revealed that the doors to the said premises were boarded up and padlocked shut. The said premises were extensively fly-posted and some of the exterior windows were smashed.

8. I also attended the said premises on   19   and I could not see that any work had been put in hand by the Defendant to remedy any of

the dilapidations specified in the said Schedule and, indeed, the said premises continued to appear completely vacant, derelict and abandoned. I noted considerable further deterioration to the said premises and there is now produced and shown to me marked " 3" a true copy of a report of my findings in that regard together with a true copy of a revised Schedule of Dilapidations in which the costs of remedial works I have

now estimated at £   , exclusive of VAT and with no allowance for contingency works.

Sworn at

This   day of   199

Before me,   a Solicitor

This Affidavit is filed on behalf of the proposed Plaintiff.

Form 7: Landlord's Originating Application seeking leave to bring proceedings under the Leasehold Property (Repairs) Act 1938

IN THE   COUNTY COURT   Case No.

In the Matter of the Leasehold Property (Repairs) Act 1938

And in the Matter of a Lease, dated   , between A.B. and C.D. of premises situate at   .

BETWEEN:

A.B.   *Applicant*

and

C.D.   *Respondent*

I,   of   , apply to the court for an order in the following terms:

An order giving the Applicant,   leave as landlord under a Lease, dated the   day of 19   and made between the Applicant of the one part and the above-mentioned C.D. of the other part, to commence proceedings in this Court against the Respondent, C.D., for the enforcement of the right of the Applicant for forfeiture and damages for breach of covenant to repair under the provisions of the said Lease and that the Applicant has the benefit of section 146(3) of the Law of Property Act 1925 in relation thereto.

The grounds on which I claim to be entitled to the order are:

1. The Applicant is the freehold owner of the premises known as   .

2. By the above-mentioned Lease, dated   , the Applicant let the said premises to the Respondent for a term of years from the   .

3. The said Lease contains (*inter alia*) the following covenants, namely: [*set out relevant repairing covenants in full*]

4. By and in a proviso contained in clause   of the said Lease, it was provided and expressly agreed (*inter alia*) as follows:
[*set out relevant portion of proviso for re-entry*]

5. The Respondent, in breach of the said covenants, has allowed various dilapidations to accrue at the said premises and on the   , the Applicant duly served upon the Respondent a notice, pursuant to section 146 of the Law of Property Act 1925 and the Leasehold Property (Repairs) Act 1938, requiring the said breach to be remedied.

6. On or about the   , the Respondent served on the Applicant a counter-notice claiming the benefit of the Leasehold Property (Repairs) Act 1938.

7. I, accordingly, apply to the court for leave under section 1 of the 1938 Act on grounds that (a) the immediate remedying of the said breach is requisite for preventing substantial diminution in the value of the Applicant's reversion and the value thereof has already been substantially diminished by the said breach and (b) the said breach can be immediately remedied at an expense that is relatively small in comparison with the much greater expense that would probably be occasioned by postponement of the necessary work and (c) special circumstances exist which render it just and equitable that leave should be given.

    The name and address of the person on whom it is intended to serve this application is Messrs.   , Solicitors for the Respondent.

My address for service is

(*Signed*)

Solicitors for the Applicant.

DATED this   day of   199 .

Form 8: Landlord's Statement of Claim: forfeiture for breach of repairing covenants following leave under the Leasehold Property (Repairs) Act 1938

IN THE HIGH COURT OF JUSTICE   199... A. No...

QUEEN'S BENCH DIVISION

BETWEEN:

A.B. Ltd.   *Plaintiff*

and

C.D.   *Defendant*

STATEMENT OF CLAIM

1. By a Lease, dated the   day of   19   and made between the Plaintiff (in the said Lease called "the Lessor") of the one part and the Defendant (in the said Lease called "the Lessee") of the other part, the premises known as and numbered   (hereinafter referred to as "the demised premises") were demised by the Plaintiff to the Defendant for a term of   years from the   at the yearly rent of £   (during the first   years of the said term and thereafter for each successive period of   years such rent as may be agreed by the parties or in default of agreement as should be determined in accordance with the provisions in that behalf contained in the said Lease) payable clear of all deductions by equal quarterly payments in advance on the usual quarter days.

2. The demised premises were let to the Defendant for use as a [factory] and for no other purpose whatsoever.

3. By and in clause   of the said Lease, the Defendant covenanted with the Plaintiff as follows:
[*set out repairing covenant in full*]

4. By and in clause   of the said Lease, the Defendant covenanted with the Plaintiff as follows:
[*set out painting covenant in full, if appropriate*]

5. By and in clause   of the said Lease, the Defendant covenanted with the Plaintiff as follows:

"To pay all expenses (including Solicitors' costs and Surveyors' fees) incurred by the Lessor incidental to the preparation and service of a Notice under sections 146 and 147 of the Law of Property Act 1925 notwithstanding forfeiture is avoided otherwise than by relief granted by the Court."

6. By and in a proviso contained in clause   of the said Lease, it was provided and expressly agreed and declared as follows: [*set out proviso for re-entry in full*]

7. In breach of the covenants referred to in paragraphs 3 and 4 hereof, the Defendant has failed [to put and thereafter to keep the demised premises and every part thereof and additions thereto and the fixtures therein and the drains soil and other pipes and the sanitary and water and heating apparatus thereof in good and tenantable repair and condition and to paint with two coats of good quality paint in a workman-like manner and in tints and colours from time to time approved by the Plaintiff all the wood iron and other parts of the demised premises (both interior and exterior) which are of the kind usually or proper to be painted as to the internal work in the third year of the said term and thereafter in every subsequent third year and as to the external work in the fifth year of the said term and thereafter in every subsequent fifth year].

PARTICULARS OF BREACH

Full particulars of the said breaches were set out in the Schedule of Dilapidations sent by the Plaintiff's Solicitors, Messrs.   , to the Defendant by letter, dated   .

8. By a Notice [delivered by hand] dated,   , and addressed to the Defendant, the Plaintiff gave notice pursuant to section 146 of the Law of Property Act 1925 specifying the said breaches of covenant referred to in paragraph 7 hereof and requiring the Defendant to remedy the same within a reasonable period of time from the date of service of the said Notice and requiring the payment of compensation in respect of the said breaches and informing the Defendant that he was entitled under the Leasehold Property (Repairs) Act 1938 to serve a counter-notice in writing on the Plaintiff claiming the benefit of that Act within 28 days from the date of service of the said Notice.

9. By letter, dated   , the Defendant's Solicitors, Messrs.   , duly acknowledged receipt of the said Notice and gave notice to the Plaintiff that the Defendant claimed the benefit of the 1938 Act.

10. By Order of Master   , dated   , the Plaintiff was granted leave under section 1 of the 1938 Act to take proceedings to enforce his right of re-entry under the said Lease of the demised premises by reason of the Defendant's breaches of the said covenants and leave also to sue for damages for the said breaches against the Defendant.

11. The Defendant has failed within a reasonable period of time or at all to remedy the said breaches of covenant referred to in paragraph 7 hereof or to make compensation to the Plaintiff therefore and by reason of the Defendant's breaches of the said covenants the Plaintiff is entitled to forfeit the said Lease and by the issue and service of the Writ of Summons herein the said Lease has become forfeited to the Plaintiff.

12. By reason of the said breaches of covenant the Plaintiff has suffered loss and damage, and the value of his reversion expectant on the determination of the said Lease has been diminished by the Defendant's failure to perform the said covenants contained in the said Lease.

PARTICULARS OF LOSS AND DAMAGE

The Plaintiff will give full particulars on discovery.

13. Further, the Plaintiff contends that by virtue of clause   of the said Lease (referred to in paragraph 5 hereof), the Defendant is bound to pay the Plaintiff's Solicitors' costs and Surveyors' fees incurred by the Plaintiff incidental to the preparation and service of the said Schedule of Dilapidations and said Notice pursuant to section 146 of the 1925 Act.

PARTICULARS OF EXPENDITURE

The Plaintiff will give full particulars on discovery.

14. The Plaintiff further claims interest pursuant to section 35A of the Supreme Court Act 1981 on the said damages referred to in paragraph 12 hereof at the rate of [15] per cent. per annum for such period as the Court may think just.

AND the Plaintiff claims:

(1) Possession of the demised premises and delivery up to the Plaintiff by the Defendant of the said Lease;
(2) Damages for breach of covenant, under paragraph 12 hereof;
(3) Payment of the said costs incurred by the Plaintiff, under paragraph 13 hereof;

(4) Interest pursuant to section 35A of the Supreme Court Act 1981 on the said damages;

(5) Such further or other relief to which the Plaintiff may in the circumstances be entitled;

(6) Costs.

Writ issued, etc.

Form 9: Statement of Claim: forfeiture for non-payment of rent

IN THE HIGH COURT OF JUSTICE   199... A. No...

QUEEN'S BENCH DIVISION

BETWEEN:

A.B.   *Plaintiff*

and

C.D.   *Defendant*

STATEMENT OF CLAIM

1. The Plaintiff's claim is for possession of the shop premises known as
, (hereinafter called "the premises") and for such other relief
as is hereinafter more particularly mentioned.

2. By a Lease, dated   , and made between the Plaintiff of
the one part and X.Y. of the other part, the Plaintiff demised the premises
to the said X.Y. for a term of   years from the   at
the yearly rent of £   during the first   years of the
said term and thereafter for each successive period of years such rent as
may be agreed by the parties or in default of agreement as should be
determined in accordance with the provisions in that behalf contained in
clause   of the said Lease payable clear of all deductions by
equal quarterly payments in advance on the usual quarter days and by
way of further or additional rent such sums as shall from time to time be
expended by the Plaintiff in insuring the demised premises in accordance
with the covenant contained in clause   of the said Lease.

3. By and in clause   of the said Lease, the said X.Y. (in the
said Lease called "the Lessee" which expression where the context so
admits is declared by the said Lease to include the persons deriving title
under the Lessee) covenanted with the Plaintiff to pay the rents reserved
on the days and in the manner aforesaid and interest at the rate of 3 per
cent. per annum above the base rate of   Bank plc for the time
being in force upon the amount of any rent unpaid 21 days after it became
due, calculated from the date such rent became due until the date of
payment.

4. By and in a proviso contained in clause   of the said Lease, it was provided and expressly agreed (*inter alia*) as follows:

"if the rent hereby reserved or any part thereof shall remain unpaid for twenty-one days after becoming payable (whether formally demanded or not) . . . then and in any such case it shall be lawful for the Lessor at any time thereafter to re-enter upon the demised premises or upon any part thereof in the name of the whole and thereupon this demise shall absolutely determine . . ."

5. Under and by virtue of an Assignment, dated the   day of 19   and made between the said X.Y of the one part and the Defendant of the other part, the Defendant became entitled to the benefit of the said Lease subject to the payment of the said rents and to the observance of the covenants and conditions on the part of the Lessee falling to be observed and performed therein contained.

6. On the   19   , the said rent reserved under the said Lease was increased to £   per year by mutual agreement between the Plaintiff and the Defendant.

7. In breach of the covenant contained in clause   of the said Lease, the Defendant has failed to pay the quarterly payments of rent due on [September 29, 1991, December 25, 1991, March 25, 1992, June 24, 1992 and September 29, 1992] and there is now due and owing by the Defendant to the Plaintiff in respect of rent down to the December 24, 1992 the sum of £   .

PARTICULARS OR RENT ARREARS

Rent due on September 29, 1991   £
Rent due on, etc.

8. In further breach of the covenant contained in clause   of the said Lease, the Defendant has failed to pay the sum of £   representing insurance premium expended by the Plaintiff in insuring the demised premises in accordance with the covenant contained in clause   thereof for the period from   to   .

9. In the premises, the Defendant is more than 21 days in arrears with the instalments of rent and additional rent unpaid.

10. By reason of the Defendant's breaches of the said covenant, the Plaintiff is entitled to forfeit the said Lease and by the issue and service of the Writ herein the said Lease has become forfeited to the Plaintiff.

11. Further, the Plaintiff claims interest on the said arrears of rent and additional rent remaining unpaid from time to time referred to in paragraphs 7 and 8 hereof at the contractual rate of 3 per cent. above the base rate of   Bank plc for the time being in force in accordance with clause   of the said Lease amounting in aggregate to the sum of £   down to the   being the date of the issue of the Writ herein.

PARTICULARS OF INTEREST

Full particulars are set out in the Statement of Interest attached hereto.

12. Alternatively to paragraph 11 hereof, the Plaintiff claims interest pursuant to section 35A of the Supreme Court Act 1981 on the said arrears of rent remaining unpaid from to time to time referred to in paragraphs 7 and 8 hereof at the rate of [15] per cent. per annum from the respective dates when the same ought to have been paid to the Plaintiff until judgment or sooner payment. The amount of interest from [September 29, 1991] to   (the date of the issue of the summons herein) being £   .

PARTICULARS OF INTEREST

Full particulars are set out in the Statement of Interest attached hereto.

AND the Plaintiff claims:

(1) Possession of the demised premises and delivery up to the Plaintiff by the Defendant of the said Lease;

(2) Payment of the said arrears of rent down to and including the payment of rent due on [September 29, 1992] amounting to the sum of £   ;

(3) Payment of the said sum of £   , under paragraph 8 hereof;

(4) Mesne profits at the rate of £   per annum (£   per day) in respect of any period from [December 25, 1992] until delivery up of possession;

(5) Payment of the said sum of £   representing interest on the said arrears of rent pursuant to clause   of the said Lease referred to in paragraph 11 hereof;

(6) Further interest on the said arrears of rent unpaid at the rate prescribed by clause   of the said Lease from (date of issue of the Writ herein) until judgment or sooner payment whichever is the earlier;

(7) Alternatively to (5) and (6) hereof, payment of the said sum of £   representing interest on the said arrears of rent pursuant to section 35A of the Supreme Court Act 1981 and continuing at the aforesaid rate from the date of the issue of the Writ herein until judgment or sooner payment whichever is the earlier;

(8) Such further or other relief to which the Plaintiff may in the circumstances be entitled;

(9) Costs.

DATED this   day of   199 .

Form 10: Landlord's summons for summary judgment: forfeiture for non-payment of rent

IN THE HIGH COURT OF JUSTICE   199.. A. No..

QUEEN'S BENCH DIVISION

BETWEEN:

A.B.   *Plaintiff*

and

C.D.   *Defendant*

LET all parties concerned attend the Master in Chambers in Room No.   , Central Office, Royal Courts of Justice, Strand, London, WC2A 2LL on   day the   day of   199   at   o'clock on the hearing of an application by the Plaintiff for final judgment in this action against the Defendant for possession of the premises set out in the Statement of Claim herein together with arrears of rent, mesne profits, interest and costs.

TAKE NOTICE that a party intending to oppose this application or to apply for a stay of execution should send to the opposite party or his solicitors to reach him not less than three days before the date above mentioned a copy of any affidavit intended to be used

DATED this   day of   199 .

This summons was taken out by Messrs.   , Solicitors to the Plaintiff whose address is   .

To the Defendant and to   .

Form 11: Affidavit in support of Landlord's application for summary judgment: forfeiture for non-payment of rent

IN THE HIGH COURT OF JUSTICE 199.. A. No..

QUEEN'S BENCH DIVISION

BETWEEN:

A.B. *Plaintiff*

and

C.D. *Defendant*

I, of , MAKE OATH and say as follows:

1. I am the Plaintiff in this action and the matters deposed to by me herein are within my own personal knowledge.

2. By a Lease, dated , and made between myself of the one part and X.Y. of the other part, premises known as and numbered were demised by me to the said X.Y. for a term of years from the at the yearly rent of [during the first years of the said term and thereafter for each successive period of years such rent as may be agreed by the parties or in default of agreement as should be determined in accordance with the provisions in that behalf contained in the said Lease] payable clear of all deductions by equal quarterly payments in advance on the usual quarter days and by way of further or additional rent such sums as shall from time to time be expended by me, in insuring the demised premises in accordance with the covenant contained in clause of the said Lease.

3. Under and by virtue of an Assignment, dated the , and made between the said X.Y. of the one part and the Defendant of the other part, the Defendant became entitled to the benefit of the said Lease subject to the payment of the said rent and to the observance of the covenants and conditions on the part of the Lessee falling to be observed and performed therein contained.

4. On the , the said rent reserved under the said Lease was increased to £ per year by mutual agreement between myself and the Defendant.

371

5. The Defendant is and was at the beginning of this action justly and truly indebted to me in the sum of £   arrears of rent and £ additional rent representing insurance premium expended by me in insuring the demised premises in accordance with the covenant contained in clause   of the said Lease as set out in the Statement of Claim herein.

6. By reason of the Defendant's breaches of the covenants contained in clauses   of the said Lease, I am entitled to forfeit the said Lease and by the issue and service of the Writ of Summons herein the said Lease has become forfeited to me.

7. I am also entitled to mesne profits in respect of the Defendant's continued occupation of the demised premises from the   at the daily rate of £   until possession is delivered up by the Defendant.

8. The demised premises comprise a lock-up shop.

9. I am advised by my Solicitors and verily believe that there is no defence to this action.

Sworn, etc.

Form 12: Landlord's Summons seeking interim payment

IN THE HIGH COURT OF JUSTICE 199.. A. No..

QUEEN'S BENCH DIVISION

BETWEEN:

A.B. *Plaintiff*

and

C.D. *Defendant*

LET all parties attend the Master in Chambers, in Room No.   , Central Office, Royal Courts of Justice, Strand, London WC2A 2LL, on   day the   day of £   199 at o'clock on the hearing of an application on the part of the Plaintiff for an Order under Order 29, Rule 10 of the Rules of the Supreme Court that the Defendant do pay the Plaintiff by way of interim payment and on account of his liability in respect of his use and occupation of the premises claimed in this action during the pendency of this action from the until final judgment herein or until further order a periodical payment of £   per week on the [Monday] of each week.

AND that the costs of an incidental to this application be the Plaintiffs in any event.

DATED this   day of   199 .

Form 13: Landlord's Particulars of Claim seeking possession of residential premises for non-payment of rent (coupled with forfeiture of contractual tenancy)

IN THE   COUNTY COURT   Case No.

BETWEEN:

A.B.   *Plaintiff*

and

C.D.   *Defendant*

PARTICULARS OF CLAIM

1. The Plaintiff is the freehold owner and is entitled to possession of the premises comprising a dwelling-house known as Flat   , [the net annual value for rating whereof does not exceed the county court limit].

2. By a written Tenancy Agreement, dated   , and made between the Plaintiff of the one part and the Defendant of the other part, the Plaintiff agreed to let and the Defendant agreed to take the said premises for the term of   years from the   at the yearly rent of £   payable by equal monthly instalments in advance on the first day of every month and also by way of further rent a yearly sum equal to the sums which the Plaintiff should from time to time pay by way of premium for keeping the premises insured against such losses and risks as are more particularly referred to in the said Agreement the said further rent to be paid on the quarter day next following payment of the premium by the Plaintiff.

3. By and in clause   of the said Agreement, the Defendant agreed to pay the said rent on the days and in the manner aforesaid.

4. By and in a proviso contained in clause   of the said Agreement, it was expressly declared and agreed between the parties that the Plaintiff should be entitled to forfeit the said Agreement and re-enter upon the said premises in the event of the Defendant failing to pay to the Plaintiff the said rent or any part thereof within 21 days of becoming due whether formally demanded or not.

5. On the first day of each of the months of   to

inclusive of 199 in respect of the period of the said Agreement ending on December 31, 199 , monthly instalments of the said rent
of £   at the rate of £   a month became payable by the
Defendant to the Plaintiff amounting in the aggregate to the sum of
£   .

6. On   , there became payable by the Plaintiff
to the insurance company in respect of the insurance of the said premises
for the half year commencing on the said date and in respect of the risks
and payments provided for by and in the said Agreement half-yearly
premium in the sum of £   and such premium was paid by the
Plaintiff in the quarter ending the   .

7. The only moneys paid by the Defendant to the Plaintiff in respect of any
of the foregoing sums due from the Defendant to the Plaintiff are the
following, that is to say:

On [	]	£
On, [etc.	]	£
		£

8. The Plaintiff has appropriated the said sum of £   in satisfaction or part satisfaction of the Defendant's liability for rent including
insurance rent accruing due at the earliest dates in accordance with the
above-mentioned provisions of the said Lease and in the premises there is
now due and owing by the Defendant to the Plaintiff in respect of rent and
insurance rent down to the   the sum of £   .

9. In the premises the Defendant is more than 21 days in arrears with the
instalments of rent unpaid.

10. By reason of the Defendant's failure to pay the said instalments of rent
as aforesaid, the Plaintiff is entitled to forfeit the said Agreement and by
the issue and service of the summons herein the said Agreement has
become forfeited to the Plaintiff.

[11. The said premises are premises to which the Rent Act 1977 applies
and by reason of the failure of the Defendant to pay the said instalments
of rent as aforesaid, possession is claimed pursuant to Case 1 of the 15th
Schedule to the said Act.]

[11. The said premises comprise a dwelling-house but the Defendant is
not entitled to the benefit of the Rent Act 1977 because the said premises
were not let as a separate dwelling.]

375

12. Further, the Plaintiff claims interest pursuant to section 69 of the County Courts Act 1984 on the said arrears of rent including insurance rent remaining unpaid from time to time referred to in paragraph 8 hereof at the rate of [15] per cent. per annum from the respective dates when the same ought to have been paid to the Plaintiff until judgment or sooner payment. The amount of interest from   to
(date of the issue of the summons herein) is

£   .

PARTICULARS OF INTEREST

[set out full particulars of interest]

And the Plaintiff claims:

   (1)   Possession of the said premises and delivery up of the said Agreement;

   (2)   Payment of the said sum of £   representing arrears of rent and insurance rent;

   (3)   Rent, or alternatively, mesne profits at the rate of £
per month (£   per day) from   until possession is delivered up;

   (4)   Payment of the said sum of £   for interest on the said arrears of rent including insurance rent at the rate of [15] per cent. per annum under section 69 of the County Courts Act 1984 and continuing at the aforesaid rate from
                    until payment or judgment, whichever is the earlier;

   (5)   Further or other relief;

   (6)   Costs.

DATED this   day of   199 .

Form 14: Tenant's Statement of Claim claiming trespass and injunction against landlord purporting to forfeit and, in the alternative, seeking relief from forfeiture

IN THE HIGH COURT OF JUSTICE   199... A. No...

QUEEN'S BENCH DIVISION

BETWEEN:

A.B.   *Plaintiff*

and

C.D.

Defendant

STATEMENT OF CLAIM

1. By a Lease, dated   , and made between X.Y. (in the said Lease called "the Landlord") of the one part and the Plaintiff (in the said Lease called "the Tenant") of the other part, all those premises being the [first floor] of the building known as   and more particularly described in the Schedule to the said Lease (hereinafter referred to as "the demised premises") were demised by the said X.Y. to the Plaintiff for a term of   years from the   at the yearly rent of £   for the period from to   and thereafter such yearly rent as should be determined as provided by clause   of the said Lease payable by equal quarterly payments in advance on the usual quarter days in every year without any deduction whatsoever and by way of further yearly rent during the said term upon demand a fair and proper proportion of the premiums paid by the Landlord for the purpose of insuring the building of which the demised premises form part against loss or damage in respect of the various risks (including fire) set out in the said Lease.

2. By and in clause   of the said Lease, the Plaintiff covenanted with the Landlord (which expression is expressed in the said Lease to include the person or persons entitled to the reversion expectant on the termination of the term thereby granted) not to use or permit or suffer to be used the demised premises or any part thereof for any purpose other than as a sweet factory.

3. By and in clause   of the said Lease, the Landlord covenanted with the Plaintiff that the Plaintiff paying the rent reserved in the said Lease and performing and observing the covenants

on the part of the Plaintiff therein contained shall and may peaceably and quietly hold and enjoy the demised premises for the said term without any interruption by the Landlord or any person lawfully claiming under or in trust for him.

4. By and in clause   of the said Lease, it was provided and expressly agreed (*inter alia*) as follows:

> "If the demised premises are so damaged or destroyed by any of the insured risks as to be unfit for occupation or use in whole or in part and the Insurance in respect thereof has not become vitiated by any act or omission of the Tenant then the rent hereby reserved or a proper proportion thereof according to the extent of the damage shall from the date of such damage or destruction and until the demised premises shall have been reinstated cease to be payable . . ."

5. The reversion immediately expectant on the determination of the said term created by the said Lease is now vested in the Defendant.

6. On or about   , the Plaintiff paid to the Defendant the sum of £   in respect of his proportion of the premiums paid by the Defendant for the purpose of insuring the said building against loss or damage in respect of the various risks (including fire) set out in the said Lease for the period from   to   .

7. On or about   , a fire took place on the ground floor of the said building causing extensive damage to the demised premises and rendering them wholly unfit for occupation or use by the Plaintiff as a sweet factory.

8. On   , the Defendant wrote to the Plaintiff stating that he had on that date taken possession of the demised premises and had forfeited the said Lease under the provisions therein contained for re-entry on forfeiture for non-payment of rent on the ground that the Plaintiff had failed to pay two quarters rent in respect of the demised premises which had fallen due for payment.

9. The Plaintiff contends that the Defendant's purported forfeiture and repossession of the demised premises was wrongful and in breach of the Landlord's covenant for quiet enjoyment contained in clause   of the said Lease and constituted a trespass upon the demised premises in that the Plaintiff was and is entitled to cease payment of the said yearly rent in the events which have happened under the provisions of clause   of the said Lease

378

(referred to in paragraph 4 hereof) for the period between the date of the said damage and until the demised premises are reinstated.

10. The Defendant has wrongfully refused to yield up possession of the demised premises to the Plaintiff who is and was at all material times entitled to possession thereof.

11. If, contrary to the Plaintiff's contention, the Defendant's forfeiture and repossession was lawful and the said Lease has been lawfully determined, the Plaintiff contends that it is just and equitable that he should be relieved from the said forfeiture for non payment of rent upon the payment thereof.

12. By reason of the Defendant's wrongful re-entry upon the demised premises, the Plaintiff has suffered loss, damage and inconvenience, full particulars whereof will be given on discovery.

AND the Plaintiff claims:

(1) A Declaration that the said Lease has not become forfeited to the Defendant and that the Defendant's re-entry was a trespass;
(2) An Injunction requiring the Defendant to quit the premises and not to interfere with the Plaintiff's quiet enjoyment thereof;
(3) An Order that possession of the demised premises be restored to the Plaintiff;
(4) Damages for trespass, alternatively damages for use and occupation, at the rate of £   per annum (£   per day) or at such other rate as the Court shall consider just from the   until possession is restored to the Plaintiff;
(5) Damages for breach of covenant for quiet enjoyment;
(6) In the event of this Court holding that the said Lease has been lawfully forfeited, an Order that upon the Plaintiff paying to the Defendant or his solicitors in this action the amount of any arrears of rent found due from the Plaintiff to the Defendant, the Plaintiff to be relieved from such forfeiture;
(7) Further or other relief;
(8) Costs.

DATED this   day of   199 .

Form 15: Tenant's Defence to Landlord's claim (see Form 8) with Counterclaim for relief from forfeiture

IN THE HIGH COURT OF JUSTICE   199... A. No...

QUEEN'S BENCH DIVISION

BETWEEN:

A.B. Ltd.

Plaintiff

and

C.D.

Defendant

DEFENCE AND COUNTERCLAIM

Defence

1. The Defendant admits paragraphs 1 to 10 of the Statement of Claim.

2. The Defendant denies that he failed to remedy the said breaches as alleged in paragraph 11 of the Statement of Claim and contends that he remedied the same by [the end of December 1992].

3. The Defendant makes no admissions as to the matters alleged in paragraphs 12 to 14 of the Statement of Claim.

Counterclaim

4. The Defendant repeats paragraphs 1 to 3 of the Defence.

5. If, contrary to the Defendant's contention, it should be found that he has failed to remedy the alleged or any breach or breaches of the said covenants within a reasonable time, the Defendant claims to be relieved from the alleged forfeiture under section 146 of the Law of Property Act 1925 on such terms as the Court shall think fit.

DATED this   day of   199 .

Form 16: Landlord's Reply and Defence to Counterclaim (see Form 15)

IN THE HIGH COURT OF JUSTICE   199... A. No...

QUEEN'S BENCH DIVISION

BETWEEN:

A.B. Ltd   *Plaintiff*

and

C.D.   *Defendant*

REPLY AND DEFENCE TO COUNTERCLAIM

Reply

1. Save and in so far as the same consists of admissions, the Plaintiff joins issue with the Defendant on his Defence.

Defence to Counterclaim

2. The Plaintiff denies that the Defendant is entitled to relief against forfeiture.

DATED this   day of   199 .

Form 17: Tenant's Summons seeking relief from forfeiture for non-payment of rent in Landlord's proceedings

IN THE HIGH COURT OF JUSTICE   199... A. No...

QUEEN'S BENCH DIVISION

BETWEEN:

A.B.   *Plaintiff*

and

C.D.   *Defendant*

LET all parties concerned attend the Master in Chambers, in Room No.
, Central Office, Royal Courts of Justice, Strand, London,
WC2A 2LL, on   day the   day of   199 ,
at   o'clock on the hearing of an application by the Defendant
for an Order:

1. That it be referred to a Master to compute the rent and arrears of rent due from the Defendant to the Plaintiff and to tax the Plaintiff's costs of this action;

2. That upon the Defendant paying to the Plaintiff or to his Solicitors in this action what the Master shall find due under paragraph 1 hereof the Defendant be relieved from forfeiture of the premises comprised in the Lease, dated   , and made between the Plaintiff of the one part and the Defendant of the other part, consequent upon the non-payment of any rent herebefore due;

3. That possession of the said premises be restored to the Defendant;

4. That all further proceedings in this action be stayed.

DATED this   day of   199 .

Form 18: Sub-tenant's Summons seeking relief from forfeiture for non-payment of rent in Landlord's proceedings

IN THE HIGH COURT OF JUSTICE   199... A. No...

QUEEN'S BENCH DIVISION

BETWEEN:

A.B.   *Plaintiff*

and

C.D.   *Defendant*

LET all parties concerned attend the Master in Chambers in Room No.
, Central Office, Royal Courts of Justice, Strand, London WC2A 2LL,
on   day the   day of   199   at
o'clock on the hearing of an application by
being a sub-tenant of the Defendant in occupation of [the first floor] of the
premises which are the subject matter of this action for an Order:

1. That [name of sub-tenant] may be joined as a Defendant in this action;

2. That [name of sub-tenant] may have vested in him pursuant to section
146(4) of the Law of Property Act 1925 the premises situate on [the first
floor] of the building known as   for a term to expire on

.

DATED this   day of   199 .

Index

Index